I0028663

Praise for *Gamestorming 2.0*

Gamestorming is one of the few facilitator resources that is never far from me. I still remember when it first came out—it was a big deal. Over a decade later, it's still always within arm's reach. I'm thrilled to see this team back at it, helping us unlock new ways of being together, make good decisions, and imagine new possibilities at work and beyond.

—*Priya Parker, author, strategic advisor, and facilitator*

The greatest instruction manual ever for ruining terrible meetings.

—*Dan Roam,*
bestselling author of The Back of the Napkin *and* Draw to Win

Meetings suck, but this book offers an alternative: tools for visual thinking to unlock your best work, together.

—*Jake Knapp,*
New York Times *bestselling author of* Sprint *and* Click

Gamestorming isn't just a toolkit—it's a shift in how we think, how we learn, and how we solve. Sun and Dave have democratized collaborative intelligence, offering a framework anyone can use to create, adapt, and thrive in ambiguity. This book helps teams—and companies—see the invisible, challenge assumptions, and turn uncertainty into momentum. If you care about creativity, culture, or high-performance collaboration, this is your new field guide.

—*Al Ramadan, CEO/founder at Play Bigger and*
bestselling author of Play Bigger *and* The Existing Market Trap

In our increasingly dynamic and unpredictable world, there's a striking paradox: the more we need clarity around our strategy and priorities, the more traditional planning approaches fall short—making the mindsets, disciplines, and practices of gamestorming not just creative exercises, but strategic imperatives for leaders who striving to build alignment and drive impact with both rigor and agility. For leaders, managers, and teams navigating today's complexity, the most serious investment they can make is mastering what Dave Gray and Sunni Brown teach in their updated version of *Gamestorming 2.0*—complete with even more examples, games, and tips on how to amplify the best of collective human ingenuity, collaboration and co-creation.

—*Lisa Kay Solomon, coauthor of* Moments of Impact *and* Design a Better Business, *Futurist in Residence, Stanford d.school*

Gamestorming is proof that play is not the opposite of work and having fun is serious business. The rules of the games inside this book will set your creative spirit free.

—*Austin Kleon,*
New York Times *bestselling author of* Steal Like an Artist

Gamestorming has become my go-to resource for workshop design, and it's been a huge inspiration in developing my work and facilitation practice. It's much more than a book—it's a movement. Gamestorming shows what's possible for teams and organizations to truly change the way they work through workshops, creativity and effective collaboration.

—*Alison Coward, author of* Workshop Culture
and founder at Bracket

When people feel seen, heard, and empowered to contribute, happiness isn't a perk—it's a product of the culture. This book helps you build that culture, one game at a time.

—*Jenn Lim, CEO/founder of Beyond Happiness,*
cofounder of Delivering Happiness, bestselling author

Asynchronous collaboration should be the new norm. This gameful way of working spares high-powered teams from yet another pointless meeting while still giving them tools to do valuable, deep work together.

—Keith Ferrazzi, #1 New York Times *bestselling author and executive team coach*

Gamestorming 2.0 is the playbook for unleashing team genius. It uses collaborative design to transform meetings into creative workspaces—deliberately shaping how people work, think, and innovate, whether you're in the same room or across the world.

—Mariano Battan, cofounder and chairman of MURAL, founder of Bocho, coauthor of Collaborative Intelligence

Back and better than ever, *Gamestorming 2.0* leads teams into the future again. You'll amplify collaboration, accelerate visual communication, and get really good at solving things together.

—Nancy Duarte, bestselling author and CEO of Duarte, Inc.

Gamestorming makes it safe to not have an answer—yet. When we're encouraged to wonder out loud, question assumptions, and think with our whole body, transformation will follow. This method offers the scaffolding that makes this kind of shift possible, at scale.

—Dr. Myriam Hadnes, CEO/podcast host, workshops.work

Gamestorming 2.0

*An Updated Playbook for Innovators,
Rule Breakers, and Changemakers*

Dave Gray and Sunni Brown

O'REILLY®

Gamestorming 2.0

by Dave Gray and Sunni Brown

Copyright © 2025 Dave Gray and Sunni Brown Ink. All rights reserved.

Published by O'Reilly Media, Inc., 141 Stony Circle, Suite 195 Santa Rosa, CA 95401.

O'Reilly books may be purchased for educational, business, or sales promotional use. Online editions are also available for most titles (*http://oreilly.com*). For more information, contact our corporate/institutional sales department: 800-998-9938 or *corporate@oreilly.com*.

Acquisition Editor: David Michelson	**Proofreader:** Kim Wimpsett
Development Editor: Sara Hunter	**Indexer:** Judy McConville
Production Editor: Christopher Faucher	**Cover Designer:** Susan Thompson
Copyeditor: Elizabeth Wheeler	**Interior Designer:** Monica Kamsvaag

July 2010:	First Edition
July 2025:	Second Edition

Revision History for the Second Edition

2025-07-16:   First Release

See *http://oreilly.com/catalog/errata.csp?isbn=9781098148089* for release details.

© Cartoons by Tom Fishburne, Marketoonist, LLC.

The O'Reilly logo is a registered trademark of O'Reilly Media, Inc. *Gamestorming 2.0*, the cover image, and related trade dress are trademarks of O'Reilly Media, Inc.

The views expressed in this work are those of the authors and do not represent the publisher's views. While the publisher and the authors have used good faith efforts to ensure that the information and instructions contained in this work are accurate, the publisher and the authors disclaim all responsibility for errors or omissions, including without limitation responsibility for damages resulting from the use of or reliance on this work. Use of the information and instructions contained in this work is at your own risk. If any code samples or other technology this work contains or describes is subject to open source licenses or the intellectual property rights of others, it is your responsibility to ensure that your use thereof complies with such licenses and/or rights.

978-1-098-14808-9

[LSI]

In memory of Michael Doyle

—Dave Gray

To Falkor

—Sunni (Sun) Brown

Contents

Foreword

My first encounter with the practice described in this book—before it was called "gamestorming"—was in a visual thinking workshop at my firm in 2007. After experiencing the value of working in this way, we immediately began to incorporate the techniques into our consulting work. Soon after, the practices became foundational inspirations as Yves Pigneur and I developed the first of what are now known as "design canvases": the Business Model Canvas.

It's easy to forget what the business landscape looked like in 2010, when *Gamestorming* (O'Reilly) and *Business Model Generation* (John Wiley and Sons) were first published, but these were groundbreaking works. Visual thinking and multisensory tools were nowhere near as mainstream as they are today. It's amazing and exciting how quickly they've been adopted into business and innovation environments. This a testament to their efficacy, so I'm glad this book has achieved the popularity it has, and I'm proud to say that Yves and I inspired one of the new chapters in this second edition.

Why does gamestorming work? How is it that these tools can be so powerful? I have trouble putting it in words. But I know that the moment people start to gather around visual tools and frameworks, the dynamic changes. Work gets faster, easier, more creative, and collaborative. It goes more smoothly and generates better results.

That's the power of gamestorming. It makes work work.

—Alex Osterwalder
Geneva, Switzerland, 2023

Preface

In 1807, the Grimm brothers began collecting folk tales that, up until that point, had never been written down. In 1812, they published a collection of 86 tales under the title *Children's and Household Tales*. By the seventh edition, the last published in their lifetime, the collection had grown to 211 tales. If not for the work of the Brothers Grimm, we might never have heard such stories as "Rumpelstiltskin," "Snow White," "Sleeping Beauty," "Rapunzel," "Cinderella," "Hansel and Gretel," "Little Red Riding Hood," and "The Frog Prince."

Jacob and Wilhelm Grimm were motivated by a few things: as philologists, they wanted to understand the linguistic elements of the stories and their sources; as historians, they wanted to record the stories as they were told in households; as storytellers, they wanted to entertain, and as Germans (although there was no single German state at the time), they were interested in understanding and developing a sense of common identity among German-speaking people.

More than 15 years ago, the coauthors of *Gamestorming* embarked on a similar project: our goal was to identify a set of emerging methods and approaches to work that had been germinating since the 1970s and are deeply entwined with patterns emerging in the way we work with information.

In an industrial society, the focus is on working with things: workers are expected to fit standardized job descriptions and perform their duties according to clear policies, procedures, and prescriptions. Knowledge work—working with information and ideas—is fundamentally different from working with things: workers are expected not so much to perform standard roles but to generate creative, innovative results that surprise and delight customers and colleagues. They are expected to not only perform a function but to design new and better products and services—and sometimes to provide dramatic, breakthrough results.

Creativity and invention have long been seen as a "black box." As a general rule, businesspeople don't typically try to understand this process. We fully expect that when designers, inventors, and other creative people go into a room with a goal, they will come out with more or less creative discoveries and results. Although when we watch them at work, we can observe some combination of sketching, animated conversations, and messy desks, the fundamental nature of what happens in that room remains mostly a mystery.

It's easy to leave creativity to the creative types and say to yourself, "I'm just not a creative person." The fact is that in a complex, dynamic, competitive knowledge economy, it's no longer acceptable to take this position. If you are a knowledge worker, you must become, to some degree, comfortable with being creative.

That may sound a bit scary, but the fact is that successful creative people tend to employ simple strategies and practices to get where they want to go. It's not so much that they employ a consistent, repeatable process that leads to consistent creative results. It's more like a workshop with a set of tools and strategies for examining things deeply, for exploring new ideas, and for performing experiments and testing hypotheses, to generate new and surprising insights and results.

So we set out, much like the Brothers Grimm, to collect the best of these practices wherever we could find them, with a special focus on Silicon Valley, innovative companies, and the information revolution.

Many of these practices emerged from a kind of "Silicon soup"—the interconnected network of Silicon Valley, where ideas and people cross-pollinate like bees in one massive hive. The practices we articulate here emerged mostly from an oral culture, passed along from person to person by word of mouth. For example, a consultant uses an approach with a client, and the client begins to employ that approach internally. Over time, as more people employ a method, it evolves into something quite different, and over time, the source of the original idea or approach may be lost. Sometimes methods are written down, and sometimes, like folk tales, they exist in many different versions in many places.

We chose to call this practice *gamestorming* because it came closer to describing the phenomenon than anything else we could think of. In the front section, Chapters 1–6, we've done our best to provide a sense of the underlying mechanics or architecture of the games we describe, as well as some design principles that may be helpful as you begin to try the practices for yourself.

It is our hope to create a volume that will be of use to the novice and the experienced practitioner alike. If you're a novice, we hope you'll find a whole new world of ideas for how to approach various challenges in your work. For the experienced practitioner, we hope you'll find some good ideas and a few things that are "new to you."

Our goal with this collection was to find the best of these tools and practices and bring them together into a single volume that could endlessly change and grow, as it has in this updated version. Gamestorming can bring teams together in person and online. While this book is written from the POV of in-person meetings, all of the games can be adapted for virtual environments. To that end, we've added tips for playing games online throughout this book.

One of our biggest challenges has been establishing the provenance of each game and sourcing it appropriately. At times, it can be very difficult to determine who first designed a tool or where it was first used. We have done our best to determine the source of each game and have made notes where possible, without distracting from the primary content. Often it seemed that we found ourselves looking at fractals of ideas with no obvious beginning or end—whenever we identified the source of a game, it seemed that it may have been derived from another, earlier source, and it always seemed that there might be a previous claimant lurking in the wings.

When we use the term "based on," the description is based on some kind of written material where we have identified a source. When we use the term "inspired by," we have identified the premise, idea, or core concept, but the game itself was based on oral histories of our own design. If we were unable to identify a source reliably, we have marked the game source as unknown. When we have invented the game ourselves, that is noted, too. If you have information or ideas about the origins of these games, please share them with us.

Due to our engagement with a larger community around this project, we added more games, refined the overall collection, and improved our understanding of the rich history of these games for this new edition. We've set up online forums at *gamestorming.com* and *nothingintheway.substack.com* where we'd like to enlist your continued collaboration. It is our hope that you will contribute games based on your personal knowledge and experience, help us clarify the history of these ideas and practices, prototype and play games alongside us, and help us better understand the fascinating history and applications of games in creative work.

Thank you for opening and exploring the world of games with us.

—Dave and Sun
Portland, OR
March 2025

Using Book Examples

Supplemental material (examples, exercises, etc.) is available for download at *https://gamestorming.substack.com*.

We appreciate, but generally do not require, attribution. An attribution usually includes the title, author, publisher, and ISBN. For example: "*Gamestorming 2.0* by Dave Gray and Sunni Brown (O'Reilly). Copyright 2025 Dave Gray and Sunni Brown Ink, 978-1-098-14808-9."

If you feel your use of examples falls outside fair use or the permission given above, feel free to contact us at *permissions@oreilly.com*.

O'Reilly Online Learning

O'REILLY® For more than 40 years, *O'Reilly Media* has provided technology and business training, knowledge, and insight to help companies succeed.

Our unique network of experts and innovators share their knowledge and expertise through books, articles, and our online learning platform. O'Reilly's online learning platform gives you on-demand access to live training courses, in-depth learning paths, interactive coding environments, and a vast collection of text and video from O'Reilly and 200+ other publishers. For more information, visit *https://oreilly.com*.

How to Contact Us

Please address comments and questions concerning this book to the publisher:

O'Reilly Media, Inc.

141 Stony Circle, Suite 195

Santa Rosa, CA 95401

800-889-8969 (in the United States or Canada)

707-827-7019 (international or local)

707-829-0104 (fax)

support@oreilly.com

https://oreilly.com/about/contact.html

We have a web page for this book, where we list errata, examples, and any additional information. You can access this page at *https://oreil.ly/gamestorming-2e*.

For news and information about our books and courses, visit *https://oreilly.com*.

Find us on LinkedIn: *https://linkedin.com/company/oreilly-media*.

Watch us on YouTube: *https://youtube.com/oreillymedia*.

Acknowledgments

We extend deep gratitude to James Macanufo, an intrepid game explorer and our coauthor on the original edition. James was instrumental in shaping the DNA of Gamestorming, designing core games and key essentials that became the backbone of our toolkit. His foundational contributions have enriched us immeasurably and they continue to elevate this practice.

We are grateful to Danyelle Faulkner, Founder & CEO of Idea Illuminations, for her valuable contributions to this second edition. Danyelle refreshed and expanded the toolkit of games and helped to translate complex facilitation techniques into engaging and practical activities. Her efforts have significantly enriched this edition.

PART I

Foundations

Why Gamestorming?

The great, transformative technologies are the ones that make the invisible visible: They enable us to see something, experience something, imagine something that we never knew existed before. Some of those examples are the telescope, the microscope, the fMRI—and even something as simple as the sail. The sail enabled us to see parts of the world and cultures that we never knew existed, and in doing so, it suddenly not only challenged our own assumptions but expanded our space of possibility.

—DR. BEAU LOTTO

If you could peer inside someone's mind, you might see a sort of matrix, an interlocking web of ideas, assumptions, biases, beliefs, and stories. In the field of neuroscience, this is called a "space of possibility." A space of possibility describes what knowledge or next steps are available to you in terms of your perception. Each individual's space is unique, built from personal, historical experiences that construct our views of reality.

The Space of Possibility

My view of the world. It's eensy-weensy, really.

Why this space matters is because it shapes who you are, how you show up, and how you live. It defines what you expect, assume, and imagine to be possible. The more nodes in your space of possibility, the more complex or nuanced it is, the more steps you can take to see things differently. If you want to expand your space of possibility, your greatest moves are to first acknowledge that your view is inherently partial—surrender to not having all the answers—and then actively occupy a state of curiosity: ask questions, wonder, get interested in the world. This will begin to open doors in your perception and give your life greater opportunity.

YOU, BEFORE   YOU, AFTER

When you start to include another person's space of possibility, wondering, asking questions, and deeply listening to their ideas, assumptions, and experiences, your space gets another chance to grow. You can imagine how expansive this space becomes when it involves an entire group of people, a collection of minds committed to inquiring, sharing, modeling, and solving problems together. It starts to feel like the sky becomes the limit.

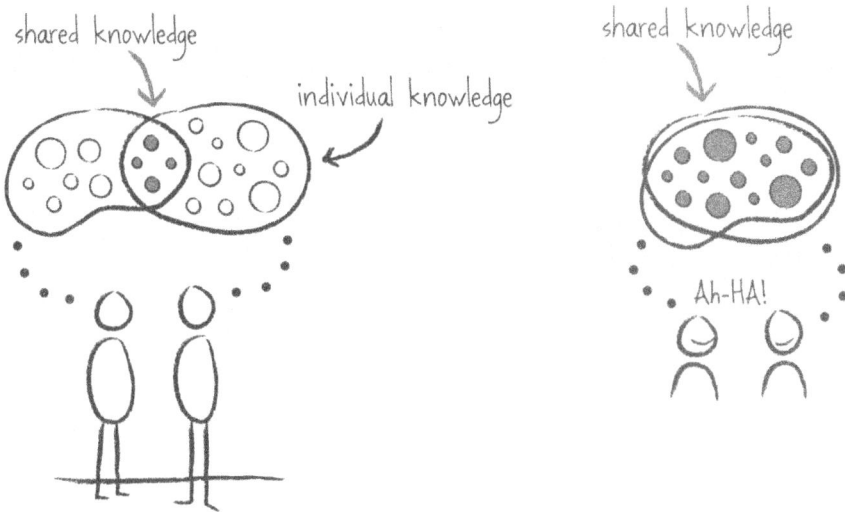

The problem is that most brains don't like to adjust perception. They don't like seeing things differently than they did before. This is because brains have a significant bias toward safety. They evolved to forecast the future based on a history of assumptions built from experience. This was a necessary safeguard against physical and existential death, one that makes perfect sense: if you were already surviving and belonging, situated well enough to sustain your life and social structures, it would be foolish and unnecessary to venture over the mountain pass. There could be a huge metabolic and social price to pay if a brain took an unnecessary risk and that risk did not pay off. Because of this bias, it can be incredibly difficult to get a brain to consider that there may be something *else*, something more, it might need to know. Unless we're trained otherwise, our brains will actively resist not-knowing in order to stay safe. So how do we get a brain to move willingly into not-knowing? How do we move not from A → B but from A → not A? How do we invite ourselves into uncertainty so we can reap the rewards of that courage?

This is what gamestorming is all about.

How We Make Not-Knowing Desirable

In pursuit of new solutions, ideas, and innovations, there is a way to make uncertainty desirable. There is a way to create conditions in which human beings—not begrudgingly but willingly—venture into new spaces of possibility, temporarily exchanging certainty for doubt in order to unlock other capacities our brain evolved to possess: collaboration, problem solving, agility, imagination, innovation, and boundless adventure. There are five features of gamestorming that tap these reservoirs of powers: thinking moves, beyond-the-brain thinking, visualization, games, and game sequences. Let's take them one at a time.

THINKING MOVES

The most reliable way to thrive in new spaces of possibility is to become agile at thinking within them. In service to that, gamestorming gives explicit agency to what we call "thinking moves." Thinking moves are metacognitive processes through which we better understand and engage with the world. There are dozens of thinking moves a brain can make. The following are examples of moves you're making all the time, often without conscious effort. Each move directs your mental activity, attempting to decipher and make meaning from whatever new context you're in. When done well, thinking moves produce the kinds of rewards an adventuring brain seeks: new resources, knowledge acquisition, breakthroughs, and surprising solutions. But rarely is a thinker *aware of and intentional about* the thinking moves they're making, so gamestorming makes thinking moves explicit, faster, easier, and shared. It helps you become strategic and purposeful about making thinking moves so that you and other "players" can choose to make them, ultimately becoming more effective at cognition itself. We do this by using visual language, games, and game sequences to help you think well beyond the brain. So what is thinking beyond the brain?

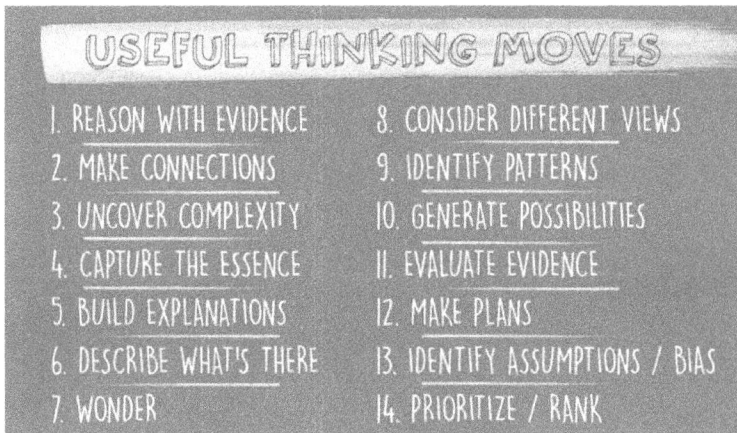

USEFUL THINKING MOVES

1. REASON WITH EVIDENCE
2. MAKE CONNECTIONS
3. UNCOVER COMPLEXITY
4. CAPTURE THE ESSENCE
5. BUILD EXPLANATIONS
6. DESCRIBE WHAT'S THERE
7. WONDER
8. CONSIDER DIFFERENT VIEWS
9. IDENTIFY PATTERNS
10. GENERATE POSSIBILITIES
11. EVALUATE EVIDENCE
12. MAKE PLANS
13. IDENTIFY ASSUMPTIONS / BIAS
14. PRIORITIZE / RANK

THINKING BEYOND THE BRAIN

Gamestorming sessions often look like the laboratories of scientists, the playgrounds of designers, or the workshops of artisans. This is because our goal is to amplify, accelerate, and augment cognition using every medium and mode at the disposal of a mammal who evolved in a four-dimensional world. In this work, thinking moves are purposefully not limited to a lonely lump of wrinkly tissue laboring and tinkering by itself. One brain alone in its skull has serious limitations to what it can do,[1] but if we extend the canvas beyond the bounds of the head, to include and be inspired by a broader field of sensory material, stimuli, and other bodies, we can light up networks well beyond the brain to awaken and enhance not just our spaces of possibility but our agility with thinking moves inside of them.

---

1 This includes limitations around memory, attention, engagement, abstraction, and persistence.

In her book *The Extended Mind*, Annie Murphy Paul (Mariner Books) unintentionally paints a perfect picture of the value in a gamestorming session like these:

> *Thinking outside the brain means skillfully engaging entities external to our heads—the feelings and movements of our bodies, the physical spaces in which we learn and work, and the minds of other people around us—drawing them into our own mental processes. By reaching beyond the brain to recruit these "extra-neural" resources, we are able to focus more intently, comprehend more deeply, and create more imaginatively— to entertain ideas that would literally be unthinkable by the brain alone.*

Because gamestorming looks fun (and often is), you can't immediately discern the power underneath, but gamestorming is cognition at its finest—simultaneously embodied, situated, and distributed.[2] It's embodied because the work welcomes the abilities of the full body: we stand, move, pose, dance, and make any and all motions with the head, hands, and body. It's situated because we build temporary environments (onsite and online), building and using artifacts that act as keepers of knowledge, mental extensions that hold information so that we can play with more of it at a time, lightening the load on short-term memory. It's distributed because it involves thinking with others, coordinating expertise and experience in a dance of dependent co-arising.[3] Players create social spaces that are collaborative and generative, spaces that emerge served by two very old human capabilities: visualization and playing games.

---

2 All of these references to cognition point to the fundamental inquiry around where the mind stops and the rest of the world begins. There currently is no unified theory on the mind or the extended mind, and certainly not on what consciousness is. What we can say with confidence is that the body, the environment, and our inclusion of other beings in an extra-neural network does much to elevate and enhance our powers of cognition.

3 Dependent co-arising or dependent origination is a term from Buddhist philosophy that speaks to the co-emergence inherent in the phenomenal world. Deeper than linear causation or temporality, dependent co-arising refers to layers of ceaseless activity that are simultaneously predictable, randomized, and chaotic.

VISUALIZATION

There is another key ingredient to effective gamestorming: visualization. Why visual language is essential is because it gives you almost immediate access to what's inside of other people's spaces of possibility. Rapid and simple sketches and doodles—spontaneous visual displays—open the black boxes of what other people are thinking and show you what the nodes are. Sketches make the invisible visible. It's hard to overstate the value of this. When knowledge that's internalized becomes externalized, we suddenly have rocks to turn over, levers to pull, anchors to drop, assumptions to check—all the sharing of mental models is suddenly at our disposal. Knowledge exploration becomes *rapidly* accelerated where visual thinking is involved. And you'll see from the game examples within the book that no real artistic skill set is required. Gamestormers can and should think of visual language as a simple doodling—the spontaneous making of marks to help us think.

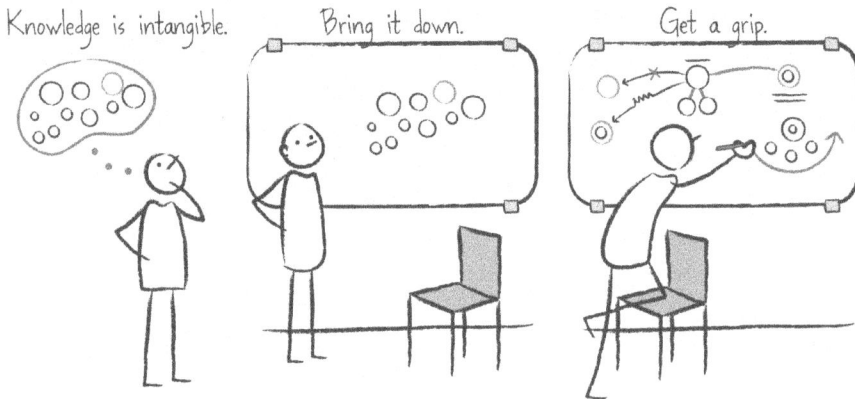

Knowledge is intangible.   Bring it down.   Get a grip.

GAMES AND GAME SEQUENCES

Last, thinking moves are mobilized by what we call *games* and *game sequences*. What a game involves is the subject of Chapter 2, so just know in advance that a game is not a trivial pursuit. We think of games as powerful and purposeful thought experiments, and a sequence of games means you are off to the races in terms of building a better anything. In our work, we use visual language as a baseline power tool, but gamestorming welcomes any and all sensory modalities that jog the mind: visual, gestural, musical, textural, emotional. If it engages the body and opens the mind, it is welcome in the room and can be used as a game. Games can and should also be invented.

What we teach in this book is for anyone to try, anywhere, at any time. We designed the technique to require very few materials, to be agile, portable, and easily democratized. It is ultimately a method—a way of life—that empowers you to see differently. It's a practice that suspends the rules of ordinary life, forgoes the limitations of ordinary reality, and invites individuals and teams into almost limitless possibility. This is an incredibly rewarding practice, almost unlimited in application and efficacy. In a short period of time, even a 20-minute meeting, this technique accomplishes some powerful things:

- Makes the invisible visible
- Creates conditions for uncertainty and celebrates it
- Leverages the power of mistake making
- Expands spaces of possibility
- Encourages and empowers us to identify and question assumptions that limit possibility
- Is inherently cooperative and collaborative, resulting in more generative social spaces
- Is intrinsically motivating and engaging

For you to step in further, first let's learn what we mean by a game.

2

What Is a Game?

Games and play are not the same thing.

Imagine you are playing with a ball. You kick the ball against a wall, and the ball bounces back to you. You stop the ball with your foot and kick it again. By engaging in this kind of play, you are learning to associate certain movements of your body with the movements of the ball in space. We could call this *associative play*.

Now imagine that you are waiting for a friend. Your friend appears, and you begin to walk down a sidewalk together, kicking the ball back and forth as you go. Now the play has gained a social dimension; one person's actions suggest a response, and vice versa. You could think of this form of play as a kind of improvised conversation, where two people are engaging each other, using the ball as a medium. This kind of play has no clear beginning or end; rather, it flows seamlessly from one state into another. We could call this *streaming play*.

Now imagine that you come to a small park and become bored simply kicking the ball back and forth. So you say to your friend, "Let's take turns trying to hit that tree. You have to kick the ball from behind this line." So you make a line by dragging your heel through the dirt, and say, "We'll take turns kicking the ball. Each time you hit the tree, you get a point. First one to five wins." Your friend agrees and you begin to play. Now the play has become a game: a fundamentally different kind of play.

What makes a game different? We can break down this very simple game into some basic components that separate it from other kinds of play:

Game space

To enter into a game is to enter another kind of space where the rules of ordinary life are temporarily suspended and replaced with the rules of the game. In effect, a game creates an alternative world, a model world. To enter a game space, the players must agree to abide by the rules of that space, and they must enter willingly. It's not a game if people are forced to play. This agreement among the players to temporarily suspend reality creates a safe place where the players can engage in behavior that might be risky, uncomfortable, or even rude in their normal lives.

By agreeing to a set of rules (stay behind the line, take turns kicking the ball, etc.), the players enter a shared world. Without that agreement, the game would not be possible.

Boundaries

A game has boundaries in time and space. There is a time when a game begins—when the players enter the game space—and a time when they leave the game space, ending the game. The game space can be paused or activated by agreement of the players. We can imagine that the players agree to pause the game for lunch, or so that one of them can go to the bathroom. The game will usually have a spatial boundary, outside of which the rules do not apply. Imagine, for example, that spectators gather to observe the kicking contest. It's easy to see that they could not insert themselves between a player and the tree, or distract the players, without spoiling or at least changing the game.

Rules for interaction

Within the game space, players agree to abide by rules that define the way the game world operates. The game rules define the constraints of the game space, just as physical laws, like gravity, constrain the real world. According to the rules of the game world, a player could no more kick the ball from the wrong side of the line than they could make a ball fall up. Of course, one could do this, but not without violating the game space—something we call cheating.

Artifacts

Most games employ physical artifacts: objects that hold information about the game, either intrinsically or by virtue of their position. The ball and the tree in our game are such objects. When the ball hits the tree, a point is scored. That's information. Artifacts can be used to track progress and to maintain a picture of the game's current state. We can easily imagine, for example, that as each point is scored, the players place a stone on the ground or make hash marks in the dirt to help them keep track of the score—another kind of information artifact. The players are also artifacts in the sense that their position can hold information about the state of a game. Compare the position of players on a sports field to the pieces on a chessboard.

Goal

Players must have a way to know when the game is over, an end state that they are all striving to attain, that is understood and agreed to by all players. Sometimes a game can be timed, as in many sports, such as football. In our case, a goal is met every time a player hits the tree with the ball, and the game ends when the first player reaches five points.

We can find these familiar elements in any game, whether it is chess, tennis, poker, ring around the rosie, or games you will find in this book, like the following example by Walt Disney called Storyboard. The Storyboard game has all the elements detailed: game space, boundaries, rules of interaction, goals, and artifact. As we go deeper into the book, you'll see how a game like this changes the structure, direction, and energy of meetings at work and situates them inside the broader landscape of business.

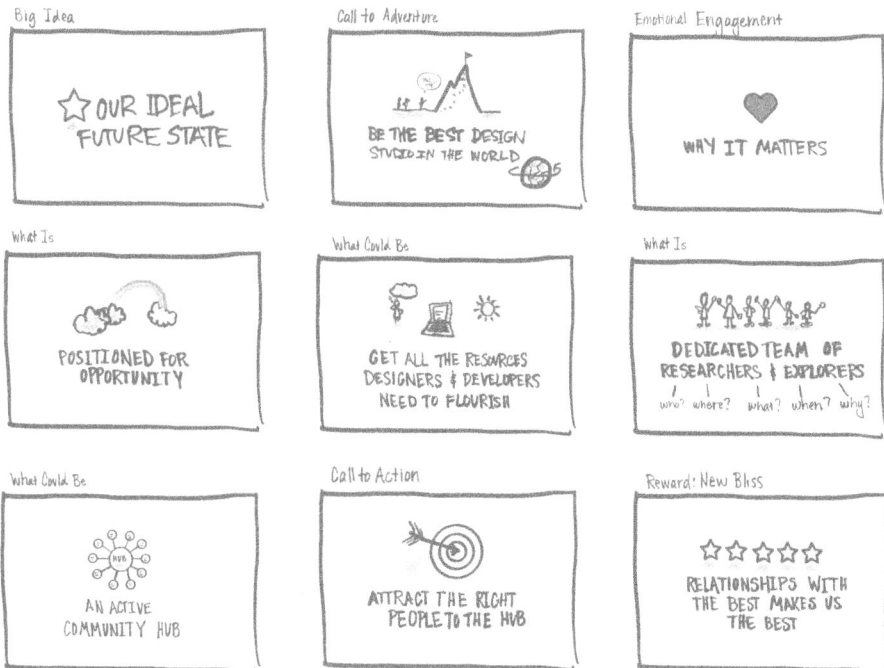

Like the Storyboard game, every game is a world that evolves in stages, as follows: imagine the world, create the world, open the world, explore the world, and close the world. Here's how it works:

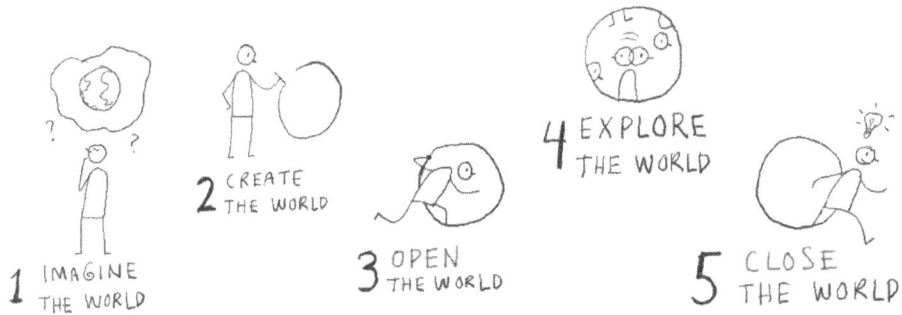

1. *Imagine the world.*

    Before the game can begin, you must imagine a possible world: a temporary space, within which players can explore any set of ideas or possibilities.

2. *Create the world.*

    A game world is formed by giving it boundaries, rules, and artifacts. Boundaries are the spatial and temporal boundaries of the world, its beginning and end, and its edges. Rules are the laws that govern the world; artifacts are the things that populate the world.

3. *Open the world.*

    A game world can only be entered by agreement among the players. To agree, they must understand the game's boundaries, rules, and artifacts—what they represent, how they operate, and so on.

4. Explore the world.

> Goals are the animating force that drive exploration; they provide a necessary tension between the initial condition of the world and some desired state. Goals can be defined in advance or by the players within the context of the game. Once players have entered the world, they try to realize their goals within the constraints of the game world's system. They interact with artifacts, test ideas, try various strategies, and adapt to changing conditions as the game progresses, in their drive to achieve their goals.

5. Close the world.

> A game is finished when the game's goals have been met. Although achieving a goal gives the players a sense of gratification and accomplishment, the goal is not really the point of the game so much as a kind of marker to ceremonially close the game space. The point of the game is the play itself, the exploration of an imaginary space that happens during the play, and the insights that come from that exploration.

Imagine the world, create the world, open the world, explore the world, and close the world. The first two stages are the game design, and the remaining three stages are the play.

You can see that a game, once designed, can be played an infinite number of times. So, if you're playing a predesigned game, there will be only three stages: open the world, explore the world, and close the world.

Gamestorming is about creating game worlds specifically to explore and examine challenges and complexities, to improve collaboration, and to generate novel insights about the way the world works and what kinds of possibilities we might find there. Game worlds are alternative realities—parallel universes that we can create and explore, limited only by our imagination. A game can be carefully designed in advance or put together in an instant, with found materials. A game can take 15 minutes or several days to complete. The number of possible games, like the number of possible worlds, is infinite. By imagining, creating, and exploring possible worlds, you will open the door to breakthrough thinking and real innovation.

The Game of Business

Let's begin by boiling the "game of business" down to its most basic components.

Business, like many other human activities, is built around goals. Goals are a way we move from where we are to where we want to be. A goal sets up a tension between a current state (an initial condition) and a targeted future state (the goal). In between is something we can call the challenge space: the ground we need to cover in order to get there.

A
•
Initial
conditions

CHALLENGE
SPACE

B
•
Target
state
(goal)

Most of the time, at work, we want to manage for consistent, repeatable, predictable results. These kinds of goals are best when they are specific and quantifiable and are best reached via a repeatable, linear process that moves from A → B. In such cases, we want to ensure that our goals are as clear and unambiguous as possible. The more specific and measurable the goal is, the better. When we have a clear, precise, specific goal, the best way to address the challenge space is with a business process—a series of steps that, if followed precisely, will create a chain of cause and effect that will lead consistently to the same result.

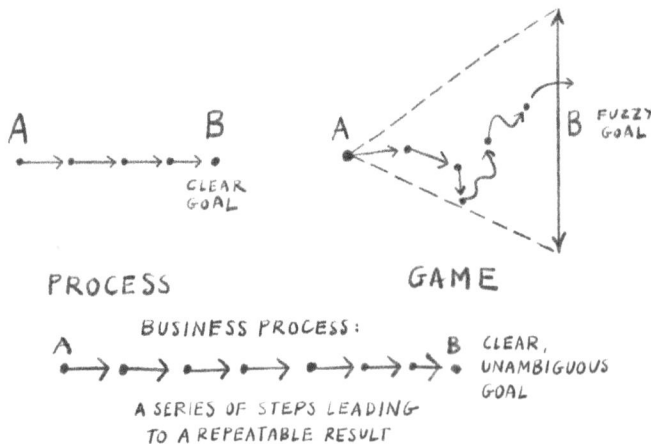

A ●→●→●→●→● B
CLEAR
GOAL

PROCESS

A ◦←→● B FUZZY GOAL

GAME

BUSINESS PROCESS:
A ●→●→●→●→●→●→● B CLEAR, UNAMBIGUOUS GOAL
A SERIES OF STEPS LEADING
TO A REPEATABLE RESULT

But in creative work, B has a different meaning. We need to manage for outcomes that can't be defined in advance. We are not seeking predictability so much as breakthrough ideas, which can't be predetermined. In any creative endeavor, the goal is not to incrementally improve on the past but to generate something new.

New, by definition, means "not seen before." So, if a team wants to truly create, there is simply no way to precisely define the goal in advance, because there are too many unknowns. Embarking on this kind of journey is akin to exploring inner and outer space—novel, infinite terrain that is at once surprising, illuminating, and challenging.

Fuzzy Goals

To move toward an uncertain future, you need to set a course. But how do you set a course when the destination is unknown? This is where it becomes necessary to imagine a future world that is different from our own. Somehow we need to imagine a world that we can't really fully conceive yet—a world that we can see only dimly, as if through a fog. In knowledge work we need our goals to be fuzzy.

Gamestorming is an alternative to the traditional business process. In gamestorming, goals are not precise, and so the way we approach the challenge space cannot be designed in advance, nor can it be fully predicted.

While a business process creates a solid, secure chain of cause and effect, gamestorming creates something different: not a chain, but a framework for exploration, experimentation, and trial and error. The path to the goal is not clear, and the goal may, in fact, change.

This is true at both a micro scale and a macro scale. Creating a complex industrial product requires the close integration of many processes. When you string a bunch of processes together, you will see a branching structure with many dependencies.

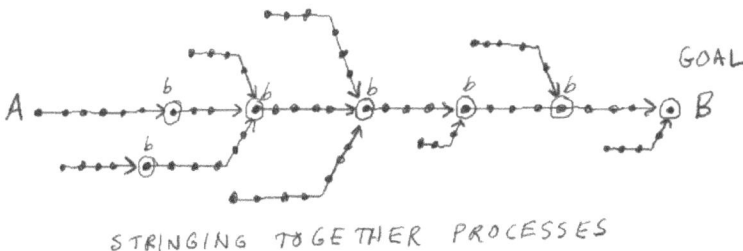

STRINGING TOGETHER PROCESSES

As long as every step is followed precisely and nothing changes along the way, you will achieve your goal reliably and predictably every time. The management challenge is one of precision, accuracy, and consistency.

Managing creative work requires a different approach. Because the outcome cannot be determined precisely in advance—and at times the goals need to shift—the project must proceed based on intuition, hypotheses, experimentation, and adaptation. This kind of approach is an accepted norm in the military, where volatile, uncertain, complex, and ambiguous environments are the norm.

We all know that the military uses games and simulations as a way to practice for war. But they also use something called a concept of operations, or CONOPS, to (1) create an overall picture of the system and the goals that they want to achieve, and (2) communicate that picture to the people who will work together to reach those goals. A concept of operations is a way to say, "Given what we know today, here is how we think this system works, and here is how we plan to approach it."

A concept of operations is a way to imagine a world.

This may seem like a big challenge, but think about our two kids playing ball: the world we create does not necessarily need to be complicated to be interesting and to help us move forward. Imagining a world can be as simple or as complex as you want to make it, depending on your goal, your situation, and the time you have available.

Unlike a large and complex process, which must be planned in advance, a concept of operations is under constant revision and adjustment based on what you learn as you go. So, yes, you need to have a goal, but since you really know very little about the challenge space, it's very likely that your goal will change as you try out ideas and learn more about what works and what doesn't.

In gamestorming, games are not links in a chain, as much as stepping stones in a fog of uncertainty. With each step, you can see a little bit further, gaining a little more clarity into the situation being explored.

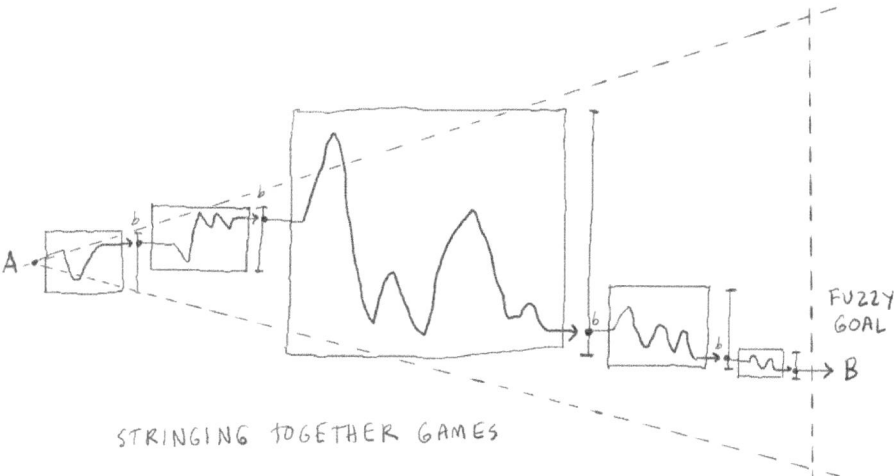

STRINGING TOGETHER GAMES

Goals, by their nature, are attempts to predict and control the future.

Specific, quantifiable goals are for production. Fuzzy goals are for search.

A startup, says entrepreneur and Stanford professor Steve Blank, is a search for a sustainable business model. How do you begin such a search? Without knowing specifically what you're looking for, it's hard to define clear, measurable goals. In search, it's not what you're seeking that matters most. It's what you find.

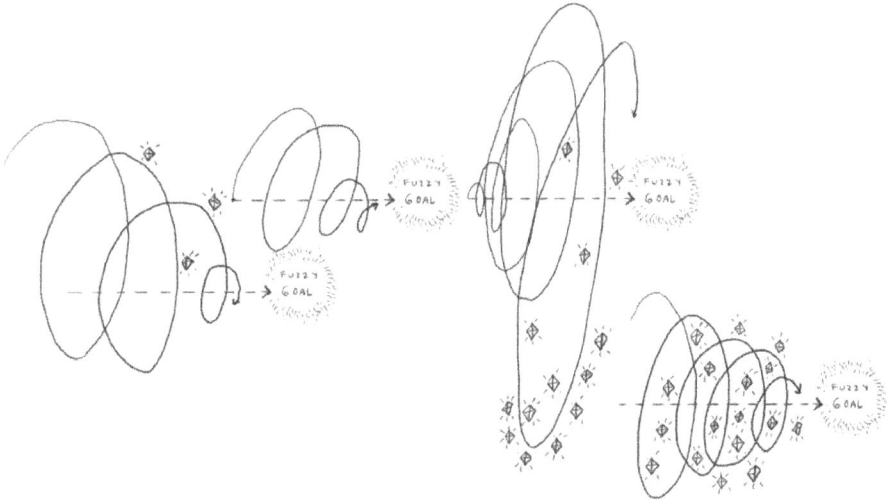

Because fuzzy goals are about creativity, sometimes, while you are searching, you discover new information that suggests a new goal, maybe even a better one. This happens all the time in creative endeavors. In the startup world, it's called a pivot.

Penicillin was discovered by accident, when bacteria in a Petri dish did not grow as expected, generating a mold instead. Plastic was invented when Charles Goodyear accidentally left rubber and sulfur on a stove. Play-Doh was designed to clean coal residue off of wallpaper. Flickr started as an online game. See Chapter 3 for a story about how sticky notes started as a failed glue project.

The possibility of discovering a pivot is one good reason to keep creative goals fuzzy and flexible.

In a paper titled "Radical Innovation: Crossing Boundaries with Interdisciplinary Teams," Cambridge researcher Alan Blackwell and colleagues identified fuzzy goals (they called this a pole-star vision) as an essential element of successful innovation. A fuzzy goal is one that "motivates the general direction of the work, without blinding the team to opportunities along the journey." One leader described his approach as "sideways management." Important factors identified by the Cambridge research team include the balance between focus and serendipity, and coordinating team goals and the goals of individual collaborators.

Fuzzy goals must give a team a sense of direction and purpose while leaving team members free to follow their intuition.

Okay, fuzzy, but how fuzzy? What is the optimal level of fuzziness? To define a fuzzy goal, you need a certain amount of ESP; fuzzy goals are emotional, sensory, and progressive:

Emotional

Fuzzy goals must be aligned with people's passion and energy for the project. It's this passion and energy that gives creative projects their momentum; therefore, fuzzy goals must have a compelling emotional component.

Sensory

The more tangible you can make a goal, the easier it is to share it with others. Sketches and crude physical models help to bring form to ideas that might otherwise be too vague to grasp. You may be able to visualize the goal itself, or you may be able to visualize an effect of the goal, such as a customer experience. Either way, before a goal can be shared, it needs to be made explicit in some way.

Progressive

Fuzzy goals are not static; they change over time. This is because, when you begin to move toward a fuzzy goal, you don't know what you don't know. The process of moving toward the goal is also a learning process, sometimes called *successive approximation*. As the team learns, the goals may change, so it's important to stop every once in a while and look around. Fuzzy goals must be adjusted (and sometimes, completely changed) based on what you learn as you go.

CHARACTERISTICS OF FUZZY GOALS

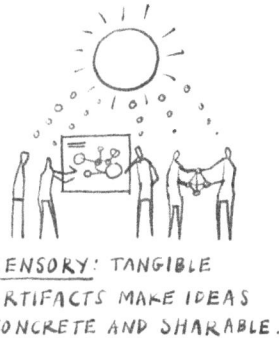

EMOTIONAL ENERGY CREATES MOMENTUM.

SENSORY: TANGIBLE ARTIFACTS MAKE IDEAS CONCRETE AND SHARABLE.

MOVEMENT TOWARD FUZZY GOALS IS PROGRESSIVE: GOALS SHIFT AS DISCOVERIES ARE MADE ALONG THE WAY.

Here are a few examples of fuzzy goals:

- A safe, snug place to sleep, wherever you are, whenever you want.
- A series of fun places to stay while you're on the road.
- A dining experience unlike anything you've had.
- A place to keep your stuff while you explore.
- A home away from home.
- Land people on the moon and return them safely to Earth.
- A faster (cheaper, more comfortable, more reliable) way to move things from here to there.

- A cure for cancer.
- A way to illuminate dark places on demand.
- Capture and store energy from the environment in a way that it can be accessed on demand.
- A way to reduce carbon in the atmosphere.
- "I have a dream that my four little children will one day live in a nation where they will not be judged by the color of their skin, but by the content of their character. I have a dream today!"
- "Be the change you are trying to create."

Innovative teams need to navigate ambiguous, uncertain, and often complex information spaces. What is unknown usually far outweighs what is known. In many ways, it's a journey in the fog, where the case studies haven't been written yet, and there are no examples of where it's been done successfully before.

You may not find what you're looking for. You might find something you're not looking for. But if you're not looking for something, you won't find anything. And the rewards are worth it.

The Shape of a Game

If you want to get started using games to effectively move toward fuzzy goals right away, you can flip to the collection of games that begins with Chapter 7 and start making things happen in your workplace. Otherwise, we can further explore what a game is. Note that once you've worked with our menu of games, you can become even more masterful by learning to design games of your own.

For now, let's start with the idea that a game has a shape. It looks something like a stubby pencil sharpened at both ends. The goal of the game is to get from the initial state to the target state, or the goal. In between you have the stubby pencil—that's the shape you need to fill in with your game design.

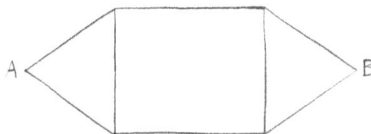

Target state

> To design a game, you begin with the end in mind: you need to know the goal of the game. What do you want to have accomplished by the end of the game? What does victory look like? What's the takeaway? That's the outcome of the game, the target state. I like to think of the target state in terms of some tangible thing, which can be anything from a prototype to a project plan or a list of ideas for further exploration. Remember, it helps if a goal is tangible; it gives people something meaningful to shoot for and gives them a sense of accomplishment when they have finished. And when they are done, they'll be able to look at something they created together.

Initial state

> We also need to know what the initial state looks like. What do we know now? What don't we know? Who is on the team? What resources do we have available?

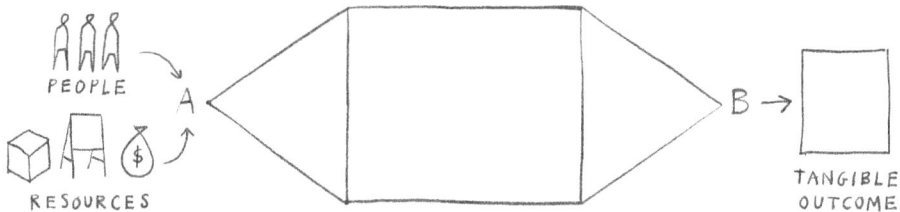

Once we understand the initial and target states as best we can (remember that many goals are fuzzy!), it's time to fill in the shape of the game. A game, like a good movie, unfolds in three acts.

The first act opens the world by setting the stage, introducing the players, and developing the themes, ideas, and information that will populate your world. In the second act, you will explore and experiment with the themes you develop in act one. In the third act, you will come to conclusions, make decisions, and plan for the actions that will serve as the inputs for the next thing that happens, whether it's another game or something else.

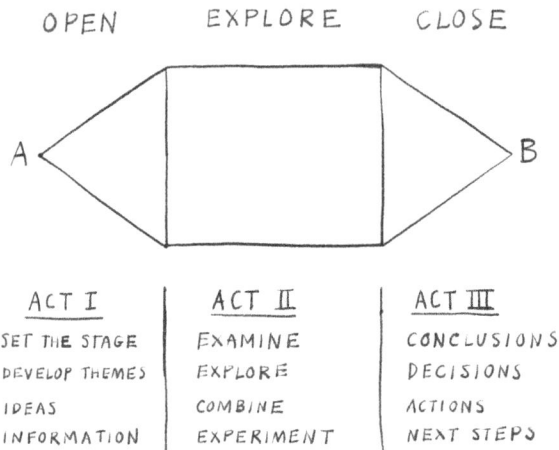

ACT I	ACT II	ACT III
SET THE STAGE	EXAMINE	CONCLUSIONS
DEVELOP THEMES	EXPLORE	DECISIONS
IDEAS	COMBINE	ACTIONS
INFORMATION	EXPERIMENT	NEXT STEPS

Each of the three stages of the game has a different purpose.

OPENING
(DIVERGENT)

Opening

The first act is the opening act, and it's all about opening—opening people's minds, opening up possibilities. The opening act is about getting the people in the room, the cards on the table, the information and ideas flowing. You can think of the opening as a big bang, an explosion of ideas and opportunities.

The more ideas you can get out in the open, the more you will have to work with in the next stage. The opening is not the time for critical thinking or skepticism; it's the time for blue-sky thinking, brainstorming, energy, and optimism. The keyword for opening is "divergent": you want the widest possible spread of perspectives; you want to populate your world with as many and as diverse a set of ideas as you can.

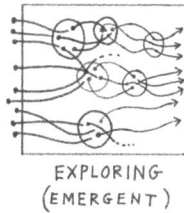

EXPLORING
(EMERGENT)

Exploring

Once you have the energy and the ideas flowing into the room, you need to do some exploration and experimentation. This is where the rubber hits the road, where you look for patterns and analogies, try to see old things in new ways, sift and sort through ideas, build and test things, and so on. The keyword for the exploring stage is "emergent": you want to create the conditions that will allow unexpected, surprising, and delightful things to emerge.

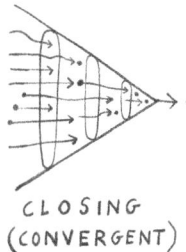

CLOSING
(CONVERGENT)

Closing

In the final act, you want to move toward conclusions—toward decisions, actions, and next steps. This is the time to assess ideas, to look at them with a critical or realistic eye. You can't do everything or pursue every opportunity. Which of them are the most promising? Where do you want to invest your time and energy? The key word for the closing act is "convergent": you want to narrow the field in order to select the most promising things for whatever comes next.

In the Storyboard game, for example, the opening stage involves thinking of a story that would qualify as a feel-good story, so it's a divergent inquiry into things that feel good or end well, leading to an ideal or target state. The exploring stage involves plotting various paths toward that ideal ending. This requires a conversation with multiple people in the same group, so the exploration becomes rich and varied. The closing state is where the value of this game really makes itself known, since it involves the participants finding patterns among the qualities and conditions that were shared across different paths. Open, explore, close. And then surprises! It would be difficult to predict a specific outcome of the Storyboard game, hence the fuzzy nature of it. What *was* predictable, however, was the emergence of plausibly useful insights into what "ideal" means to this particular team.

Now that you're situated in the shape and momentum of a game, Chapter 3 takes you to the heart of the matter: the energy, structure, and essentials to help your gamestorming practice come to life.

3

Gamestorming in Practice

If you want to do anything well, you need to practice. Gamestorming is no different. Like playing a musical instrument, it's something you do with your body as much as your mind. The more you practice, the better you will get.

In music, it's helpful to know about certain things, like how to read sheet music, play scales, and keep time. These things can seem like a lot at first, but in time, and with practice, they become second nature.

In this chapter, we will cover foundational concepts and ideas that will be useful whenever you design or facilitate a gamestorming session. Let's start with energy.

Energy

EVERYTHING STARTS
WITH ENERGY.

Everything in the universe starts with energy. Without energy, nothing happens. And in a meeting or event, energy is just as important. In gamestorming, we are talking specifically about the mental, emotional, and physical energy that participants bring when they come to a gamestorming session. That's the energy you have available, and whether you waste it or use it productively will make the difference between a great meeting and a mediocre one.

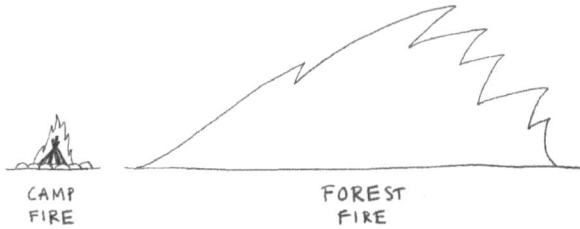

CAMP
FIRE

FOREST
FIRE

Energy can take many forms. Consider a campfire versus a forest fire. They are made of the same thing, but a campfire is controlled and generates heat and warmth, while a forest fire is out of control and causes pain and suffering. Meetings are like this too. We've all been in "brainstorming sessions" that feel like wildfires, bursting with energy but chaotic and out of control. And too much control can be just as bad as too little. Some meetings are so tightly controlled that they stifle all creativity.

Structure

Energy will follow the path of least resistance.

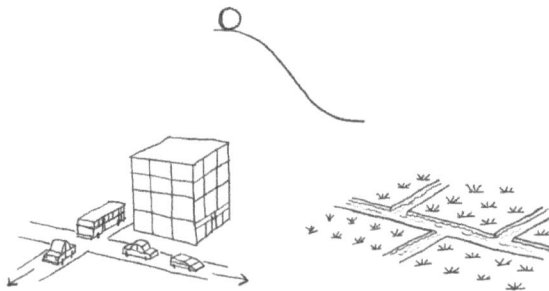

ENERGY FOLLOWS
THE PATH OF LEAST RESISTANCE

Energy left to itself will tend to run out of control or burn itself out. Harnessing energy requires some thinking about structure. Depending on what you want to do, you might think about that structure in different ways. One of the most powerful things about gamestorming is that it is a collection of lightweight, easy-to-build structures that you can use to harness energy in order to get different kinds of results.

DIFFERENT STRUCTURES
YIELD DIFFERENT RESULTS

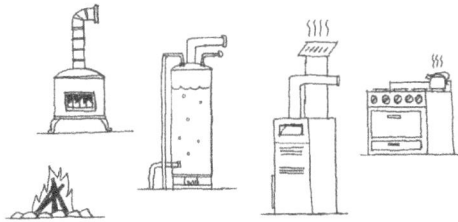

In the physical world, we have many different kinds of structures to harness energy for different purposes. A wood stove is a nice all-around tool that generates heat and a surface for cooking. A campfire is a temporary structure that's easy to build out of natural materials. Water heaters, stoves, and furnaces are more permanent structures that we use because we plan to rely on them for a long period of time.

Meeting structures can be more temporary or more permanent. Gamestorming as a toolkit is designed to make it easy for you to create temporary structures for a particular purpose, using materials that are easily "scavenged" in most work environments, like sticky notes, index cards, whiteboards, flip charts, and so on.

STRUCTURE OF MEETING SPACE

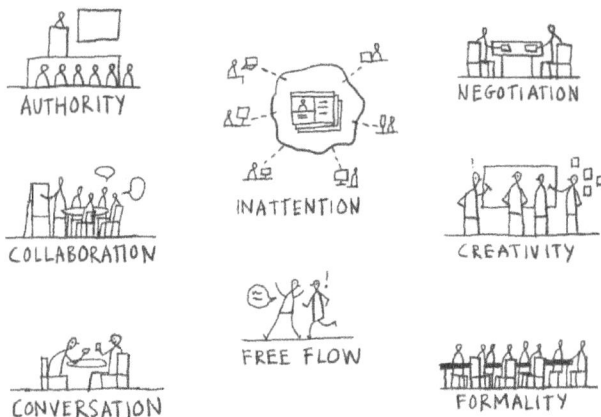

AUTHORITY

INATTENTION

NEGOTIATION

COLLABORATION

CREATIVITY

CONVERSATION

FREE FLOW

FORMALITY

Remember, energy follows structure. The layout of the room matters quite a bit. Different meeting structures will facilitate different kinds of energy flow. A room organized to highlight a presenter will create a differential between the speaker and the audience. It's clear who's in charge of the conversation. Easily accessible devices like laptops and phones will tend to dissipate attention. Putting people on opposite sides of a table may be conducive to negotiation but may hinder collaboration. Moving the focus to a flip chart or whiteboard can bring out creative energy as people work side-by-side and focus on shared work. A walk or a coffee-shop conversation will encourage open, free-flowing conversation, and people may feel more free to share more personal and intimate information. A formal meeting room will tend to reinforce existing hierarchies.

WHAT KIND OF RESULT DO YOU WANT?

NEW IDEAS

AGREEMENT

TOUGH DECISIONS

PROBLEM-SOLVING

UNRAVELING COMPLEXITY

PLANNING

When you think about the structure you want for your meeting or event, consider what you want to achieve. Do you want new ideas, or would you rather focus on planning based on what you already know? Gamestorming provides many kinds of structures beyond the room. Many gamestorming activities use "game boards"—visual frameworks for structuring information—that you can use to create frames for thinking, creativity, and conversation.

The structure you create will determine where and how the energy flows. The way you set up the room is one kind of structure. The agenda, or run-of-show, is another. A well-designed gamestorming agenda is not just a sequence of activities that follow each other, but a set of activities that create a story and build on each other from beginning to end. The output of each activity flows seamlessly as inputs into the next activity, with each exercise feeling like the inevitable next step, until the conclusion is reached.

Natural Energy Flows

There are some biological factors that simply affect all people, and the better you can understand these basic constraints, the more effective you will be.

BRIGHT AND STIMULATING ENVIRONMENTS

Natural light, if you can get it, is more comfortable and conducive to creative work than fluorescent light. Look for rooms with big windows and high ceilings. A friend once told us, "High ceilings create room for big ideas."

Don't just fill the room with the traditional pale yellow stickies, if you can help it. Bright-colored stickies and colored markers—anything you can do to make the room feel inviting and fun—will alert people that you are embarking on an adventure.

ENERGY GRADIENTS

Most people—between 55 and 65 percent of the population—reach peak energy between mid-morning and mid-day, with a mid-afternoon dip. Keep that in mind when you schedule your work sessions, and you'll tend to get better results.

TIME-BOXING

We also have pretty short attention spans. We are most attentive at the beginning of a meeting, and our attention starts to wane after about 10 minutes, after which attention drifts, until it spikes at the end of the meeting. You can take advantage of this natural human dynamic by designing an agenda so that there's a change-up in activity every 10 to 15 minutes. Frequent change-ups is a kind of cheat code. The shift from one activity into the next is like a reset button, refreshing people's energy and refocusing their attention.

INTROVERT AND EXTROVERT ENERGY

Energy doesn't work the same way for everyone. Introverts naturally recharge and store up energy when they are working alone, and their energy drains as they work with others. Extroverts are exactly the opposite: working with others charges their batteries, while working alone tends to drain them.

Since most meetings are social and full of talking, they can be more draining for introverts than for extroverts. But you can improve the balance and sustain a group's energy for much longer periods if you design a rhythm that allows both introverts and extroverts to recharge.

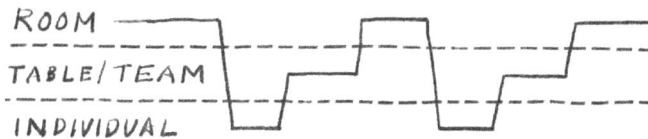

A simple rhythm that works really well is to start with an idea or activity for the entire group, then give people something they can do quietly as individuals (like writing ideas on sticky notes), then move to something they can talk about together in small groups (at their table or in breakout rooms), and follow that with something that realigns the larger group. This cadence, moving from the room to individuals to tables or teams and back to the room again, allows the whole group to stay aligned while giving everyone a chance to recharge and refresh along the way.

Opening and Closing

Opening and closing is the way you orchestrate your gamestorming activities. Like breathing, it underlies every activity, giving them rhythm and life. The way you begin something sets the stage for everything that comes afterward. A good opening creates a sense of anticipation for what comes next. Opening invites participation and exploration.

The way you end things is equally important. Closing invites reflection and decisions about next steps.

Think about the opening and closing arguments in a court trial. The purpose of the opening is to establish a frame of reference, set the context, and lay out the themes that will be explored in the trial. The closing argument sums things up and prepares the way for the jury or judge to make a decision.

Opening is just what it sounds like—it's a beginning. To open is to get people thinking and spark their imaginations. To open, you need to create a comfortable environment where people feel invited and welcome so that they will open their minds and explore possibilities they may not have considered before. Closing is about bringing things to a conclusion, moving from thinking mode into doing mode. Closing is about making choices and decisions. Breaking out/reporting back are forms of opening and closing: you open or break out to find divergent ideas and perspectives, and you close or report back to share ideas and realign with the group.

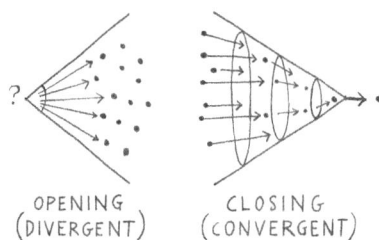

OPENING
(DIVERGENT)   CLOSING
(CONVERGENT)

Here are some risks to be aware of:

Don't open and close at the same time.

>   You can't be creative and critical simultaneously. People's minds just don't work that way. When you are exploring creative possibilities, you need to shut down the judging, critical part of your mind, and when you are making difficult choices, you should not try to be creative. Keep them separate and do them in order.

Close everything you open.

>   If you open something, you must close it, or you will risk losing the energy of the group. Opening can feel overwhelming. If you open and don't close, people may feel as if you have opened Pandora's box: there are too many opportunities and no plan to tackle them. If people do work in a breakout session, they will be disappointed if they don't have a chance to share it with others, and you may miss an important learning opportunity.

>   Sometimes closing can be as simple as saying, "This thread doesn't seem to be taking us anywhere, so let's not waste any more time on it."

Artifacts

As you begin to collect, sort, and organize information, it can quickly become overwhelming. How do you keep track of it all? In archeology, an artifact is anything made or shaped by a human hand—especially when it has archaeological or historical interest. In gamestorming, an artifact is any tangible, portable object that holds information. An artifact can be anything from a piece of paper to a sticky note or index card. Artifacts make it easier to keep track of information by making it a part of the environment.

The pieces in any game, such as cards, counters, and dice, are artifacts. When you do something as simple as moving salt and pepper shakers on a tabletop to tell a story, you are transforming them into artifacts for the sake of your tale.

The importance of these artifacts as an aid to thinking can easily be illustrated if you imagine yourself playing a game of chess while blindfolded. It's possible to hold the positions of all the pieces in your mind's eye for a time—and most chess masters can do it for an entire game—but it's much easier to have the pieces displayed on a board in front of you. The shape and color of each piece, and its position relative to the board and to the other pieces, contain a rich set of information that can help you make better decisions about the game.

Artifacts are carriers of meaning; just like chess pieces on a board, they make knowledge or information explicit, tangible, portable, and persistent. When you write an idea on a sticky note, you are creating an information artifact. When you have created many such artifacts, they can become more or less useful depending on how you distribute them in your environment. The more information you can store in material objects or the environment, the more your players' minds are free to engage with the situation at hand.

STICKY NOTES

In 1968, Dr. Spencer Silver, a scientist at 3M, developed a low-tack, reusable adhesive. For years, he promoted it within the company in the hope of turning it into a product. The adhesive was strong enough to hold papers together but weak enough that they could easily be pulled apart without tearing. He promoted it as a spray, or as a surface for bulletin boards where papers could be attached and removed without the use of pins.

Silver was not having much luck promoting his invention until he ran into Arthur Fry, who sang in his church choir and was frustrated that the small slips of paper he used as bookmarks kept falling out of his hymnal. Fry realized that the adhesive was perfect for keeping his bookmarks attached to the hymnal without damaging the book. And thus, the Post-it and many sticky-note progeny were born.

The sticky note is one of the most useful tools in gamestorming because it allows you to break any complex topic into small, movable artifacts that you can then distribute into physical space by attaching them to your desk, walls, doors, and so on. This allows you to quickly and easily explore all kinds of relationships between and among the atoms and to keep these various alternatives within your visual field while you are working.

It's easy to see the value of being able to distribute information into your environment in this way by looking at all the ways people use sticky notes in their daily lives. Want to remember to bring something to work? Leave a sticky note on the inside of the front door to remind you. Want to remember which items to pick up on the way home? Leave a sticky note on your phone. Need to remember how to get somewhere? Write the directions on a sticky note and stick it to your steering wheel. Want to leave a message for someone at work? Leave a sticky note on her computer screen.

Placing artifacts into the environment like this is a way to put ideas into context in a way that's dynamic. Combinations can stay fixed for as long as you want them to, and can also be shuffled or reconfigured at a moment's notice.

Artifacts like sticky notes and index cards have the same kinds of properties as a deck of cards. They can be spread out in various combinations. They can be shuffled into random order. They can be distributed into groups. Endless permutations and combinations are possible.

NODES

A node is an important kind of artifact. A node can be pretty much anything, when seen as part of a larger system. As a knowledge explorer, when you create artifacts, you will usually be thinking of them as elements in something larger. In the opening stages of any inquiry, the first order of business is to generate as many artifacts—nodes—as possible, so you want to begin from as wide an angle as possible. We call this kind of exercise node generation.

the post-up

One method for generating nodes is called the Post-Up (see a full description in Chapter 7). To post up, you begin with some kind of fire-starter to set the parameters that define your list. To start with a simple example, imagine that you are going shopping and need to create a list of groceries. You could start with a simple question: "What do I need from the store?" Instead of a typical brainstorming session, where people call out ideas and a facilitator makes a list that everyone can see, you ask people to generate their ideas silently, using sticky notes—one idea per note.

Doing this accomplishes two goals. First, since it's an opening exercise, you will get a more diverse set of ideas by asking people to generate them silently. Second, by asking people to write each idea on a separate sticky note, you are generating a set of modular, movable artifacts that you will later be able to shuffle, sort, and reorganize.

When people are finished generating ideas, ask them to take turns going up to a flip chart or whiteboard and sharing their ideas with the group, as follows: read each sticky note aloud and place it on the board where everyone can see it. Notice that this post-up process is a version of breaking out/reporting back. The breakout begins when you ask people to start writing ideas, and the report-back ends when everyone has finished sharing ideas and the board is filled with sticky notes.

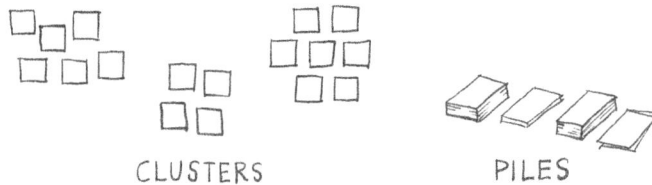

CLUSTERS   PILES

Let's say you have generated a bunch of nodes—most likely index cards and sticky notes or some combination of them—and you want to explore some different combinations. What can you do? You can shuffle them. You can group them by sorting them into piles or clusters (a cluster is simply a pile that's spread out so that you can see everything in the pile).

LINKING

Another way to organize nodes is to link them together in various ways, in much the same way as the web is organized by the links that connect pages and ideas to one another. For example, you could link nodes together in a chain that represents a process, like a flowchart, or link them conceptually, such as you might do in a mind map. With sticky notes and a whiteboard, you can start to create flows and structures like these:

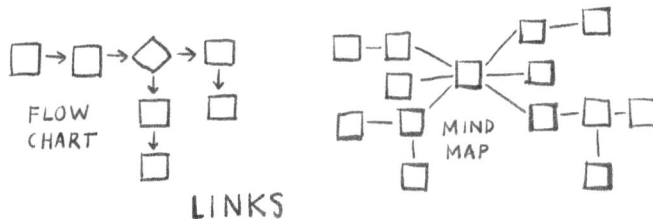

LINKS

Meaningful Space

Academic Yuri Engelhardt introduced the term "meaningful space," which gives us a great framework for considering the relationships among artifacts: "The key feature distinguishing graphics from text is 'meaningful space'—the use of spatial relations to convey information."[1]

White to mate in 2 moves.

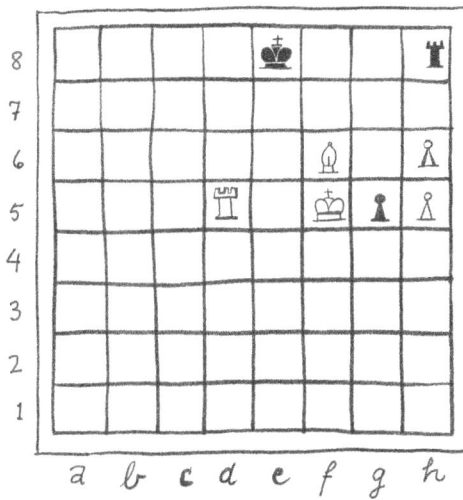

Imagine trying to play chess without a board. A game like chess relies not only on the meaning of the pieces but also on the ever-changing relationships they have to each other in space. The grid of the chessboard creates a meaningful space as cleanly and as surely as the grid on any map. Both the grid and the pieces are integral and essential to the game.

---

1 Yuri Engelhardt, "Meaningful Space: How Graphics Use Space to Convey Information," *Proceedings of Vision Plus 4, School of Design* (1998): 108–126.

Just like every other game, chess creates a world that players can explore together. The chessboard (meaningful space) creates the boundaries of the world, and the pieces (artifacts) populate the world.

The rules of the game govern what is and isn't possible in the world. Chess players agree to enter the world in order to explore the possible permutations and combinations and try to achieve their goals, which, in the case of chess, are achieved at the expense of the other player. However, in gamestorming, more often, the players share a common goal.

In gamestorming, meaningful space can be created anywhere: on a whiteboard, flip chart, or piece of paper; on a tabletop or in a room. It's a way of framing any space to make relationships within it more meaningful. The grid, like the grid of a chessboard, is one of the most common and useful ways to organize space. You can see grids all around you; we use grids for everything from planning cities to managing the numbers in our spreadsheets.

Affinity mapping is a common method that uses meaningful space to sort a large set of nodes into a few common themes. It is a way to rapidly get a group of people aligned about what they are working on together. First, generate a set of nodes using the Post-Up game or some other node-generation method (see Chapter 7).

Next, create a meaningful space by dividing a whiteboard or other visual area into three columns. Ask people to sort the sticky notes into three columns that "feel like they belong together" without trying to name the columns. It's important that they not try to name the columns. Naming the columns too early will force them back into familiar, comfortable patterns. Remember that in creative work, we are trying to help people generate and see new patterns. While people are sorting, you may ask them to try to eliminate redundancies by placing similar sticky notes on top of each other. Sometimes the sticky notes don't fit neatly into three columns, and you may want to create more columns to accommodate the differences. You should do this sparingly, though, because too many categories will defeat your purpose, which is to find some common themes.

The three (or more) columns serve as a meaningful space, a set of "empty buckets" that people can use to sort their ideas, kind of like a cubbyhole desk or one of those change-sorting machines you see sometimes at carnivals.

Affinity Mapping

Having a business meeting without artifacts and meaningful space is like meeting blindfolded with your hands behind your back. Yes, you can do it, but why would you want to?

Now let's add to this equation the concept of meaningful, organized space, such as what you might find in a board game, or on a tennis court or golf course. Think about what these organized spaces make possible: they allow the position of artifacts to have a precise meaning that is dependent on their position.

Note: Meaningful space is a concept introduced by visual thinking researcher Yuri Englehardt in his important book and PhD thesis, *The Language of Graphics* (2002).

BORDERS

Borders are lines that frame a space. They create edges that separate one thing from another. A border can be as simple as a line down the center of the page that separates the pros from the cons. By drawing a box or a circle, you create a border that separates the inside from the outside. Borders are imaginary lines. You can see borders on a map, but if you go to the real place that's represented on the map, you won't see a line drawn on the ground.

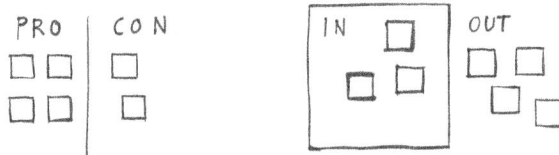

PRO | CON   IN   OUT

BORDERS

Nevertheless, borders are so important that for many people, they are worth fighting wars over.

AXES

An axis gives meaning to direction within a space. One common example is the compass points on a map. By convention, north is usually up, unless otherwise noted. Now, in addition to the borders that separate things like countries, we have a common language for navigating within the given space.

Unlike a border, which simply separates one thing from another, an axis is a line of force. It has direction. North may be indicated by a small arrow in the corner of a map, but nevertheless, the idea influences the entire map. North is "up" not only in the corner but all over the map.

SEQUENCE

PRIORITY
IMPORTANCE

Like the north arrow on a map, many axes are not explicitly depicted but are implied by convention. For example, in Western countries, people read left to right, so when you do something like place a bunch of sticky notes in a left-to-right sequence, many people will assume that you intend them to be read in sequence.

Similarly, if you organize things from top to bottom, many people will assume that you have ranked them in order of importance (at least, in the West).

Many methods for organizing ideas have implied axes that are not explicitly depicted. The org chart, for example, has an implied axis where up represents "reports to" and down represents "authority over"; and the conference brackets in a sports tournament have an implied time axis that goes from left to right.

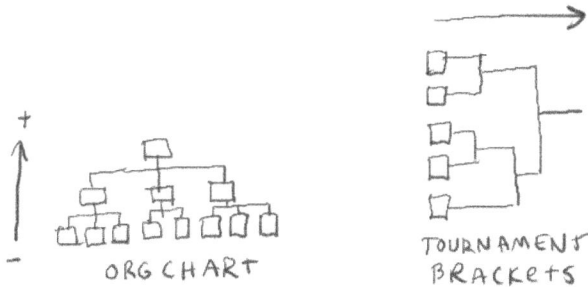

ORG CHART

TOURNAMENT BRACKETS

CIRCLES AND TARGETS

Circles and target shapes can be useful when you want to approximate how close you are to a stated goal. Like an archer shooting arrows at a target, you can estimate how close or how far a certain artifact is from the center you are aiming for. You can use concentric rings and axes in combination to delineate both degree and lines of force.

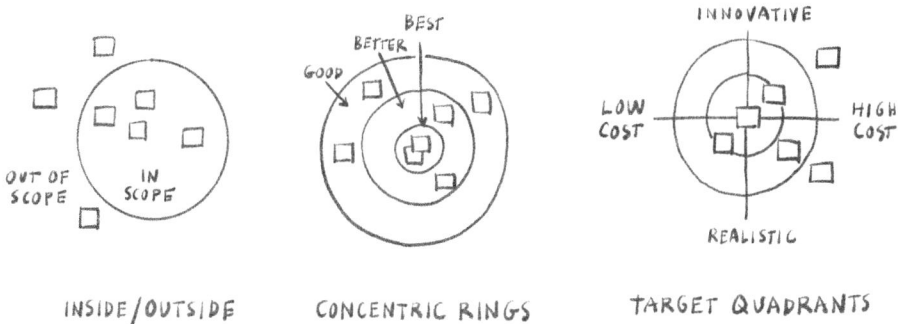

INSIDE/OUTSIDE

CONCENTRIC RINGS

TARGET QUADRANTS

METRIC VERSUS ORDERED SPACE

To illustrate the difference between metric and ordered space, think about how we measure time. When we talk about the days of the week or the months of the year, we are making an either/or kind of distinction. "What day is it?" is an either/or question. Either it's Monday, or it's Tuesday, and so on. When we talk about the time of day, we are talking about something that's much more relative and is dependent on who is asking the question and in what context. We might answer "noonish" or we might answer "12:01:36," depending on the context. That's because calendar time is ordered (we care more about sequence than precision), and clock time is measured (we care more about precision than sequence).

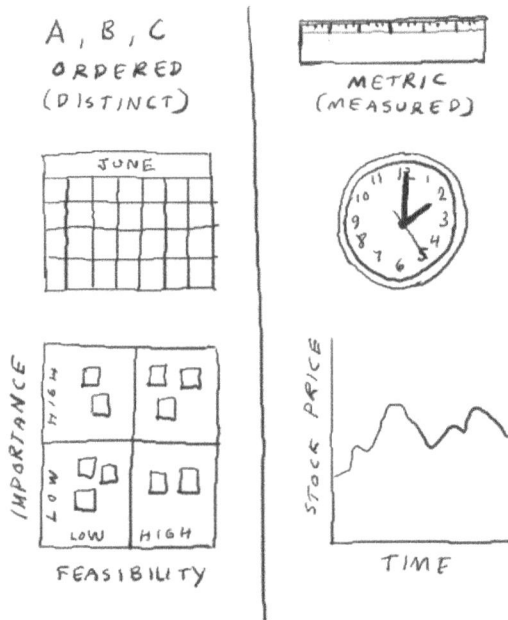

Metric space is space that we measure with more or less precision. Ordered space is space where we care more about the order of things than their precise position. For example, in a footrace, it's usually very important who came in first, second, and third. The exact times may be important also, but probably less so. If the first-place runner came in an hour before the second-place runner, and the second-place runner came in only minutes before the third-place runner, the order of their finishing is the same, as though they all finished within seconds of each other.

In meaningful space that's metric, we care about things that are absolute, like height, weight, length, distance, speed, temperature, and so on. In meaningful space that's ordered, we care more about categories and relationships: Is it higher or lower? Heavier or lighter? Longer or shorter? And so on.

GRIDS

The grid is simply what you see when you look at a chessboard, checkerboard, spreadsheet, or soldiers on parade. Rows and columns, rank and file. The file or column is the vertical line. When people march in single file, it means they have lined up in a column, like the lines you see in the grocery store or the bank. The row or rank is the horizontal line. In combination, rank and file make up a grid, one of the most useful methods for organizing information.

Grids come in all shapes and sizes. You can use grids to organize physical space, such as the gridlines on a map. You can use a grid to formulate a search, such as in the game of *Battleship*. You can use a grid to lay out a web page or a magazine page. You can use it to do your bookkeeping or to organize any set of numbers into columns and rows. One very useful form of grid is created by breaking a square into quadrants to organize information according to two criteria. Another useful method is to use a grid to sort things into columns or rows.

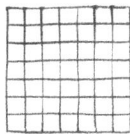 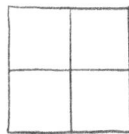 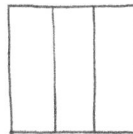 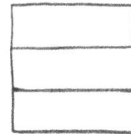

GRID   QUADRANTS   COLUMNS   ROWS

LANDSCAPES AND MAPS

Sometimes it makes sense to think of information in terms of a landscape. Every business is on a journey of some kind, going from one place to another, and every marketplace is a landscape with its own unique perils, challenges, and opportunities. What journey is your business on? What does the road ahead look like? What obstacles lie in the immediate future? What is farther down the road? What forces help drive you forward? What forces hold you back?

David Sibbet, of The Grove Consultants International, uses a tool he calls the Graphic Gameplan to help teams think through their challenges.[2] The Graphic Gameplan uses a precisely designed set of meaningful spaces to organize people's thinking and move from ideas to action. Challenges are represented as a rough landscape, actions as an arrow, success factors as wheels, goals as a target, and so on.

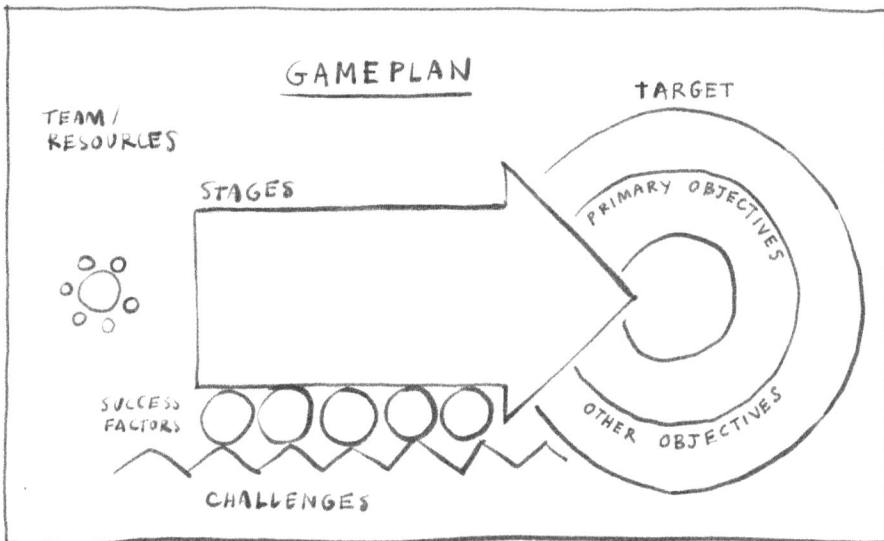

GRAPHIC GAMEPLAN DESIGNED BY DAVID SIBBET

---

2 The Graphic Gameplan is one of many Graphic Guide® templates designed by David Sibbet of The Grove Consultants International. You can order templates at *https://www.thegrove.com*.

METAPHOR

Another way to organize information is to formulate analogies and conceptual links with other things. Your information space can be represented by a house, an airplane, a building, an animal, a ship, a restaurant, or anything else that will help you break out of habitual thinking patterns. A good metaphor comes with a set of associations that will change your perspective and help you think differently about a topic. A metaphoric structure can help you ask new and thought-provoking questions that you may not have considered before.

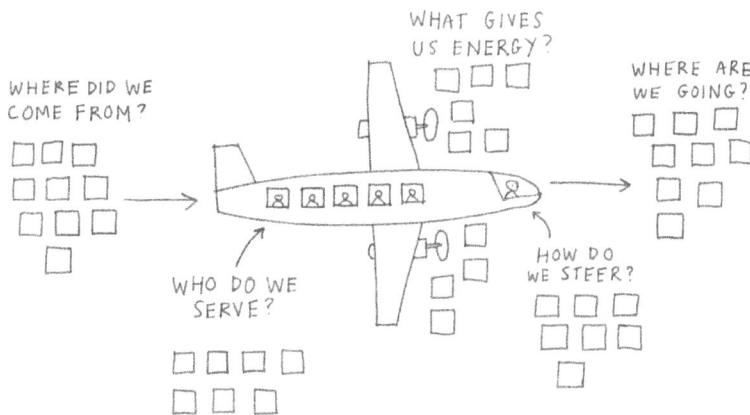

For example, a house is a common metaphor that leads to questions such as: What are the foundations? What are the columns and beams that support the roof? What covers us? What is the floor, the walls?

One danger in this kind of exploration is getting too connected to, or too rigid about, the metaphor—everything does not need to be force-fit into the metaphor.

For example, Dave once worked with a recruiting company that was using fishing as a metaphor for recruiting. That's a solid metaphor, and it's useful as long as it generates thought-provoking questions. But you're sinking too low when you start asking questions like: "Does this mean we see the people we are recruiting as food? That we are baiting them and that they will end up worse off?" No, it doesn't. It's a metaphor, a tool for thinking. Don't let people overthink it or you can easily go down a rabbit hole.

Note: Dave has created a library of visual frameworks, which you can view online for free at *https://visualframeworks.com*.

Sketching and Modelmaking

When we start talking about metaphors, like houses and airplanes, some people start feeling a bit uncomfortable. After all, maybe you signed up to be a facilitator, but that doesn't mean you're an artist. Right?

Well, we'd like you to reconsider that. Sun wrote an entire book—a prequel to *Gamestorming*—on making spontaneous visual marks to help yourself think, without needing to feel like an artist or creative. If you can warm up to the idea of sketching and modelmaking, a whole new world of possibilities opens up that will make your explorations more enjoyable and productive and your meetings richer and more visually engaging.

Sketches and models are simply different kinds of artifacts. A sketch can be a drawing, as in a pencil sketch. It can be a short skit, as in a comedy sketch. It can be a roughly described outline, as in "he sketched out a plan" or "she sketched in the details." What do all these meanings have in common? What is the nature of a sketch?

The defining characteristics of a sketch are its informality, looseness, and brevity. A sketch is a preliminary activity that may or may not lead to a more refined, finished version. A sketch is a rapid study, an exploration. An artist might do hundreds of sketches before settling on one idea for deeper examination. Sketching is a way to quickly explore ideas by making them more tangible or concrete.

A good sketch has just enough information to get an idea across, and no more. But sketching out ideas cannot be the sole domain of the artist, sculptor, or actor. Most of us convey our thoughts verbally or in writing, but this is only one channel of communication, and limiting our ideas to a single channel is a serious constraint on thinking.

A quick introduction to visual language (for example, see the visual alphabet discussion in the next section) can help people get over the psychological "I can't draw" barrier, to feel more comfortable expressing ideas visually or symbolically.

Sketching can also include other kinds of modeling exercises, such as a quick improvised skit or physical modelmaking with modeling clay and pipe cleaners.

The key is to make things real with minimal effort. Rapid paper prototyping is a way to sketch software interfaces. Designers create mockups of computer interfaces using sticky notes, paper, and cardboard, which they can then use to test and try various user interactions.

VISUAL LANGUAGE

In school we are taught that the fundamental things we need to learn to be successful in our society are reading, writing, and arithmetic. The first several years of public education focus primarily on these fundamentals. In an industrial world, where every worker functioned as a standardized cog in a corporate machine, this may have made sense.

But today's challenges aren't standard. As we have discussed, work today often must address unknowns, uncertainty, and ambiguous challenge spaces where solutions are not clear or standard, and where the ability to create and discover is more important than fitting an established mold.

Nearly every human endeavor, when examined, reveals evidence of the importance of visual language. In legal proceedings, visual aids help juries decide complex cases. Filmmakers create storyboards to help them bring screenplays to life. Medical illustration helps surgeons and other medical professionals learn their trade. The road signs we navigate by, the interfaces on our computer screens, and the logos that help us find the stores and brands we like are all examples of visual language in action. Even your driver's license would be useless without the image that represents you and confirms that, yes, the person in the picture is in fact the person this card identifies.

We think sketching is a core practice of gamestorming. It's an important element of creative thinking, and anyone can do it. You don't need any special skills. You can start with a pen and paper. That doesn't mean it's easy, any more than reading, writing, and arithmetic are easy; you will need to apply yourself. But we have found that the biggest hurdle for most people is confidence. If you can bring yourself to dive in and start drawing, the rest will take care of itself. So, with that in mind, here are a few concepts and exercises that you can use to start building some basic drawing skills. Once you are familiar with these concepts, you can use the same exercises to bring colleagues and other groups quickly up to speed.

Now, grab a pen and a piece of paper, and let's do a few exercises.

Note: Dave has created a free primer with video lessons (*https://xplaner.com/visual-thinking-school*).

THE VISUAL ALPHABET

Let's begin with the visual alphabet, a kind of proto-alphabet of visual shapes that you can use to construct any kind of visual. It's made up of 12 shapes—the "letters" of the visual alphabet—called *glyphs*. If you can draw these 12 shapes, you can draw anything else you can imagine.

The first six glyphs are linear. They can be linked to each other in a sequence or chain; they are open shapes that flow naturally together, so we call them *flows*. Their names are point, line, angle, arc, spiral, and loop. Try drawing them now.

The next six glyphs are closed shapes. When a line closes in on itself, it tends to feel more like a solid object, because the border of a closed shape separates it from the background, like an island. Closed shapes are distinct from the environment that surrounds them, which gives them the illusion of form, so we call these shapes *forms*. Their names are oval, seed, triangle, rectangle, house, and cloud. Try drawing them now.

With these 12 glyphs, you can draw anything. The number of possible combinations is infinite. Hard to believe? Let's prove this in a few steps. First, see if you can make the letters of the alphabet using just the 12 shapes of the visual alphabet:

ABCDEFGHIJKLMNOPQRSTUVWXYZ

Satisfied? From 12 come 26. And now the numbers:

1 2 3 4 5 6 7 8 9 0

Now let's try something more difficult. Look around you, wherever you happen to be at the moment. Pick out a few simple objects and see if you can draw them using just the shapes from the visual alphabet:

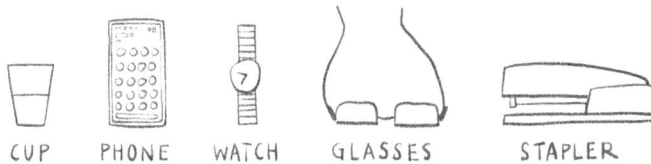

CUP   PHONE   WATCH   GLASSES   STAPLER

Notice that the images in the preceding figure are labeled. Pictures don't need to carry all the semantic weight of whatever you are trying to convey. This is a key difference between drawing and visual language. Drawing in an artistic sense is about fooling the eye—making things appear like they appear in nature. Visual language is about conveying meaning. By labeling anything that might be otherwise ambiguous or confusing, you make it easier for people to understand what you are "drawing about."

DRAWING PEOPLE

Now let's try something a little more difficult. One of the most common things you'll need to draw, since you'll be communicating with people, is, yes, people. Just about anything you want to communicate visually will probably require images of people at one point or another

Most of us can use the glyphs of the visual alphabet to draw a simple stick figure, like this:

The problem arises when you try to draw something more complex, such as people doing something more than just standing there. Usually when you want to draw a person, it's because you want to show an action—for example, somebody eating dinner, using a vending machine, driving a car, or riding a bicycle.

Let's start by drawing a picture of somebody mailing a letter.

First, imagine yourself mailing a letter. Pick up a piece of paper and pose yourself in that position to see how it feels. You might want to do it in front of a mirror or ask a friend to take a picture at first. Or if it's easier, you can find a picture on the internet or in a magazine. Over time, with practice, you will be able to imagine and draw people without posing or reference.

Pay special attention to the angle of the body; it conveys the essence of the action. Think about what you notice first when you see a person in the distance. It's the position of the body that conveys a person's attitude as much as anything else. Most people draw a stick figure by starting with the head and adding the body afterward. This way of drawing a stick figure will almost always result in a big-headed, stiff stick figure.

When drawing a person, you will get a much better effect if you start with the center of gravity and work outward. Draw a rectangle to represent the trunk of the body, trying to keep it at approximately the same angle.

In his notebooks, Leonardo da Vinci kept careful notes about the importance of the body's attitude and how it can be used to convey meaning:

A picture or representation of human figures ought to be done in such a way as that the spectator may easily recognize, by means of their attitudes, the purpose in their minds. Thus, if you have to represent a man of noble character in the act of speaking, let his gestures be such as naturally accompany good words; and, in the same way, if you wish to depict a man of a brutal nature, give him fierce movements; as with his arms flung out towards the listener, and his head and breast thrust forward beyond his feet, as if following the speaker's hands. Thus it is with a deaf and dumb person who, when he sees two men in conversation— although he is deprived of hearing—can nevertheless understand, from the attitudes and gestures of the speakers, the nature of their discussion.

—LEONARDO DA VINCI

The next most prominent feature is the legs; they connect the person to the ground and have the most impact on the body's position. Draw a line to represent the ground and add lines for the legs and feet to connect the body to the ground.

The next most important element to conveying attitude is the hands. We use our hands for nearly everything we do. Have you ever heard the advice given to public speakers to use their hands and to gesture to help them reinforce their meaning? The same principle applies to stick figures. Now try drawing the arms in position. A small circle is usually sufficient to represent the hands. Don't forget to add the letter, or our trip to the mailbox will be wasted.

Now take a look at the angle of the neck and head relative to the rest of the body. Notice that they are at different angles. Unless you are a soldier standing at attention, this is nearly always the case. We are constantly turning our heads to see better, to listen carefully, and so on. See if you can draw the head and attach it to the body with a single line at the right angle.

Now that we have finished the figure, we can think about the face. Think about the various smiley faces and other emoticons you can make on a computer keyboard. Those same combinations will suffice for nearly any facial expression you want. Adding a short line for the nose will help you show which direction the head is pointing. This can be especially important when you want to show two people interacting with each other.

You can use the same principles you learned earlier to make the mailbox, by combining basic shapes from the visual alphabet. In the United States, our mailboxes look like R2-D2 of Star Wars fame. Depending on where you live, yours may differ.

We hope this short demonstration has convinced you that basic sketching skills are not out of your reach. Once you become comfortable with the preceding exercises, you can use them to help others become more comfortable with sketching their ideas. In numerous workshops, we've found that you can get through these exercises with a group in about 10 to 15 minutes. In the time it takes for a brief coffee break, you can familiarize a group with these concepts and get them comfortable enough to begin sketching out their ideas.

PERSPECTIVE

One thing that often intimidates people is the notion of perspective. We've found it helpful to describe the three primary methods that have been used to create a sense of visual space in the history of art. The one we are most familiar with is linear perspective, developed during the Italian Renaissance. The invention, or perhaps we should say "discovery," of perspective is credited to the artist and architect Filippo Brunnelleschi around 1425.

Linear perspective creates the illusion of space by imitating the view seen by the eye from a particular vantage point. The artist draws a line representing the horizon at eye level and then establishes vanishing points along that horizon. You can use these vanishing points to construct almost any scene and give an illusion of depth that immerses the viewer in the scene.

But linear perspective is only one of three principal methods that artists have used through the centuries.

Parallel perspective is another form of pictorial grammar that originated in China and predates linear perspective by hundreds of years. In parallel perspective, construction lines do not converge to points on the horizon but are drawn parallel to each other so that the scene appears to go on indefinitely in all directions. This is a way of showing a scene as though seen from above and has the advantage that everything in the image can be drawn to the same scale. This is sometimes called God's perspective because of the aerial view that can be extended infinitely in all directions.

An even earlier form of pictorial space emerged thousands of years before either linear or parallel perspective. This way of organizing images was more similar to written language and perhaps found its purest expression in the art of ancient Egypt, so we like to call this Egyptian perspective. Instead of drawing things as we see them, it involved drawing things in their ideal form, as they might be seen by the mind. If something was most recognizable from the side, it was drawn in profile; if it was most recognizable from the top, it was drawn from that perspective. This Egyptian form of perspective is by far the most common across all societies and cultures since the earliest times. Children will naturally draw things this way unless they are taught a different method. For many uses it is the clearest and easiest to understand, and for most people it's the easiest to learn and apply quickly.

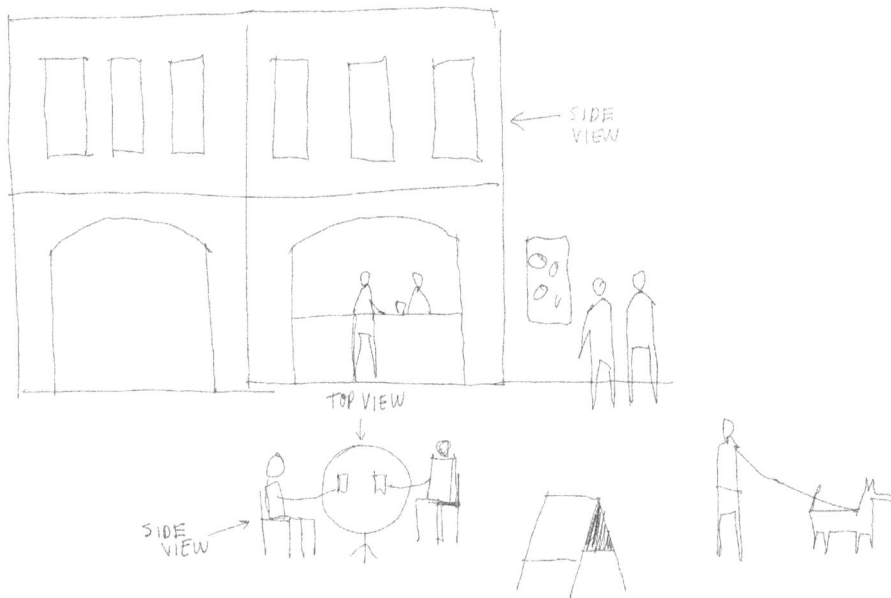

To draw in the Egyptian perspective, all you need to do is think like a child. Draw things the way they appear in your mind's eye, without worrying about whether they resemble reality. The idea in Egyptian perspective is to capture and convey the essence of the object. A drawing of a cat doesn't need to look like a cat so much as it must convey the idea of a cat. The letters in the word *CAT* convey an idea without any resemblance whatsoever, and you can convey the same concept pictorially with a very small number of simple shapes.

How many ways can you sketch a cat?

THERE'S MORE THAN ONE WAY TO SKETCH A CAT!

As you begin to develop your visual language skills, consider carrying a notebook, as Leonardo da Vinci did, to record your observations and reflections. Here's his advice on the matter:

> *Go about, and constantly, as you go, observe, note and consider the circumstances and behavior of men in talking, quarreling or laughing or fighting together; the action of the men themselves and the actions of the bystanders, who separate them or look on. And take a note of them with slight strokes in a little book which you should always carry with you... for the forms, and positions of objects are so infinite that the memory is incapable of retaining them, wherefore keep these [sketches] as your guides and masters.*
>
> **—LEONARDO DA VINCI**

Randomness, Reversal, and Reframing

Not everything comes to us in order. It's rumored that William S. Burroughs determined the order of the pages in his book, *Naked Lunch*, by throwing the manuscript in the air and assembling the pages in the order he picked them up. Agatha Christie would write down scenes for her novels, assign each scene a letter, and try them in random sequences to find the best order. Martin Luther King kept his ideas for speeches and sermons on note cards so he could shuffle and rearrange them as needed.

The human brain is a pattern-making machine. We seek and find patterns everywhere we look. Leonardo da Vinci used to find inspiration by looking at stains on the wall:

> *I cannot forbear to mention...a new device for study...which may seem trivial and almost ludicrous...[but] is extremely useful in arousing the mind...Look at a wall spotted with stains, or with a mixture of stones... you may discover a resemblance to landscapes...battles with figures in action...strange faces and costumes...and an endless variety of objects....*
>
> **—LEONARDO DA VINCI**

We are so good at finding patterns that once we find one, it can be difficult to see anything else. Creating randomness is a way of fooling the mind so that you can more easily search for new patterns in familiar domains. By shuffling the deck, reversing the order, or reframing the familiar, you create enough space for new ideas and opportunities to emerge.

Randomness is an essential element in any kind of creativity. The shuffling and recombination of genes, for example, is an essential element in the variation and selection that leads to the emergence of new life forms. The same principle works in the realm of thought and ideas.

A map of the world with south at the top, for example, invites new thinking about the relationships among nations.

One reason to use modular artifacts such as index cards and sticky notes is that they facilitate randomness; they can be easily shuffled, resorted, and rearranged to generate new patterns and ideas.

Firestarting

How do you get the energy going?

Firestarting is anything you can do that ignites people's imagination and creates a call to adventure. In the wilderness, the way you start a fire is very important, and in gamestorming, the same is true. Start a fire in the wrong way or in the wrong place, and you may soon find that things are out of control—you can have a raging forest fire on your hands. By the way you initiate an inquiry, you can inspire the kinds of thought, reflection, emotion, and sensation that are most likely to get you the result that you want.

The most common and powerful firestarter is a question. A good question is like an arrow you can aim at any challenge. The way you frame a question will lay out a vector, a line of inquiry that points in a certain direction. There are many kinds of questioning techniques, and they bear careful study and practice. You can use them to change people's perspectives on a problem, drill down to expose root causes, elevate a conversation to a higher plane, and many other things.

If people are gathering for the first time, one of my favorite firestarter questions is "What brings you here?" This is especially useful for a group that's just forming, because it is the one thing that you can be sure everybody has in common. Everyone is there, and you can be pretty sure everybody is there for a reason.

Another common firestarter is called fill-in-the-blank, in which you craft a short phrase or sentence and ask people to fill in the blank like they would on a test. For example, if you want to explore customer needs, consider how customer needs are typically expressed. A fill-in-the-blank to explore customer needs could be written as "I want _____," "I wish _____," or "I wonder _____."

Setups

One of the hardest things for people who are new to facilitating is learning how to give simple, clear instructions for an exercise. It seems simple enough when you read the instructions in the book, but somehow, when you get in front of a group, it can be hard. There are two tips that we have found get people over this hump pretty quickly.

The first tip is that you don't have to give all the instructions at the very beginning. If you have 30 minutes for an exercise with three steps, don't give people all three steps at once. It's much better to give the instruction for the first step, give people time to do it, and don't give the instruction for the second step until people have finished the first. This keeps people from getting confused.

The second tip is to practice your setups. It might seem like the instructions are pretty simple, but you'll find people have all kinds of questions that you didn't anticipate. Practice your setups with friends and colleagues in low-risk settings, and you'll be much better prepared when it comes to game time.

Asking Questions

Perhaps nothing is more important to exploration and discovery than the art of asking good questions. Questions ignite people's passions and energy; they create heat; and they illuminate things that were previously obscure.

In life and in business, we are often in a position where we want to go from point A to point B. When the path from A to B is clear, we can draw a straight line and be done with it. Whether that path is easy or difficult is beside the point.

A   B

A question is one half of an equation, where the other half is usually unknown. If the question is "How do we get from here to there?" and the answer is known, the equation is fulfilled and we have our answer. We can draw a straight line from A to B. This is the process answer, where we describe the path from A to B as a series of steps.

A ————————————————————→ B

When the path from A to B is unclear, we have a different kind of challenge. If we ask the same question, "How do we get from here to there?" we need to face the fact that we don't know the answer. The answer in fact may be not only unknown but also unknowable: not all questions are answerable.

Crossing this kind of challenge space is a journey into the unknown, like crossing a desert or sailing into uncharted waters. When you begin, it's impossible to know how near or far the answer—if there is an answer—may be. There are five kinds of questions for finding your way in complex challenge spaces: opening, navigating, examining, experimental, and closing questions.

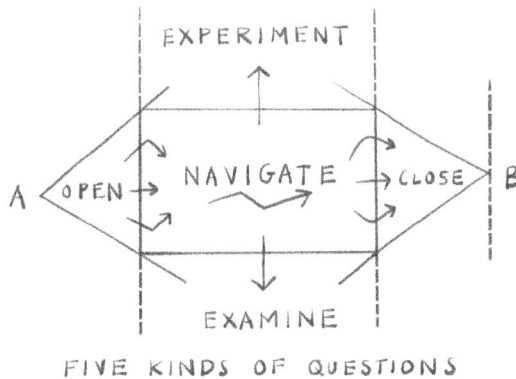

FIVE KINDS OF QUESTIONS

As we've seen, in any knowledge game, you must open the world, explore the world, and close the world. In between points A and B, you must navigate as best you can to ensure that you are making the progress you want. In the next section, we define categories of questions that move you effectively through that challenge space and offer a few example questions for each category. We'll dive deeper into the use of questions (and offer more examples relative to meeting design) in Chapter 4.

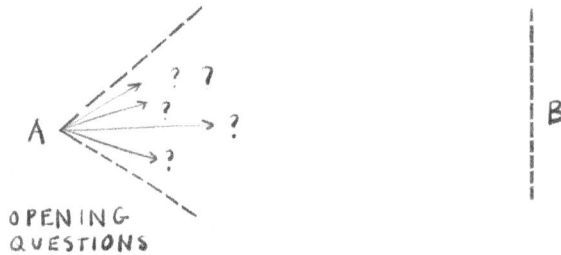

A   OPENING
     QUESTIONS

B

OPENING QUESTIONS

Opening questions are intended to open a portal into the game world. The opening stage of your game is the first act, where the players get to know each other and, together, you identify the main themes you want to explore in the next stage. The trick of opening is to get people to feel comfortable with the process of working together while generating as many ideas as possible. If they know each other too well, they will have trouble breaking out of the traditional limits of their collective culture, and their ideas will be too similar. If they are complete strangers, they will generate a lot of diverse ideas but may have trouble working together as a team.

OPENING

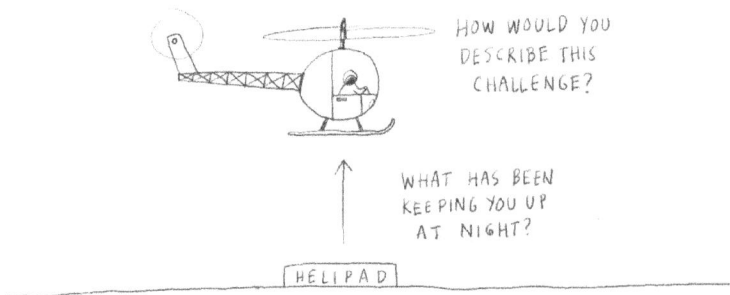

HOW WOULD YOU DESCRIBE THIS CHALLENGE?

WHAT HAS BEEN KEEPING YOU UP AT NIGHT?

HELIPAD

As a facilitator, the questions you have allow you to channel the energy and flow of the group. Imagine your role as a helicopter pilot, like a tour guide, creating a flow and perspective on the group's focus and energy. When you open, you are taking off, beginning the tour. This is a great chance to create energy, get ideas flowing, and ensure that you are taking people where they want to go.

The idea behind an opening question is to generate ideas and options, to provoke thought and reveal possibilities, to jump-start the brain. Good opening questions open doors to new ways of looking at a challenge. The feeling you are striving for is a sense of energy and optimism, where anything is possible. A good opening is a call to adventure.

For example, you might start by brainstorming a list of questions about the challenge space. Focus on quantity, not quality. Withhold criticism and welcome unusual or controversial ideas. Look to build on ideas and combine them to make them better.

The focus of opening questions is to find things you can work with later. Imagine yourself with a big basket that can hold an infinite number of ideas. If you find something, don't ask if it's useful; just put it into the basket. The more ideas and variation you have, the better.

Here are some examples of opening questions:

- "How would you define the problem we are facing?"
- "What kinds of things do we want to explore?"
- "What are the biggest problem areas?"

NAVIGATING QUESTIONS

Navigating questions help you assess and adjust your course while the game is underway. For example, summarize key points and confirm that people agree to ensure that you understand and that the group is aligned.

DID I UNDERSTAND
THAT CORRECTLY?

IS THIS A
PRODUCTIVE
DISCUSSION
THREAD?

NAVIGATING

When you facilitate a group, you are responsible for the flow. Is your plan working? Are people engaged? Is the team fatigued? Are they frustrated or sapped of energy? Take a break and check in. Ask them questions that will help them see how difficult the problem is or how far they have come.

Are you getting where you need to go? Have you made as much progress as you had hoped? Are people still feeling connected to the project? Ask them!

Before you ask too many navigating questions, keep in mind that you may have more experience navigating complex challenge spaces than some of the other people in the room. You may have a better sense of how far along you are than they do. If you are the captain of the ship, it may make people nervous if you express too much doubt.

Navigating questions set the course, point the way, and adjust for error. Here are some examples of navigating questions:

- "Are we on track?"

- "Did I understand this correctly?"

- "Is this helping us to get where we want to go?"

- "Is this a useful discussion thread?"

- "Should we table this for now and put it on a list of things to talk about later?"

- "Does the goal that we set this morning still make sense, or should we make some adjustments based on what we have learned so far?"

NAVIGATING

IS THERE SOME
TENSION AROUND
THIS TOPIC?

HOW ABOUT
A SHORT
BREAK?

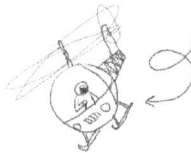

If things feel like they are going off track, take a pause and ask a navigating question or two. You can always suggest a short break and check in with leaders, sponsors, or key stakeholders, to see if they are happy with the conversation or would like to change course.

There are two big questions that are worth asking whenever you come across something new. First, what is it? And second, what can I do with it? The first question has to do with examination, while the second deals with experimentation.

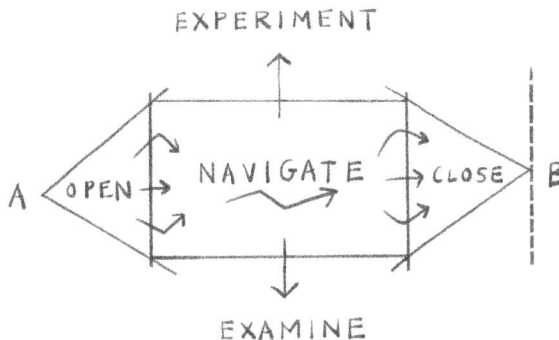

EXPERIMENT

A OPEN NAVIGATE CLOSE B

EXAMINE

EXAMINING QUESTIONS

Examining questions invoke observation and analysis. What is it? What is its nature? The more closely you look at something, the better you can examine it. Examining questions narrow your inquiry to focus on details, specifics, and observable characteristics. They make abstract ideas more concrete by quantifying and qualifying them. You can imagine an examining question as a lens that allows you to zoom in to a topic so that you can see more detail. Usually, it's good to begin an exploration by examining and challenging your fundamental assumptions.

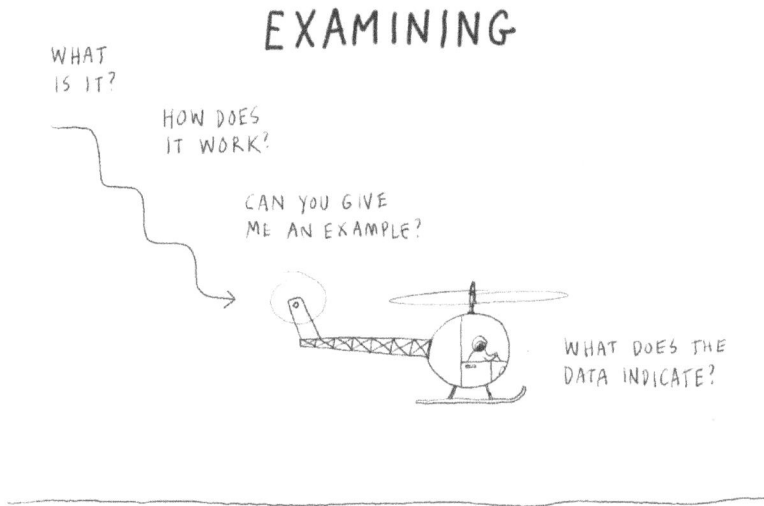

Examining questions are great when you feel the conversation is too vague or abstract to be actionable. They bring you closer to the ground by focusing on concrete details and examples.

If your idea were a rock, examining questions would help you understand things like its weight, color, size, shape, and chemical makeup.

Here are some examples of examining questions:

- "What is it made of?"
- "How does it work?"
- "What are the pieces and parts?"
- "Can you give me an example of that?"

- "What does that look like?"
- "Can you describe it in terms of a real-life scenario?"

EXPERIMENTAL QUESTIONS

Experimental questions invoke the imagination. They are about possibility. What can we do with it? What opportunities does it create? Experimental questions are concerned with taking you to a higher level of abstraction to find similarities with other things, to make unlikely and unexpected connections. Whatever "it" is, experiment with it. Try to break it, throw it, spin it, invert it, and so on.

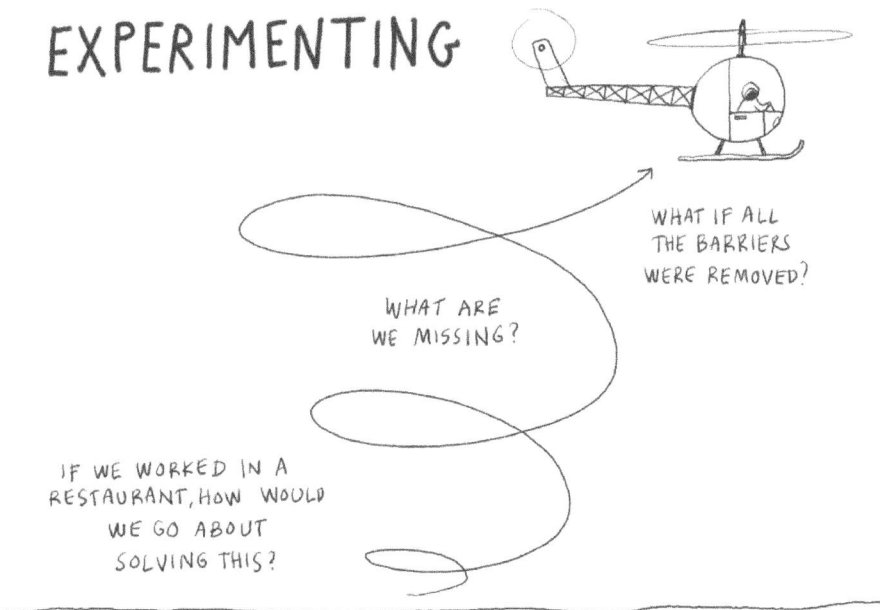

EXPERIMENTING

WHAT IF ALL
THE BARRIERS
WERE REMOVED?

WHAT ARE
WE MISSING?

IF WE WORKED IN A
RESTAURANT, HOW WOULD
WE GO ABOUT
SOLVING THIS?

Experimenting questions are useful if you feel like the conversation is getting bogged down in details and analysis. They create more distance and make room for more creative thinking.

If your idea were a rock, experimental questions would ask "What can I do with this that's beyond the obvious?" For example, you could use it to hammer a nail, or you could throw it, make noise with it, and so on. One day someone asked questions like this, came up with the idea for the pet rock, and made a million dollars.

Here are some examples of experimental questions:

- "What else works like this?"
- "If this were an animal (or a plant, machine, etc.), what kind of animal would it be, and why?"
- "What are we missing?"
- "What if all the barriers were removed?"
- "How would we handle this if we were operating a restaurant?
- What if it was a hospital?"
- "What if we are wrong?"

You can think of this as a matter of altitude. When people are getting too caught up in the details, spark the imagination and bring them up a level with some experimental questions. If they are up in the clouds and need a bit of grounding, bring them down with some examining questions.

CLOSING QUESTIONS

Closing questions serve the opposite function from opening questions. When you are opening, you want to create as much divergence and variation as possible. When you are closing, you want to focus on convergence and selection. Your goal at this stage is to move toward commitment, decisions, and action. Opening is about opportunities; closing is about selecting which opportunities you want to pursue. That means eliminating lines of inquiry that don't seem promising, assigning priorities, and so on. Now is the time for critical thinking.

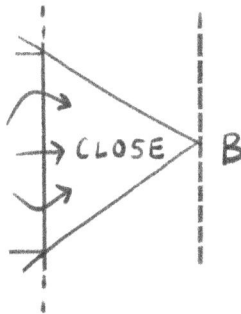

Closing is like coming home. You are tired but you want to end the day with a sense of accomplishment. What have you achieved? What have you accomplished? The natural need for a feeling of accomplishment is one of the reasons why tangible outcomes are so important in gamestorming. The fact that people have created something tangible—even if it's simply a report or to-do list —helps the group maintain momentum and generate energy for the next phase of activity.

CLOSING

HOW WOULD YOU PRIORITIZE THESE?

WHAT'S FEASIBLE IN THE NEXT TWO WEEKS?

WHO WILL TAKE RESPONSIBILITY FOR DOING THAT?

HELIPAD

Closing questions are useful as you get toward the end of your tour, for forcing decisions and generating next steps.

People want to know: Where is the artifact? What is finished? What comes next? What will tomorrow look like?

Here are some examples of closing questions:

- "How can we prioritize these options?"
- "What's feasible?"
- "What can we do in the next two weeks?"
- "Who is going to do what?"

Improvisation

To improvise is to make it up as you go along, to make do with whatever happens to be available, to proceed without a plan. Like a jazz musician, you compose and create simultaneously. When you improvise, you create in the moment, responding intuitively to the environment and your inner feelings. You let go. By letting go of your assumptions and biases, you open a path to new ideas, new practices, and new behaviors. You consciously forget what you know in order to elicit spontaneity, serendipity, and surprise.

It may appear that jazz is totally free and spontaneous, but behind the scenes, jazz has a rigid structure that creates the scaffolding for the freeform activity. Gamestorming provides such a scaffolding. Concepts like opening and closing, the use of meaningful space and artifacts, and every one of these practices will help you create structure and space for spontaneous activity.

Improvisation is a way of thinking with your body. In role-play, you take on the role of a character, imagine a situation, and act as you think your character would act in that situation. Putting yourself in another person's shoes helps you to empathize with that person's goals and challenges and can lead to insights and better solutions.

Bodystorming (see game description in Chapter 7) is a kind of improvisation in which players construct (sketch) a makeshift world using cardboard, chairs, or whatever is at hand, and then act out scenarios within that world in order to understand it better.

In the early 1990s, user experience designer Jared Spool and several colleagues developed a design game in which players worked together to design a prototype of an interactive kiosk using cardboard and paper. The purpose of the game was to help designers learn how paper prototyping could speed up their design process.

Because of the fleeting, impermanent nature of the ideas generated by these kinds of exercises, it can be very helpful to have some recording equipment handy, such as a video camera, a small tripod, and perhaps a microphone. If you plan to be doing a lot of this, you may want to invest in more professional equipment. There's a balance to be struck here: while recording sessions is a way to create tangible artifacts that represent temporal experiences, it may also take some of the spontaneity out of the improvisation.

If anything most resembles gamestorming in its purest form, surely it's improvisation. As a group, the players work together to create a world and explore it with their intuition and their entire bodies.

Improvisation is a big word with lots of meanings—it means different things to different people and in different contexts.

When you are faced with the unexpected, to improvise is to be in the moment, to proceed without a plan. It is to make do with whatever is at hand, to use your ingenuity to develop makeshift solutions to unanticipated problems. Thus, improvisation skills are survival skills. It's a common problem for any explorer: when you don't know what to expect and you need to anticipate anything and everything, what do you bring?

In jazz and theater traditions, improvisation involves laying out a basic structure and then creating spontaneous compositions that weave within and around that structure to create harmonious, beautiful, and sometimes complex sounds and scenarios. In this context, improvisation's beauty lies in its spontaneity and variety.

In gamestorming, improvisation is important in both ways—the ability to quickly respond to unanticipated or emergency situations as well as to develop spontaneous compositions around a baseline rhythm or structure. We'll take both in turn:

Responsiveness to the unexpected

> The gamestorming practices listed in this chapter are a great set of methods that will apply to nearly any unexpected situation. If you have your core supplies handy (flip charts, markers, sticky notes, dot voting, paper, index cards) and you have mastered the core skills (questions, use of artifacts and meaningful space, sketching and improvisation), it will be a rare circumstance that will throw you off your feet. There's a great calm and confidence that comes from knowing that you have the tools as well as the skills and are prepared for any situation.

Variations on a theme

> Like almost the entire gamestorming toolkit, improvisation is a matter of some basic skills combined with a lot of practice. It is the goal of this section to lay out some basic principles and practices that will help you create simple, loose structures and guide people through the process of exploring them improvisationally—that is, with the kind of spontaneity and freedom that involves the physical senses in the process of discovery and develops and hones the intuitive sense.

The idea of bringing improv into a business context may seem intimidating, but the challenges are mostly in your mind. You're already improvising at work.

In *GameChangers: Improvisation for Business in the Networked World (Gamechangers)*, improv expert Mike Bonifer reminds us that all of life is improvisation: from a conversation at the dinner table to the way we respond to unexpected situations, improv is natural; we do it all the time.

To get people warmed up, Bonifer suggests a game he calls Gibberish. Here's how it works. Divide a group into teams of two or three people. Give the first team a slip of paper describing a scene—a role and a goal for each player—and ask them to act it out while everyone else watches. But here's the rub: they can't use words. They can only use gibberish sounds and other things like actions, body language, and tone of voice to convey their meaning. The round is over when the audience guesses what the scene is about. Do the same with each team (with different scenes, of course) until everyone has had a go.

The point of this game is to strip away what Bonifer calls the *layers of cosmetic meaning*—the talking and data that so many business conversations revolve around—in order to reveal the deeper layers of communication that are always there but often go unnoticed, like tone of voice, body language, and action.

At its core, an improv game isn't different from any other kind of gamestorming activity: you need to open the world, explore the world, and close the world. In this sense, it's the same. But in another sense, it's different: improv is not so much about the outcomes as it is about the experience—an experience that, ideally, will lead to insight.

Underlying structure is important to improv in the same way that bones are helpful to muscles or trees are helpful to vines; in order to loosen up and let yourself go, you need something to innovate around, or else you will simply create chaos.

Jazz musicians improvise music around a steady beat or theme. Basketball players improvise around the boundaries of the court and the rules of the game. The beauty and success of these improvisational activities would not be possible without the underlying structure that supports and contains them.

The theme is the thing you want to explore, and the scene is the thing that gives you a structure to improvise around. There are four elements of a scene: the setting, the characters, the characters' objectives, and props.

For example, let's say you want to find a way to improve the public transportation system in your city, and you want to use improv to explore some possibilities. That's your theme: getting around using public transportation.

Before you can start to improvise, you need characters, goals, settings, and props. Let's start with goals. You could brainstorm a list of situations in which people would need public transportation: one person needs to do their grocery shopping, another needs to visit a friend, another wants to see a movie or get to work. Next, you could brainstorm a list of characters. One person is retired, another is a surgeon, and so on. Now, settings: one person is at home, another is in a park. Finally, props: one person has a mobile phone, another does not.

Now, imagine that you color-code four sets of index cards so that the goals are one color, the characters are another color, and so on. You could shuffle the cards and ask people to choose one card of each color. Once everyone has their objectives, you could take turns acting out the scenes. After each scene, you could have a short discussion about its implications.

One challenge with improv is that because its nature is so experiential, the learning is in the doing. An improv experience does not naturally generate a tangible artifact as an outcome. But this is not an insurmountable problem. You can assign a person to videotape the scenarios as you act them out, or ask someone to take notes or even make some storyboard sketches to capture the essence of the things you have discovered.

Selection

Toward the end of any meeting, you will get to a point where it's time to make choices about which ideas will be pursued and which will be discarded. You can't do everything, and so eventually you will need to winnow a large set of ideas or options down to a smaller, more manageable set.

Voting can be a good way to do this. We're all familiar with raising our hands or using a secret ballot to vote on things, but when you have a massive amount of information that you need to cull, there are better, faster ways to use voting to do this. For example, you can give everyone 10 small, round stickers and ask them to stick them on the things that interest them most. When they are out of stickers, they are out of votes.

Voting with stickers (as in the dot voting game in Chapter 7) is an example of a form of currency. Circular stickers are like money that players can distribute among a group of things, to help them decide what matters most to them. Imagine your grocery list again, and imagine that you have a very long list but a limited amount of money. If you had unlimited funds, you could buy everything you wanted, but the fact that your funds are limited forces you to make choices— sometimes difficult ones.

People have a natural tendency to bite off more than they can chew. We are naturally optimistic. But when people do this, they easily become overwhelmed, and then nothing is accomplished in the end. Voting and currencies help people make the difficult choices about what is important to them. By giving people stickers or asking them to make marks that represent their votes, you can make the preferences of a group visible and explicit so that they can see where everybody stands and move more quickly to decisions.

Another way to boil down a set of ideas is to sort information according to priority. Forced Ranking (see Chapter 7) prioritizes a list of items by "forcing" them into a linear rank: most important to least important, first to last, and so on. For example, imagine your grocery list again. You could force-rank the list by organizing items by cost, from most expensive to least expensive. You could also force-rank the items in order of priority, from most important to least important. If you have a limited amount of money to spend, you could compare both lists to determine the best way to spend your money.

Many virtual meeting and whiteboard tools have functions or plug-ins that enable dot voting, polls, and more. You can even have people vote on something in chat, for example by using numbers to register their votes.

Try Something New

The best way to hone your knowledge in exploring skills is to keep yourself honest. You won't discover and invent anything unless you get used to taking risks and trying new things on a regular basis. Make it a practice to try at least one new thing every time you gamestorm. It will keep you honest, force you to continuously develop and improve, and keep things fresh and alive for you. You won't inspire others unless you can stoke your own fires.

Think of gamestorming as a toolkit that allows you to plug pieces together in different ways, depending on the way the action is going. The game is the game until it changes. A seasoned knowledge explorer will quickly abandon a game that isn't working and smoothly transition into another. You can think of each game as a scene in a play—or a skit. The players need to have their heads in the game to make real, meaningful progress.

In a gamestorming environment, you might move from a role-playing game to a board game to a building game in quick succession. The games are not ends in themselves, but building blocks that help you get from one point to another. Like a team of soldiers building a pontoon bridge to cross a river, you create a game when you need it, use it for as long as it is useful, and then discard it when you no longer need it. It's like building a ladder one step at a time because you aren't quite sure where you're going—in fact, it's like a cartoon character building a ladder to nowhere.

Be in the now. Look around and grab something, patch it together, make a game from the simplest tools. The game will move you forward. You don't need to know the final destination; only the next step in the journey. Just keep your eye on the fuzzy goal—the mountaintop, the imagined thing over the horizon—and the next step, the next game, that moves you one step in approximately the right direction.

Practice

We started this chapter by talking about practice.

You can think about practice in two ways. First, in the sense of a profession or skill, as in a consulting practice, a law practice, or a medical practice. Gamestorming is a practice in this sense. If you're reading this book, you can think of yourself as a gamestorming practitioner.

Second, you can think of practice as an ongoing commitment to develop, hone, and maintain the skills that are necessary within a discipline. This is the kind of practice we mean when we talk about Zen practice or piano practice or basketball practice. To build your gamestorming skills, you will need to practice.

Mastery of a practice is not something that can be gained simply by studying a book or attending a workshop, and gamestorming is no exception to this rule. The reason that athletes practice, and actors and musicians rehearse, is to build the confidence and muscle memory so that the skills become second nature, fluid, and easy. The more you can practice in low-stakes environments, the more confident you will be when it's game time. If you can approach gamestorming as a practice, worthy of careful study and ongoing skill-building work, you will find a path to rich rewards and personal fulfillment at work.

In this first section of the book, we wanted to focus on the fundamentals of gamestorming and the underlying principles that make it work. We didn't want to simply write a book of recipes for people to follow blindly without understanding them. That would defeat our purpose, which is to encourage a shift in how work is done—from a process-centric model that's about predictability and consistency to a game-centric model that recognizes the complexity and unpredictability of a digital world.

In the second part of the book, Chapters 7–10, we have compiled a list of the best games we know. We hope you will peruse them, try them in your workplace, and continue to modify and improve them. If you have ideas, comments, or questions, you can join conversations and communities at *http://gamestorming.com* and *https://nothingintheway.substack.com*.

Welcome to the world of practice!

4

Designing Workshops and Meetings

Whether we're conscious of it or not, ordinary life has rules. Secret signals, implicit norms, and explicit codes of conduct form what cultural psychologist Michele Gelfand calls a *primal template of culture*—an elegant way of describing *how we do things around here*.

Meetings also have cultural templates. They're revealed in our default versions of gathering at work, which almost no one seems to delight in. Meetings as we know them tend to be too tight or too loose, too vague or too prescribed, too joyless or too chaotic—and definitely far too frequent. Few organizations have solved the meeting puzzle in terms of people, process, path, and product, so meetings end up being almost tragicomic, unsatisfying for most attendees most of the time. This is hardly a revelation. Meetings are the butt of countless jokes about modern work. At best, they're a groan-worthy, minor inconvenience. At worst, they're a sign of partial attention, scattered focus, oblivion, and disrespect.

Disrupting the Default Meeting Template

When entrepreneur David Hieatt was designing the culture of Hiut Denim inspired by Cal Newport's research on deep work,[1] he drafted a set of team guiding principles. One standout on the list: protect employees from dumb meetings. As the CEO of 37 Signals pointed out, "Five people in a room for an hour isn't a one-hour meeting. It's a five-hour meeting." Designing this time well matters, and that's why this book exists: to positively disrupt default meeting templates and share a unique, multisensory, effective approach to bringing people together and making them glad they came.

SHOULD WE SCHEDULE OUR NEXT ZOOM MEETING OR JUST HIT OURSELVES REPEATEDLY IN THE HEAD WITH A HAMMER?

© marketoonist.com

Accomplishing that doesn't have to be complicated. You don't need to be a seasoned meeting planner or any version of a meeting guru to quickly improve on the default experience. If we decide to, any one of us can counteract the life-draining forces of ordinary meetings. Any one of us can identify a problem that warrants a meeting, gather the energies of a group, and help point that energy in a valuable direction. By now you know that we do this through games, and we call our practice *gamestorming*.

---

1 Cal Newport's advocacy of what he calls "deep work" is an antidote to the continuous partial attention many of us are plagued with. The idea of "deep work" is just as it sounds: it's cognitively rich work that purposefully blocks time and minimizes distractions in order to accommodate sustained, meaningful focus that results in higher productivity and more valuable output. Notably, Newport puts typical meetings in the category of "shallow work," a position we would not dispute.

It should be stated outright that it's okay to be allergic to the words "game" or "gaming" at work. Games have varied connotations that aren't associated with this practice, including zero-sum competition, psychological manipulations, and hidden agendas or, on the flip side and God forbid, having fun. Discouragingly, it's the last one that seems to be the most taboo!

On the surface, work is a four-letter word that designates not enjoying yourself, and managers don't necessarily applaud us for having a good time. In Chapter 2, however, you learned how we define a game. Our kind of game is one that positively disrupts the default meeting template by approaching any challenge through a series of thought experiments—multisensory, interactive, intentional thought experiments. Gamestorming makes things happen, and if fun is a natural byproduct, so be it. Learning and solving *should* be fun—it makes problem solving more fluid and effective. Gobs of research supports this,[2] and so does direct experience.

We've applied this method for more than 20 years, and its aliveness continues to surprise us. As one of our global gamestormers expressed, "[This practice] inspired me, and a whole community of people, to understand how we can be (should be) together when fully immersed in collaboration at work. It changed how we viewed "work." It brought creativity, design and co-creation to a new group of people to show them what's possible."[3]

Structures of Meetings

When you're designing a meeting or workshop in the gamestorming way, you want to think like a composer, orchestrating the activities to achieve harmony between creating, reflecting, thinking or analyzing, connecting, and decision making while staying focused on the goals, fuzzy or otherwise. There's no "right" sequence of games to build each experience, which is partly why they're full of creative potential. The aim is to compose a meeting flow that's conducive to

---

2 Explore the research of Stuart Brown, M.D., Kathy Hirsh-Pasek, Marc Bekoff, Jean Piaget, Dorothy and Jerome Singer, and Jaak Panksepp, and this from a 2023 *Newsweek* article by Adam Piore titled "Do You Play Enough? Science Says It's Critical to Your Health and Well-Being": "An embracing of joy and play is overdue, and not just because it feels good. Scientists have learned through a panoply of studies that the drive to play is a biologically hard-wired tool, common to almost all mammals, to promote experimentation, imagination, exploration and creativity. Play activates the reward centers of the brain, floods the rest of the brain with feel-good chemicals like dopamine and oxytocin and triggers the release of powerful neural growth factors that promote learning and mental flexibility. It causes stress hormones to drop, mood to lift and has an energizing effect."

3 Alison Coward, Founder & CEO, Bracket

engaging the unique group you're working with, and useful for the situation you're working on.

You've been exposed to opening, exploring, and closing as a basic, core meeting (and game) structure that helps you build a meeting flow that moves toward ideal outcomes.

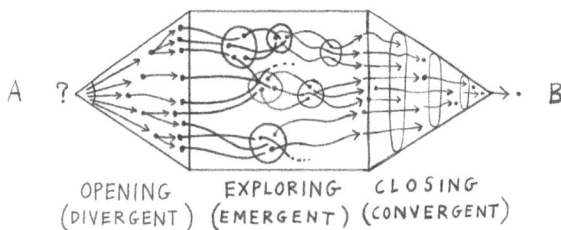

OPENING   EXPLORING   CLOSING
(DIVERGENT) (EMERGENT)   (CONVERGENT)

In more robust gaming sessions, games are played in series in which the outcomes of one game create the initial conditions for the next. A daylong onsite workshop, for example, could be filled with multiple games linked to each other. The following visual shows a meeting in which three games are played in a row. You see that each game has a clear stage of opening, exploring, and closing, and the outcome of each game becomes the input for the next. This kind of meeting is straightforward and simple, generally easy to design and facilitate.

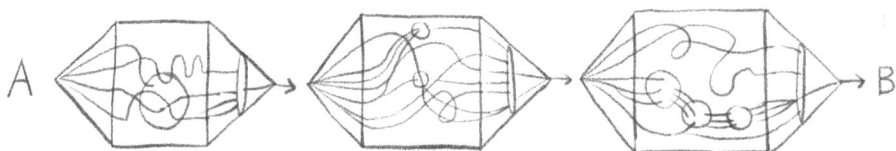

The next visual shows a meeting that involves three longer, more intensive games interlinked with two shorter ones. The shorter games could be palate cleansers, so to speak, giving the group a chance to socialize, reflect on what just took place, do something playful or connective, or down-shift intellectual gears before returning to intensive work. In that image, you can see that the overall meeting, like the last one, points toward one main goal.

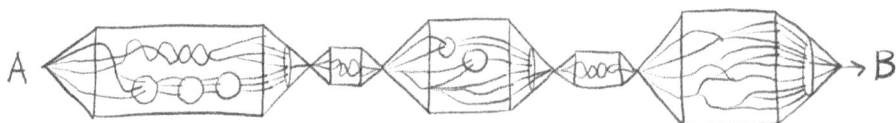

There are other meeting structures, however, particularly with a larger group, in which it makes sense to pursue multiple goals, or goals categorized as explicit and task-oriented versus implicit and social-relational. A key technique for these types of meetings that's a faithful companion for opening and closing is breaking out/reporting back, during which a group or groups temporarily splinters off the larger group, breaking into subgroups to play a game or two and then converging to report the outcome of their efforts to the plenary. This approach is useful because it respects different obligations of unique groups, allowing them to become purposefully focused and more dynamic, and it often increases the variety of emergent ideas since multiple games are played in parallel. Breaking out/reporting back also has the upside of giving people an opportunity to reflect. In breakout groups, players can work on individual exercises without it feeling disruptive to the cohesion of the entire group.

This next visual shows a meeting of this nature during which an initial, opening session leads to three distinct goals pursued in parallel working groups using breaking out/reporting back to come together at crucial junctures. At the end of the series, the three working groups' outcomes are reported to the larger group, and all goals converge ultimately into the bigger, shared goal.

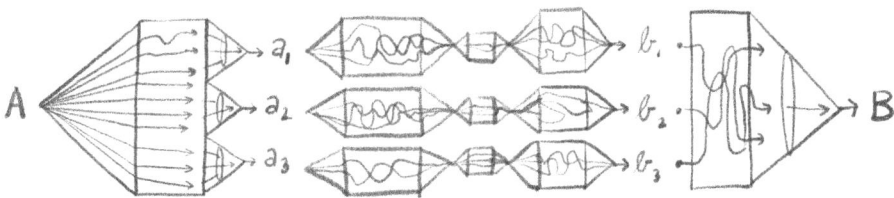

Ideally, you're starting to see how the structure of open, explore, close is like a fractal for both games and meetings. It replicates and lends itself to a variety of structures that give groups energy, purpose, and direction.

This visual shows a meeting in which the outcomes of the first game generate inputs for five games, which then generate inputs for two games, which generate the input for a single, longer game at the end. This sequence suggests a workshop with multiple needs best served by subgroups working in parallel. As you gain confidence in gamestorming, you'll be inspired to take more risks and design more fluently relative to identified goals.

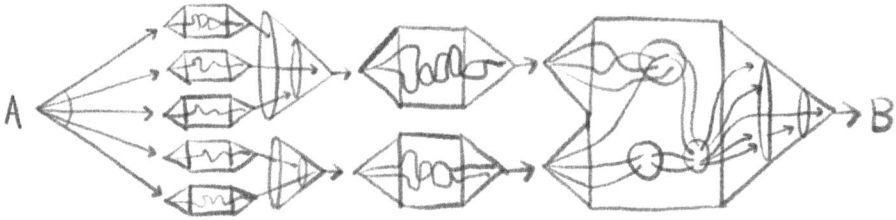

Next you see one daylong game in which a big portion of the morning is spent on divergent activities, generating a plethora of ideas and information, and the exploration phase is split into two parts with a break for lunch. The group breaks bread together at four tables for informal conversation and reflection on the morning's activities before going into the afternoon session. Lunch is followed by an afternoon of convergent activities that flow into one single outcome. This kind of meeting structure is great for a group in which all players have an interest and/or a stake in the problem being tackled and, therefore, should be together for the duration.

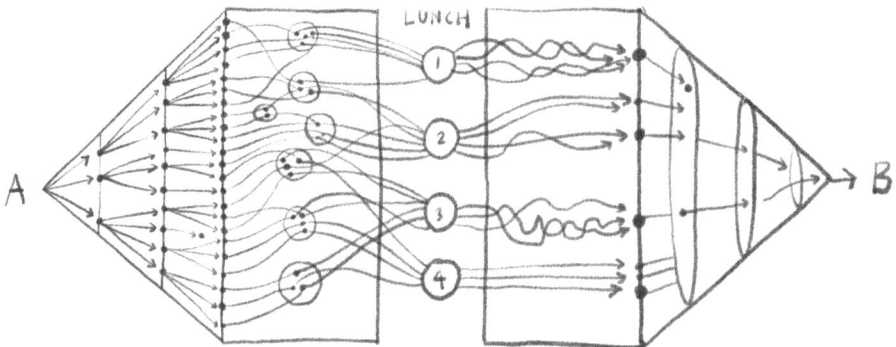

In meetings that support knowledge work, there are no guarantees of what's to come. Collaborators may search for something they won't be able to find, and they'll almost certainly find things they don't expect. Sometimes, players will make discoveries while games are underway that reveal a legitimate need to change direction. This last visual shows an initial opening and exploration that unearthed a goal the team didn't anticipate, so the group spontaneously agreed to break into two subgroups, one pursuing the original goal and the other pursuing the discovered goal. It can and does happen, so gamestorming facilitators roll with the waves and stay the course. It's all part of the process.

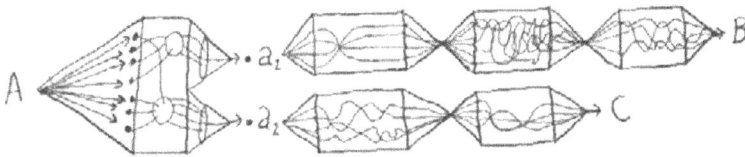

The 7Ps

In this book, we're not aiming to build an army of hard-nosed, clinical meeting technicians. We're aiming to democratize visual thinking and experiential ways of working, to empower every person to improve any meeting experience. To that end, we want to outfit you with tools of various shapes and sizes. Gamestorming goes deeper the more you practice, so the first technique that can build real confidence is our tool called the 7Ps.[4]

---

4 The 7Ps was an innovation by our original coauthor, James Macanufo.

Think of the 7Ps as the tool to consult any time you're tasked with bringing people together. It's a recipe to transform not just one meeting but potentially your entire meeting culture! Like a great meal, a great meeting requires planning in advance. The 7Ps is your secret recipe, one you can count on and return to to increase the odds of a crowd-pleaser. Let's take a walk through each of the Ps so you can slowly take them in, beginning with that North Star: purpose.

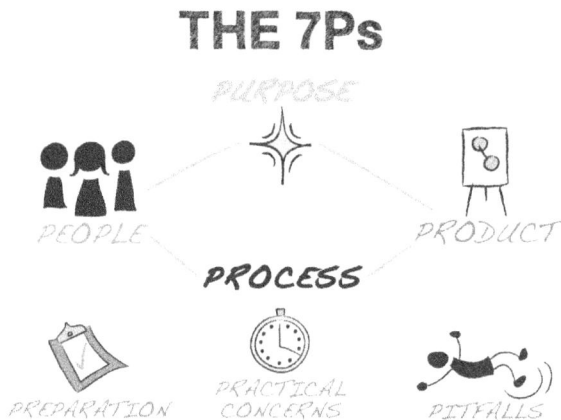

PURPOSE

I know some of you reading the word "purpose" will be surprised at the requirement to include it. Surely people don't bring others together without knowing why they're doing it?! Indeed, we do it all the time. Some of us are social creatures, and we gather people out of our own biological requirement for extroversion. Some of us are people who have to think out loud with others—verbalizing, externalizing, and socializing thoughts in order to think better. Some of us are spread thin and moving so fast we haven't slowed down long enough to consider what the hell is going on. And still others of us are so accustomed to the absurd and pointless default meeting template that we're unconscious to it, resigned to our fate.

To be a gamestormer is to become conscious of the default meeting template and own your conditioning around it. This doesn't have to involve a huge leap. Determining the purpose of a meeting can take 30 seconds if you know your team, the context, and the project or strategic initiative y'all are focused on. Simply imagine yourself in a room with those stakeholders and ask yourself the essential question, *Why are we here?* You can often get a good insight right away. In this case, it's the upstream act of *choosing to pause in order to make the purpose explicit* that can require some effort.

In other situations, the discernment of purpose may require a bit of mental gymnastics. The latter, more complex circumstance, is worth examining.

We've discussed that a gamestorm can take anywhere from 30 seconds to four or five days or beyond. Shorter meetings—those that last 20 to 60 minutes, for example—are relatively easy to design. But as the time spent lengthens, the number of stakeholders increases, and/or the size of the challenge being addressed scales upward, the arc of an experience will need to be more crafted in order to be valuable, and determining a meeting's purpose(s) will first require two crucial skills: great questioning and deep listening.

Sensing interviews illuminate meeting goals

People responsible for a meeting or workshop toward the longer end of the time spectrum will generally have a sense of what they want to accomplish, but it can become the job of a game facilitator to seriously kick the tires on their perceptions and assumptions before designing, or helping design, the meeting experience. We use what we call "sensing interviews" to help them begin. Those interviews involve the kinds of questions you read about in Chapter 3.[5] Like any good design scoping process, the aim of these interviews is to help a person responsible for the success of a meeting precisely identify two types of meeting goals: explicit and implicit.

---

5 Opening, navigating, examining, experimental, and closing

Explicit meeting goals are those that directly point to a tangible deliverable(s). These are goals that, if not met during the time spent, would make the meeting a failure in the eyes of the stakeholder or client. A tangible deliverable might include a process map for onboarding new employees, the establishment of criteria for a future product, a revisioning of an old vision statement, or consensus around next steps for an ongoing campaign.

Implicit meeting goals are the subtle and subterranean, often equally and sometimes more important, goals of the time spent together. These types of goals include relationship building, deeper onboarding, the reification of cultural or desirable norms, the smoothing over of known conflict, changing perceptions, social bonding, and so on. Both of these types of goals matter, and they tend to matter more as the duration lengthens.

When designing a meeting, many people blow past this process of discernment and jump right into meeting design, or they identify explicit goals but neglect putting attention on implicit goals. Both moves are a mistake. It's far better to be patient, go slow, and ask intelligent, bold, and nuanced questions at this scoping stage. If you do, you'll have more confidence that when you put together a sequence of games, you're helping the group solve the right problem, the one that would best serve their needs at this juncture.

Types of sensing interview questions

There are scores of books that offer examples of excellent questions aiming for discovery, so don't imagine there's some "best set" of inquiries. This stage of meeting design is much more about your willingness to engage in clear, sometimes courageous, probes and pay close attention to the responses while minimizing the overlay of your biases, or at least bringing them to awareness and putting them on the table for inquiry. It is then your task to help the meeting lead or client (or yourself, if it's your meeting) *sense into* what's needed—intellectually, emotionally, intuitively, operationally, and strategically. Most likely, they already have the first-level answer to the purpose of the meeting but could use space, time, and supportive attention to go a few levels down, homing in on a deeper knowing, kind of like a heat-seeking missile.

The most important aspect of the questions you ask while in sensing mode is that they be open-ended. Ideally, some of the questions involve the client telling real-world stories—about the team, the culture, the state of the organization, why this meeting now, what efforts the team has made in the past to attend to the challenge, and so on. Your job at this stage is to create conditions for deeper insights to become available, then capture that wisdom as it emerges, reflect it back to the meeting lead, and design for it.

The following are more examples of the sensing questions we previously defined in Chapter 3. It helps to have rigorous question sets, and we've used these many times to discover the purpose and goals of a meeting or workshop so we can design more intelligently. Keep in mind these are just examples; they're not the Holy Grail. It's always a useful endeavor to exercise *your* muscles for imagining and inventing questions.

Opening questions Recall that opening questions provoke thought and reveal possibilities, opening doors to new ways of looking at a challenge. Here are some examples of opening questions to help you design a meeting:

- What are your hopes or desires for this workshop/session/meeting/gathering?
- What is *really* prompting the desire to arrange this meeting?
- In this scenario, what would a wildly successful meeting look like?
- If you could accomplish a surprising amount of objectives in this period of time, how would you do it?
- For this session, what's relevant about the state of the organization? What's relevant about the state of the industry?
- Paint me a picture of what would happen if this meeting didn't take place.

Navigating questions Navigating questions set the course, point the way, assess, adjust, and correct for errors.

- If we were to get the group to this desired insight or understanding, where might we go from there?
- If you had to kill one of your meeting-goal darlings, which one would go first? Second?
- What aspect of this session is expendable if we were to run out of time for any reason?
- How would you redesign the stakeholder groups if you wanted teams to help identify unseen obstacles in other teams' worlds?

Examining questions You read in Chapter 3 that examining questions are about observing and analyzing, focusing on details and specifics, and noting observable characteristics. To examine the possible best direction of a meeting, you might ask questions like the following:

- What has caused past brainstorms to fall short or fail? What have been distractions from or impediments to the robust exchange of ideas?

- Describe the interpersonal dynamics among the people attending this session. Say something about their familiarity with each other, their history, or the history of the team's role in the bigger picture of the organization.

- What has made past sessions successful? What conditions or dynamics helped ensure the desired outcomes were reached?

- What are current changes or trends happening in the industry that influence this group's thinking?

- What elements of your product, service, or experience are up for reexamination?

Experimental questions Experimental questions are powerful questions because they invoke imagination, take people to higher levels of abstraction, and purposefully awaken the possibility of seeing or doing things differently. These questions might be related to the goals of a meeting or to the experience design of a meeting itself.

- What if success for this project were completely redefined?

- What would happen if we left leadership out of this meeting?

- How might you add a constraint in order to boost creative thinking?

- What if the user base for this product were another community entirely?

- Imagine a scenario in which your users became your advisors.

- How would this meeting be conducted if we designed it using no slides and including no planned presentations?

Closing questions Remember that closing questions converge and select, rank options, and help people move toward commitment, make decisions, and take action.

- Are you present to anything you're not saying about this meeting and the people participating?

- Here are explicit and implicit goals that have come up in this conversation... Can you give us your perspective on them? Do some need to be edited, added, or removed?

- Rank these outcomes of the meeting in no uncertain terms.

- Even though this meeting is positioned as an exploratory, open-ended brainstorm, can you speak to meeting outcomes that leadership is ultimately aiming to drive people toward?

In sensing interviews, the richness of an answer or response is so profoundly influenced by the power of a question that these question categories bear repeating. Developing your ability to inquire with texture and depth will very much serve your gamestorming skills. At the end of the day, each game, in its own way, asks a question and leverages group intelligence to respond to that question. And as a game facilitator, your opportunity is to skillfully curate those games—to help players open, explore, and close those worlds—one after the other in a meaningful path we call a game sequence. We'll go over game sequences in the section called Process. First, let's examine that second requirement for designing great meetings: deep listening.

Deep listening

Deeply listening to another person is a gift to that person and to ourselves. To quote author David Augsburger, "Being heard is so close to being loved that for the average person, they are almost indistinguishable." Now, as a gamestormer, it's not your work to learn to love your client, but it is your work to listen closely to them before you attempt to build an experience that serves. This section is about the listening work that needs to happen *in order to* design a fantastic meeting or workshop, but it's also relevant to note that deep listening is a crucial skill for leading and facilitating that meeting as well, if that ends up being part of your role. Great facilitators are necessarily great listeners. Learning to listen deeply will serve you well in every area of your gamestorming practice—from beginning to end—and also in your life. Let's look closer.

The following infographic shows a model for listening inspired by Sun's collaborations with therapists, coaches, spiritual directors, and great facilitators. There's a lot to it, so review it at your leisure. The headline is that *deep listening happens in the absence of our own judgments and opinions.* It is easy to allegedly "listen" with our personal internal chatter running in the foreground of our minds, issuing all sorts of evaluations, retorts, assessments, and critiques. It takes practice to listen with that in the background, or better yet, to listen with it not running at all. The outer circle of this infographic designates what it looks like to not be listening. When we're being emotionally honest with ourselves, we can see how much that outer ring resonates with how we usually operate.

Where we aim to go is toward the inner circles. As we move closer to the center, which is the seat of deep listening, our own egoic pursuits start dropping away. We learn to stop listening for our turn to speak, to stop listening solely to assert ourselves and show our dominance or intelligence, and we learn to start listening with the sole aim of intimately knowing someone else's view of the world.

For many people, a quick hack to do this thing that sounds, and is, pretty hard is to think of yourself as an anthropologist. Take a backward step and try to remove yourself from the action of the moment. If we can shift into observing mind, we have a better shot at softening our own perspectives and ideas and making space for someone else's. Anthropologists don't necessarily listen with empathy, but they do try to pay attention with a more receptive mind. They try and drop preconceived notions of what they're witnessing and make space for information at least slightly less polluted by personal interpretation. It can be done with commitment and a little effort. Luckily, opportunities abound to practice, and you can always check your view of reality by summarizing your perceptions and running them by your client and other trusted collaborators.

getting precise about definitions or categories and missing the bigger point (connection)

offering an opinion with very little context

leaping to solve someone's problem without being asked

hijacking the story and making it about ourself

making assumptions about what's true for someone

suddenly becoming an expert on what someone's facing

right away introducing an unrelated subject matter

trying to usher the conversation along due to our own discomfort

having an agenda for how they should fix the problem while pretending you're open to ideas

dismissing someone's direct experience because 'that can't be true'

being emotionally oblivious to a person's vulnerability in the moment

trying to change people's emotions rather than just being with them

dismissing or minimizing ('oh, you'll survive')

labeling emotions people are experiencing before they've named them for themselves

comparing or ranking someone's pain or experience ('well, it's not as a bad as X, Y, Z')

* LETTING GO OF ASSUMPTIONS AND EXPECTATIONS OF HOW THE PERSON SHOULD BE

* NOT NEEDING SOMEONE TO CHANGE FOR YOU TO BE OKAY

* BEING ABLE TO ACCURATELY REFLECT WHAT'S BEING SAID

* STAYING OBSERVANT, NOTICING BODY LANGUAGE AND MICRO-EXPRESSIONS

DEEP SELF
PRISTINE AWARENESS
* PURE PRESENCE *
* DON'T-KNOW MIND *
* THE OBSERVER *

* STAYING CENTERED, CLEAR, CALM, AND CONNECTED TO THE PERSON SHARING

* CONSISTENTLY BRINGING YOUR ATTENTION BACK TO THE PERSON WHEN YOUR MIND WANDERS

* OCCUPYING A MIND OF CURIOSITY

LISTENING

NOT LISTENING

CENTERFORDEEPSELFDESIGN.COM

The skills of great questioning accompanied by deep listening shape the container for solid meeting design. Gamestormers working toward mastery should purposefully prioritize and strengthen these capacities. They're among the secret sauces for compelling meeting design, and they help cement a real sense of purpose as we work to solve problems together. When we get into process, the value of these skills will be even more apparent. First, though, let's talk about people.

PEOPLE

If we had a dollar for every time a friend or colleague texted me behind the scenes to say "Why the hell am I in this meeting?" it's safe to say we'd have an extra vehicle. Just as it's common for the purpose of a meeting to be poorly or undefined, it's also common for a smattering of the right *and* wrong people to be in attendance. But as noted, a one-hour meeting involving five people is a five-hour meeting, so it pays literally and socially to steward the participant list.

For most meetings, this exploration doesn't require a concerted cognitive effort. Is this person directly involved with what's being discussed? Will they have something crucial to contribute? Would their absence create a strategic, tactical, or logistical problem?

For explicit meeting goals, you might think in terms of questions and answers. Who are the people you need in the room to answer the questions you have? For implicit meeting goals, you can think in terms of relationships, influence, and group needs. Whose presence encourages openness and transparency? Whose leadership qualities give people courage? Who has deep experience with the landscape being explored in the meeting? Who inspires curiosity? Who is the keeper of the history we need to know for this session? Even if that person or group isn't responsible for the final deliverable, their presence may create a much-needed fluidity, or add valuable but more subtle knowledge, to help that deliverable emerge and improve.

Consider both types of meeting goals—explicit and implicit—and weigh those goals against the know-how, presence, and gifts of each possible participant. Then choose wisely. Choose even more wisely if the meeting has constraints you can't correct for—like a requirement to travel, physical space limitations, time-zone restrictions, or needs for confidentiality. If the participant list is necessarily limited by these kinds of constraints, it's important to designate post-session communicators or communication deliverables—people or artifacts that can convey the informational and actionable exchanges if everyone you wanted to couldn't attend.

PROCESS

Designing the arc of experience for a meeting is one of the two main areas where gamestorming chops get refined—the other is in the arena.

Paths of play in iterating meeting flows

The overarching question related to process is *What sequence of games will inspire, compel, and move this group in an engaging and intelligent way toward the meeting's purpose, goals, and product?* There are truly infinite answers to that question. Games and game mechanics are endless, which means process design is the most divergent and creative P among the 7Ps. It's also where you as a game facilitator have the most opportunity to collaborate in advance with stakeholders or attendees, if either of those options makes sense.

Our teams have designed a surprising number of game sequences over the last 17 years, and we've run those sequences with groups ranging from 4 to 5,000 people in built environments of every shape and size—board rooms, museums, auditoriums, theaters, classrooms, rooftops, and offices almost as small as closets. The world of games is boundless and very much choose-your-own-adventure, as long as you keep the endgame in mind and are present to the norms of the culture, even as you may seek to expand them.

The following are examples of meeting agendas we've sculpted in diverse ways using software like Excel, SessionLab, Trello, and Mural, or good old-fashioned sticky notes. The impression we're hoping to convey here is that when complete, agendas stitch together a group experience, taking people through an arc of time that's structured and scaffolded by chains of events in the form of games. Agendas of any complexity will go through multiple drafts and iterations—you're taking initial swipes at paths of play—so it's useful to embrace that reality as you begin. It's also useful to see a few agendas so you get the sense that they can be built in any number of ways. We're agnostic about the tool you use to draft and document your agenda or meeting flow. What matters chiefly are those structures of opening, exploring, and closing we discussed in Chapter 3 and that you've imagined and built the world well.

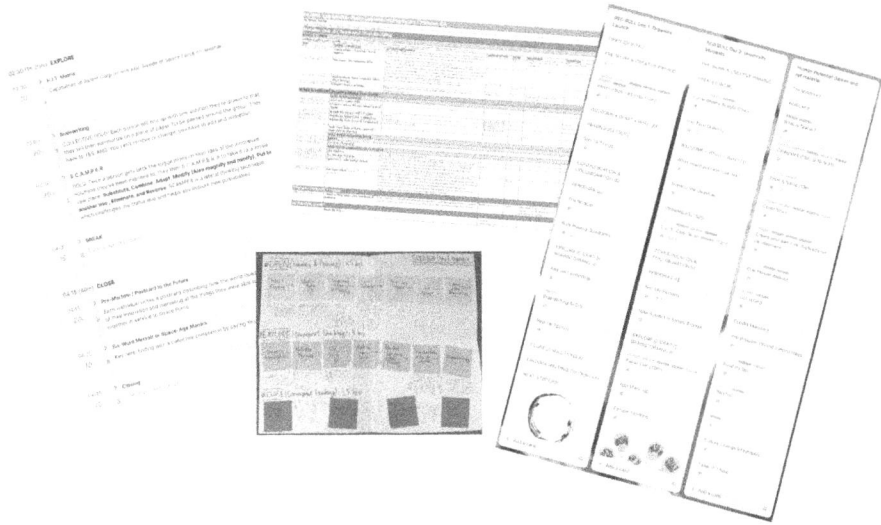

What also matters is how each individual game selected interacts with the games that come before and after, and how the combined sequence of games serves the participants as well as the meeting goals. The following image represents one game—for example, The Blind Side—and it reminds you how each game is its own self-contained unit of activity and energy, a unique thought experiment ushering us toward a (sometimes fuzzily defined) horizon.

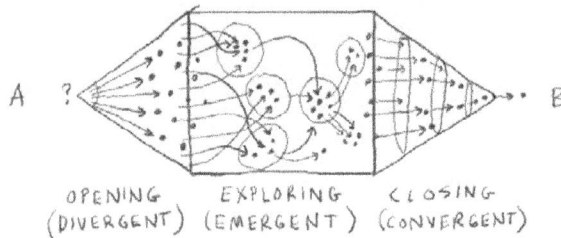

You'll see in the game sections of this book that there are durations assigned to each game, so as you try on different paths of play, make note of those durations, since your agenda is ultimately contingent on the amount of time you have with a group. Even short meetings—perhaps a meeting with three games, each lasting approximately 15 minutes—provide an opportunity to do something good, or even great. Participants working in a gamestorming fashion almost always emerge more energized, and you can easily turn something like a typical stand-up meeting into a fantastic gamestorm.

The vast majority of your design decisions will be fueled by those early sensing interviews. That discovery process informs the depth of your understanding, and it's the ground from which purpose, goals, and product spring. When you get down to brass tacks and start plotting a possible sequence of games for a meeting, the sky is truly the limit, and there are key areas to be mindful of as you consider game selection. These three things must be explored in order to arrive at even a prototype of meeting design:

- Duration
- Insight/purpose
- Game mechanics

When you start the design process, you'll almost always know the total amount of time you have with a group, and that's typically where you're most constrained. That part is relatively easy. It's knowing the emergent insights that tend to come from particular games, understanding how they work, and then selecting and sequencing them that requires a mental and imaginative workout.

Insight/purpose of a game

As noted earlier, every game is a unique and an individual thought experiment, out of which comes a set of semi-predictable insights that respond to the input or provocation of that game. For example, the input of the thought experiment of Pre-Mortem is a single question, *What could possibly go wrong?* The output is a collection of thoughts and ideas from the group about that very thing. For a game sequence to be coherent, that output needs to flow with ease into the opening of the next game, almost like a chapter in a storybook.

Using the example of Pre-Mortem, let's say the group has brainstormed potential missteps and is leaning into the next game. The question is what game(s) might be useful to open right after they've generated these insights? There are many diverging options. Your next game could involve a thought experiment around co-defining specifically what they're trying to do. Or the group might be served by turning their attention to what things have actually gone wrong in the past and extracting lessons learned. Or the next game could double down on what could go wrong, asking the group for hellish scenarios to go the distance in using our powers of catastrophizing.

The aim here is to use the content generated by a game to keep the energy moving. A good game sequence will leverage the information surfaced from one game and move it, often seamlessly, into the next. As we work to build an agenda game by game, time block by time block, we ask ourselves some key questions:

- What does this particular game help the participants do? What kind of thinking move[6] does it help them make? What are the learning outcomes and insights of this game?

---

6 The language of "thinking moves" is found in the book *Making Thinking Visible: How to Promote Engagement, Understanding, and Independence for all Learners*, funded by Harvard's Project Zero, by Ron Richhart (John Wiley, 2000). Also referred to as "thinking routines," these moves refer to habits of mind and cognition that support learning and engagement.

- What is *useful and needed* at this node in the meeting experience? Do the participants need information in order to take action? Do they need time for reflection on something they just absorbed? Do they need to socialize about their insights and create together? Once we have a sense of what's needed or what would serve at each turning point in a meeting agenda, we can evaluate games based on that need.

- If we chose the game, does it flow nicely after the one before? Does it segue well into the one that comes after? Did the game before set this game up for success, and does this game set up the next game for success, too? Does this game sequence flow? If so, how well?

To take it to an even more attentive depth, because gamestorming is ideally deployed with attention to learning styles, energy levels, and the spectrum of introversion and extroversion, you might also consider the following:

- Is this an individual game or a collaborative game? Do introverts need downtime at this intersection in the agenda?

- How intense or challenging was this game for them mentally? Would this be a good moment in the agenda for lightheartedness or levity?

- What sensory modalities are involved? Visual? Auditory? Musical? Kinesthetic? Mathematical?

- How long have we been in this room or game space? Does the group need to shift their attention entirely? Go outside to change states and come back to try again?

- Does this game feel like something that would resonate with the culture we're facilitating for? If not, does it help them expand and grow in ways that will be useful?

- If leadership needed to intervene with a presentation, thus disrupting our game flow, does this game follow nicely with the content of their keynote or talk and still meet the needs of our agenda?

Game mechanics

The mechanics of a game refer to just what it sounds like—the working parts of a game that give it its own locomotion. Mechanics are about how the game runs on a functional level. To take this entirely out of abstraction, let's look at the simple game Post-Up. Post-Up involves players generating ideas related to a question, writing one idea per sticky note in response to that question, and posting all of their sticky notes on a wall. The mechanics of that game are simple: Jot down an idea. Post the idea on the wall. The output of that motion are flurries of sticky notes that show individual ideas.

To move into the next game, those sticky notes, or the information on them, needs to somehow become usable. So, do you cluster all of those sticky notes in terms of similarity? Do you move them to different walls related to roles? Does someone read them aloud while breakout groups choose which idea they want to pursue? The mechanics of the closing of one game need to be sorted with the opening of the next.

In an uncomplicated or seamless world, the mechanics of a game wouldn't require serious attention, and often you can get by without pinpoint precision. The information generated can readily be transferred to the next context. Other times, you'll need to really think through how the artifacts of each game may need to be pulled along, sometimes across multiple games, to arrive at the endgame in a meaningful way. There are a couple of crucial questions to ask relative to game mechanics:

- What materials are needed to successfully run a game, and are they already in place, or does it require effort or a predesigned object or artifact?

- What artifacts will emerge from a game, and how will those artifacts be plugged into and inform the next game?

Selecting and sequencing games

How we think about game selection and game sequencing is multifaceted. For your typical stand-up team update, you can select games that you know play well together and have become "old reliables." These may be core games or games for exploring like Forced Ranking and Stop-Start-Continue. But for a meeting that has more potential, there are considerations for game selection that include a crucial understanding of the insight/purpose of the game, the game mechanics, and, perhaps obviously, its duration. In each game chosen, those aspects of it need to thread together effectively throughout.

The following is a game-boarding template that can help you consider a game sequence. This is an experimental space for you to write names of potential games, plot them on this board, and then evaluate how that arc of experience would feel for the group. Does it accomplish all that you've set out to do? Does it lead them toward the goal, however fuzzy? Does it honor the purpose of you all getting together? Does it engage as many of their senses as possible? If so, then you may well be on to something.

GAMEBOARDING TEMPLATE

• **Instructions:** Write the name of a game on a 2"x2" sticky note and sequence multiple notes to design your own meeting. Shuffle the games around to create different meeting outcomes. If you don't have 2"x2" sticky notes, draw this template on paper, a whiteboard or a flip chart and use any size sticky notes available.

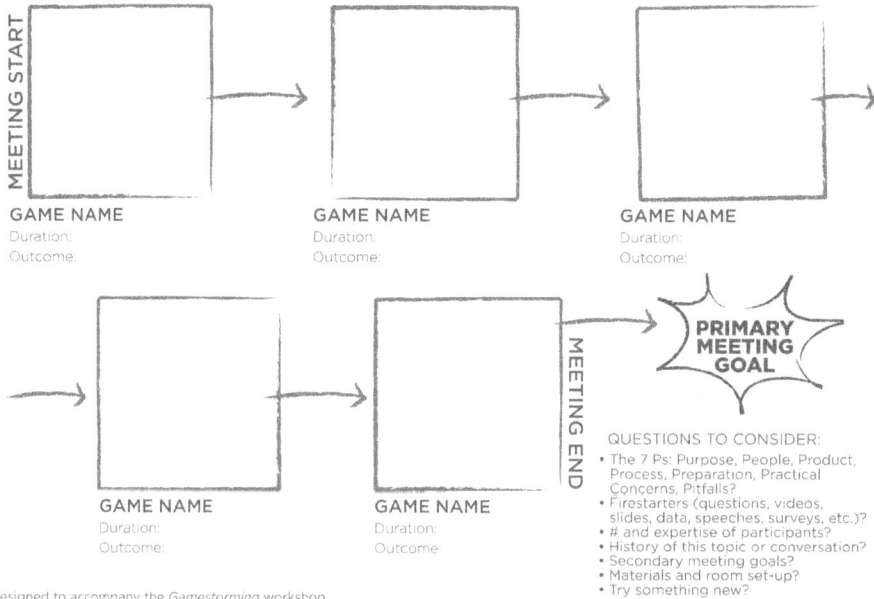

MEETING START

GAME NAME
Duration:
Outcome:

GAME NAME
Duration:
Outcome:

GAME NAME
Duration:
Outcome:

MEETING END

GAME NAME
Duration:
Outcome:

GAME NAME
Duration:
Outcome:

PRIMARY MEETING GOAL

QUESTIONS TO CONSIDER:
• The 7 Ps: Purpose, People, Product, Process, Preparation, Practical Concerns, Pitfalls?
• Firestarters (questions, videos, slides, data, speeches, surveys, etc.)?
• # and expertise of participants?
• History of this topic or conversation?
• Secondary meeting goals?
• Materials and room set-up?
• Try something new?

*Designed to accompany the *Gamestorming* workshop.

The more you build up your encyclopedia of games (and eventually, gain confidence in inventing your own!), the more options you have to build a dynamic and impactful experience. Take creative and intellectual risks. Don't play it safe with games you already know and love. Honor the energy and attention of the people in the room by really contemplating the efficacy and process of what you have designed. Think of yourself like a chef putting together the best possible menu for the situation at hand. How can you best delight? How can you best serve?

Practice giving simple, clear instructions

One of the most common ways gamestorming meetings can go awry is in the narrative framing. Each game has a unique nature and ways to enter in and engage with it, so it's useful to understand the nature of the game from your own experience and have a script in your mind (or on paper!) with clear guidance or instruction. Verbally draft the script for each game in advance of the meeting. Try to keep instructions simple. Resist the urge to ask people to remember multiple steps. If you want people to take multiple steps, we suggest you reduce their cognitive load by breaking the game steps into short sequences. For example, if you want people to do an activity with three steps, have them do the first step and then reconvene and make space for questions or reflections, before moving on to the next step.

PRODUCT

The meeting product is the high-value, tangible deliverable that ultimately shapes the arc of experience. It's that which you can sink your teeth into, that which you can wrap your mind and hands around once a meeting closes. The product, therefore, is the thing that gives you confidence in choosing the directionality of your meeting even while, in true gamestorming fashion, that direction may include some diversions, some exits and re-entries, maybe even some meanders. Remember this image?

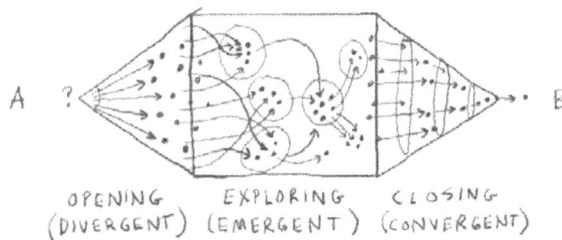

OPENING   EXPLORING   CLOSING
(DIVERGENT)   (EMERGENT)   (CONVERGENT)

Your meeting's purpose—why you're there, the implicit and explicit goals of the meeting—is directly influenced by the desired product, in that the product is the tangible endgame, and the meeting's purpose should be harmonious with that endgame. The product *can* be qualitative or subjective, something like helping the team to bond, but more often than not, clients or stakeholders want a specific *thing*. They want a budget hammered out; they want a strategy document; they want a signed team declaration of values.

Every step of the way, the process you design is intended to get them there in ways both tactical and creative. What's good about thinking of a meeting in terms of including a product is the clarifying effect that knowledge has. When participants know they're responsible for producing something actionable or deployable after getting together, they tend to buckle down and focus.

PREPARATION

This P doesn't refer to *your* preparation as the game facilitator or meeting lead. You'll find that insight in process. This P refers to ways you might help the participants prepare for the workshop. In reality, unless there's a cultural mandate or a really motivated team, many participants won't carve out the time to do preparation, even if it's brief (unless their failure to do so will somehow show in the end product—and you can design for that). Nevertheless, some participants will do work in advance, and it can help to seed the upcoming conversation with information that orients, inspires, or informs.

Examples of information that helps people prepare might be reviewing a slide deck that shows the latest market trends, scanning a whitepaper about nanotechnology, watching a short documentary about a company that gets culture right, responding anonymously to survey questions that can be shown in session, recording a video for people to review at their leisure, or asking people to source examples of products that inspire them and may contribute to ideation in an innovation session. We live in a multimedia world, so we often encourage meeting planners to take advantage of that. You can get usefully informed on some aspect of a meeting through a YouTube video, a Substack post, or a podcast.

Take note: if you're going to make the success of the meeting contingent on people doing their pre-work, give them fair notice—multiple days in advance. And make the relationship between the content they're consuming and the purpose and product of the meeting itself abundantly clear. In other words, motivate them and set them up for success through clear communication.

PRACTICAL CONCERNS

© marketoonist.com

Practical concerns are just that—the nuts and bolts, the time, place, and material requirements for a meeting to be successfully executed. Your game sequence will take place inside of some environment—analog or digital—so that environment and its resources need to be known as roundly as possible. A short story will drive this point home.

One of the authors of this book—Sun—is credited with being the first person to bring graphic recording and graphic facilitation to the South by Southwest (SXSW) Film Conference in Austin, Texas. She introduced large-scale visual thinking to the organizers in 2009 and worked with them for several years. Eventually, other practitioners were inspired and got involved, so visual-thinking teams spread into various avenues of the conference.

Here's an example that stresses the importance of considering the practical concerns. One of the later visual-thinking teams for SXSW lived in New York and hadn't been onsite in Austin or designed visual-thinking sessions in the flesh at the conference, which resulted in a sizable blooper: the team made unconscious assumptions about the physical space. They didn't anticipate the sheer size of the convention center in which the conference was held and didn't ask for site maps for sessions inside or outside of the convention center.

As you might imagine, this seemingly simple omission affected the outcome in a significant way. This team had agreed to be the visual practitioners for any session SXSW requested, resulting in another error that could have been anticipated in the preparation stage. They dramatically underestimated how long it would take to move a team member and their visual materials from one room to another. As a result, team members were all over the place. They were late to many of the sessions, missed some of them entirely, arrived at some without meeting supplies, and they were scrambling, running around, trying desperately to make it all work. The team members grew sweaty, exhausted, and frustrated, and that, of course, impacted performance.

This was a foreseeable outcome, had they anticipated one of the most crucial questions involving meetings in the real world: the dimensions of physical space. One basic error like this can have a cascade effect on almost everything, so be rigorous about asking logistical questions. Don't just imagine the space you're working in—get pictures of it. Find the dimensions or site map online. Ask the hotel onsite event coordinator to send you everything they have about the space. Find out where the stage will be. The speakers. How much privacy do you have? What size tables are you working with? Will people need microphones? How and when might other traffic be moving through? What is there to project slides onto? How far away are breakout rooms? WHERE ARE THE BATHROOMS? WHERE IS COFFEE?! And what are the equivalencies in digital meetings?

All of that will need to come together for a hearty gamestorming session. Sometimes it's simple—your team is simply assembling in your regular reserved space—and other times much of this is handled by reliable, vetted people or even an events team. But sometimes it's not. Know what you're getting into and check your assumptions.

Even though other folks who aren't responsible for the meeting may not understand your questions, when planning a meeting onsite or online, be thorough almost to a fault. Ask questions of people on the ground and in the know, even if they roll their eyes about your fixation on login protocols, room acoustics, the food menu, or lighting. When the people finally arrive in the room and they're ready to get to work, the less surprises, the better. There are detailed meeting checklists for onsite and online gamestorming sessions. Start with those and modify them as you develop your personal approach and style.

PITFALLS

In many ways, pitfalls are the result of what happens when we don't spend sufficient time considering the other Ps. Pitfalls can be technical, social, logistical, political, material, and financial. There are myriad ways to unintentionally misstep, so whether you're gamestorming in the real world or a digital environment, it behooves you to try to anticipate pitfalls of various shapes and sizes.

As you start to experiment with gamestorming in the true arena of meetings and workshops, you'll quickly discover that the diversity of possible pitfalls is boundless, so agility and improvisation ultimately become your best friends. We can tell that someone has become more masterful at meetings when they're unflappable no matter what happens, and they stay calm and meet each moment. It takes time, experimentation, and trust to get there. En route to greater confidence, anticipating and scenario-planning pitfalls is a very good practice. Edward De Bono calls this "black-hat thinking" anticipating what could go wrong—or you can think of it as a light version of red teaming—a model for roundly challenging significant aspects of a plan.

The following are examples of common pitfalls that can be avoided with a little preparation:

- Not having detailed knowledge of either the onsite location or the online equipment and its functionality.

- Leaving the design of the agenda until just a few days before a workshop that's either large, long, or complex.

- Letting one group overwhelm the presence or contributions of another without having a plan to address that circumstance.

- Failing to consider who's sitting where, with whom, and why.

- Not connecting meaningfully with your cofacilitator in advance to discuss how you'll "dance" together if X, Y, or Z occurs.

- Neglecting to consider the acoustics and lighting in the room.

- Inviting the wrong people or forgetting to invite the right people.

- Being insensitive to power dynamics.

- Avoiding an elephant in the room that's occupying everyone's awareness and making it difficult for them to focus.

- Being oblivious to cultural norms. This doesn't mean you obey them all the time—it can be healthy to challenge norms for the sake of learning—but to sustain the confidence of the group, be aware of what norms you're challenging and why.

- Including too many people on the design team.

- Socializing with the wrong stakeholders or with too many stakeholders to figure out the meeting's purpose and goals.

- Not getting clear on the requirement for materials—gamestorming is a multisensory, hands-on way of working. If you have 16 round tables in a session and only two flip charts and four markers, well, you see the problem. If your digital whiteboard has game spaces that only accommodate 20 sticky notes and each group is likely to generate 100 sticky notes per game space, that's also a problem.

PRACTICE THE 7PS IN A MEETING ABOUT MEETINGS

To enhance your love for the 7Ps, we've included a rapid approach to help identify *which* meetings in your team or organization you could immediately rework with some gamestorming mojo. Knowing which meetings are ripe for transformation can help you step in faster—and recruit the right folks for an ideally low-hurdle creative risk.

Post-Up

Start by brainstorming all the types of meetings you've noticed in your organization. Think through a typical day, week, month, quarter, year. How many distinct kinds of meetings can you recall? Write one meeting type per sticky note.

Prioritize

Use the Impact/Effort Matrix to prioritize these meeting types. Which meetings require the least effort to change? Which meetings have the most impact on culture and behavior? Select the meeting(s) you want to rethink and redesign.

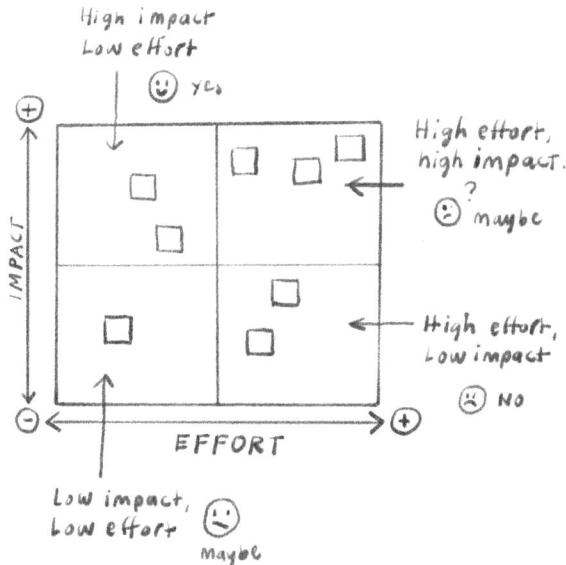

Going meta on the 7Ps

Once you've assessed which meetings are the first candidates for gamestorming makeovers, use the 7Ps to imagine their redesign. This gives you a chance to get your feet wet before going all in on complex meeting structures. The following is a visual architecture to re-create and doodle around on:

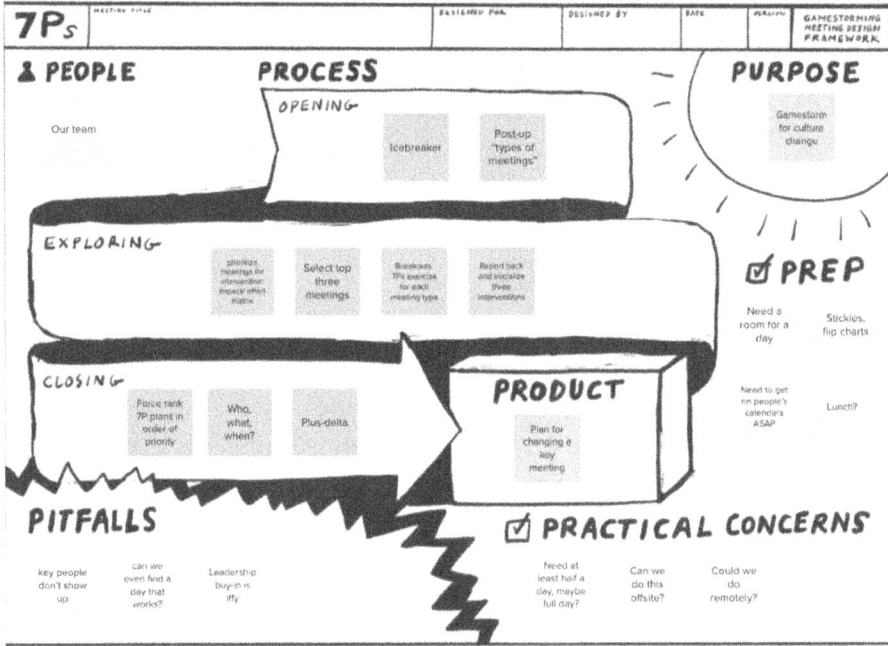

Once you've seen the 7Ps, ideally they feel so natural that they almost immediately become intuitive, like a language you once knew but somehow forgot. We cannot stress enough how helpful it is to anchor your meeting design with this tool. It is the scaffolding on which good (or at least better) meetings are built. Keeping it in mind any time you plan to gather is one way to demonstrate respect for the people you've invited.

Virtual Meetings

In gamestorming trainings, one question consistently comes up: *How can we use this with virtual, distributed teams?* If there are silver linings to the COVID-19 pandemic, one is that the technology for virtual meetings advanced rapidly since we first published this book in 2010, and the other is that so has knowledge workers' facility with them. Most people are now accustomed to meeting and collaborating virtually, and many have dedicated home offices with cameras and microphones. They're increasingly well-versed in getting things done together online. For good reasons—better teaming, collective solving, aligning around projects—many people aim to elevate online meetings, but they often imagine that digital environments constrain or limit what's possible. Thankfully, that doesn't have to be the case. Digital environments are wide-open fields of possibility, and they can amplify thinking, creativity, and collaborative problem solving with a bit of preparation, planning, and basic facilitation skills. Virtual spaces, while certainly different from real-life environments, can nevertheless support gamestorming in playful and powerful ways. There are seemingly infinite game spaces that can be designed and game mechanics that can be facilitated (you'll see a few examples below). That said, virtual meetings do come with a different set of constraints and opportunities. In crucial ways, there's no real substitute for meeting in person, but if your team is distributed, there's a lot you can do to introduce gamestorming principles and practices for significantly better engagement and productivity.

GAMESTORMING FOR VIRTUAL MEETINGS AND EVENTS

Since virtual meetings are their own animal and need to be approached differently, how can you use gamestorming to design and facilitate better online meetings and events? First, we have to address the technology. Two tools we've found indispensable are video meeting apps, like Zoom or Microsoft Teams, and online whiteboards such as Mural or Miro. These tools work really well in combination, allowing people to see and hear each other while providing spaces for them to work and think. One salient feature of Zoom, relative to group connection, is that people's video feeds can be minimized but visible while working on the whiteboard. As a facilitator, this helps you read the room while people think together, sensing and pacing along with their progress and, of course, making it possible to ask questions and advance the discussion as needed. Once you've situated your technology and have a sufficient sense of fluidity using it, you can address what's needed to make it gameful.

CONSIDERATIONS FOR THINKING VIRTUALLY IN GROUPS

In these next sections, we include screenshots from real virtual sessions that use Zoom and Mural or Miro to fire your imagination around what you can do. We also address the basics for getting up and running using gamestorming in what are now fairly common working environments.

The merits of virtual whiteboards

Our minds extend well beyond the boundaries of our skulls, and you can understand virtual whiteboards to be extensions of the group's hands, hearts, and minds. These spaces are highly useful thinking and working companions since they can hold game spaces, game mechanics, agendas and timing, content generated by players, facilitation tools, artifacts needed for discussion, and so on. Collaborative whiteboards are powerful places because they scaffold all of those things to support group work while also being persistent. You can organize your working space in advance of a meeting, and it will remain online indefinitely for later check-ins, updates, and elaborations. The structures you build can also be easily duplicated, used an infinite number of times for future meetings, or modified for new ones. You can harvest the text people input on sticky notes (which is also easier to read) and, thanks to AI, you can summarize it and place it in other documents to advance follow-on goals.

Online whiteboards also include features useful to facilitators like timers, dot voting, private mode, summoning the group to a specific place, and the ability to lock down elements you don't want to be moved.

Last, most digital whiteboards can be made democratic, meaning they allow for individual contributions to have equal participation and fair influence—confidentially if the user names are anonymous. This feature makes it possible for unpopular but perhaps much-needed insight and information to be shared, and there are typically few opportunities for workers to safely do that. There's a lot to be said on the merits of digital collaboration spaces; the gamestormer's real task is leveraging all that they offer to make a meaningful experience for participants.

Create meaningful game spaces for people to work in

When designing a virtual meeting, it's imperative to consider the design of the game spaces. As we noted earlier, online whiteboards like Mural and Miro make it possible to build compelling thinking and working spaces using visual templates, game structures, infographics, metaphors, process and system maps, you name it. Virtual whiteboards support many different types of thinking spaces, ensuring that your meeting is interesting, valuable, and connective.

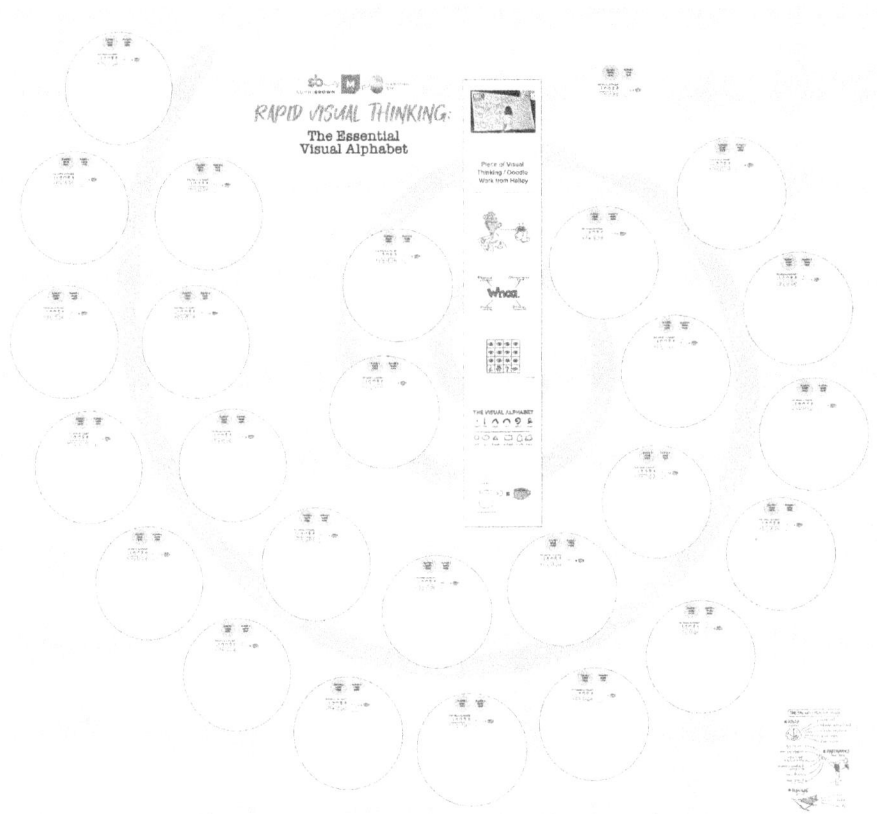

ALL PARTS OF YOU ARE WELCOME.

WE ALL CONTAIN MULTITUDES AND LIFE CAN GET MESSY, SO MIXED EMOTIONS ABOUT A TOPIC ARE NOT ONLY NATURAL, BUT DERIVATIVE OF FINELY-TUNED SURVIVAL SKILLS. AS YOU RUN INTO COMPLEXITY, THERE WILL BE PARTS OF YOU THAT ARISE IN RESPONSE. THESE PARTS WON'T ALWAYS AGREE ON WHAT TO DO OR HOW TO FEEL, BUT EACH DESERVES A CHANCE TO BE HEARD. IN THE IMAGE BELOW, THE INDIVIDUAL VOICES IN YOUR HEART AND HEAD HAVE A PLACE AT THE TABLE. CHOOSE A COMPLEX TOPIC FOR THE CENTERPIECE AND WRITE OR DOODLE IN FRONT OF EACH CHARACTER WHAT HE OR SHE WOULD SAY ABOUT THE TOPIC. LET THEM BE THEIR MOST HONEST. ADD PATTERNS AND COLORS THAT MIGHT RESONATE WITH THEIR POINT OF VIEW. EXHALE. EXPRESS. THEY HAVE SOMETHING THEY NEED YOU TO KNOW.

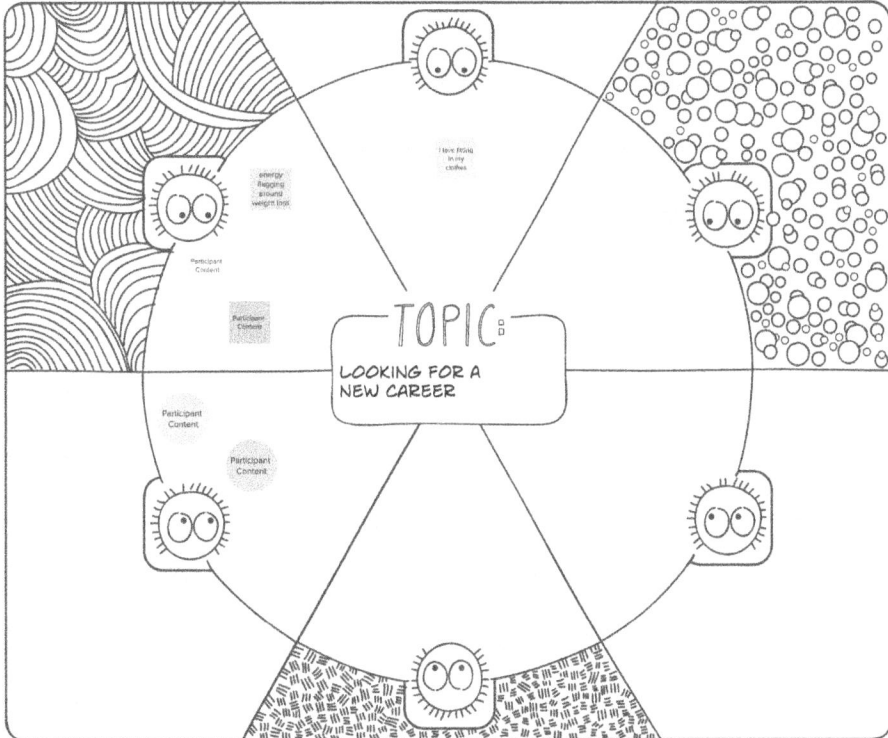

When using digital whiteboards for online facilitation, you'll need to make room for each game, exercise, or task included in your agenda. Design and build your game spaces by populating the board in advance with game boards, visual architectures, or templates (you can even use scenes from films or video games) and include any documents, videos, or presentation decks you'll need to refer to in the meeting.

The following is an example of a multiplayer gameboard, along with an expanded view of one player's game space:

NOTHING IN THE WAY

(SUN'S SUBSTACK FACILITATION SPACE)

EXAMPLE EXPLORATION SPACE

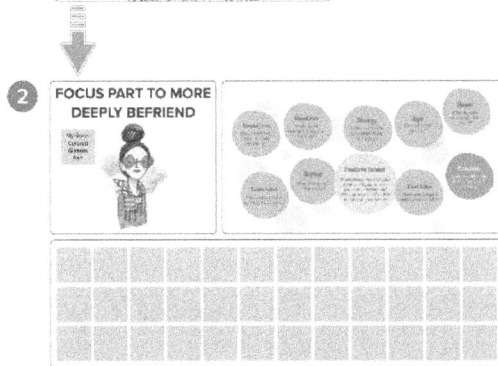

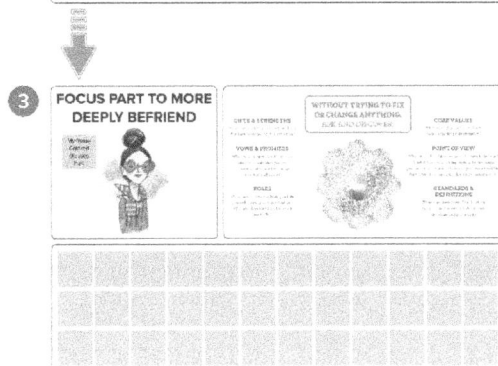

1 ALL PARTS OF YOU ARE WELCOME.

TOPIC OR DILEMMA

2 FOCUS PART TO MORE DEEPLY BEFRIEND

3 FOCUS PART TO MORE DEEPLY BEFRIEND

WITHOUT TRYING TO FIX OR CHANGE ANYTHING,

If it's a longer meeting or a complex problem-solving experience and the board starts to feel overwhelming, you can make certain sections invisible or simply hide them by covering them with a white rectangle, revealing them as their time comes. Strive for a level of engagement that piques the participants' interest but doesn't dizzy them or make them want to sneak off and play upcoming games before it's time. As a facilitator, the main aim is to have the materials you need to support the experience, a sequence of game spaces that people can work within, the ability to articulate the game mechanics, and minimal distractions.

There are so many possibilities for building game spaces that it's also appropriate to have fun designing spaces for people to think in. For example, when we hosted a meeting about holiday experiences, we built a candy store and asked people to pull off the shelf and place on a table which candy they lusted after when they were young and what features of that candy made them irrational and why. In a meeting about note-taking, we visualized a knowledge garden for people to explore, with prompts for things to think about, like sources of knowledge, seeds of new ideas, harvesting fruits, and so on. Someone in that session noticed we forgot a compost pile for old ideas and added it! One of the great things about metaphors is that they encourage people to see something habitual in a new way and they empower people to extend the metaphor for deeper understanding.

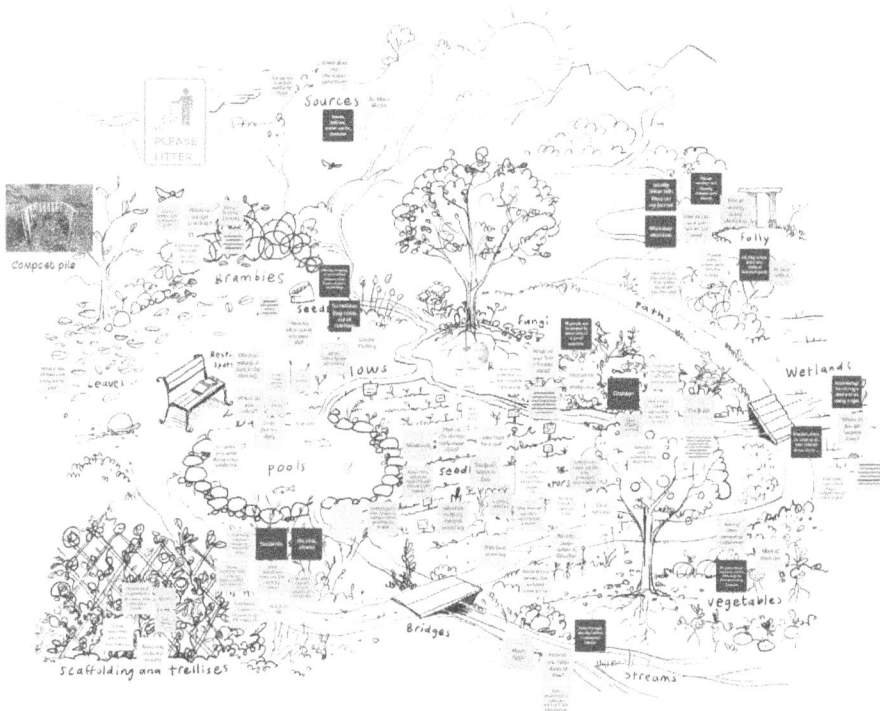

To give you a sense of how wide open the playing field is in digital environments, one more example of a thinking space is shown next. To create the feeling of a museum or art gallery, we used drawing skills to show security guards (you can also search for photographs and insert them) and asked people to contemplate things they collect. Players had five minutes to themselves, and we played relaxing music in the background while they populated the space with their ideas. All of these unique game spaces can and should be welcomed; the question is what you as a facilitator will come up with to resonate with the group.

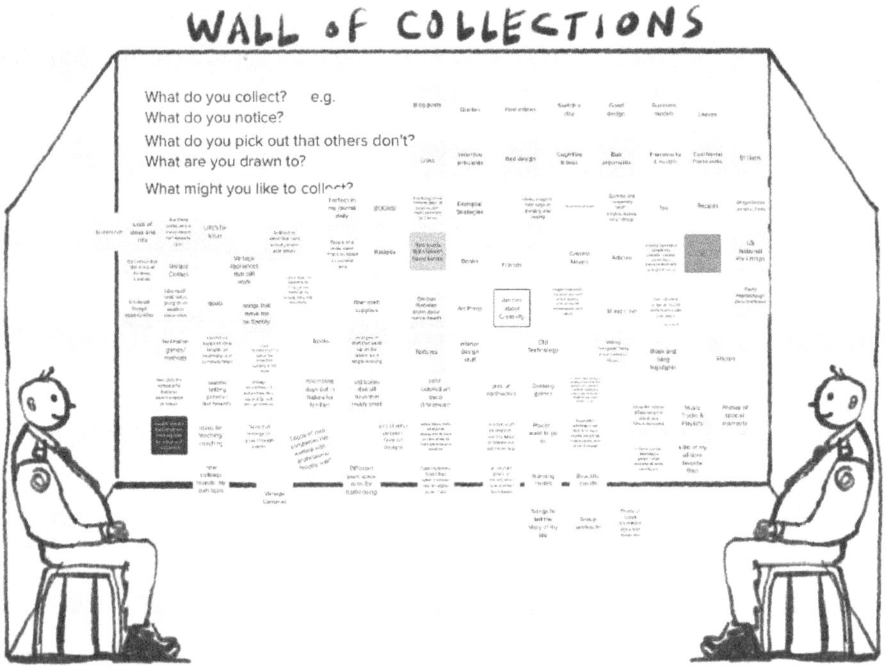

Provide things for people to think with

The most common "thing" to capture thoughts of the group is the sticky note, and the ability to work with sticky notes is a core element of the gamestorming toolkit, whether working in real life or digitally. Sticky notes allow people to express their perspectives and ideas in a modular, concise way, and they can be shuffled, arranged, configured, and organized in surprising ways. Online whiteboards like Mural make this as easy as double-clicking the background. But you don't need to limit yourself to sticky notes. You can and should use the doodling and drawing tools provided in the apps, and also include background data in the form of documents, spreadsheets, slide presentations, and web links, simply by copying the URLs and pasting them into the whiteboard.

Game mechanics

Game mechanics are silent partners not to be underestimated in terms of the attention they warrant. It's crucial to think through how each game is played because, remember, the output of each game becomes the input for the next! There are basic but highly disruptive bloopers we can make, like not having the number of game boards match the number of attendees or not anticipating and making room for the sheer amount of sticky notes that can be generated by one person or one thought experiment, and bigger bloopers we can make, like not locking down the right components of built visual structures and therefore unleashing mayhem on our board.

For meetings that are weekly, fairly simple, or predictable, these kinds of things don't require too much pre-planning, but if you are the gamestormer responsible for conducting any experience, few things should surprise you in the moment unless the culture of your team or your client can embrace that. Ideally, you've not only premeditated and built your game spaces, but you've also tested them—walking through them in your mind's eye or literally playing them in advance—as if they were being facilitated live.

Breakout rooms

Virtual video apps like Zoom and Microsoft Teams allow you to create breakout rooms for small-group work and discussions, and thank goodness. This opens up possibilities for meeting design in diverse and wonderful ways. Think of breakout rooms as smaller working cells, pop-up spaces for quiet, more enhanced, or more intimate collaborations. The option of breakout rooms comes with quite a few ways to amplify a meeting. You can use the smaller groups to process and socialize ideas and information outside of the sometimes stressful large-group environment. You can convert them into quiet but not isolated learning spaces, like libraries, in which people can lower their energy but still work together quietly or speak on an as-needed basis. You can create breakout rooms with entirely different purposes—one perhaps being an Ideation Room, another being a Break-Things Room, another being a Contemplate Room, and another being a Recharge Room. You can even use breakout rooms for playful games like Tag! or Scavenger Hunt if the setting allows people to come and go as they please. The breakout-room feature in Zoom and Teams is about much more than just making smaller groups. It's about using these temporary microcultures to open, explore, and close games in ways that keep unique learners engaged while moving the agenda along. You'll need to be mindful of bringing people back at junctures relevant to the overarching experience, so, as you craft your meeting agenda, consider when those junctures make the most sense and whether or not breaks around them would be useful.

Last, it's a general best practice to keep instructions for breakout rooms simple since the players will be temporarily in their own worlds without a lead facilitator. That said, the technology now enables sharing of audio, video, and slides across breakout rooms, so you can more comfortably leave people to their own devices for longer, letting them work "on the side" without your support since they can hear your broadcasted voice and see any visual facilitation instructions.

Agendas and onboarding

If people are new to collaborating and working in online whiteboards, it's helpful to carve out time at the beginning of the meeting for people to get comfortable with the tools and ask questions about them. Be sure to leave a little extra time for random noise as people enter the virtual space, fiddle with their technology, and get accustomed to the virtual environment. You can and should combine this quick onboarding with firestarters, too. For example, make an open space on the whiteboard and ask people to find and place an emoji that expresses how they're feeling right now, or create a sticky note with something they're thinking about, or choose gifs of animals that represent the one they feel most like today. Consider both the culture of the group and the goals of your gamestorm to tailor your firestarters to those contexts and give people a low-stakes, lighthearted way to try out the tools.

If you pay attention to what happens as they onboard, you'll get a good sense of how capable people are with the technology. Based on what you see, you may ask people participating to provide additional support via private chats or through live demos, or adjust the game mechanics, if necessary. Depending on the complexity and intensity of the session, you can also send helpful "how-to" videos in advance or embed them in the whiteboard and watch them together before you begin. Be mindful that the game mechanics of each game in your experience design are conducive to the know-how of the group. It's perfectly suitable to help them stretch and grow into learning the software, but you don't want your experience to make demands that stall the process or frustrate the players. It's a balancing act, and something to be mindful of in advance.

In terms of letting people know what is the "what and when," the simplest way to show the agenda is by using sticky notes with approximate times for each section. The following is an example of a sticky-note agenda:

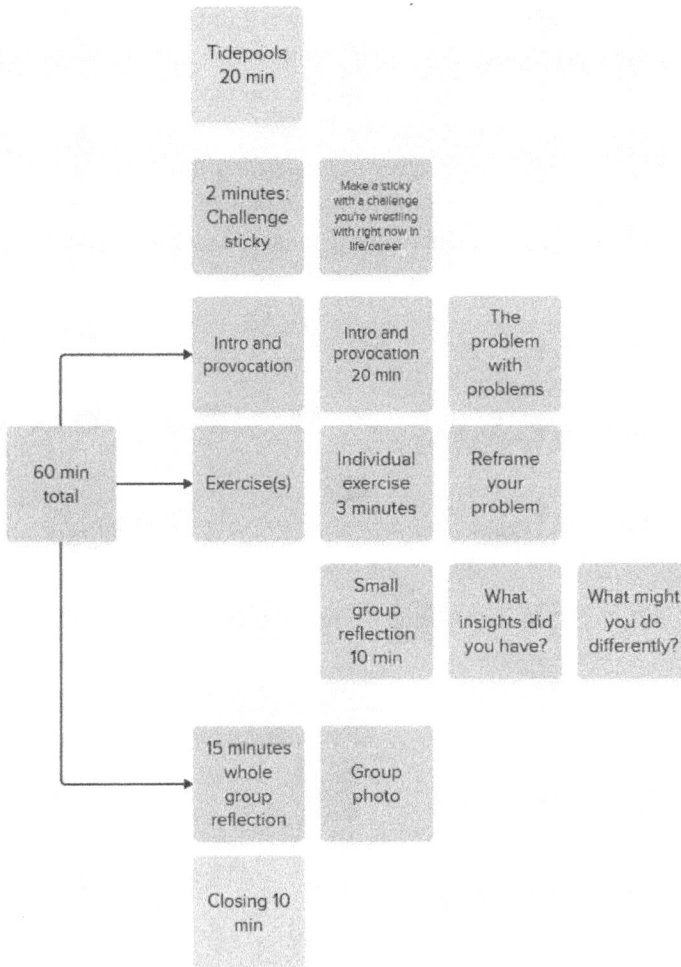

Note that each section of the meeting has an estimated time, and the exercises are briefly described. There's enough here for the facilitator to remember everything, keep the timing on track, and make sure that nothing is left out. There's also enough for the players to know what to expect and to plan breaks or other tasks accordingly. When you get people into the shared space, you can summon them to this simple visual and set expectations around what will be happening. A pie chart agenda is also useful, or a schedule made possible by the software you're using, as in the bottom post-it in the previous image and the outline in Mural shown next.

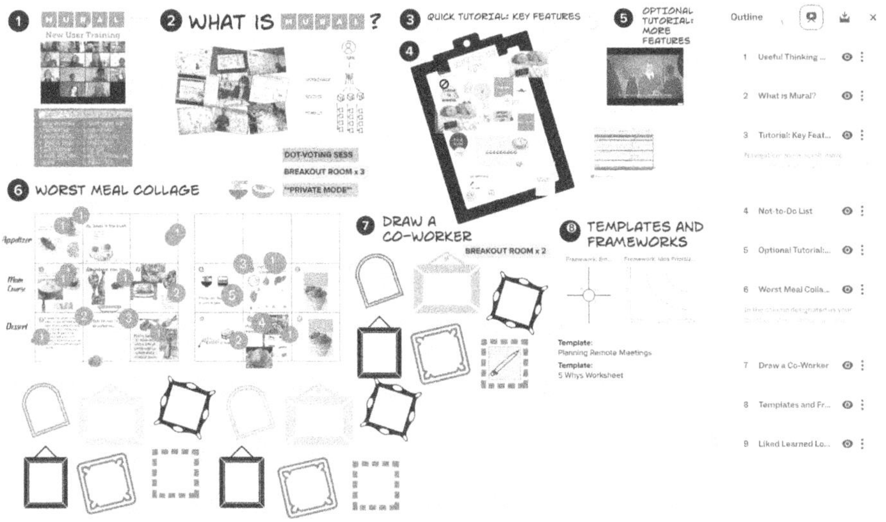

Energy tolls

Energetically, virtual meetings take a toll on people. There's more cognitive load and distraction in these environments, and fewer opportunities for spontaneous, often restorative, connection. After much experimentation, we concluded that virtual gamestorming meetings are optimized in 90-minute sections, which can be sequenced across days to accommodate more robust agendas. Most people are accustomed to hour-long (fairly pointless) meetings, so claiming 90 minutes allows you to maintain a useful degree of intensity and focus. We've observed that when a meeting goes over 90 minutes, attention and energy start to wane and you enter a point of diminishing returns. You can conduct successful workshops, even intense ones such as strategic planning sessions, by changing what would normally be a two-day offsite into a weeklong sprint, for example, scheduling morning and afternoon sessions with breaks and homework between sessions.

A note about hybrid meetings

You *can* support the same meeting simultaneously in analog and digital environments, but we don't recommend it. Gamestorming works best when everyone occupies the same space and the opportunities to contribute are relatively equal. Hybrid meetings are extremely difficult to level-set in this way.

If a hybrid meeting is unavoidable, understand that the in-person participants have an advantage in terms of contributing and steering the direction of the meeting. If the facilitator is online, it's difficult to guide and contain their energy while attending to the layers of technology and the needs of online participants. If the facilitator is in the room, it's too easy to lose touch with the online participants.

There are a couple of things you can do to mitigate the inevitable asymmetry of hybrid meetings, however. You can create the same game spaces in both environments, using an online whiteboard and projecting the whiteboard on a screen for in-person participants working in parallel on physical walls. Or you can invite people in the office to bring their laptops and work on a shared digital whiteboard while they're physically together and their colleagues are distributed. This scenario would ideally have a camera and microphone set up in the physical working room so remote participants can see what's going on and speak to the people who are in the same room with each other. If the meeting is equally important to all participants, consider simply allowing everyone to work from home the day of the meeting or, if possible, requiring everyone to attend in person.

Each opportunity is a judgment call, contingent on the urgency and significance of the meeting, but gamestorming has an ethos of making participation as equal as possible, so we encourage you to help hybrid meetings choose an identity—entirely digital or entirely analog—rather than straddling a suboptimal, messy middle. What we know for sure is that remote work is rapidly becoming a fixture of modern life—the savings on travel, food, lodging, and physical materials make it compelling—so gamestormers who embrace the design and facilitation of virtual meetings will serve themselves and future players well. Virtual meetings are ultimately an opportunity to expand the boundaries of gamestorming and leverage the power of technology, combined with imagination, to offer quality sessions for people trying to think better together.

PRIOR PREPARATION PREVENTS POOR PERFORMANCE

Sun's stepfather was in the Marines, and he reminded her (often!) that prior preparation prevented piss-poor performance. Stated differently, ninety percent of the success in any gamestorming meeting is based on that P, of preparation: how you think about and plan the meeting in advance. As a designer of the group's experience, you are charged with discerning ideal outcomes, choosing participants, considering energy and expectations, setting up the game spaces and working areas, and being clear on timing, mechanics, and game sequence. (This is in addition to skillfully guiding the group's energy when you're in the live session!) When you lean into all of that, you are building worlds that make new things possible, and the planning shows respect and appreciation to those who attend. Use your imagination. Take risks and experiment. Try to enjoy the learning process. There is so much treasure that can emerge.

5

The Design Canvas

Gamestorming is more than a book. It's a collaborative way of life, a sweeping invitation to make work more visible, sharable, engaging, and meaningful. We've been workshopping and teaching gamestorming since before it had a name. In fact, the original working title for *Gamestorming* was "The Visual Thinking Playbook."

One of the early adopters of this approach and evangelists for the movement was Alex Osterwalder, known for producing the best-selling book *Business Model Generation* with coauthor Yves Pigneur, which featured the Business Model Canvas (John Wiley and Sons). This canvas was shared in the first edition of *Gamestorming*, and both books came out in 2010. Gamestorming was introduced to Alex in a workshop in Geneva in 2007, and he quickly saw the value and supported it. Since that (fantastic!) year, the Business Model Canvas has taken the world by storm and created a new category of artifact, a hands-on tool (a kind of game board) called the design canvas, defined and explored in the following section. This category is so useful that it has been rapidly adopted by consultants, practitioners, and facilitators all over the world, and there are now hundreds, if not thousands, of design canvases, available for every imaginable personal and professional use.

This rapid proliferation has also created quality problems. Design canvases have a tendency to look similar to one another. Many are ultimately just worksheets labeled as "canvases." It's very hard, superficially, to tell a good canvas from a bad one by simply looking at it.

As one person put it, "Everyone has a canvas now, and they're all bad."

The design canvas is a new innovation in group work. When designed correctly, a design canvas can be an incredibly powerful tool. When poorly designed, it works like a bad consultant: it may make a good first impression but ultimately provides a weak, derivative, or meaningless framework; gives you bad advice; leads people to make bad decisions; and sometimes can even generate disastrous results.

In this chapter, we will answer the following questions:

- What is a design canvas?
- How is it different from any other template or game board?
- Why and when would you choose a game board versus a canvas?
- What does "good" look like?
- How might you develop a design canvas from scratch?
- How might you transform an existing game board into a design canvas, and why would you want to?
- How can you evaluate a design canvas, to separate the good from the bad?

What Is a Design Canvas?

A design canvas is like a supercharged game board that incorporates rigorous business thinking and is developed more like software, involving prototyping, testing, and an iterative development process, to create a game board that's more robust, clearer in its intended use, more self-explanatory, and easier to use.

A design canvas has the following qualities:

- It has a clear intended purpose that is self-evident.
- It incorporates rigorous business thinking, theory, and research around a specific purpose (like designing a business model).
- It visually represents a group of concepts and ideas to make a structured, coherent, meaningful, self-contained, sharable work space.

- It's created like software, using a design and development process that includes prototyping, testing, and iterative development with feedback from users, often released in versions, beginning with low-stability alpha and beta stages and evolving to stable versions.

- It includes instructions within the canvas itself, making it self-explanatory and, to some degree, self-facilitating.

- It has clear authorship, a designated "single source of truth."

- It's often accompanied by real-world examples and case studies.

How Is a Design Canvas Different?

Let's compare the Business Model Canvas to see how it differs from a typical game board, using the Speed Boat game designed by Luke Hohmann, and described in his book, *Innovation Games* (Addison-Wesley Professional).

Although the purpose is clear in Luke's book (making complaint sessions more constructive), Speed Boat is a flexible concept, an extendable metaphor that can take many forms and be adjusted for a broad range of situations.

A quick web search for "speed boat templates" revealed many visual formations and use cases, including project retrospectives, evaluating products and services, determining team strengths and weaknesses, and so on. Many were actually sailboats, not speed boats!

While all of these "speed boats" clearly have many things in common, they are not self-explanatory. The Speed Boat game requires a facilitator or consultant who knows the game and is able to teach it to others, or at the very least, a set of instructions or "recipe" like those found in *Gamestorming*.

In his excellent playbook, *Innovation Games*, Luke emphasizes creativity, describing how teams created different variations, including one where the team used barnacles to represent customer complaints.

Speed Boat is a game that's optimized for flexibility, fun, and engagement. It can be morphed and modified in an infinite number of ways, for a wide variety of uses. That's what the Speed Boat game was designed for, and that kind of use is encouraged.[1]

In contrast, the Business Model Canvas is more stately, spare, Spartan, almost boring.

It is for one thing and one thing only. Its title makes a clear statement about what it is for—representing and creating a business model.

It is structured according to clear visual logic, a value chain, with the supply side on the left, the customer demand side on the right, and a value proposition in the middle that connects them. Costs and revenue are the foundations that support the other blocks.

It is self-evident and includes the instructions for its own use. Each of the nine boxes includes a clear title, stating what that box represents, and a set of questions to answer for that box, as well as sufficient space for ideation.

---

1 Image credits: Drawbridge Innovations, Eamon O'Rourke, Deb Mrazek, João Costa Ribeiro, Cara Holland (graphicchangeacademy.com), and 60 Bits Consulting.

The authorship is clear, with a link to follow for anyone who wants to do due diligence on the tool.

Although you can certainly sketch it on a whiteboard or flip chart (and people do), it is presented as a finished product. It is "locked down." The Business Model Canvas, by its very finish, format, and nature, discourages modifications and derivatives.

There are aspects of the Business Model Canvas that are difficult to see just by looking at it. This is the "good consulting" or deep structure that underpins the tool, including underlying business logic, which maps to the visual logic, and the rigorous development process used to ensure that it delivers on its promise.

Alex Osterwalder and Yves Pigneur conducted an extensive literature review, identified all the existing business model categories, and consolidated them into an ontology with categories that were mutually exclusive and collectively exhaustive. They ran workshops to test and evolve the ontology and language, applying it to numerous case studies, and continually revised it until it was clear and intuitive for users.

There's no way to know this by simply looking at the result. Like a great hardware device or software application, its simplicity hides a lot of necessary complexity. There are only two ways to evaluate these hidden qualities:

1. Try it to see if it works for you. This might be the best way to go on projects where the failure risk is low.

2. Trust. When the stakes are high, you should ask yourself whether you trust the tool designer. A good question to ask is this: If they had not created a design canvas, would you hire them for a project in this area?

Canvas or Game Board?

So why and when would you choose one over the other? And when designing a game, should you make a game board or a canvas? Which is better?

Well, neither is better or worse. They are simply different. A game board often leaves a lot of room for personalization and customization for a particular client or use case. A design canvas will tend to put a design meeting "on rails"— if your problem fits well with the purpose of the canvas, follow the recipe and you'll tend to get the promised result. But remember, a design canvas is only as good as its creator, and the web is full of scammers as well as legitimate toolmakers. The responsibility is on you to do your homework and make sure you're not introducing your team to snake oil in a pretty can.

If you're a creator, it's a good idea to start with a game board. This is a low-risk realm with a lot of wiggle room, where the marketplace will give you a lot of freedom and forgiveness. It also gets you to a good starting place, something you can test and iterate on until you know what you're working with. Once you have something you know is working, you can consider whether to "evolve it" into a design canvas. We'll share an example of how to do that later in this chapter.

What Does "Good" Look Like?

A good design canvas should meet some basic criteria. Some are surface qualities that are easy to evaluate. Other criteria are "under the hood" and require a little more due diligence on the user's part.

The first set of criteria is about surface qualities. These are things you should be able to evaluate without doing a lot of research:

Purpose

Is it clear what the tool is for? A good canvas is a functional tool, with a clear purpose, designed to do a specific job within a broader context.

Authorship

Is it clear who created it? Does it point back to the author or a website where you can learn more?

Visual logic

Are the categories clear? Do they make sense? Is the language clear and easy to understand? Does the visual arrangement make sense? It includes its own instructions, so it is self-explanatory and self-facilitating.

The second set of criteria has to do with the tool's deep structure. Evaluating the deep structure "under the hood" of a design canvas will require you to dig deeper and ask the kinds of questions you would ask a consultant you're about to hire for an important project:

Credibility

Who is the creator? What experience and expertise have they demonstrated? Can they provide references, testimonials? Would you hire them for a project in this area?

Theory, research, practice

Where did this come from? What theory, research, or practical knowledge is "built-in" to the tool? Does the creator clearly explain this?

Visual logic

Can the creator explain the logic behind the visual arrangement? Does it reflect a clear business logic, or is it just a series of boxes like you might find in a tax form?

Provenance

Can the creator explain the history of the tool and articulate the development process, or did they just pull it out of thin air? Does the creator have a practice community that regularly tested the tool and its iterations and is that know-how accessible? Can the creator explain any criticism of the validity of the tool and how he reflects on it? This includes demonstrated results, case studies, examples, testimonials, and so on.

As a user, it's fair to ask questions about a tool's authorship, credibility, provenance, and historical results. You want to do your best to determine whether it's a solid tool or snake-oil gobbledegook, dressed up in a flashy suit.

How to Develop a Design Canvas from Scratch

Dave was lucky enough to work with Alex directly to create a new design canvas completely from scratch: the Culture Map. This project started when Dave pointed out that any time an established company creates a new business model, they will need to evaluate whether their culture can deliver on that promise. There are numerous examples of companies that developed the right idea and were unable to execute for culture reasons.

Alex agreed, and we embarked together on a project to develop a design canvas for evaluating and designing culture. Step 1 was to state this project in the form of a recipe. This should be step 1 for any canvas. Here are the remaining steps for creating a design canvas:

1. Define a clear purpose for the tool. What job will it do for users? What problem will it solve? When and where will it be useful?

2. Conduct an extensive review of all the theory, research, and practical "how-to" knowledge you can find. What has been tried and failed? Where do experts agree, and where do they disagree? Where they disagree, do you favor one theory over the others? In the case of the Culture Map, we chose a theory called exploratory inquiry, one of several competing theories about culture.

3. Create a testable prototype as early in the process as possible. It doesn't have to be perfect, and your first attempts will probably fail. That doesn't matter, though, because you'll be learning. Whenever possible, do at least one test with experts in the domain, and another with "novice" end users. You will learn different things from each.

4. In your testing, resist the urge to facilitate or help. Tell people the purpose of the tool and then give them a task. Note where people question the validity of the canvas in any way or are confused or have lengthy conversations about what words mean. A good design canvas will be self-evident, self-explanatory, and self-facilitating.

5. Don't be afraid to go back to the drawing board and start over from scratch. The Culture Map went through many iterations before we found a combination that worked. Like the Business Model Canvas, the end

result is deceptively simple, but the process to get there was a long one. It's useful to remember the words of Apple founder Steve Jobs: "Put complexity where it belongs."

Here is a kind of "visual history" to give you a sense of the design process from the first sticky notes to the current version of the Culture Map:

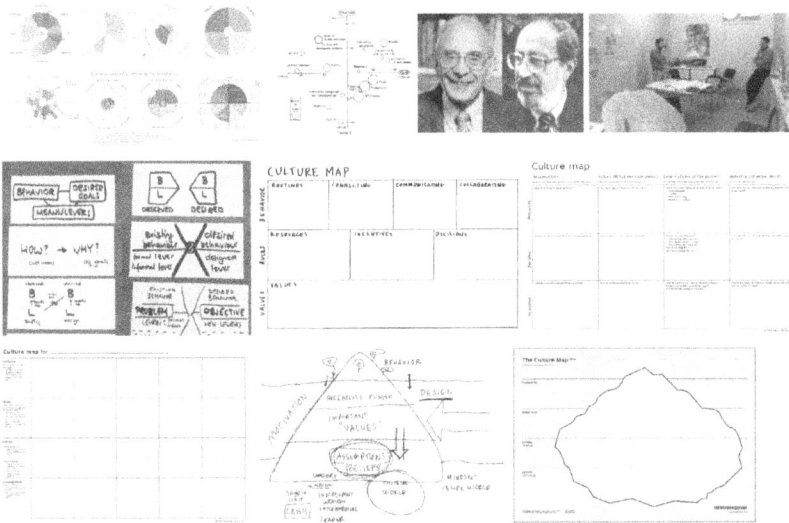

How to Evolve an Existing Model, Framework, or Game Board into a Design Canvas

Let's say you don't have a canvas, but you have a game board that seems to work really well. Does it make sense to evolve this into a canvas? Here are a few guidelines and an example of a time when Dave did exactly that.

We've looked at Luke Hohmann's Speed Boat game as an example of how a game concept can be loose and expansive and make room for fun and playful customizations, interpretations, and translations into various use cases. Speed Boat is a great example because it's a powerful and extensible metaphor that can work for many contexts and situations. It is open enough to contain multiple possible concepts. For example:

- Wind, sails, motor, oars: What's propelling us forward?

- Anchor, barnacles, headwinds: What's holding us back?

- Islands, ports, destinations: Where did we come from? Where do we want to go next?

- Sharks, underwater reefs, and obstacles: What are the risks/hazards?

- Currents, winds: What are the forces/trends we can work with? Forces/trends that are working against us?

- North Star: What is our purpose? How do we navigate?

As you've discerned, the boat is a broad, extensible metaphor. You can look at the previous web-search examples and see the wide variety.

As a contrast, let's look at the Empathy Map, which we described in the first edition of *Gamestorming*. Here's the game board we published in the first edition:

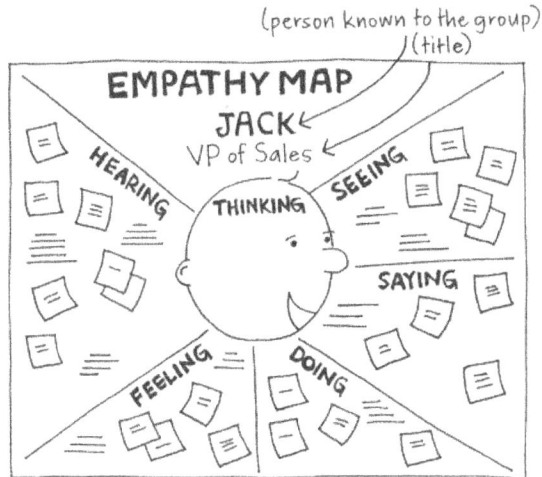

Now let's see what shows up in a quick web search for "empathy map." The following is a representative sampling:[2]

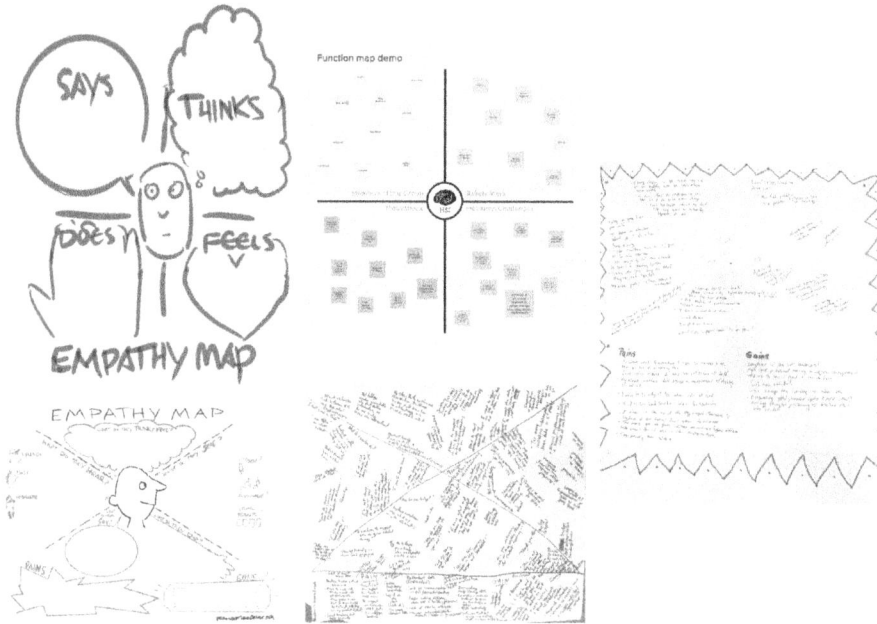

Notice that the range of game boards that showed up in our search is much more consistent than when we searched for the "speed boat" game board. There is variety, but not a lot of difference between one game board and another. The variation is not so much a rich exploration of an expansive metaphor as a kind of annoying inconsistency. Which one is right? As a user, how would you know which one is the right one, or best for you? How would you choose one game board or template over another? They all look pretty much the same. With this kind of selection, it really does feel arbitrary—one seems as good as the next.

That brings us to an important aspect of a design canvas. It provides a "single source of truth." If you search for "Business Model Canvas," you will see some variation, but not much. And you will find the definitive version on Wikipedia. The creators of the Business Model Canvas are easy to find. Their

---

2 Image credits: Krys Blackwood, NASA JPL Human Centered Design, Matt Strock (*mattstrock.com*), and Lisa Rothstein

contact information is right there on the canvas itself! Like an artist, the author of a canvas tends to sign their work.

Going back to the Empathy Map, it's clear that the variety of formulations out there on the web doesn't provide a lot of additional value. The variation isn't helpful, and it doesn't improve the utility of the Empathy Map as a tool or extend the variety of situations and contexts where it can be useful. It just adds unnecessary complexity, confusion, and noise.

Remember our criteria? A good design canvas has a clear purpose. The Empathy Map is a tool that was designed for a specific purpose, to solve a problem, and it solves that problem well. The variety isn't helpful, because none of the variations improve the tool, the quality of the experience, or the outcomes in any substantial way.

With the Business Model Canvas as an example, Dave set about applying the skills he learned developing the Culture Map to the problem of "canvasizing" the Empathy Map to improve the quality of the experience and provide a "single source of truth."

The single source of truth creates a lot of positive feedback loops. Perhaps most obviously, it is a way to ensure that the author gets credit for their work and compensated if they so desire. But there are more reasons. It also provides users with an authority to go to when they have questions and want to understand the deep structure that's "under the hood" of the canvas. Every tool has a history, a story about where and why it came to be, and why it is designed the way it is, and the Empathy Map is no exception. When you know where the map came from, you can contact the creator to ask questions. This happens more than you would expect.

Additionally, being the "source of the truth" provides creators with a feedback mechanism so they can see how their canvas is used, improve it based on user feedback, and develop variations when there is a valid need. For example, based on feedback, the creators of the Business Model Canvas recognized that mission-driven organizations needed a way to develop models that were not primarily financial, and in response to that need, they created a variation called the Mission Model Canvas. Finally, when appropriate, it reduces unnecessary confusion, complexity, fog, and noise in the marketplace.

Here's Dave's redesigned version, now called the Empathy Map Canvas:

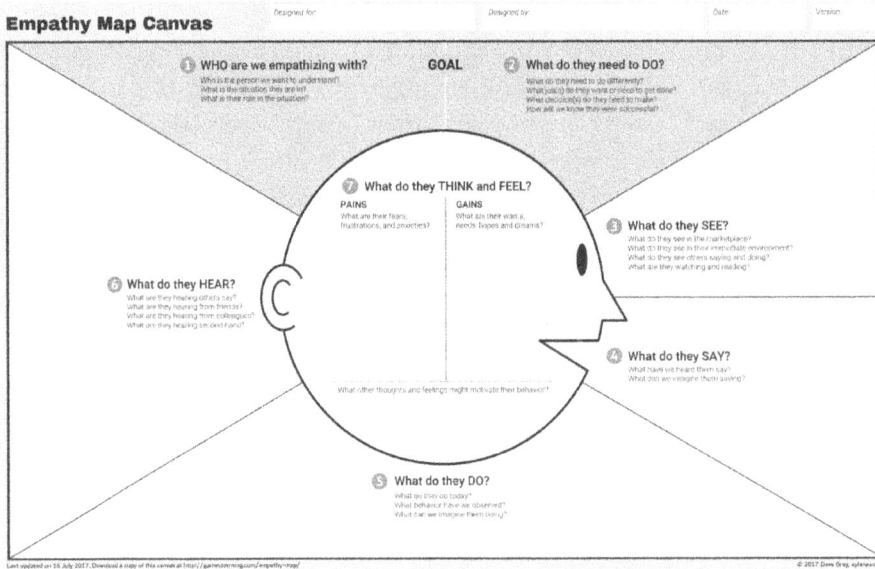

Attentive gamestormers may note that the new Empathy Map Canvas contains elements from not just one but three games from the original book: WhoDo, the Empathy Map, and the Pain-Gain Map. The reason for this is that these games are always done together in this sequence and that all three exercises are necessary to get the right outcome.

Thus, we can now encapsulate a solid chunk of meaningful work into one visual framework. We can point to a tool that has a clear purpose and is self-evident, self-explanatory, and self-facilitating, and we know exactly where to go to learn more and ask questions. (And they do! In fact, Dave just got a question today via LinkedIn.) In addition, Dave can see how his canvas is performing in the world and make improvements or new variations if the need arises.

How to Evaluate a Design Canvas

We've already discussed how you can ask questions to evaluate a canvas as a user. You can evaluate the surface qualities, and for the deep structure, you can ask the creator questions or ask yourself whether you trust them.

But what if you want to create a design canvas? You want to design a great tool that's useful for others. You've gone through the steps we listed, and you've developed a design canvas that you feel is pretty strong. What's the best way to see how you're doing? How can you improve it, make it better?

Happily for us, Alex Osterwalder and Yves Pigneur have thought deeply about this problem and have created an assessment tool that you can use to help you create a high-quality design canvas. It's a way to give yourself a grade.

Here is an adaptation of their design canvas assessment tool (*https://oreil.ly/G8DlX*), which is available through the company Osterwalder founded and leads, Strategyzer:

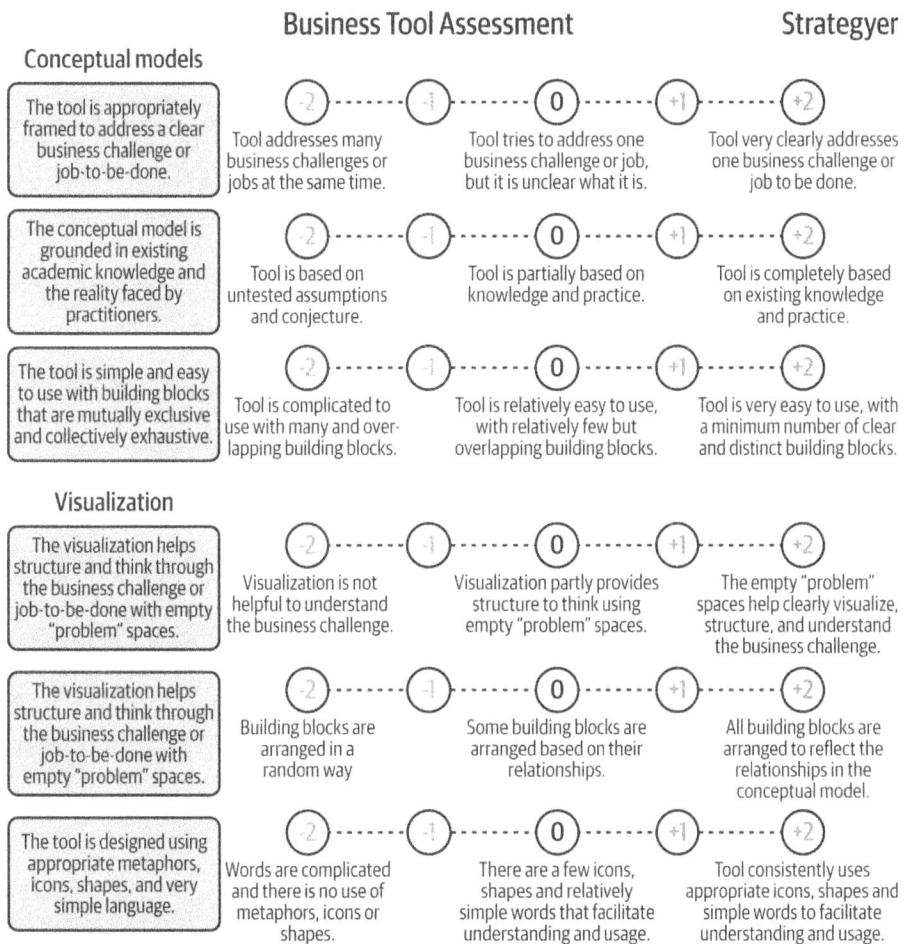

Business Tool Assessment — Strategyer

Conceptual models

The tool is appropriately framed to address a clear business challenge or job-to-be-done.
(-2) — (-1) — (0) — (+1) — (+2)
- -2: Tool addresses many business challenges or jobs at the same time.
- 0: Tool tries to address one business challenge or job, but it is unclear what it is.
- +2: Tool very clearly addresses one business challenge or job to be done.

The conceptual model is grounded in existing academic knowledge and the reality faced by practitioners.
(-2) — (-1) — (0) — (+1) — (+2)
- -2: Tool is based on untested assumptions and conjecture.
- 0: Tool is partially based on knowledge and practice.
- +2: Tool is completely based on existing knowledge and practice.

The tool is simple and easy to use with building blocks that are mutually exclusive and collectively exhaustive.
(-2) — (-1) — (0) — (+1) — (+2)
- -2: Tool is complicated to use with many and overlapping building blocks.
- 0: Tool is relatively easy to use, with relatively few but overlapping building blocks.
- +2: Tool is very easy to use, with a minimum number of clear and distinct building blocks.

Visualization

The visualization helps structure and think through the business challenge or job-to-be-done with empty "problem" spaces.
(-2) — (-1) — (0) — (+1) — (+2)
- -2: Visualization is not helpful to understand the business challenge.
- 0: Visualization partly provides structure to think using empty "problem" spaces.
- +2: The empty "problem" spaces help clearly visualize, structure, and understand the business challenge.

The visualization helps structure and think through the business challenge or job-to-be-done with empty "problem" spaces.
(-2) — (-1) — (0) — (+1) — (+2)
- -2: Building blocks are arranged in a random way
- 0: Some building blocks are arranged based on their relationships.
- +2: All building blocks are arranged to reflect the relationships in the conceptual model.

The tool is designed using appropriate metaphors, icons, shapes, and very simple language.
(-2) — (-1) — (0) — (+1) — (+2)
- -2: Words are complicated and there is no use of metaphors, icons or shapes.
- 0: There are a few icons, shapes and relatively simple words that facilitate understanding and usage.
- +2: Tool consistently uses appropriate icons, shapes and simple words to facilitate understanding and usage.

Business Tool Assessment

Strategyer

User experience

The tool helps map an existing business challenge or design a desired state.

- (-2) Tool is not not helpful to map and understand the business challenge for an existing or desired state.
- (0) Tool helps map and understand the business challenge, but it is difficult.
- (+2) Tool creates a simple shared language to map and understand the business challenge.

The tool can be used to analyze, test and critique the business challenge.

- (-2) Tool is not helpful to analyze, test or critique of the business challenge.
- (0) Tool is somewhat helpful to analyze, test or critique of the business challenge.
- (+2) Tool is very helpful to analyze, test or critique of the business challenge.

The tool can be used to communicate and share the business challenge.

- (-2) Tool is not helpful to communicate and share the business challenge.
- (0) Tool helps communicate and share the business challenge, but it is difficult.
- (+2) Tool creates a simple shared language to communicate and share the business challenge.

Flexibility

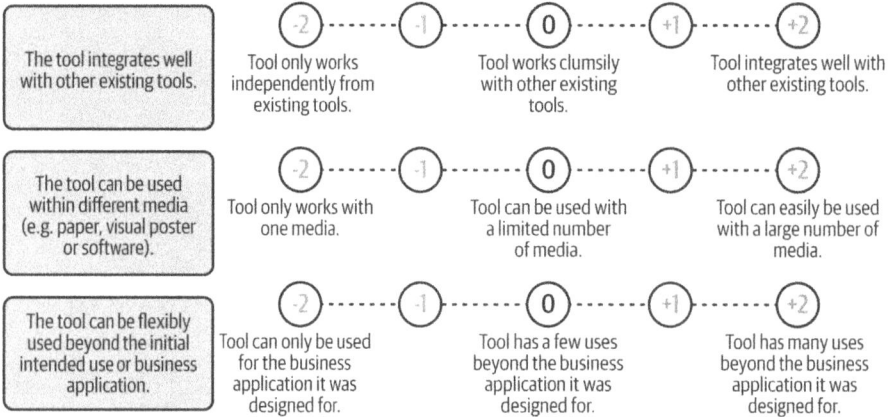

The tool integrates well with other existing tools.

- (-2) Tool only works independently from existing tools.
- (0) Tool works clumsily with other existing tools.
- (+2) Tool integrates well with other existing tools.

The tool can be used within different media (e.g. paper, visual poster or software).

- (-2) Tool only works with one media.
- (0) Tool can be used with a limited number of media.
- (+2) Tool can easily be used with a large number of media.

The tool can be flexibly used beyond the initial intended use or business application.

- (-2) Tool can only be used for the business application it was designed for.
- (0) Tool has a few uses beyond the business application it was designed for.
- (+2) Tool has many uses beyond the business application it was designed for.

Summary

A design canvas is a tool for structured group thinking. It is different from other templates and game boards in some specific ways. It has a surface structure, which is self-evident and self-explanatory, including the following:

- A clear purpose rooted in a well-defined problem and a "job to be done."
- An organized workspace with a visual logic that presents a coherent whole.
- It includes within itself all instructions necessary to use it.
- It references sources and/or creators to create a "single source of truth."

It also has a deep structure, which is not visible or self-evident, including the following:

- A basis rooted in theoretical, research-informed, and/or practical know-how.
- An underlying structural business logic that supports the visual logic.
- A development process that includes prototyping, testing, and iterative development, with feedback from users.

Use a game board when you are early in the process, still figuring out what the different use cases are, and when you want to provide users with a great degree of freedom and flexibility to customize your framework for their own purposes.

Invest extra energy to develop a design canvas when you have a framework that has a clear purpose and solves a specific problem and after you have tested it thoroughly with users to ensure it is self-evident, self-explanatory, and easy to use (self-facilitating).

A design canvas has great power, and with great power comes great responsibility. Don't invest that extra energy unless you are willing to sign your name to the work and defend your design decisions. You should be prepared to articulate the theory or practical know-how that supports the design and answer questions about the business logic and how it is expressed in the visual structure. You should also be ready and willing to make improvements and adjustments based on feedback from users.

When you think you're done, you're probably not! Take the extra step and ask people you trust to evaluate your design canvas with the Strategyzer design canvas assessment tool (*https://oreil.ly/G8DlX*).

6

Gamestorming for Culture Change

Let's say you're excited about gamestorming. You're at least interested and curious, or you wouldn't be reading this book. And maybe you're thinking, "This is all very interesting, but I don't think it would work here." Or maybe you're wondering just how you could make it work for you, about whether you could introduce it at work, and how you might do that. Gamestorming is a natural culture-shifting activity. Indeed, it can be a Trojan horse for a host of cultural shifts. The better you understand the cultural aspects of gamestorming, the more successfully you can use it to change your culture.

What Is Culture?

Our working definition for culture is this: "Culture is the way we do things around here." Every organization, division, department, satellite office, depot, warehouse, factory, retail store—in fact, every group of people that spends time doing anything together will develop, over time, a way that they do those things. That's what we mean when we talk about culture. Culture is all around you, all the time.

Why Is Culture Important?

We swim in culture like fish swim in water. It gets so you don't notice it. The longer you've been in a culture, the harder it can be to see it clearly. And that can actually be dangerous. By its very nature, culture helps you focus on the things that are important and reduce or eliminate distractions. To improve focus and productivity, cultures ignore things that don't matter to them. When the world around you changes, though, those "distractions" might matter. They might matter a lot.

A changing surrounding environment can be very difficult to see from inside your culture. Often, it's the newcomers and outsiders who can see your culture most clearly. Unfortunately, they are also usually the people with the least power to change things.

Fortunately, gamestorming is a set of tools and techniques that can give powerless and marginalized people more voice and visibility. If you're in a situation like this, gamestorming can help. If you happen to be an insider with power with the prescience to see a big shift coming, even better. Gamestorming can be a powerful tool for culture change, if you understand how and why it works.

How Gamestorming Shifts Culture

As we write this second edition, gamestorming is already a global phenomenon. The book has sold over 150,000 copies in English and has been translated into 9 languages. In the ten years since the book was published, we have seen gamestorming flourish in every kind of organization, from small startups to large global corporations, in just about every industry and numerous fields of knowledge we're aware of.

Introducing gamestorming into a company will inherently begin to shift culture. In fact, gamestorming itself can be viewed as a tool for culture change. Meetings are an integral element of every organization, and because gamestorming is designed to change meeting culture, it will naturally create a shift in the rest of the culture as well.

It's important to realize that gamestorming is not culturally agnostic. It comes out of the box already bundled with a bunch of cultural characteristics and properties. Like any culture, gamestorming focuses attention on some things, at the expense of other things. The better you can understand these tradeoffs, the better you will be able to make gamestorming work for you.

What Gamestorming Is and What It Is Not

Gamestorming will help you create a culture that is dynamic, creative, collaborative, reflective, and inclusive. It has a tendency to flatten hierarchies, create a more intentional meeting culture, and make room for a greater diversity of voices and perspectives. If you want to move your culture in this direction, gamestorming can help.

By its very nature, gamestorming creates work products—visual artifacts that carry information like business models, strategies, roadmaps, and so on—that are highly accessible, sharable, and configurable. They make it easier for teams to share information and collaborate across organizational silos and between different disciplines. They encourage experts to make their work understandable and fungible for different audiences across your organization.

Gamestorming will not help you if you want to reinforce your hierarchy and respect for the chain of command, keep information in silos or walled off, reduce questions, or enforce internal controls and compliance, although it can be a way to get more people involved in the design of such systems, and generate more buy-in as they are created and deployed.

GAMESTORMING ENGAGES THE FULL PERSON

Gamestorming is designed to get people out of "talking heads" mode. It uses things like sticky notes, index cards, markers, scissors, flip chart pads, objects and artifacts, and other tools to coax people away from their laptops, out of their seats, to get them working with their bodies as well as their minds.

Positives: Gamestorming engages people physically by encouraging them to move around and use the visual space of walls, whiteboards, and windows. Even in virtual environments, it employs visual workspaces like virtual whiteboards. It makes space for introverts who like to have time to think quietly, as well as extroverts who like to talk things out. It employs techniques like turn-taking to make space for multiple thinking styles and perspectives and to ensure that everyone has a voice.

The flip side: Gamestorming is a multimodal practice, which is to say that it ignites and employs as many of our senses as possible, often leaning heavily on visual sense-making. You may need to adapt some games to include participants who are visually or physically impaired in order to support their learning process and path. Essentially all games can be modified to accommodate different senses and still arrive at the crux of the game, whether you're working online or in person.

GAMESTORMING MAKES INFORMATION EXPLICIT AND TANGIBLE

Gamestorming turns walls, whiteboards, and windows into spaces for visual thinking. This makes ideas, information, and work products visible, tangible, modular, and explicit.

Positives: The visual thinking aspect of gamestorming increases common awareness of each other's work and facilitates connections. It makes it easier to rearrange and reconfigure things. People can more easily see who is working on what, how they are configured, what progress is being made, and what is going on.

The flip side: When confidentiality and privacy are major concerns, when dealing with trade secrets, for example, it is not always wise or fruitful to have work plastered visibly all over the walls. And because it requires wall space and extra materials, like sticky notes, it can be hard to make it work in some environments.

GAMESTORMING INSPIRES CREATIVITY AND THE FREE FLOW OF IDEAS

Gamestorming encourages a free flow of ideas with things like silent reflection and sketching, post-up conversations, and using sticky notes to rearrange and reconfigure systems and processes.

Positives: The free-flowing spirit of gamestorming encourages people to share their ideas, to speak up, to rethink and rearrange, to share their thinking "in process" by making it visible and reconfigurable. This creates space for fresh thinking, new ideas, and more engagement, passion, and energy in meetings.

The flip side: Once they are "out of the box," ideas can be difficult to contain. The free-flowing nature of much of the work we do is focused on teamwork, and as such, it can be difficult to determine who is responsible for what, or who gets the credit. In cultures that focus on rewarding individual achievement, this can create challenges. It can also be hard to capture and document the work in traditional software systems and workflows.

GAMESTORMING ENCOURAGES COLLABORATION AND CONSENSUS

Gamestorming uses mechanisms like turn-taking, dot voting, spectrum mapping, and forced ranking to enable group consensus and decision-making.

Positives: The democratic style you see in a gamestorming meeting helps ensure that no one person can dominate a meeting, making space for everyone to have a voice and contribute to decisions. In a gamestorming session, every voice is heard, and groups can more easily collaborate and come to consensus on priorities and other work decisions.

The flip side: Democracies may be more inclusive than authoritarian systems, but they also move more slowly and are easier for people with contrarian intentions to manipulate. They can create space for people to air grievances that might be best dealt with in other channels. Gamestorming tends to make things more transparent, and that can include deep rifts and conflicts that can be disruptive.

TO GAMESTORM OR NOT TO GAMESTORM?

Is gamestorming right for you? You must decide that for yourself. As the designers and authors of this book, it should be clear that we believe the advantages far outweigh the disadvantages. In balance, we feel the tradeoffs are well worth it for most organizations and teams.

Gamestorming creates culture and connection while getting work done. It creates a meritocracy where the best ideas bubble up and tend to win. Startups and innovation labs benefit greatly from the energy, engagement, and free-flowing ideas that gamestorming generates.

Larger, more hierarchical, process-driven organizations can have more issues with gamestorming. But let's face it, many of these kinds of organizations have become overly rigid and ossified over time and could use some fresh air in their stuffy halls and conference rooms.

Gamestorming is a natural fit for dynamic, generative, volatile industries like tech. It's no accident that this book is published by O'Reilly, a publisher focused primarily on the ever-changing and fast-shifting technology sector. It's where we belong.

How to Create the Shift

So let's say you have decided that gamestorming is for you. What should you look for? What should you do? Where to begin? How will you know it's working?

SET THE STAGE

Gamestorming creates a culture of collaboration and connection. It works best when people come together to do work. That means meetings and events. Meetings are central to any kind of group work activity, but they don't have a great reputation. People complain about them. People avoid them. But they are a fact of life in just about every organization.

This "meeting malaise" also plays to a core strength of gamestorming and can be a help as you introduce it. You can set the stage for culture change by spending more time *before* your meetings, thinking about how you can build gamestorming into your meeting design. This has the additional advantage of forcing you to think through the outcomes you want out of every meeting you participate in, because you can't design an agenda until you are clear on what you want.

Part of setting the stage is also making sure that the materials are available. Gamestorming makes copious use of sticky notes, markers, whiteboards, flip charts, and so on. The last thing you want in a gamestorming session is to run out of materials. You will want to make sure your rooms are well-stocked with materials and, ideally, a copy of the *Gamestorming* book. Assuming culture change is your goal, we recommend you have a supply of these on hand and encourage people to "steal" this book. Leave extra copies lying around if you can. The more copies of this playbook are floating through the work environment, the better your chances of success.

If you're meeting virtually, think through every element of the session, and create a "game board" that's pre-populated with as much information as you can determine in advance. Make time to test your tech in advance if possible. Be prepared for some "onboarding" time, as people learn how to use new tools.

REMOVE BARRIERS

Gamestorming does require some advance thinking and some "staging" of the space you will use in your meeting. Sometimes architectural elements can get in the way. For example, a meeting room might have a large table that makes it difficult for people to use the walls. Or there might be pictures on the walls, or rules that constrain behavior. Sometimes the walls are fabric, and sticky notes just won't stick.

With ingenuity, you can work around most of these problems. But the more you can remove them in advance, the better. For example, in your meeting invite, you can suggest that people wear comfortable clothes, or ask them to leave their laptops behind. Check out rooms in advance. If the room is problematic, do your best to move the meeting to another room.

If your meeting is virtual, test software in advance to make sure you don't have any firewall or software licensing issues that might get in your way.

DESIGN INTERVENTIONS AND EXPERIMENTS

We designed gamestorming when we were consultants. We had to "parachute in" to many different organizational cultures, set up camp, and get work done quickly and effectively. We created it in such a way that we could bring everything with us, make just about any space work, and leave no trace behind when we left.

This makes gamestorming very suitable for quick experiments, and even "stealth mode" sessions where you want to actively push the boundaries of what's acceptable. So consider the culture you are working within and what you can get away with.

Every culture is different, and we have seen many approaches that work. You might want to start with a single event like a team offsite, where people are already expecting something different. You might start with a regular weekly meeting, or a monthly lunch-and-learn session. You could try the "leaflet campaign" approach, where you simply put the book and some sticky notes into meeting rooms and see what happens.

CREATE A LOW-RISK SPACE FOR PRACTICE AND PLAY

Gamestorming is a new way of working for many people, and not everyone takes to it right away. Consider creating some low-risk spaces for people to play around with new ideas. When we first introduced gamestorming in our own consultancies, we created a weekly session called "visual thinking school"—two hours every week devoted to playing with new ideas, new activities and exercises, and playful experimentation. We invited people from outside the company, and this was critical to keeping it playful, fresh, and alive.

Which brings us to another point. Don't think of gamestorming as something that is just for work. You can bring it into your home, church, club, or other social organization and create space that way too.

PERSISTENCE

Culture is the sum of the embedded habits and routines of a team or organization. It's not realistic to expect it to change overnight. Steady progress is more important than spectacular successes. Prioritize your efforts, and focus on accumulating small wins over time.

Every time you introduce gamestorming into a meeting is a chance to collect feedback. As much as possible, we like to end every meeting using the Plus-Delta game, by asking people to share at least one thing that worked well for them and at least one idea for making it better next time.

PATIENCE

Focus on one intervention at a time. Show people that you are listening to their concerns and objections as you go.

For example, start collecting your plus-deltas, not just compliments but complaints and objections that you hear about gamestorming. Put them on sticky notes and start a "Pluses and Deltas" wall. Encourage people to share their thoughts for the wall on sticky notes. This is a bit subversive but effective...even the people who share their concerns will find themselves gamestorming! And this is a good way to show people that even detractors will be heard.

How to Know It's Working

Over the years, we have seen gamestorming introduced into many, many organizations. Every organization is different, of course, and what counts for a "win" in one organization might not seem like much compared to some others. But wherever you work, and whatever you do, if you put your head, heart, and hands into it, you are bound to see some progress. And wherever you start, progress is a more important measure than any other.

One executive told us he measures progress by how much sticky note activity he sees on the walls, and we think that is as good a measure as any. The great thing about gamestorming is how visual, and hence visible, it is. When it's working, you will see it, in the halls and on the walls. Once you start working in this way, it's hard to go back.

When those around you see people having fun and getting more work done at the same time, they will start wondering how they can do it, too. And when they are ready to ask the questions, you will have answers for them. And that's what culture change is all about: showing people a better way.

PART II

The Collection

7

Core Games

We've included a short list of games in this chapter that work well in any situation, reliable techniques that add value every time and never let a group down. These are what we call Core Games. They're simple enough to show up as "moves" in other games.

Post-Up

OBJECT OF PLAY

The goal of this game is to generate ideas with silent sticky note writing and make them visible.

NUMBER OF PLAYERS

1–50 people

DURATION OF PLAY

1–20 minutes

HOW TO PLAY

There are many ways to work with ideas using sticky notes. Generating ideas is the most basic play, and it starts with a question that your group will be brainstorming answers to. For example: "What are possible uses for Product X?"

Write the question or topic on a whiteboard. Ask the group to brainstorm answers individually, silently writing their ideas on separate sticky notes. The silence lets people think without interruption, and putting items on separate notes ensures that they can later be shuffled and sorted as distinct thoughts. After a set amount of time, ask the members of the group to stick ("post-up") their notes to the whiteboard and quickly present them.

If anyone's items inspire others to write more, they can stick those up on the wall too, after everyone has presented.

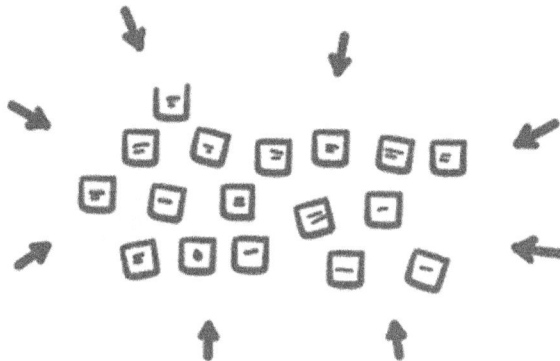

STRATEGY

Set a timer, one that's short enough to encourage spontaneous thinking. What is top of mind? Write one idea per sticky note. There are no wrong answers, and all ideas are welcome. Keep writing as thoughts emerge during or after the session—sometimes insights emerge when you've cleared space in your mind and think you have nothing left. Facilitators wait for the timer, or notice when the group seems complete. Generating ideas is a first step. From here you can create an affinity map, begin to structure, and further organize and prioritize the thoughts that are now visible.

TIPS FOR PLAYING ONLINE

Add blank sticky note "packs" to your digital whiteboard to set the board, reduce friction, and encourage brainstorming. Depending on what you want to accomplish, responses can be color coded by person or anonymous. Anonymous responses add an element that can't be accomplished in real life, further leveling the room. Generating responses in "private mode" or using individual space on the board can mimic the private thinking or "individual brainstorming" that happens in IRL.

The Post-Up game is based on the exercises in Rapid Problem Solving with Post-it® Notes *by David Straker (Lund Humphries).*

Affinity Map

OBJECT OF PLAY

Most of us are familiar with brainstorming—a method by which a group gener-ates as many ideas around a topic as possible in a limited amount of time. Brainstorming works to get a high quantity of information on the table. But it begs the follow-up question of how to gather meaning from all the data. Using a simple affinity diagram technique can help us discover embedded patterns (and sometimes break old patterns) of thinking by sorting and clustering language-based information into relationships. It can also give us a sense of where most people's thinking is focused. Use an affinity diagram when you want to find categories and meta-categories within a cluster of ideas and when you want to see which ideas are most common within the group.

NUMBER OF PLAYERS

Up to 20 people

DURATION OF PLAY

Depends on the number of players, but a maximum of 1.5 hours

HOW TO PLAY

1. On a sheet of flip-chart paper, write a question the players will respond to along with a visual that complements it. Conduct this game only when you have a question for the players that you know will generate at least 20 pieces of information to sort.

2. Ask each player to take 10 minutes to generate sticky notes in response to the question. Use index cards on a table if you have a group of four or fewer. Conduct this part of the process silently.

3. Have the players post-up ideas on a flat, visible surface.

4. Have players sort the ideas into columns (or clusters) based on categories, themes, and relationships. Involve the group in the process as much as possible. Have the players approach the wall to post their notes—it saves time—and allow them to do an initial, general sorting in columns or clusters.

5. Create a sticky-note "parking lot" close to the display for ideas that don't appear to fall into a natural category. Redundancy in ideas is OK; don't discard sticky notes because they're already represented. It's helpful to leave repeated ideas posted since it indicates to the group how many people are thinking the same thing. At this stage, ask the players to try to avoid searching for higher categories and simply to focus on grouping the information based on the affinities.

6. Once the content is sorted, ask the group to suggest categories that represent the columns you've created and write the categories they agree on at the top of the column (or near a cluster if you chose a cluster rather than a column display). Don't let the players spend an inordinate amount of time agreeing on a name for a category. If there's disagreement over "Facilities" versus "Infrastructure," write them both. If the players produce categories that are significantly different, pay attention to which category gets the most approval from the group and write that one. Your visual may end up looking like the one shown here.

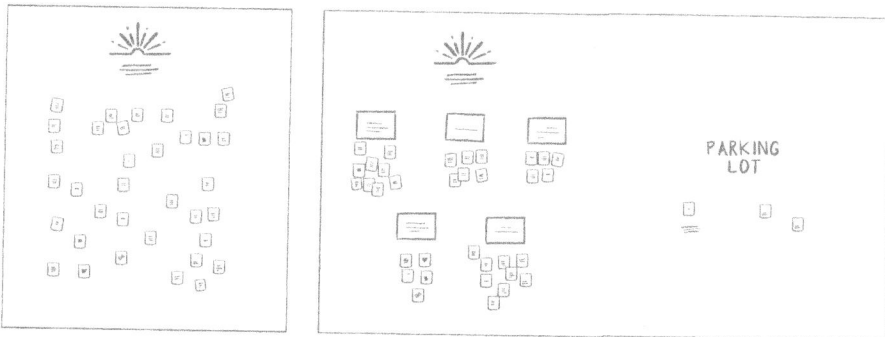

STRATEGY

The value of the Affinity Map game increases when two conditions are met. The first is that the players generate multiple data points, ideally with good information. The second relates to the quality of the sorting. The cleaner the players' insights when they form relationships within the content, the better the categories will be.

Fun, optional activity: Run through the Affinity Diagram game once, complete with categorizations. Then ask the group to reshuffle the sticky notes and recombine the ideas based on affinities they didn't notice in the first round.

Sometimes affinities within content are crystal clear, so the sorting becomes less pivotal, but when those relationships are more nuanced, it's more important that the sorting process is done well. In a situation in which there are many ways to "affinitize" information, assume a stronger facilitative role. Ask questions about the columns or clusters to clarify the group's thinking and steer them toward an appropriate number of categories. If there are too many, the data gets watered down. If there are too few, the analysis gets watered down. Help the players find the sweet spot.

TIPS FOR PLAYING ONLINE

Groups can work together to make categories and will begin to naturally do this during the post-up process in step 3. Size, color, outlines, bolding, etc., can be used to quickly designate categories and shuffle ideas.

The affinity diagram was devised by Jiro Kawakita in the 1960s. It is also referred to as the KJ Method.

Card Sort

OBJECT OF PLAY

Card sorting is a practice used frequently by information architects and designers to gather and structure inputs for a variety of purposes. In a common use of card sorting, information for a website is put onto the cards, and the sorting helps create categories for navigation and the overall architecture. The method works just as well for creating slides for presentations, or at any point where information needs to be sorted and organized in a sensible way.

The applications of card sorting are numerous, and in use it works similarly to Post-Up and affinity mapping. Card sorting can differ from these methods, however. First, the cards are generally prepared in advance, although participants should be allowed to create their own while sorting. Second, the cards are a semi-permanent artifact and can be used as a control over several exercises with different participants to find patterns among them.

NUMBER OF PLAYERS

Small groups or individuals

DURATION OF PLAY

30 minutes or more, depending on the number of cards and participants

HOW TO PLAY

Use 3×5 index cards or similar. For a typical sorting exercise, aim for 30–100 cards in total; more than this range will likely overwhelm the participants, and fewer may not be meaningful enough to be worth the effort.

On each card should be a succinct bit of information; enough to tell the participants what it is and no more. Putting too much information on a card will slow down the sorting; not enough will cause confusion and will slow down the process even more.

Give the group the shuffled deck and a stack of blank cards. Describe the overall organization challenge, and ask them to sort the cards into groups that go together. If they think something is unclear or missing, they may alter a card or create a new one. Once they have created the groups, ask them to name them and describe them.

There are variations of sorting—including asking the group to rank the items from most to least desirable or to organize the cards into two categories such as "must have" and "nice to have." You may also ask the group to sort cards into a predefined set of categories, to test their validity.

STRATEGY

Although the Card Sort game won't tell you everything you need to know about a set of information, it will help reveal the thought process of participants. In this sense, it's more about people than information. Only after a number of sorting exercises with a number of groups will larger patterns appear. It uses a core gamestorming practice of organizing tangible artifacts and visual collaboration.

TIPS FOR PLAYING ONLINE

Groups can work together to make categories and, because we are humans, we will begin to naturally sort them and attempt to create order and meaning. Digital environments allow for quick duplication, rearranging, and editing of information and ideas for processing by humans or AI. Information can be infinitely distilled or expanded in structure.

Card sorting is a common practice of information architects and designers of complex systems. Its actual source is unknown.

The 7Ps Framework

In preparing for battle I have always found that plans are useless, but planning is indispensable.

—DWIGHT D. EISENHOWER

OBJECT OF PLAY

Every meeting deserves a plan and someone focused on creating the environment for a shared outcome. Note that a great plan can't guarantee a great outcome, but it will help lay down the fundamentals from which you can adapt. Sketch out these fundamentals by using the 7Ps framework.[1]

NUMBER OF PLAYERS

Small groups or individuals

DURATION OF PLAY

15–45 minutes

HOW TO PLAY

Use these items as a checklist. When preparing for a meeting, thinking through the 7Ps can improve focus and results, even if you have only a few moments to reflect on them.

Purpose

> Why are you having this meeting? Facilitators and leaders need to be able to state this clearly and succinctly. Consider the urgency of the meeting: what's going on, and what's on fire? If this is difficult to articulate, ask yourself if a meeting is really necessary.

People

> Who needs to be there, and what role will they play? One way to focus your list of attendees is to think in terms of questions and answers. What questions are we answering with this meeting? Who are the right people to answer the questions?

---

1 We elaborate on this framework thoroughly in Chapter 4, "Designing Workshops and Meetings".

Process

What agenda will these people use to create the product? Of all the 7Ps, the agenda is where you have the most opportunity to collaborate in advance with the attendees. Co-design an agenda with them to ensure that they will show up and stay engaged.

Product

What specific artifact will we produce out of the meeting? What will it do, and how will it support the purpose? If your meetings seem to be "all talk and no follow-through," consider how a product might change things.

Preparation

What would be useful to do in advance? This could be material to read in advance, research to conduct, or "homework" to assign to the attendees.

Practical Concerns

These are the logistics of the meeting—the where and when and, importantly, who's bringing lunch.

Pitfalls

What are the risks in this meeting, and how will we address them? These could be as simple as ground rules, such as "no laptops," or specific topics that are designated as out of scope.

STRATEGY

- Each of the 7Ps can influence or change one of the others, and developing a good plan will take this into account. For instance, if you have certain participants for only part of a meeting, this will change your process.

- Get others involved in the design of the meeting. Their participation in its design is the quickest route to its effectiveness.

- Recurring meetings can take on a life of their own and stray from their original purpose. It's a healthy activity to revisit "Why are we having this meeting?" regularly for such events.

- Make the 7Ps visible during the meeting. These reference points can help focus and refocus a group as needed.

- Have a plan and expect it to change. The 7Ps can give you a framework for designing a meeting, but they can't run the meeting for you. The unexpected will happen, and as a leader you will need to adapt. Thinking things through thoroughly ahead of time will help you be flexible and calm.

TIPS FOR PLAYING ONLINE

Add a 7Ps template to your digital whiteboard for individual planning or invite others to add ideas and discuss as a small group in advance of a meeting. This digital artifact can be easily built on to bring structure and clarity to the conversation with a broader group.

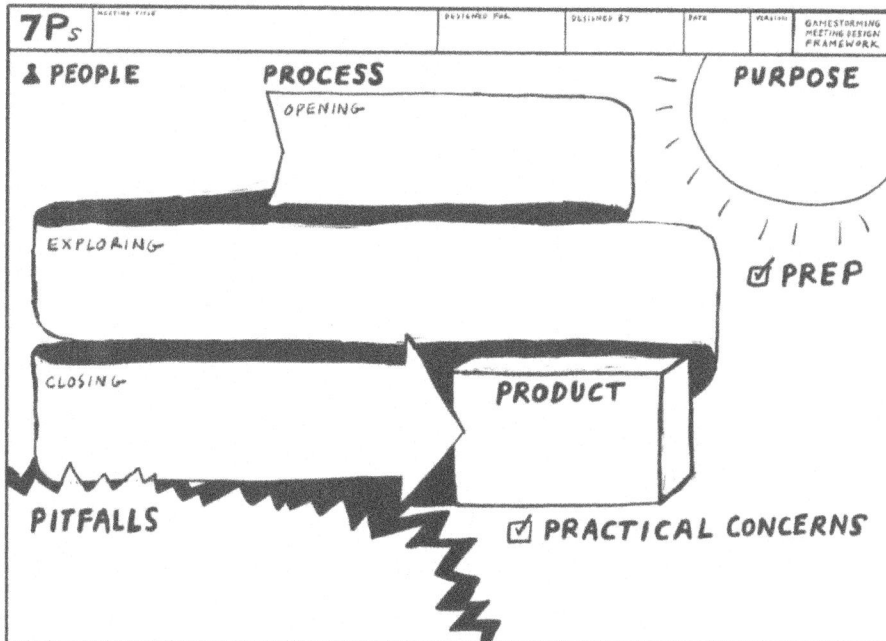

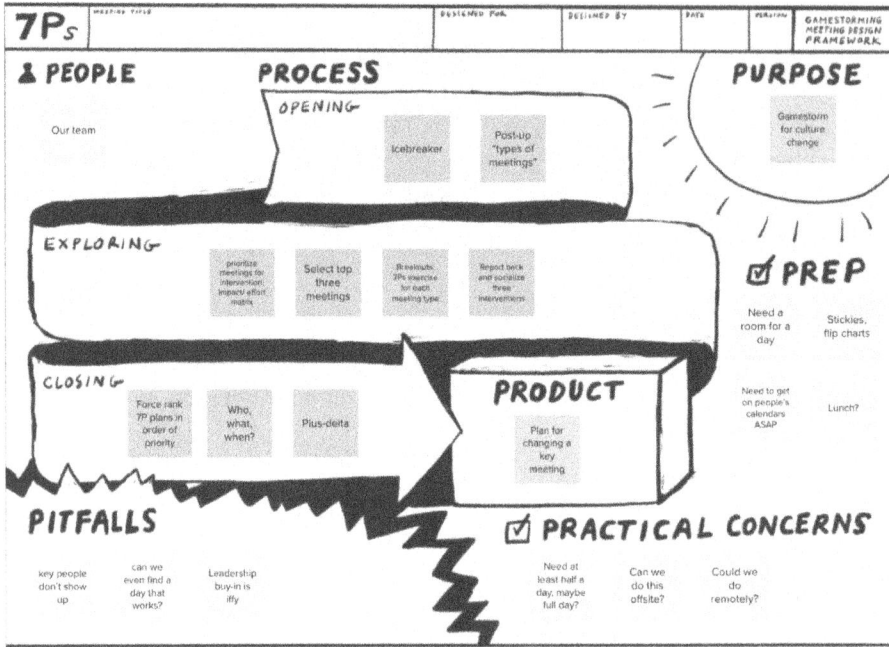

The 7Ps framework is credited to James Macanufo.

Empathy Map

OBJECT OF PLAY

The object of this game is to quickly develop a customer or user profile.

NUMBER OF PLAYERS

3–10 people

DURATION OF PLAY

10–15 minutes

HOW TO PLAY

Personas help focus a group's attention on the people involved in a project—often the customer or end user. Although creating an empathy map is not the rigorous, research-based process that is required for developing personas, it can quickly get a group to focus on the most important element: people.

In this exercise, you will be creating a study of a person with the group. Start by drawing a large circle that will accommodate writing inside. Add eyes and ears to make it into a large "head."

1. Ask the group to give this person a name.

2. Ask the group to describe the goals this person wants to achieve—what objective are they trying to accomplish?

3. Label large areas around the head: "Thinking," "Seeing," "Saying," "Doing," "Feeling," and "Hearing."

4. Ask the group to describe—from this person's point of view—what their experience is, moving through the categories from seeing through hearing.

5. The goal of the exercise is to create a degree of empathy for the person with the group. The exercise shouldn't take more than 15 minutes. Ask the group to synthesize: What does this person want? What forces are motivating this person? What can we do for this person?

STRATEGY

The group should feel comfortable "checking" each other by referring back to the empathy map. When this happens, it will sound like "What would so-and-so think?" It's good to keep the empathy map up and visible during the course of the work to be used as this kind of focusing device.

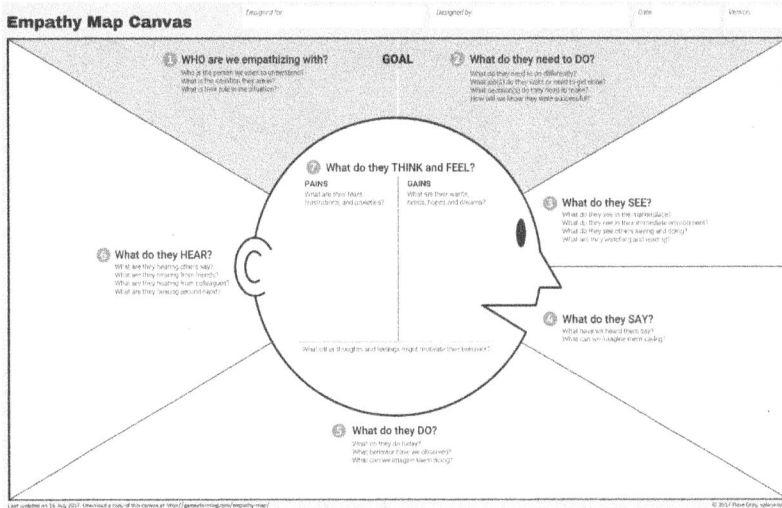

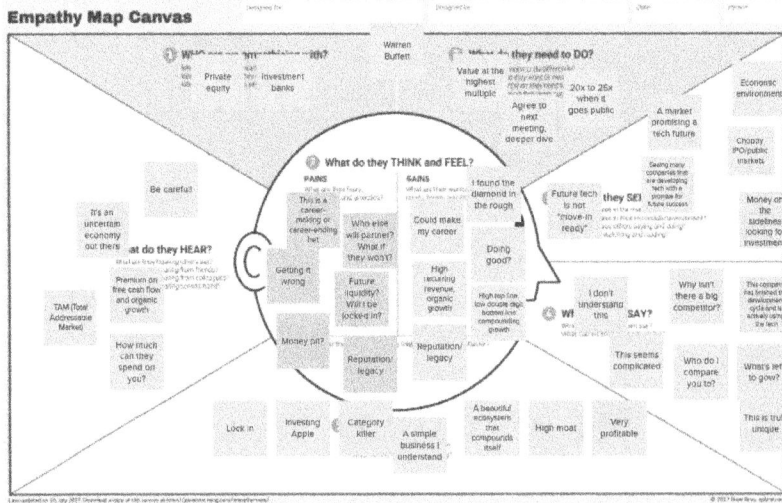

TIPS FOR PLAYING ONLINE

Populate the Empathy Map Canvas as a group, or divide participants into smaller groups or pairs to complete. Add the canvas to a digital whiteboard tool and populate it using sticky notes.

The Empathy Map game was developed by XPLANE, and the Empathy Map Canvas is credited to Dave Gray.

Carousel

OBJECT OF PLAY

This game has been designed to gather facts and opinions from the participants on different aspects of the issue at stake. It will help gain and share insight from all points of view, since everyone will have had the chance to contribute.

NUMBER OF PLAYERS

At least two people

DURATION OF PLAY

15 minutes to an hour depending on the amount of participants

HOW TO PLAY

1. Prepare 5–10 flip charts where you address different aspects of the topic at hand. On each flip chart, you address a certain aspect of the issue by posing a powerful question about it. These questions should be impersonal and ask for facts and opinions. Focus on "what," "when," and "how" questions.

2. Spread the flip charts through the entire room, making sure there is enough distance in between to allow group discussions between participants without disturbing the others too much.

3. Quickly introduce the topic at hand and go through the questions of each flip chart, making sure everybody understands the questions correctly.

4. Ask participants to split into pairs, or groups of up to 5 people if you have a bigger group. You should have one group per flip chart/question.

5. Ask each group to answer the question by adding their ideas, facts, and opinions on the flip chart, with images, writing, or sticky note artifacts in such a way that it is possible for others to interpret the data presented.

6. Give each group 2–3 minutes of time to add their information, and then rotate to the next flipchart (clockwise or counterclockwise).

7. Repeat until each group has answered all the questions.

8. Give the entire group another 5–10 minutes to review all the generated content and move to the next step: prioritization and/or deeper research into some of the ideas generated.

OUR INDUSTRY
IS IMPORTANT
BECAUSE...

⑥

WHAT I LOVE MOST
ABOUT MY DAILY LIFE
AT WORK IS...

①

WHAT DO I BELIEVE
WILL BE TRUE 10 YEARS
FROM TODAY?

⑤

AUG.
8th

② HOW DID I HAVE
FUN LAST YEAR?

④

③

WHAT TRENDS
ARE IMPACTING OUR
BUSINESS?

WHAT I HEAR
OUR CUSTOMERS
SAY ABOUT US...

STRATEGY

By limiting the time a group has to answer a question, you will make them focus on the most important things. The idea is not to gather all information per participant but to gather meaningful information as a group. This gathered information will form the basis for a prioritization and/or deeper research into some of the ideas and opinions.

TIPS FOR PLAYING ONLINE

As with in-person play, Carousel works really well online as a core opening or exploring exercise. It is good for priming thoughts and mindset, while quickly getting the pulse of the group on topics that are relevant for the goals of the meeting. Facilitators can reveal questions in sequence or let participants choose which question to answer.

The original source of Carousel is unknown.

Bodystorming

OBJECT OF PLAY

Bodystorming is simply brainstorming, but done with the body. It may look different depending on the preparations and location, but in the end, all bodystorming is fundamentally about one thing: getting people to figure things out by trying things out.

A group may explore one of the techniques described next to get their feet wet with bodystorming. They may move through them in order, from observing and learning to ideation and prototyping, although this is not a strict sequence. Each level of bodystorming will help break the pattern of analyzing ideas around a conference table and get people closer to developing things that will work in the real world.

HOW TO PLAY

Bodystorming takes place in three phases.

Level 1: Go observe

Go to the key location to do your work. If you are developing an idea for a coffee shop or a shopping mall or a hospital, go there and do your work as you would normally. The environment will present idea cues and authentic information that would never emerge from conference room brainstorming.

For example, say a group is charged with improving the student experience on a college campus. Although they may conduct interviews or other research, they may start by going to a few campus locations and "blending in" with the surroundings while going about their usual work. It's important that the group does not zero in on any specific analysis so that they will be open to the cues that the environment presents.

Level 2: Try it

Use role-play and props to develop an idea. In this exercise, a group physically "acts out" an experience by using whatever they have on hand or can acquire. The group focuses on how they interact with each other, their surroundings, and makeshift artifacts, testing existing ideas and uncovering new ones.

For example, say a small group is asked to "reimagine the evening news." Using each other as the actors, the audience, the news anchors, and the television itself, they improvise a script that plays out the experience as they conceive it could be. There are a couple of steps to this:

1. Identify and assign critical roles. For any experience, identifying the "customer" or "user" role is a good way to get started. This participant (or group of participants) becomes the focal point and main character of the bodystorm. Other critical roles will present themselves. "Who wants to be the internet?" is not an uncommon question to hear.

2. Improvise the experience. Bodystorming is physical and progressive: as the group starts to put their thoughts into action, they will naturally ask simple and important questions by acting them out, often leading to the unexpected. We can use the evening news scenario as an example:

   Q: "OK, so how do you watch the evening news?"

   A: "I don't have a television. Also, I'm usually out jogging."

   Q: "Oh. Do you have your phone on you?"

   A: "Always. I'm listening to music."

   Q: "OK, what if this happened...who wants to play the phone?"

   In a completely improvised scenario, the group should keep in mind the principal rule of the game: building on each other's inputs. "Yes, and..." will generate more progress than "Yeah, but..." thinking.

In some uses of bodystorming, a group will act out a script prepared in advance. In these cases, an equal amount of planning and, often, providing props to build an environment is key. For example, if it's a coffee shop, set up the counter and chairs. If it's a park or outdoor area, strongly consider going there.

Level 3: Reflect on what happens, and why

By enacting the experience, the participants will naturally explore new possibilities and uncover flaws or assumptions about how an idea could work. This is valuable both during the process itself and afterward: by documenting the exercise on video, the participants may later "watch the reel" to discuss key points.

1. Go observe

2. Try it

3. Reflect

STRATEGY

Choose the right level of bodystorming at the right time for the group. Because bodystorming asks participants to take a big step away from the typical conference table mode of thinking, they may need to get comfortable with more structured sessions first, armed with scripts and specific roles, before stepping into complete improv. In all cases, the exercise itself will be more memorable than the customary problem-solving session and will help generate empathy that comes from "embodying" the experience.

TIPS FOR PLAYING ONLINE

The full multisensory experience is less readily available online, but it can be adapted. Break into smaller groups than you would in person. Experiment with real-life scenarios connecting online and offline environments, using pen and paper, and break away from the computer for periods of time—go look for an item in the physical environment, turn off the cameras, switch to audio-only and move around, etc.

The term "bodystorming" was coined by Colin Burns at the Conference on Human Factors in Computing Systems (CHI) '94 in Boston, Massachusetts.

Storyboard

OBJECT OF PLAY

This game asks players to envision and describe an ideal future in sequence using words and pictures. Storyboarding as a technique is so versatile that it can be used to show any topic, not just an ideal future. But it is particularly powerful as a visioning exercise since it allows players to imagine and create possibilities. The players tell a story with a happy ending, planting tiny seeds for a different future. You can also use storyboarding to let employees describe their experience on a project, to show approaches to solving a problem, or to orient new employees on policies and procedures—its uses are limited only by the imagination.

NUMBER OF PLAYERS

8–20 people

DURATION OF PLAY

45 minutes to 1.5 hours

HOW TO PLAY

Before the meeting, determine the topic around which the players will craft their "ideal" story. Once the meeting starts, divide the group into pairs or groups of three or four, depending on the size of the group. Provide markers, pads of flip-chart paper, and stands.

1. Tell the players that the purpose of this game is to tell the other players a feel-good story. The topic of the story is "The Ideal Future for [blank]" —for a team, a product, the company, whatever you decided beforehand. The players' assignment is to visually describe the topic and narrate it to the group.

2. After the groups are established, give them 20–25 minutes to (1) agree on an ideal state, (2) determine what steps they would take to get there, and (3) draw each step as a sequence of large images or scenes, one per sheet of flip-chart paper.

3. Give the players a two-minute time warning, and once the time is up, bring them back together. Ask for volunteers to tell the story first.

4. After all the groups have presented, ask them what's inspiring in what they heard. Summarize any recurring themes and ask for observations, insights, and "*ahas*" about the stories.

Big Idea

☆ OUR IDEAL FUTURE STATE

Call to Adventure

BE THE BEST DESIGN STUDIO IN THE WORLD

Emotional Engagement

♥ WHY IT MATTERS

What Is

POSITIONED FOR OPPORTUNITY

What Could Be

GET ALL THE RESOURCES DESIGNERS & DEVELOPERS NEED TO FLOURISH

What Is

DEDICATED TEAM OF RESEARCHERS & EXPLORERS
who? where? what? when? why?

What Could Be

AN ACTIVE COMMUNITY HUB

Call to Action

ATTRACT THE RIGHT PEOPLE TO THE HUB

Reward: New Bliss

☆☆☆☆☆
RELATIONSHIPS WITH THE BEST MAKES US THE BEST

STRATEGY

As the leader of this game, be sensitive to the fact that many of the meeting participants will freak out when you tell them that large-scale drawing is involved. Reassure them that the story is the point of the exercise and that the images play a supporting role. They can use words as captions to clarify the images and they can also select the "artist" within their group so that not everyone has to put marker to paper. (But it's more fun for those who do.) Finally, remind them that they aren't allotted sufficient time to create a da Vinci anyway, so stick figures work perfectly well.

For the presentation format, there are various options. Breakout groups can post each sheet of flip-chart paper in a row around the room and walk along the row as they tell the story. They can also leave the flip-chart pad intact and flip the pages over the stand as they narrate. They could choose to hang the sheets in rows and cover them, using one group member to act as a "Vanna White" and create a series of voilà moments. Tell them to have fun with it—they aren't being graded on their stories (although you could make it a contest if it's that kind of crowd). The process of creating and sharing the stories is what matters.

TIPS FOR PLAYING ONLINE

The storyboard can include images, drawings, icons, diagrams, etc., that can be pulled in from other sources. A storyboard is often the initial blueprint for persuasive presentations and is a natural precursor to well-designed slides.

Walt Disney is credited for this activity. His need to animate Steamboat Willie *in 1928 led to the process of storyboarding—a story told in sequence on a wall covered with a special kind of board. He found it to be an effective way to track progress and improve a story.*

Forced Ranking

OBJECT OF PLAY

When prioritizing, a group may need to agree on a single, ranked list of items. Forced ranking obligates the group to make difficult decisions, and each item is ranked relative to the others. This is an important step in making decisions on items like investments, business priorities, and features or requirements—wherever a clear, prioritized list is needed.

NUMBER OF PLAYERS

Small group of 3–10 people

DURATION OF PLAY

Medium to long; 30 minutes to 1 hour depending on the length of the list, the criteria, and the size of the group

HOW TO PLAY

To set up the game, participants need to have two things: an unranked list of items and the criteria for ranking them. Because forced ranking makes the group judge items closely, the criteria should be as clear as possible. For example, in ranking features for a product, the criteria might be "Most important features for User X." In the case of developing business priorities, the criteria might be "Most potential impact over the next year."

If there are multiple dimensions to a ranking, it is best to rank the items separately for each criterion and then combine the scores to determine the final ranking. It is difficult for participants to weigh more than one criterion at a time, as in the confusing "Most potential impact over the next year and least amount of effort over the next six months." In this case, it would be best to rank items twice: once by impact and once by effort.

Although there is no hard limit on the number of items to be ranked, in a small-group setting the ideal length of a list is about 10 items. This allows participants to judge items relative to one another without it becoming overwhelming. By making the entire list visible on a flip chart or whiteboard, participants will have an easier time ranking a larger list.

To play, create a matrix of items and the criteria. Each participant ranks the items by assigning them a number, with the most important item being #1, the second most important item #2, and so forth, to the least important item. Because the ranking is "forced," no items can receive equal weight.

CRITERIA	RANKING

MOST IMPACT

$$3 + 2 + 2 + 1 = 8$$
$$1 + 1 + 3 + 2 = 7$$
$$2 + 3 + 1 + 3 = 9$$

} • Individual rankings

MOST IMPORTANT FEATURE

$$2 \quad 3 \quad 1 \quad 2 = 8$$
$$3 \quad 2 \quad 3 \quad 1 = 9$$
$$1 \quad 1 \quad 2 \quad 3 = 7$$

} • If there's a tie, get group consensus in a second round

Once the items have been ranked, tally them and discuss the prioritized list and next steps.

STRATEGY

Creating a forced ranking may be difficult for participants, as it requires that they make clear-cut assessments about a set of items. In many cases, this is not the normal mode of operation for groups, where it is easier to add items to lists to string together agreement and support. Getting people to make these assessments, guided by clear criteria, is the entire point of forced ranking.

TIPS FOR PLAYING ONLINE

Forced ranking works well online. Create a template, and add participant names to the top of the ranking section for voting. Then, in the session, add the top ideas to be ranked. Give the group 3–5 minutes to add their name and rankings and then create totals and discuss results as a group.

The original source of the Forced Ranking game is unknown.

Dot Voting

OBJECT OF PLAY

In any good brainstorming session, there will come a time when there are too many good ideas, too many concepts, and too many possibilities to proceed. When this time has come, dot voting is one of the simplest ways to prioritize and converge upon an agreed solution.

NUMBER OF PLAYERS

At least three people; in larger groups, tallying votes will be more time-consuming

DURATION OF PLAY

1–5 minutes

HOW TO PLAY

First, the group needs a set of things to vote on! This may be something they have just developed, such as a wall of sticky notes, or it may be a flip-chart list that captures the ideas in one place. Ask the group to cast their votes by placing a dot next to the items they feel the most strongly about. They may use stickers or markers to do this.

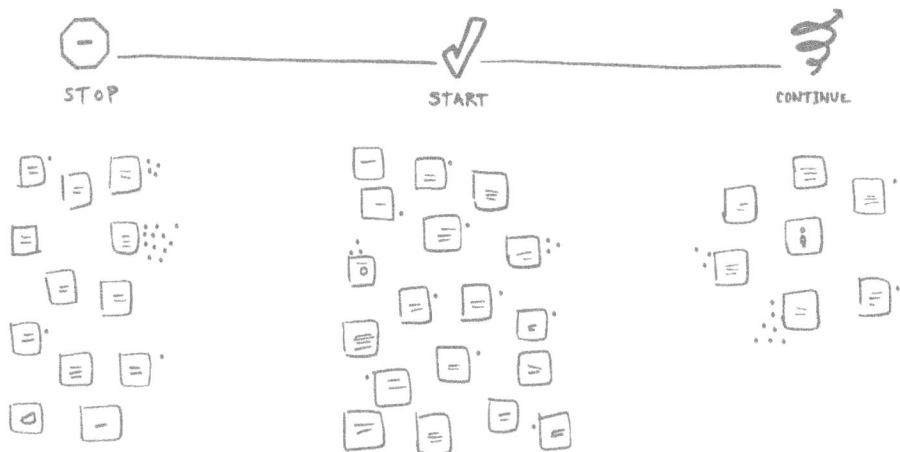

Participants cast their votes all at once, and they may vote more than once for a single item if they feel strongly about it. Once all the votes are cast, tally them, and if necessary, make a list of the items by their new rank.

This prioritized list becomes the subject of discussion and decision-making. In some cases, it may be useful to reflect on ideas that didn't receive votes to verify that they haven't been left behind without cause.

STRATEGY

This technique is used to collaboratively prioritize any set of items. It could be used to hone a list of features, to agree on discussion topics, or to choose among strategies and concepts. Giving participants five votes is enough to be meaningful while still asking for individual prioritization; however, this is not a hard rule.

TIPS FOR PLAYING ONLINE

The mechanics of in-person dot voting can be re-created online. Voting features are also built into most digital whiteboards and collaboration tools. Consider whether you want anonymity when choosing which method to use online.

The original source of the Dot Voting game is unknown.

WhoDo

OBJECT OF PLAY

The objective of this game is to brainstorm, plan, and prioritize actions.

NUMBER OF PLAYERS

1–10 people

DURATION OF PLAY

20–45 minutes

HOW TO PLAY

Who do you want to do what? Almost any endeavor of substantial impact requires seeking help from others. Developing a WHO + DO list is a simple way to scope out the undertaking.

1. Start with the vision. Write out or visualize the big goal.

2. Draw a two-column matrix and write "WHO" on the left and "DO" on the right.

3. Ask: Who is involved in making this happen? Who is the decision-maker? Whose support is needed? Who has the needed resources? Who may be an obstacle? These individuals or groups are your list of WHOs.

4. The DOs are often harder. For each WHO, ask: What do they need to do, or do differently? What actions will build toward the big goal? Sharpen each WHO in the list until you have a desired and measurable action for each.

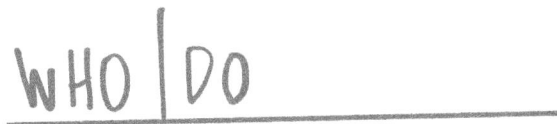

WHO | DO

Given all of the possible WHOs and DOs, which are the most important? Who comes first? How will you know when it is complete and if it was successful?

STRATEGY

Bias yourself toward action. When brainstorming DOs, there is a tendency to slip into the easier mode of "we just want them to understand." Most often, when you want people to understand something, it's because you want them to change something or learn something that they can then "DO." Ask yourself, or the group, "What will happen once they understand?" Don't shortchange what you are really looking for: action.

TIPS FOR PLAYING ONLINE

This game works well online and is helpful for carrying the meeting forward with action. Use tagging to capture committed action items for each participant.

The WhoDo game is credited to Dave Gray.

8

Games for Opening

Opening is taking the first step into an empty space. Games that open are focused on framing and describing the bounds of that space and then jumping headfirst into it. In some cases, they foster the spark that produces a large and diverse set of ideas. In other cases, they quickly map out the space, time, and scope to be explored. Some are complete exercises that stand on their own, and others are building blocks that can be composed into larger forms. When you're facing a blank space, the most difficult mark to make is the first one.Games that open make that mark and serve up the deluge that comes after.

3-12-3 Brainstorm

OBJECT OF PLAY

This format for brainstorming compresses the essentials of an ideation session into one short format. The numbers 3-12-3 refer to the amount of time in minutes given to each of three activities: 3 minutes for generating a pool of observations, 12 for combining those observations into rough concepts, and 3 again for presenting the concepts back to a group.

Essential to this format is strict time keeping. The "ticking clock" forces spontaneous, quick-fire decisions and doesn't allow for overthinking. With this in mind, a group that is typically heavily measured in its thought process will benefit the most from this exercise but will also be the hardest to engage.

Given its short duration (30 minutes total for 10 participants), 3-12-3 Brainstorming can be used as an energizer before diving into a longer exercise or as a stand-alone, zero-prep activity. It works equally well in generating new ideas as in providing improvements to existing ones.

NUMBER OF PLAYERS

This is a fast exercise that gets slower as more participants are added. With up to 10 people working as partners, the speed of the exercise makes it an energy builder. Working beyond ten players may require creating groups of three instead of pairs to keep from getting slowed down.

DURATION OF PLAY

21–30 minutes, depending on number of participants

HOW TO PLAY

You will need a topic on which to brainstorm ideas, boiled down to two words. This could be an existing problem, such as "energy efficiency," or it could be focused on creating something new, such as "tomorrow's television."

Although the two words could be presented as a full challenge question, such as "How will tomorrow's television work?" it is best to avoid doing this right away. By focusing on two words that signify the topic, you will aim to evoke thinking about its defining aspects first, before moving onto new concepts or proposing solutions.

To set up the game, distribute a stack of index cards and markers to all the participants. Everyone should have a fair number of cards available. The game should begin immediately after the rules have been explained.

3 Minutes: Generate a Pool of Aspects

For the first three minutes of the exercise, participants are asked to think about the characteristics of the topic at hand and to write down as many of them as they can on separate index cards. It may accelerate the group's process to think in terms of "nouns and verbs" that come to mind when thinking about the subject, or to free-associate. As in all brainstorming, no filtering should be put on this phase, in which the goal is a large pool of aspects in a small window of three minutes.

12 Minutes: Develop Concepts

At this point, the group is divided into pairs. Each team draws three cards randomly from the pool. With these as thought starters, the teams now have 12 minutes to develop a concept to present back to the larger group.

If the two topic words are sufficient to explain the challenge, the clock starts, and the teams begin. If there is any doubt, reveal a more fleshed-out version of the topic's focus, such as "How will we become more energy-efficient next quarter?"

In developing concepts to present, teams may create rough sketches, proto-types, or other media—the key is in preparing for a short (three-minute maximum) presentation of their concept back to the group.

3 Minutes: Make Presentations

When presenting to the larger group, teams may reveal the cards that they drew and how the cards influenced their thinking. Again, tight time keep-ing is critical here—every team should have a maximum of three minutes to present their concept. After every team has presented, the entire group may reflect on what was uncovered.

STRATEGY

Speed is key. Many traditional brainstorming techniques can be slowed down or fouled entirely when time is not of the essence, despite the best intentions of par-ticipants. Additionally, speed helps prove the value of what can be accomplished in short bursts—often the important aspects of good ideas can be captured very quickly and do not require laborious discussion before first coming to light.

After presenting concepts back to the group, teams may do a number of things. They may dig deeper on an individual concept or try to integrate the ideas into each other. They may vote on or rank the concepts to decide which to spend more time developing. Often, concepts coming out of this exercise are more memorable to the participants, who are bonded in the time-driven stress of creating together.

TIPS FOR PLAYING ONLINE

The 3-12-3 Brainstorm game works well online. Each pair should have their own space to iterate and develop their concepts. Online play for this game can easily be extended to continue refining the concepts developed.

The 3-12-3 Brainstorm game is credited to James Macanufo.

6-8-5

OBJECT OF PLAY

Rarely are ideas born overnight. And for an idea to become a great idea, it takes considerable work and effort to develop. Part of the reason we end up with under-developed ideas is that we stick with the first good idea we have, rather than taking the time to explore complementary approaches. 6-8-5 is designed to combat this pattern by forcing us to generate lots of ideas in a short period of time. The activity can then be repeated to hone and flesh out a few of the best ideas.

NUMBER OF PLAYERS

Two or more people

DURATION OF PLAY

5 minutes to play each round + 15-20 minutes for discussion

HOW TO PLAY

1. Before the meeting, prepare several sheets of paper with a 2×2 or 2×3 grid. You want to create boxes big enough for players to sketch their ideas in but small enough to constrain them to one idea per box. Prepare enough paper for everyone to have about 10 boxes per round.

2. As the group is gathering, distribute sheets of paper to each player. Or instruct the group on how to make their own 2×2 or 2×3 grid by drawing lines in their notebook.

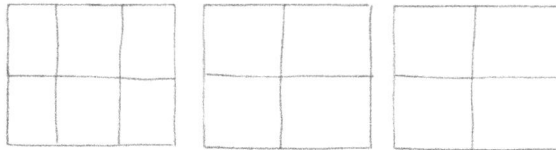

3. Introduce the game and remind players of the objective for the meeting. Tell players that the goal with 6-8-5 is to generate between 6 and 8 ideas (related to the meeting objective) in five minutes.

4. Next, set a timer for five minutes. Tell the players to sit silently and sketch out as many ideas as they can until the timer ends—with the goal of

reaching 6–8 ideas. The sketches can and should be very rough—nothing polished in this stage.

5. When the time runs out, the players should share their sketches with the rest of the group. The group can ask questions of each player, but this is not a time for a larger brainstorming session. Make sure every player presents their sketches.

6. With time permitting, repeat another few rounds of 6-8-5. Players can further develop any ideas that were presented by the group as a whole or can sketch new ideas that emerged since the last round. They can continue to work on separate ideas or begin working on the same idea. But the five-minute sketching sprint should always be done silently and independently.

STRATEGY

6-8-5 is intended to help players generate many ideas in succession, without worrying about the details or implementation of any particular idea. It's designed to keep players on task by limiting them to sketching in small boxes and working fast in a limited amount of time. 6-8-5 can be used on any product or concept that you want to brainstorm, and it produces the best results with a heterogenous group (people from product, marketing, engineering, design...).

6-8-5 works great in the early stages of the ideation process, and it's often followed by a debrief and synthesis session or by another gamestorming exercise to identify the most fruitful ideas given the team's business, product, or end-user goals.

TIPS FOR PLAYING ONLINE

Draw digitally, or ask participants to write in their notebooks or on blank paper. Once drawings are complete, ask participants to hold up their drawings or take photos of their ideas and add them to a shared board.

6-8-5 has been used in design studio workshops for rapid ideation. This game is credited to Todd Zaki Warfel (http://zakiwarfel.com).

Altitude

OBJECT OF PLAY

Sometimes it can be difficult to keep a meeting on track when people have a hard time staying focused at the right level. People can find themselves "down in the weeds" or stuck in operational details when the meeting is supposed to be strategic. Conversely, they can find themselves being too abstract and strategic when operational detail is exactly what's needed. You can use Altitude to agree on expectations and keep people focused at the right level to serve the goals of the meeting.

NUMBER OF PLAYERS

Any number of people can play this game

DURATION

Five minutes

HOW TO PLAY

1. Create a chart like the one shown next:

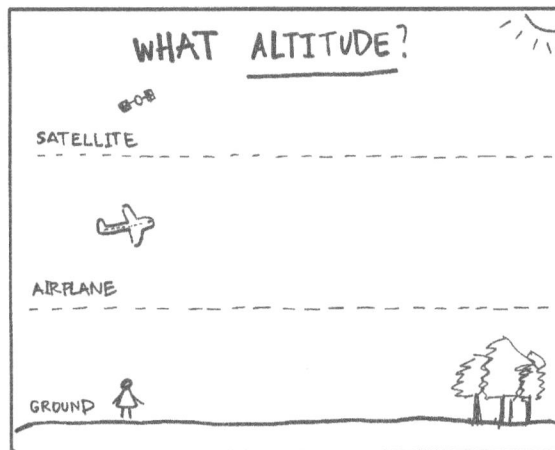

2. Give everyone a sheet of paper. Ask, "Who knows how to make a paper airplane?" and ask for a show of hands. If there are people who don't know how, either show them or ask someone at their table to do so. Now

ask everyone to make a paper airplane. If time permits, you might offer them a chance to test their planes to make sure they fly.

3. Reveal the altitude chart, and ask the group to define what they mean by the satellite level, the airplane level, and the ground level. For example, if people say that the satellite level is too high but the ground level is too detailed, ask them for examples of the kinds of things that they would consider to be at the right altitude. Then ask them for examples of things that would be too low or too high.

4. When you have reached some consensus on the right altitude level, put a mark on the page to represent the "right" altitude.

5. Now tell people that whenever they notice the conversation going too high (abstract, vague, strategic) or too low (down in the weeds, tactical, operational), they can float their airplane, and that will be a signal to the group.

STRATEGY

Meetings often go off track when someone pulls conversations into the wrong "altitude." When this happens, people often tune out, or even leave. In most meetings, there is no simple, easy feedback mechanism people can use to keep the meeting on track. Giving people such a feedback mechanism (and making it fun) makes it easier for people to weigh in, keeping the meeting on track.

TIPS FOR PLAYING ONLINE

Make the Altitude game card-referenceable during the rest of the session. Instead of flying a paper airplane through the room, add an emoji to your zoom video, or participants can make a paper airplane to have next to them during the meeting and hold up on camera to signal the group has drifted into a new altitude. The contrast of offline work alongside a virtual meeting can offer engagement, act as a nice change of pace, and help hold attention as a result.

The Altitude game was created by Dave Gray.

The Anti-Problem

OBJECT OF PLAY

The Anti-Problem game helps people get unstuck when they are at their wit's end. It is most useful when a team is already working on a problem but they're running out of ideas for solutions. By asking players to identify ways to solve the problem opposite to their current problem, it becomes easier to see where a current solution might be going astray or where an obvious solution isn't being applied.

NUMBER OF PLAYERS

5–20 people

DURATION OF PLAY

30–45 minutes

HOW TO PLAY

1. Before the meeting, find a situation that needs to be resolved or a problem that needs a solution.

2. Give players access to sticky notes, markers, index cards, pipe cleaners, modeling clay—any supplies you have around the office that they could use to design and describe solutions.

3. Break large groups into smaller groups of three to four people and describe what they'll tackle together: the anti-problem, or the current problem's opposite. (For example, if the problem is sales conversion, the players would brainstorm ways to get customers to avoid buying the product.) The more extreme the problem's opposite, the better.

    Optional activity: Bring a list of smaller problems and decrease the amount of time allotted to solve them. Make it a race to come up with as many solutions as the group can churn out—even if they're outlandish.

4. Give the players 15–20 minutes to generate and display various ways to solve the anti-problem. Encourage fast responses and a volume of ideas. There are no wrong solutions.

5. When the time is up, ask each group to share their solutions to the anti-problem. They should stand and display any visual creations they have at this time or ask the others to gather around their table to see their solutions.

6. Discuss any insights and discoveries the players have.

STRATEGY

This game's purpose is to help teams evaluate a problem differently and break out of existing patterns, so make the anti-problem more extreme than it really is, just to get people thinking. And don't worry if the players don't generate many (or any) viable or actionable solutions. Obviously, those would be a boon to the game, but the intention is not to eliminate a complex problem in 30 minutes. The intention is to give people a new approach that can lead to a solution when they have time to think after the meeting is over. Or, since this game tends to naturally segue into a conversation about the real problem, you could use any extra time to start that conversation while the players' ideas are ignited. Note: there may be some unexpected "aha moments," as people could discover that they're applying a solution that's actually contributing to the current problem. Whoops!

TIPS FOR PLAYING ONLINE

Build a board to establish a group working space and set the tone of the activity. Set up the activity as a group as you would offline, and be thoughtful, with clear communication on what to do in breakout groups (of 5–7 people). Add instructions in the chat and to the board to help groups work efficiently. Participants are always invited to the chat or back to the main room for clarification. Facilitate group sharing of solutions on the board and add a space to organize insights and highlight discoveries to be leveraged.

The Anti-Problem game is based on an activity called Reverse It, from Donna Spencer's design games website (https://oreil.ly/rsQZN).

Brainwriting

OBJECT OF PLAY

Some of the best ideas are compilations from multiple contributors. Brainwriting is a simple way to generate ideas, share them, and subsequently build on them within a group. Access to multiple hands, eyes, and minds can yield the most interesting results.

NUMBER OF PLAYERS

5–15 people

DURATION OF PLAY

30–45 minutes

HOW TO PLAY

1. In a space visible to the players, write the topic around which you need to generate ideas and draw a picture of it. An example of a topic might be "Employee Recognition Program."

2. Distribute index cards to each player and ask them to silently generate ideas related to the topic and write them on the cards.

3. As they complete each idea, ask the players to pass that idea to the person on their right.

4. Tell the players to read the card they received and think of it as an "idea stimulation" card. Ask them to add an idea inspired by what they just read or to enhance the idea and then pass again to their right.

5. Continue this process of "brainwriting" and passing cards to the right until there are various ideas on each card.

   Optional activity: Ask the players to write an idea on a piece of paper and then fold it into an airplane and fly it to another participant. Continue writing and flying the planes until each piece of paper has several ideas. Conclude with steps 6 and 7.

6. Once finished, collect the cards and ask for help taping them to the wall around the topic and its picture.

7. Have the group come to the wall to review the ideas and draw stars next to the ones they find most compelling. Discuss.

Optional activity: Create an idea gallery in the room using flip-chart pads and stands. Ask players to write as many ideas on the sheet as they can and then wander around the room and add ideas to the other sheets. Continue this process until each sheet has a good number of ideas.

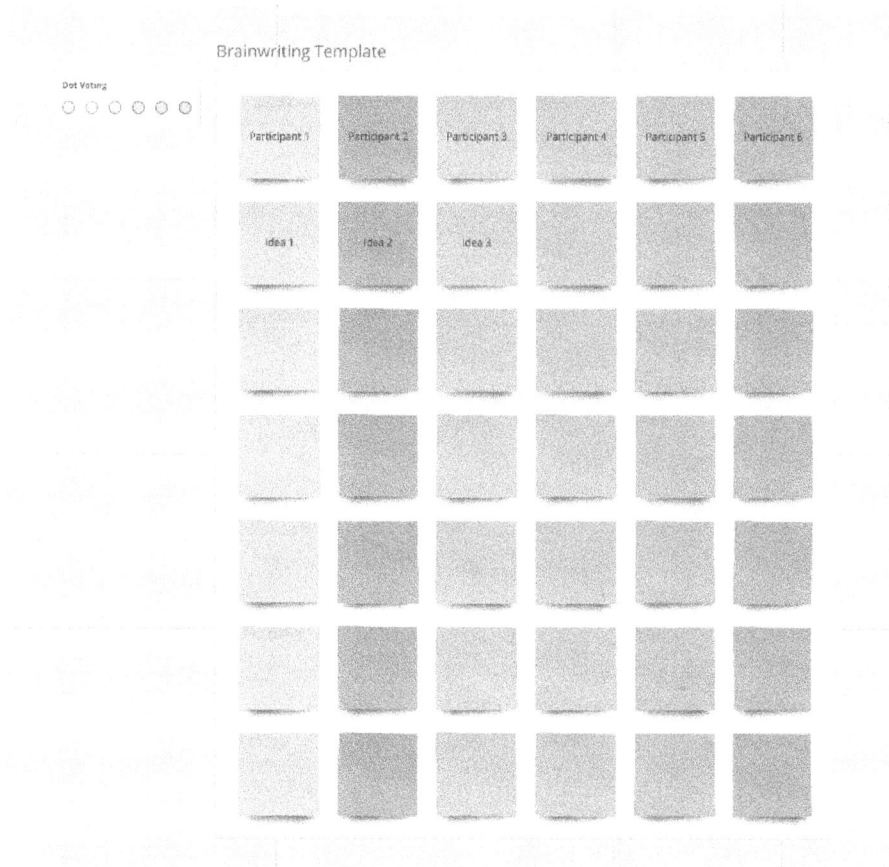

Brainwriting Template

Dot Voting

○ ○ ○ ○ ○ ○

Participant 1	Participant 2	Participant 3	Participant 4	Participant 5	Participant 6
Idea 1	Idea 2	Idea 3			

STRATEGY

In a typical group setting, extroverts tend to dominate the verbal contributions. And while their contributions are certainly important, it can be difficult to hear from quieter players who also have something valuable to offer. Let the players know that this play is intentionally silent. It affords the quiet people the opportunity to generate ideas without having to verbalize to the whole group, and it gives you certainty that you'll hear from every player in the room. Brainwriting also allows ideas to emerge *before* being critiqued and creates a space for them to be cocreated, with multiple owners; therefore, there's a greater chance of follow-through.

TIPS FOR PLAYING ONLINE

Google Docs can be used for Brainwriting, or use a template like the following one from Miro with spaces for each participant and color coding for additional clarity.

The Brainwriting game is based on the same-named activity in Michael Michalko's Thinkertoys *(Ten Speed Press). Horst Geschke and associates at the Battelle Institute in Frankfurt, Germany, developed a variety of these creative-thinking techniques referred to as "brainwriting."*

Code of Conduct

OBJECT OF PLAY

This game has been designed to help set the right culture in a group of people and help build mutual trust. It will empower all participants to act upon the results of this game.

NUMBER OF PLAYERS

Up to 30 people

DURATION OF PLAY

+/– 30 minutes

HOW TO PLAY

1. Write down the words "Meaningful" and "Pleasant" in the middle of a flip chart or whiteboard.

2. Ask everyone to shout out what they believe makes something meaningful and pleasant.

3. As participants are providing thoughts and ideas, record the information given in a mind-map structure. Note: try to use images and words.

4. Quickly review each of the ideas recorded and make sure everybody has the same understanding of the idea at hand. If necessary, adjust the item to avoid misunderstanding.

5. Now, review and ask the participants how they could carry out these ideas during the meeting or workshop. Record the items addressed with the label "Actions."

6. End the game by pointing out that this code of conduct was co-created by everyone. Every participant has the responsibility to make sure the group respects this code and has a part in making the meeting or workshop meaningful and pleasant.

Optionally, you could ask people if they want to take ownership of one of the actions registered. But note, be aware that this may cause a typical human reaction from the others: "It is this person's problem to monitor, not mine anymore."

STRATEGY

Make sure everybody contributes to the making of the mind-map. If you believe the group is not strong or comfortable enough for this, you could substitute the shouting of ideas with letting everyone write down their ideas in silence combined with an affinity map to achieve similar results, which can then be recorded in the mind-map. It will take some time to create this shared code of conduct, but it will help groups of people where there is little to no trust and openness to break through the initial barriers.

The same concept can be applied to not just a meeting, but a project or initiative. Reminding everyone of the core values to be built on and used in their interactions and decisions can help keep everyone aligned and result in better decision making.

This activity makes perspectives that are usually implicit explicit, and it becomes the group's working agreement. Once the mind-map is complete, the group's "norms" have been established. As a facilitator, remind the group of the importance of defining this common language and code of conduct and commend them on their efforts to work together effectively as a team.

The mind-map can be further refined as the main norms the group wants to carry into future sessions. This works well for forums and small teams.

TIPS FOR PLAYING ONLINE

This game translates well online. Create a mind-map with sticky notes or images, a drawing tool, etc. Encourage participation from everyone. Ask participants to unmute to encourage shouting out ideas or cocreate the map together.

This game is based on principles from drama therapy and organizational psychology. The forming, storming, norming, and performing (FSNP) model is a model of group development that describes the stages a group goes through as it forms and becomes effective.

Context Map

OBJECT OF PLAY

We don't truly have a good grasp of a situation until we see it in a fuller context. The Context Map, therefore, is designed to show us the external factors, trends, and forces at work surrounding an organization. Once we have a systemic view of the external environment we're in, we are better equipped to respond proactively to that landscape.

NUMBER OF PLAYERS

5–25 people

DURATION OF PLAY

45 minutes to 1.5 hours

HOW TO PLAY

1. Hang six sheets of flip-chart paper on a wall in a two-row, three-column format.

2. On the top-middle sheet of flip-chart paper, draw a representation of the organization under discussion. It can be as simple as an image of your office building or an image of a globe to represent a global marketplace. Label the picture or scene.

3. On the same sheet of paper, above and to the left of the image, write the words "POLITICAL FACTORS." Above and to the right, write the words "ECONOMIC CLIMATE."

4. On the top-left sheet of flip-chart paper, draw several large arrows pointing to the right. Label this sheet "TRENDS." Include a blank before the word "TRENDS" so that you can add a qualifier later.

5. On the top-right sheet of flip-chart paper, draw several large arrows pointing to the left. Label this sheet "TRENDS." Again, include a blank before the word "TRENDS" so that you can add a qualifier later.

6. On the bottom-left sheet, draw large arrows pointing up and to the right. Label this sheet "TECHNOLOGY FACTORS."

7. On the bottom-middle sheet, draw an image representing your client(s) and label the sheet "CUSTOMER NEEDS."

8. On the bottom-right sheet, draw a thundercloud or a person with a question mark overhead and label this sheet "UNCERTAINTIES."

9. Introduce the context map to the group. Explain that the goal of populating the map is to get a sense of the big picture in which your organization operates. Ask the players which category on the map they'd like to discuss first, other than TRENDS. Open up the category they select for comments and discussion. Write the comments they verbalize in the space created for that category.

10. Based on an indication from the group or your own sense of direction, move to another category and ask the group to offer ideas for that category. Continue populating the map with content until every category but TRENDS is filled in.

11. The two TRENDS categories can be qualified by the group, so take a quick poll to determine what kinds of trends the players would like to discuss. These could be online trends, demographic trends, growth trends, and so forth. As you help the players find agreement on qualifiers for the trends (conduct a dot vote or have them raise their hands if you need to), write those qualifiers in the blanks next to TRENDS. Then continue the process of requesting content and writing it in the appropriate space.

12. Summarize the overall findings with the group and ask for observations, insights, "ahas," and concerns about the context map.

STRATEGY

It's up to the players to paint a picture of the environment in which they sit, but as the meeting leader, you can help them generate content by asking intelligent and thought-provoking questions. Conduct research or employee interviews before the meeting if you need to. The idea is to portray a context that is as rich and accurate as possible so that the players gain insight into their environment and can subsequently move proactively rather than reactively. The players can populate the categories other than TRENDS on the context map in any order, so note their starting point and pay attention to where they focus or generate the most content—both can indicate where their energy lies. But keep in mind that this activity is designed to generate a display of the external environment, not the internal one. So, if you notice that the discussion steers toward analyzing the internal context, guide them back to the outside world. There are other games for internal dynamics. The Context Map game should result in a holistic view of the external business landscape and show the group where they can focus their efforts to get strategic results.

TIPS FOR PLAYING ONLINE

Create one group context map (preferred), or separate maps for small groups to populate and discuss in breakout rooms.

This game is based on The Grove Consultants International's *Context Map Leader's Guide (https://oreil.ly/8Tujc).*

Cover Story

OBJECT OF PLAY

Cover Story is a game about pure imagination. The purpose is to think expansively around an ideal future state for the organization; it's an exercise in visioning. The object of the game is to suspend all disbelief and envision a future state that is so stellar that it landed your organization on the cover of a well-known magazine. The players must pretend as though this future has already taken place and has been reported by the mainstream media. This game is worth playing because it not only encourages people to "think big" but also actually plants the seeds for a future that perhaps wasn't possible before the game was played.

NUMBER OF PLAYERS

Any

DURATION OF PLAY

Depends on the number of players, but a maximum of 90 minutes

HOW TO PLAY

1. Before the meeting, draw out large-scale templates that include the categories shown on the following image. Your template doesn't need to look exactly like this one; you can be creative with the central image and the layout. Just be sure to keep the categories intact. The number of templates you create depends on the size of the group. At the most, allow four to six people to work on one template together.

2. Explain the object of the game to the players and define each category on the template:

"Cover" tells the BIG story of their success.

"Headlines" convey the substance of the cover story.

"Sidebars" reveal interesting facets of the cover story.

"Quotes" can be from anyone as long as they're related to the story.

"Brainstorm" is for documenting initial ideas for the cover story.

"Images" are for supporting the content with illustrations.

3. Break the players into groups of four to six and make sure there are markers and one template for each group. Tell the players that to populate the template, they can either select a scribe or write and draw on it together.

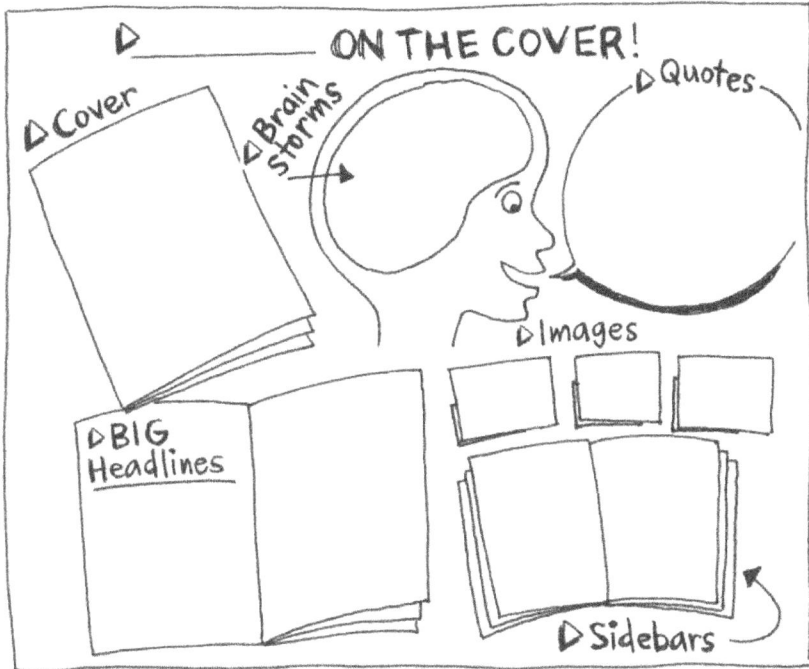

4. Ask the players to imagine the best-case scenario for their company and to take that scenario one step further. Request that they spend five quiet minutes imagining their own stories before they work together to agree on one. Give the groups 30–45 minutes to generate this "story of the year" and represent it on their template.

5. Reconvene the breakout groups and ask for volunteers to present their visions first. Give each group 5–10 minutes to share what they imagined was written in the story and the supporting elements.

6. Note any common vision themes and areas of agreement. Ask for observations, insights, and concerns about the future state.

Optional activity: ask two players to role-play an interview based on the content from their "On the Cover" template, as though the magazine sent a reporter to interview an important character in the story.

STRATEGY

This game is about the wildest dream for the organization—that has already happened! So, when you set up this game as the meeting leader, speak about their "successes" with enthusiasm and in the past tense. Encourage the players to use the past tense in their brainstorming and story creation. And don't let the group go into analysis mode. This game is not about logic, pragmatism, or parameters. Cover Story is an open-ended, creative-thinking exercise, so tell the players to be wary of any "reality checks" from other players. And as the small groups present their visions to the large group, note and discuss any common themes that arise. These themes—however fantastical—are telling, because commonalities reveal shared hopes and also plant seeds for real possibilities. If this play is part of a longer group process, post these visions around the room so that they serve as reference points for continued ideas and inspiration.

TIPS FOR PLAYING ONLINE

This game works easily and well online. Re-create the template by rapid-doodling a version of it and invite players to add images, symbols, sketches, headlines, or example publications, etc. The important thing to remember is that this is about visioning and declaring. A variation on this game was created by Sunni (Sun) Brown and is shown next. In this variation, participants are given the front and back covers of a book and asked to respond to two questions—one current and one either celebratory or aspirational.

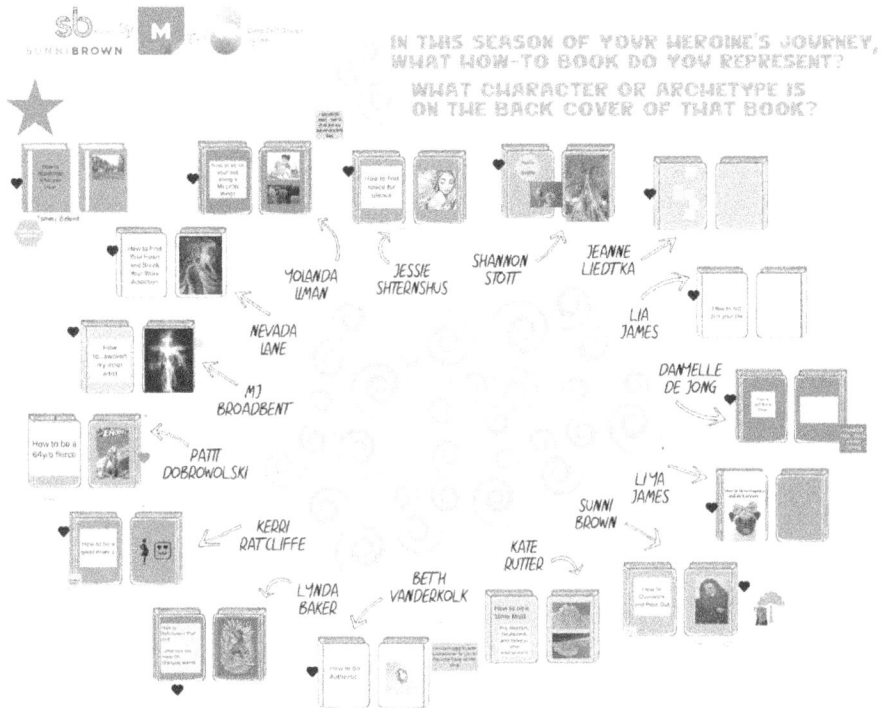

The Cover Story game is based on The Grove Consultants International's *Leader's Guide to accompany the* Cover Story Vision Graphic Guide *(https://oreil.ly/ZMMtC).*

The variation on this game referenced in the template shown was invented by Sunni (Sun) Brown, inspired by the book The Heroine's Journey: Woman's Quest for Wholeness *by Maureen Murdock (Shambhala). Example facilitated by Sunni (Sun) Brown for Mural.*

Day in the Life

OBJECT OF PLAY

Many of us make the mistaken assumption that others see what we see and know what we know. No one in the world shares your internal system map of reality. The best way to compare notes, so to speak, is to actually draw an external representation of what you think is happening. Day in the Life gives players an opportunity to better understand other players' roles and responsibilities. It helps chip away at silos and introduces the novel idea that we may be seeing only one reality: ours. It helps immensely to show what we see to others so that we can start to share a reality and work on it together.

NUMBER OF PLAYERS

8–20 people

DURATION OF PLAY

30 minutes to 1 hour

HOW TO PLAY

1. Give all players access to flip-chart paper, markers, and sticky notes. Ask them to take 30 seconds to write one of their job responsibilities (e.g., create the company newsletter or devise a marketing strategy for Product X) on a sticky note and stick it to their shirt.

2. Have the players wander around the room and pair up with someone whose job responsibility they're the least familiar with or that they're curious about. If you have an odd number of players, join them to even it out.

3. In pairs, ask the players to take turns drawing their best representation of how they envision the other person's workflow around that job duty. They can use simple circles, boxes, and arrows to make flowcharts, or they can get creative, but they cannot interview the other player or ask any clarifying questions while they're drawing. Give them 5–15 minutes to draw quietly.

4. When the time is up, give each player five minutes to share their drawing with the other person and describe what it means.

5. Then give the pairs 5–10 minutes each to clarify or agree on the realities of each other's drawing. They should also take time to discuss where the

areas of ease, friction, and interactions with others fall in the process. They can elaborate and draw on the other person's visual at this point, or the original creator of the visual can add content as their partner shares.

6. Ask for volunteers to show their visuals to the larger group and to describe some of their insights and observations.

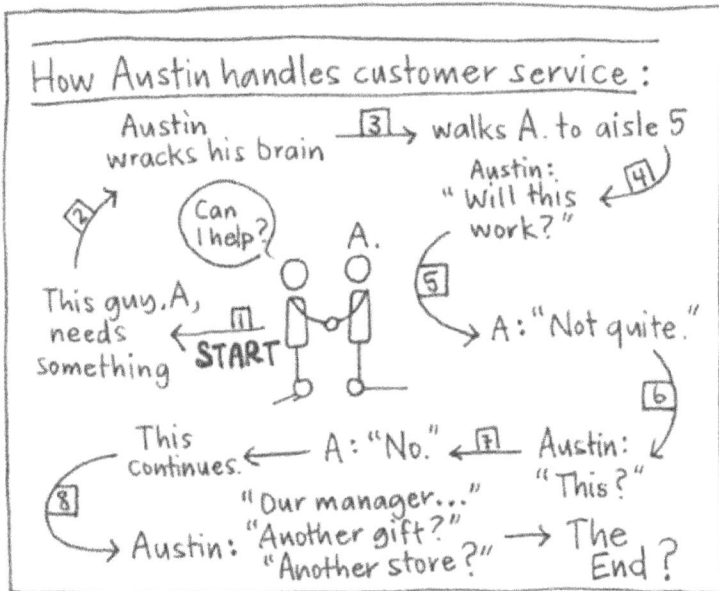

STRATEGY

To be maximally effective, this game has one requirement: the players should represent a range of positions or job responsibilities within an organization. The game rapidly loses its value if all the participants have the same, predictable workflow, like processing an undisputed insurance claim. The idea is to *educate* each other on the realities of their work duties and to help break down silos across organizational areas. Once the insights start coming out, this game can significantly increase the understanding and appreciation of others' work. And it can be even more effective when you have players who have to work together but historically have had little insight into—or even patience with—their colleagues' processes.

Most people feel comfortable drawing basic shapes and workflow-related diagrams since these are common in company life. If, however, players balk at having to draw, tell them they're welcome to rely only on words, but they'll miss an opportunity to make a simple picture of someone else's "world" at work.

TIPS FOR PLAYING ONLINE

Create a game board for participants to join. For step 1, add your sticky note to a space on the board. For step 2, review the board and move your sticky note to whichever breakout group you choose. This will go quickly. Facilitators set up the activity as a group then invite the pairs to breakout rooms for step 3. Bring the group back together to set up steps 4 and 5 in breakouts. To set up step 6, bring the group back and ask participants to take a photo of their drawing and add it to the board. Then, invite volunteers to describe their visuals to the larger group.

The source for Day in the Life is unknown.

Draw the Problem

OBJECT OF PLAY

On any given day, we prioritize the problems that get our attention. Problems that are vague or misunderstood have a harder time passing our internal tests of what matters and, as a result, go unaddressed and unsolved. Often, meetings that address problem solving skip this critical step: defining the problem in a way that is not only clear but also compelling enough to make people care about solving it.

Running this short drawing exercise at the beginning of a meeting will help get the laptops closed and the participants engaged with their purpose.

NUMBER OF PLAYERS

Works best with small groups of 6–10 people

DURATION OF PLAY

20–30 minutes

HOW TO PLAY

Each participant should have a large index card or letter-sized piece of paper. After introducing the topic of the meeting, ask the participants to think about the problem they are here to solve. As they do so, ask them to write a list of items helping to explain the problem. For example, they may think about a "day in the life" of the problem or an item that represents the problem as a whole.

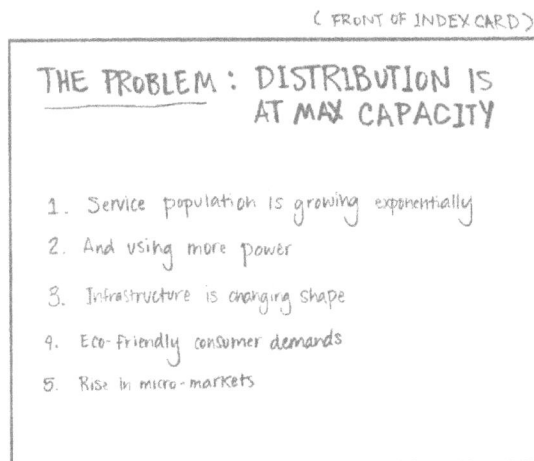

(FRONT OF INDEX CARD)

THE PROBLEM : DISTRIBUTION IS
                    AT MAX CAPACITY

1. Service population is growing exponentially
2. And using more power
3. Infrastructure is changing shape
4. Eco-friendly consumer demands
5. Rise in micro-markets

After a few minutes of this thinking and reflection, ask the participants to flip over their paper and draw a picture of the problem, as they would explain it to a peer. They may draw a simple diagram or something more metaphorical; there are no prizes or punishments for good or bad artistry. The drawing should simply assist in explaining the problem.

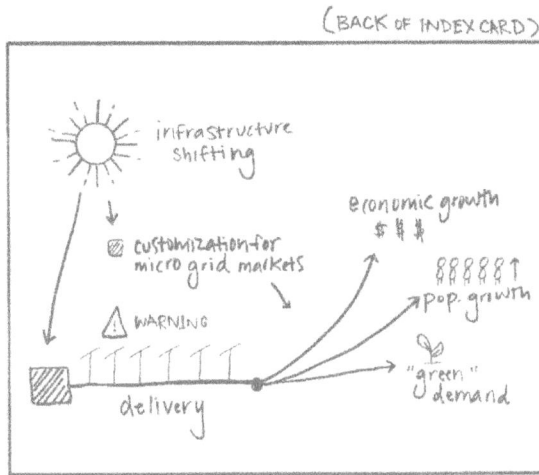

When everyone is finished, have the participants post their drawings on the wall and explain them to each other. While the group shares, note any common elements. After the exercise, the group should reflect on the similarities and differences and work toward a shared understanding of the problem.

STRATEGY

This warm-up does not result in a problem definition that will satisfy an engineer; rather, it engages participants in defining the challenge in a simplified form. It is a first step in bringing a group together under a common purpose, elevating the problem above the noise to become something they care to solve.

TIPS FOR PLAYING ONLINE

Use a digital whiteboard to sketch and arrange, or draw on paper. Add digital sketches to a shared board, or add a photo of the sketch paper to the board.

The Draw the Problem game is credited to James Macanufo.

Draw Toast

OBJECT OF PLAY

You can use the Draw Toast exercise to introduce people to the concepts of visual thinking, working memory, mental models, and/or systems thinking. This also works as a nice warm-up exercise to get people engaged with each other and thinking visually. Plus, it's fun!

NUMBER OF PLAYERS

Any number of people can play this game.

DURATION OF PLAY

10–15 minutes.

HOW TO PLAY

On paper or index cards, ask people to draw "How to make toast."

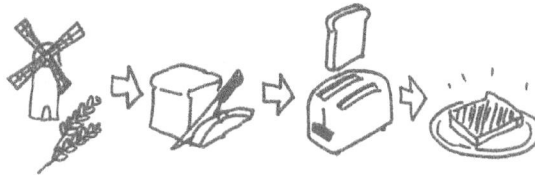

After a couple of minutes, ask people to share their diagrams with each other and discuss the similarities and differences. Ask people to share any observations or insights they have about the various drawings. You are likely to hear comments about the relative simplicity or complexity of the drawings, whether they have people in them, how technical they are, how similar or different they are, and so on.

Depending on why you are doing the exercise, you may want to point out the following:

- Note that although the drawings are all different, they are all fundamentally correct. There are many ways to visualize information, and they all enrich understanding rather than being "right" or "wrong."

- Although the drawings are different in content, they tend to be similar in structure. That is, most drawings of mental models tend to contain three to seven elements, connected by lines or arrows.

STRATEGY

The main point of this exercise is to demonstrate the power of visual thinking to represent information.

Visualizations of this kind tend to be easily understandable, although they are visually as rich and diverse as people. Pictures can be fundamentally correct even though they are quite different. There is no "one right type" of visualization.

When people visualize a mental model, they usually will include 5–7 elements, linked together by lines or arrows. The number of elements tends to correspond to the number of things people can hold in their working memory, also known as short-term memory (see the paper "The Magical Number Seven, Plus or Minus Two" (*https://oreil.ly/x_UPj*) for more information).

This is also a nice warm-up exercise that is fun and gets people talking to each other.

There is an excellent TED talk by Tom Wujec (*https://tomwujec.com*), which you may want to watch in preparation. It may also be useful to show the talk to the group in sessions as a way to share insights after the exercise. Tom also has a page with ideas for extending this exercise into group problem solving, which you can find at DrawToast.com.

TIPS FOR PLAYING ONLINE

Have participants draw on paper and show or upload an image of their work or draw digitally. This works with online collaboration tools as well. Encourage players to draw, rather than just describe the process with words.

The Draw Toast exercise is credited to Dave Gray.

Fishbowl

OBJECT OF PLAY

Often during meetings we bring together stakeholders who aren't familiar with each other's perspectives or aren't accustomed to listening to each other without offering an immediate response. In some cases, stakeholders may even be meeting for the first time. In scenarios like these, it's not surprising that it can be difficult for people to engage in a rich and meaningful conversation. The Fishbowl game is an effective way to activate attention—to prime our natural listening and observing skills so that a more substantive conversation can take place.

NUMBER OF PLAYERS

Medium to large groups

DURATION OF PLAY

40–45 minutes

HOW TO PLAY

1. Before the meeting, think of a topic that could be served by a group discussion and write down questions associated with it.

2. Find a room with a good amount of open space and clear out anything other than chairs.

3. Create a handout similar to the following:

4. Arrange the chairs in two concentric circles in the room, as shown in the following figure. The inner circle seats the players engaged in conversation; the outer circle seats the players acting as observers.

5. Introduce the game and assign "observer" or "player" status to each person. Give everyone a pen and a handout (but mention that the handout is used only in the observer role). Ask the participants to sit in the circle relative to their assigned role.

6. Announce the topic of the game and ask the players to take 15 minutes to have a discussion around it. Use the questions you generated before the meeting to start the conversation and keep it moving. Make sure the players know that their responsibility is simply to converse in the circle. Make sure the observers know that their role is to pay close attention and to write on the handouts all discussion points and evidence that come out of the conversation.

7. When 15 minutes are up, ask the group to switch seats and switch roles. Then start another 15-minute discussion on the same topic or a different one.

8. After both conversations have completed, ask for volunteers to share the information they gathered and ask them to describe their experiences on the inner versus outer circle.

People are well versed in having conversations; what most of us aren't used to is listening, observing, and being accountable for our observations. The Fishbowl game, therefore, is about engaging skills that in many of us have become rusty. So, despite that it may look as though the action happens in the players' conversation, the action in this game happens in the outer circle, with the observers. As the group leader, be clear with the group that this is a listening and observing exercise. If there were a point system (and there is decidedly not), points would be awarded to those who most accurately logged the conversation that took place —not to those who made the most comments in the discussion. Talk to the group about their experience of being silent and paying attention. What was difficult about it? What was easy? How did it affect their perception of the topic and the other players? Use the Fishbowl exercise as a segue to a heightened give-and-take between stakeholders.

TIPS FOR PLAYING ONLINE

Share the handout as a Google Doc or create a template to populate in an online board. Instruct participants who are in the fishbowl to keep their cameras on and observers to cover their camera with a sticky note (preferably blue).

The Fishbowl game is based on ideas from the Facilitator's Guide to Participatory Decision-Making, *by Sam Kaner et al. (Jossey-Bass).*

Forced Analogy

OBJECT OF PLAY

We understand things by grouping them with other things of similar type and function. An airplane is similar to a helicopter; they're both flying things. Both are more similar to a bird, which is also a flying thing, than any of those things are to an earthworm, which is a crawling and tunneling thing. The Forced Analogy game breaks these hard-wired categories and allows us to see things from a different angle, opening new possibilities in problem solving and idea generation.

NUMBER OF PLAYERS

1–10 people

DURATION OF PLAY

15 minutes to 1 hour

HOW TO PLAY

Participants set up the exercise by generating a random list of things—animals, objects, or people. Write these items on individual index cards. For each item, write some of its qualities or attributes—for example, "An airplane flies through the air, moves along predefined routes, and has an autopilot feature." Likewise, an oak tree would be noted for its branching structure, its deep roots, and its ability to grow from a very small seed.

Participants shuffle the cards and distribute them randomly. They then use the cards to develop analogies to the problem or issue at hand, asking:

- How is this problem similar to [random object]?
- How would I solve this problem with [random object]?

Participants may also work through one analogy as a group, as in "How would we use a paperclip to solve our data integration problem?"

STRATEGY

A truly random list of objects will push the boundaries of the group's mindset and create new perspectives. If needed, this list can be created in advance of the game itself by an unbiased nonparticipant.

TIPS FOR PLAYING ONLINE

To distribute cards randomly, facilitators assign items to participants in private mode and reveal the assignments at once when private mode is turned off.

The source of the Forced Analogy game is unknown.

Graphic Jam

OBJECT OF PLAY

Words become more challenging to visualize as they become less literal. For example, the words *computer* and *necktie* offer immediate imagery. But the words *strategy* and *justice* are more abstract and lend themselves to broader visual interpretations. Graphic Jam is an all-purpose visualization game that you can conduct before many other games as a warm-up, but it's also a useful game in itself. Visualizing abstract concepts supports logo development, presentation design, website design, metaphor development for e-learning, and so on. It exercises the visual part of our cortex—which accounts for 75% of our sensory neurons—and turns on parts of our minds that don't get much action in a typical business setting. Why does that matter? Because business is getting more complex. Being able to use your mind's eye to see and show problems—and solutions—will be a sought-after skill.

NUMBER OF PLAYERS

5–15 people

DURATION OF PLAY

30 minutes to 1 hour

HOW TO PLAY

1. Establish a large, flat, white display area for this game. Give all players access to sticky notes and index cards.

2. Ask them to take 1–2 minutes to write words *on the index cards* that they have difficulty conceptualizing and drawing, like "quality" or "teamwork." Ask for one word or phrase per index card.

3. Gather all of the contributions, shuffle them, and then select one card and read it aloud to the group. Tape it up in the white space.

4. Ask the players to reflect on the word and draw a visual representation of it *on a sticky note* so that it can be posted on the wall. Give them 2–3 minutes to do so.

5. Have the players approach the white space and post their sticky note under the index card with the related word.

6. Repeat steps 3–5 until all or most of the words have been read aloud. If you draw repeat words or synonyms of previously drawn words, draw again until you get a fresh concept.

7. By the end of the game, you'll have a gallery space of visualized concepts. Ask the group to spend time looking at how others interpreted the words.

8. Referring to the sticky notes, lead a group discussion by asking what certain images mean and how the artist related that image to the word that was read aloud. Ask players to discuss which words were easier to visualize than others and why. Close by asking them how they might see visualization skills applied in their daily life and work.

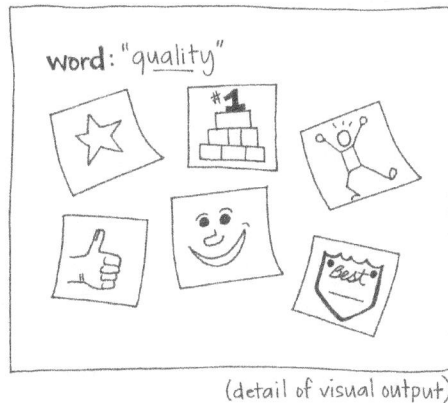

(detail of visual output)

STRATEGY

It is highly likely that the words the players contribute to this game will be on the abstract end of the spectrum. Note that the amount of time you'll need for this game depends on the number of players, the number of words each player generates, and the complexity of the word concepts. Use your best judgment on how long to spend conducting a Graphic Jam session. And when you decide it's time to call it quits, ask the group if there are any burning concepts they'd like to see visualized. If so, take a few more minutes with the group to tackle them. When the game is over, give the players a chance to converse with each other about the creative processes and techniques they use to conjure ideas and imagery.

TIPS FOR PLAYING ONLINE

Ask participants to add their words to a defined space on the board. The facilitator then zooms out so the details of the sticky notes aren't visible and randomly selects a subset of the stickies to move to a new area. Have the players draw on sticky notes IRL and add a photo to the board, or draw digitally on a sticky note.

The Graphic Jam game was inspired by the same-named activity created by Leslie Salmon-Zhu, cofounder of the International Forum of Visual Practitioners.

Hero's Journey Agenda

OBJECT OF PLAY

The Hero's Journey Agenda is a unique and different way to lay out the agenda for a meeting or workshop that creates a sense of adventure and builds anticipation for the meeting.

NUMBER OF PLAYERS

One, usually the facilitator, created live in front of a group

DURATION OF PLAY

10–15 minutes

HOW TO PLAY

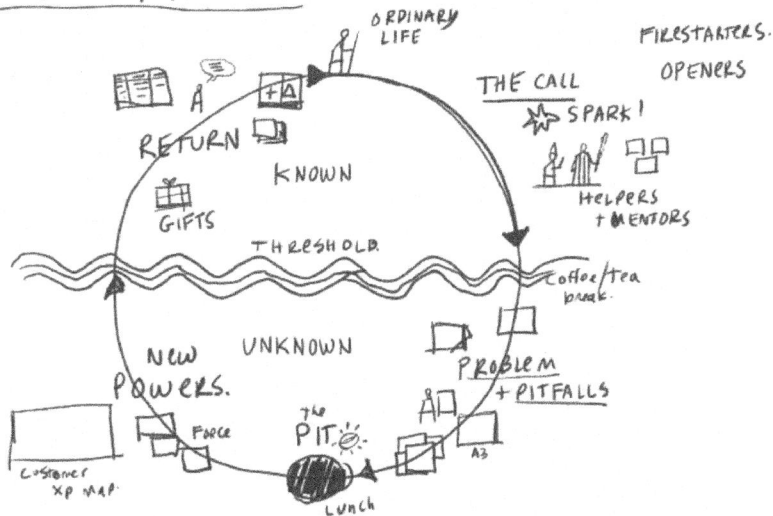

We include a script, but this exercise works best if you make it your own, using a story you love and that you feel your audience will be familiar with, like a favorite fairy tale or movie.

1. Draw a large circle on a whiteboard or flip chart. Tell people, "This circle represents all the things we're going to do today. We're starting up here (point to the top of the circle), and we're going to take a hero's journey." Depending on who is in the room, you can actually talk about it in terms

of Star Wars or Lord of the Rings or another story you expect the group to be familiar with.

You can also say, "Any story, any epic adventure follows this basic format. This is something that a guy named Joseph Campbell came up with. He wrote a book called *The Hero with a Thousand Faces*, which you can look up. Basically, the hero's journey works like this. You begin in ordinary life. This is where everyone is when coming into a meeting. We're actually in our ordinary lives right now, and we're going to do some special work and we're going to be moving outside of ordinary life."

2. Draw a stick figure at the top of the circle. Now say, "The hero's journey basically has two big components to it. There is the known world, which is made up of the things that we kind of already know, the regular work, and so forth. There's the unknown, which are the things that we hope we will discover and explore during the course of this meeting." Draw a wavy line to represent the boundary between the known and unknown.

"This is called the threshold. It's the threshold between the known and the unknown."

3. Now say, "Here we are on the hero's journey. The first thing in the hero's journey is the call to adventure. That is where we talk about things like: What are we going to do? What's the work that we're going to do? Why is it important? What brings us to this point?" Write "The Call" at around one o'clock on the circle, and talk about the purpose of the meeting. You may want to ask people why they came and what their expectations are.

4. Now draw a couple of stick figures at around two o'clock, and say, "In the beginning of any story, you're going to find the helpers and the mentors. You've got, whether it's Dumbledore or Gandalf or Obi Wan, whoever that character is, the droids, the characters that are going to help you. These are the characters that are going to help you find your way." Helpers can be things like teaching people how to use sticky notes in a certain way. There are a lot of gamestorming tools in this category. We call them openers. So you can tell people, "We're going to meet our helpers and mentors." Those helpers might be tools, or people, experts that we might bring in. It could be a keynote speaker.

5. Next, you will talk about crossing the threshold between the known and the unknown. "Now, where we cross the threshold, that's usually a good time for a coffee break. It's the end of the morning, coffee or tea, depending on what country you're in. Maybe both. We're going to have a break." You can draw a coffee cup or a teacup here.

6. Now say, "Next, we're going to start getting into the trials and tribulations. We call this 'problems and pitfalls.' It's the part of the journey where you're exploring the problem space." There may be all kinds of activities or things that you're going to do here. You might be brainstorming, you might be working stuff out, might be drawing a map of the system. There are a bunch of things that you can do to explore this problem space. In a story, you're going to find all kinds of challenges: you have to climb the mountain, you have to fight the trolls, all the things that have to happen to move the story forward.

   Write the words "Problems and pitfalls," and draw some explosions here, or barbed wire, or something representing problems and pitfalls, at four and five o'clock on your circle.

7. Now write the word "Pit" and draw a pit at the bottom of the circle. The pit, in a day-long meeting, might be lunchtime.

   "Every story has its pit. The belly of the whale, the cave. I just call this the pit. We've hit the bottom. This can be a tough space to be, because we've just opened up all these problem spaces and issues and things that we have to deal with. It may feel like we're never going to get home. The pit is also the place where Bilbo Baggins finds the ring. It's the place where the deep reflection, the real powerful learning can also happen. Over lunch might be a good time to explore what is down here in the pit. What are we feeling like? What are the emotions?"

8. Now write "Powers" and draw some stars, or a superhero stick figure with a cape, something that represents powers, around seven or eight o'clock, and say, "We come out of the pit after lunch, and we're creating new powers. We're solving problems. We've learned how to use the force. We're now solving problems, we're creating solutions, we're working on things together. The kind of tools we might be using here would be a customer experience map, a service blueprint; we might be designing, we might be prototyping a product. This is where we're actually getting cool results out of the meeting, but we still have to take that back to work."

9. Now write "The return" at around ten o'clock, and say, "That's part of the hero's journey, too, the return to ordinary life. We have to go back and cross the threshold again. This time is all about those powers that you're bringing back. We want to come back to the workplace with gifts. Think, new ideas, new thoughts. We want to spend some time thinking about, 'How do we take this back to work?'"

This is the part of the meeting where you make some time for the group to think together about how they are going to bring the new ideas from the meeting back into the organization. What am I going to do in my next meeting? How am I going to explain this to my team? You might actually work on the PowerPoint together or work on some documents that are about sharing what you actually did during the meeting.

10. At this point you can close the exercise by asking people if they have any thoughts and additions before you proceed with the meeting.

STRATEGY

This is a very powerful way to set up an agenda for a relatively large-scale session of work. Spend some time up-front on this. Draw it out and talk through it with key stakeholders, either before the meeting or at the beginning of the meeting. It is also a good litmus test to help you think through the goals of your meeting. If you can't answer questions like "What's the call to adventure? What are the problems we want to explore? What are the things that we want to find? What are the things that we want to bring back to work?" or if you can't imagine the team thinking through these questions at the beginning of a meeting, then it's legitimate to ask yourself, should we really have this meeting?

The Hero's Journey Agenda seems to work really well, not only for designing the agenda but for making sure you have all the major bases covered and creating positive energy and enthusiasm for the whole endeavor.

TIPS FOR PLAYING ONLINE

This can be drawn live by the facilitator in an online meeting, or drawn in advance and revealed in sequence or expanded on live.

The Hero's Journey Agenda was created by Dave Gray. It was inspired by the concept of the hero's journey, popularized by Joseph Campbell.

Heuristic Ideation Technique

In this simple game, participants use a matrix to generate new ideas or approaches to a solution. The game gets its name from three heuristics—or rules of thumb—of idea generation:

- A new idea can be generated from remixing the attributes of an existing idea.
- A new idea is best understood by describing its two essential attributes.
- The more different or surprising the combination of the two attributes, the more compelling the idea.

NUMBER OF PLAYERS

1–10

DURATION OF PLAY

15 minutes to 2 hours

HOW TO PLAY

To set up the game, participants decide on two categories of attributes that will define their matrix. For example, a toy manufacturer might look at its product line by type (vehicles, figures and dolls, puzzles, and instruments) and by type of play (racing, simulation, construction). Participants use these lists to populate a matrix, creating a grid of new possible combinations.

TOY IDEAS	Vehicles	Dolls	Puzzles	Instruments
Racing	Slot cars	Wind-up	Speed Puzzle	???
Simulation	Flight Simulator	Voodoo Doll??	???	"Join the Band"
Construction	Model Kit	Paintable	3-D	Build-an-Instrument

In playing the game, participants look across the cells for unusual or surprising combinations. These become the seeds of new ideas.

STRATEGY

Some combinations that at first seem absurd are worth examining more closely: a toy that combines puzzle pieces with a racing element might seem counterintuitive, but there are classic games built around that principle. After looking across the matrix for such combinations, a group may then develop fast prototypes or sketches that explore the possibilities. Consider that *G.I. Joe* came to life conceptually as a "doll for boys."

TIPS FOR PLAYING ONLINE

Use images instead of words to describe the combinations; use AI to make images that don't exist or to find additional combinations once all ideas have been exhausted.

The technique used in this game was documented by Edward Tauber in his 1972 paper, "HIT: Heuristic Ideation Technique—A Systematic Procedure for New Product Search."

History Map

OBJECT OF PLAY

Organizations naturally look ahead to anticipate progress. But the past can be as informative as the future. When an organization undergoes systemic or cultural change, documenting its history becomes an important process. By collecting and visualizing the components of history, we necessarily discover, recognize, and appreciate what got us where we are today. We can see the past as a guiding light or a course correction for our future. The History Map game shows you how to map moments and metrics that shaped your organization. It's also a great way to familiarize new people with an organization's history and culture during periods of rapid growth.

NUMBER OF PLAYERS

10–50

DURATION OF PLAY

30 minutes to 1.5 hours

HOW TO PLAY

1. Using flip-chart paper and markers, draw a continuous timeline along the bottom of several pages. Hang the paper end to end along a wall. Write the years under the timeline and include an appropriate starting point—don't go back 75 years if you don't need to. Choose a longer time increment, 5- or 10-year windows, if your organization has a long history, and be sure to leave enough space in between years for writing, drawing, and posting content. Leave extra space for years that you know people have more knowledge of or that were years of significant growth or change in the organization.

2. Ask each player to write their name and draw a self-portrait on a sticky note and post it on the wall above the year they joined the organization. As the participants approach the wall for post-ups, ask questions and encourage storytelling about first impressions of the company or why they joined. Note when you see "old-timers" approaching the wall. The richness of their experience can educate the group, so be sure to request that they share a story. Old-timers: never map a history without them.

Optional activity: Before they post the sticky notes, ask the group to stand up and form a line based on when they joined the organization. Let them discover who came on board when and let the line self-organize based on these discovery conversations. Ask for their thoughts and observations once the line is sorted.

3. Ask questions to the group about the following, and build the history map by plotting their answers using text and images:

   — Company successes

   — Lessons learned

   — Changes in leadership and vision

   — Culture shifts

   — Trends in the marketplace

   — Structural reorganizations

   — The ebb and flow of regulations

   — Shifts in revenue and number of employees

   — Major projects

   — Major investments

   — Etc.

4. If you're not comfortable drawing improvisationally, establish icons before the meeting to categorize events for easy visual recognition. (For example, you can use stars for successes, arrows for increases or decreases in revenue or employees, a toolbox for projects, etc.) As you add content, refer to items you're adding and ask open-ended questions about them to keep the conversation going.

5. Summarize the findings and ask the players what they learned and why they believe the history of an organization is important. Look for emergent patterns in the life of the organization and verbally relate the history to the future. Request the thoughts, feelings, and observations of the players.

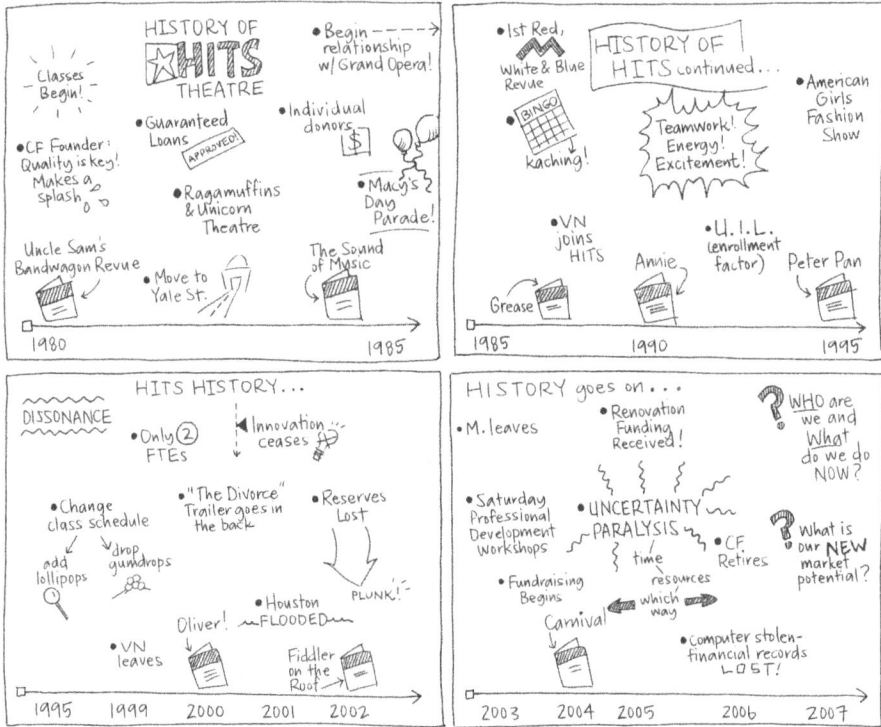

HISTORY OF ★HITS THEATRE

Classes Begin!

• CF Founder: Quality is key! Makes a splash!

• Guaranteed Loans APPROVED!

• Ragamuffins & Unicorn Theatre

Uncle Sam's Bandwagon Revue

• Move to Yale St.

• Begin relationship w/ Grand Opera!

• Individual donors $

• Macy's Day Parade!

The Sound of Music

1980 ——— 1985

• 1st Red, White & Blue Revue

• BINGO kaching!

• VN joins HITS

Grease

HISTORY OF HITS continued...

Teamwork! Energy! Excitement!

• American Girls Fashion Show

Annie

• U.I.L. (enrollment factor)

Peter Pan

1985 ——— 1990 ——— 1995

HITS HISTORY...

DISSONANCE

• Only 2 FTEs

◄ Innovation ceases

• Change class schedule

add lollipops   drop gumdrops

• "The Divorce" Trailer goes in the back

• Reserves Lost

• Houston FLOODED

Oliver!   PLUNK!

• VN leaves

Fiddler on the Roof

1995   1999   2000   2001   2002

HISTORY goes on...

• M. leaves

• Renovation Funding Received!

WHO are we and What do we do NOW?

• Saturday Professional Development Workshops

• UNCERTAINTY PARALYSIS

time   resources

• CF Retires

which way

What is our NEW market potential?

• Fundraising Begins

Carnival

• computer stolen— financial records LOST!

2003   2004   2005   2006   2007

STRATEGY

Mapping a history should be an enjoyable experience for the meeting leader and the participants. It's a time for storytelling, reflection, and appreciation of the life and experience of the organization. While you're helping the group document the history, set a supportive tone and encourage camaraderie, storytelling, and honesty—even about the hard times. And if the meeting runs relatively long, leave the history map posted so that the players can review it during a break and continue to breathe life into it. Let the story build even when you're not conducting the story session.

To make the creation of the map logistically easier for you as the meeting leader, follow these tips:

- Always be aware of the level of institutional memory in the meeting. If you're running a game that would work better with experienced employees, include them. If you're running a game that would work better with new eyes and fresh ideas, include newer employees. Pay attention to the knowledge and experience levels of the players as it relates to your desired outcome. Brand the history map with the company's logo and write a phrase beforehand that sums up the current vision and culture.

- Draw major events on the map beforehand to use as conversation starters.

- Use sticky notes for events where people are unsure of the dates or metrics so that you can log more accurate information later.

TIPS FOR PLAYING ONLINE

Create a board or space on the board for this game and pre-populate it with the company logo, important images, and digital elements reflecting the company's branding to help set the tone. Allow participants to bring in additional visual representations of achievements and other digital elements.

The History Map game is based on The Grove Consultants International's Graphic History Leader's Guide (*https://oreil.ly/m5aVi*).

Hopes & Dreams

OBJECT OF PLAY

Hopes & Dreams is an opening exercise that helps frame the time, prime minds, and reveal dynamics. The approach and opening question remain the same, but the second and third questions will vary depending on the goals of the session.

NUMBER OF PLAYERS

2–12 people

DURATION OF PLAY

15 minutes

HOW TO PLAY

Use a whiteboard or arrange flip-chart paper, and draw three nested boxes. You, as the facilitator, explain that the group will start with a quick game to get warmed up. Everyone should find their favorite color sticky note and a marker.

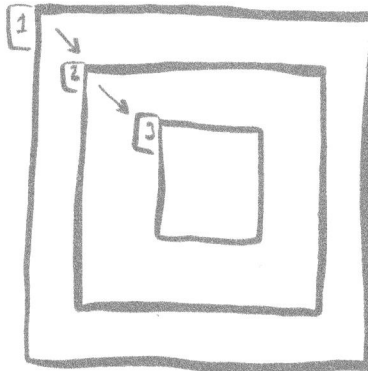

1. Invite players to warm up and write their name and primary role on a sticky note. Now, on a separate sticky note, what's their "secret sauce," "super power," or whatever unique magic they have, that makes them great in that role? Allow just a couple of minutes to respond, whatever is top of mind. When the group has their answers, invite them to post-up to the outer box, labeled "1."

2. Now, ask players to consider what they want to get out of the next year. What's top of mind? This is timed for three minutes. One idea per sticky note. (The time horizon could also be the end of the project, quarter, etc., if a short time horizon is more appropriate given the context of the session.) When the group has their answers, invite them to post-up to the outer box, labeled "2."

3. Finally, ask players to consider what they want to get out of the time together during the session. Give the group a couple of minutes, and then post-up answers to the core box, labeled "3."

4. Now, ask everyone to take a look at the responses. As a facilitator, highlight a few that stand out. Ask for clarification, watch for alignment, and anchor these things in your mind. Let the group know we all now have tangible ideas to measure against to know if we've been successful and hold each other accountable.

STRATEGY

Hopes & Dreams works well at a fast pace and is effective at setting the tone and providing important markers to refer back to. This game taps into appreciative inquiry, positive priming, and positive positioning. Asking broad questions about goals after this, combined with the time limitation, can help participants tap into their subconscious awareness without overthinking the complexities that come with actually bringing the ideas to fruition. As a facilitator, use the outer rings for context for the rest of the session and to get to know a group of people. Mentally refer to the core topics from step 3 throughout the session to help orient the group toward these objectives, and bring the group back to them at the end to collectively check in on whether they were accomplished and if further discussion is needed.

Make sure there is enough space in the center for at least one sticky note per participant. While the participants are generating ideas for each section, the facilitator reads the responses from the last round to get a feel for the group and the topics at hand.

TIPS FOR PLAYING ONLINE

This game works well online. Add a template to a shared board and play as you would offline. There is even more opportunity to use the ideas in the center box to inform and adapt the session to meet expectations and to check in on whether the groups' goals were accomplished or where additional follow-up might be needed.

The Hopes & Dreams game was created by Dave Gray and adapted by Danyelle Faulkner.

I Notice, I Wonder, It Reminds Me of...

OBJECT OF PLAY

I Notice, I Wonder, It Reminds Me of... is a structure and practice for honing observational skills and practicing active listening and appreciative inquiry. It's a thinking routine that can encourage deeper observations and connections. Participants are encouraged to develop curiosity and engage with their environment.

NUMBER OF PLAYERS

Two or more people

DURATION OF PLAY

20–30 minutes

HOW TO PLAY

Talk to the group about observational skills and how they translate to mindfulness through noticing the world around us at any given moment. If possible, go outside into nature. During a walk, instruct participants to pick an object that interests them.

1. Either individually, or in pairs, make observations about the object. Begin the sentence "I notice," and then describe what you observe with your senses.

2. Each individual shares for a few minutes, then begins to explore the object more. Begin the next sentence with "I wonder," and discuss what piques your curiosity.

3. Share for a few minutes, then make connections. Begin the next sentence with "It reminds me of" and discuss what it brings up for each individual.

STRATEGY

The I Notice, I Wonder, It Reminds Me of... game is based on powerful prompts to observe more deeply, ask better questions, and make interesting connections. Play this game in nature for the multisensory experience to engrain the observations in your mind.

TIPS FOR PLAYING ONLINE

This game can work well as a prompt during a break in an online meeting. Instead of taking a walk in the "natural world" outdoors with a partner, invite participants to explore the "natural world" of their remote working space. Can they find something to notice and appreciate in the environment they are so familiar with? After a defined period of time, split the group into pairs in breakout groups to discuss their observations.

The I Notice, I Wonder, It Reminds Me of... game is based on well-known thinking routines in educational curricula. The creator of the routine is unknown.

Let's Count

OBJECT OF PLAY

The goal of the activity is for an entire room to try to count to the number 10—out loud—one number at a time, with one person speaking at a time, without anyone talking over someone else.

NUMBER OF PLAYERS

Three or more

DURATION OF PLAY

5–7 minutes

HOW TO PLAY

1. Instruct the group that they will count, 1, 2, 3... and so on until 10.

2. Explain that the goal of the activity is for the entire room to try to count to the number 10—out loud—one number at a time without anyone talking over someone.

3. If two people say a number at the same time, the group gives one big clap; then we start over with "1."

4. The facilitation tone is positive and lighthearted. Keep going! Typical frustrations for players include going too fast, no one is listening, trying to establish dominance with voice, not getting a chance to play.

5. Once the group gets to 10, celebrate! Congratulate them on completing the game as a team.

6. Then, invite them to make observations. Who did they show up as in that activity? Did they take over, or sit back? How did the group come together to solve the problem? What cues were used to communicate?

STRATEGY

We all play certain roles in our interactions in the world and on teams. Let's Count helps prime for self-awareness. It's energizing and introduces playfulness while revealing personalities and group dynamics. Let's Count works well to open for sessions involving agility, collaboration, and strategy.

TIPS FOR PLAYING ONLINE

This game works well online, ideally with cameras on. Notice how layers of technology may require clearer communication, more silence, etc., and how teams naturally adapt to meet the objective in whatever environment they're in.

The Let's Count game is credited to Shannon Stott from Improv On | Off The Stage.

Low-Tech Social Network

OBJECT OF PLAY

The object of this game is to introduce event participants to each other by co-creating a mural-sized, visual network of their connections.

NUMBER OF PLAYERS

Large groups in an event setting

DURATION OF PLAY

25 minutes to create the first version of the network; the network remains up for the duration of the event and may be added to, changed, or studied throughout.

HOW TO PLAY

To set up the game, all participants will need a 5×8 index card and access to markers or something similar to draw their avatar. They will also need a substantial wall covered in butcher paper to create the actual network.

1. An emcee or leader for the event gives the participants clear instructions: "As a group, we are going to build the social network that is in the room right now. We're going to use this wall to do it. But first, we need to create the most fundamental elements of the network: who you are. Start by taking your card and drawing your avatar (profile picture) that you'll be uploading to the network. Save room on the bottom of the card for your name."

2. **Create the avatars.** After a short period of time (and probably some laughter and apologies for drawing ability), the participants should have their avatars and names created. At this point, the emcee may add a variation, which is to ask the group to also write two words on the card that "tag" who they are or what they're interested in at the event. If the Trading Cards game was played, ask players to get their trading cards and add information.

3. **Make the connections.** Next, the emcee directs participants to stand up and bring their cards and a marker to the butcher paper wall and then "upload" themselves by sticking their card to the wall.

4. The next task is simple: find the people you know and draw lines to make the connections. Label the lines if you can: "friends with" or "went to

school with" or "went mountain climbing with." This continues for a time and is likely to result in previously undiscovered links and new friends.

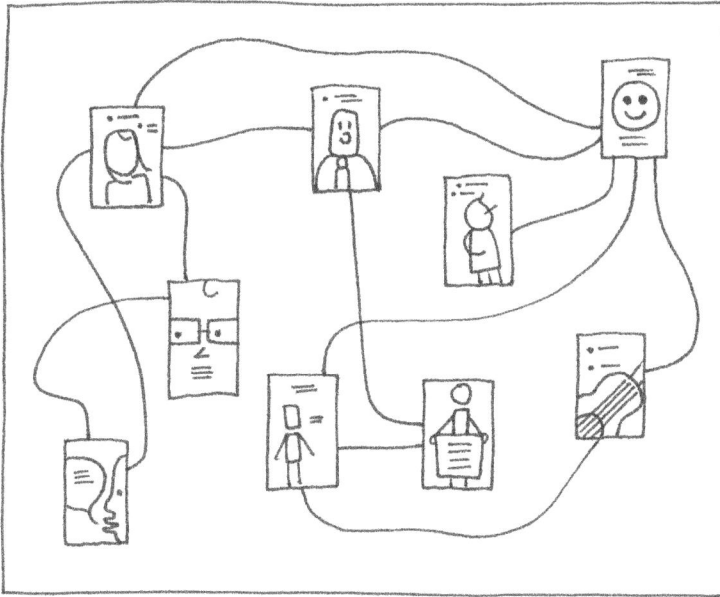

STRATEGY

The initial network creation will be somewhat chaotic and messy, resulting in a mural that has a lot of spaghetti lines. Over the course of the event, participants may browse the network. Encourage this, and see what new connections are made.

TIPS FOR PLAYING ONLINE

Use an online whiteboard and draw lines to make connections. Digital elements like links to more information, tagging, coding, comments, or embarrassing photos with your connections can further illuminate connections in the network. Invite participants to small breakout rooms after the initial network has been established to discuss the connections and add new ones. Repeat this a couple of times with new breakout rooms and then discuss notable revelations as a group.

Dave Gray created this game for the Meshforum Conference in 2006.

Mission Impossible

OBJECT OF PLAY

To truly create something new, we must challenge constraints. In this exercise, participants take an existing design, process, or idea and change one foundational aspect that makes it "impossible" in function or feasibility. For example:

- "How do we build a house...in a day?"
- "How do we create a mobile device...with no battery?"
- "What would a browser be...without an internet connection?"

NUMBER OF PLAYERS

Small groups

DURATION OF PLAY

45 minutes to 1 hour, depending on the size of the group

HOW TO PLAY

When a problem is interesting and important, we naturally rise to the occasion. To set up the exercise, develop a question in advance that engages both the emotional and the rational parts of the brain. A mobile device without batteries would be an engineering feat (rational) and a make-the-world-better proposition (emotional). Write down the question you choose for the group and explain the challenge.

For the next 30 minutes, working in pairs or small teams, the groups develop approaches to accomplishing the "impossible." They may consider these broad questions, or you can develop a set that is more specific to the challenge:

- What new benefits or features might emerge from this constraint?
- Why is this a typical constraint or requirement? Is it just a customary assumption?
- What are the core elements in conflict?
- Can the conflicting elements be eliminated, replaced, or altered in some way?

- Is there anything that can happen before or after to change the parts in conflict?
- Can time, space, materials, motion, or the environment have an effect?

At the end of the 30 minutes, groups present their concepts to each other. Following this, a reflective discussion about both common and uncommon approaches should yield a list of possible solutions to be explored further. Closing and next steps should include this follow-up work.

STRATEGY

This challenge works well for thinking through assumptions and obstacles in a product or a process. When a product is languishing and needs to be reimagined, this technique will help challenge basic assumptions about its design. In cases where processes are slow or overloaded, the "fire drill" question of "How would we do this in a day?" can be a powerful framing device.

TIPS FOR PLAYING ONLINE

Using the same instructions, send participants in pairs or small teams to breakout groups to discuss and present their concepts to each other. Give each breakout group a space on the board to capture their thoughts and present their concept to the group.

The Mission Impossible game is credited to James Macanufo.

Object Brainstorm

OBJECT OF PLAY

Objects play a special role in brainstorming. A tangible object helps externalize the thought process, just as sketching or role-play does, but often in a more immediate and concrete way. Because objects suggest stories about how they might be used, they make a great starting point for free association and exploration.

NUMBER OF PLAYERS

Any

DURATION OF PLAY

30 minutes or more

HOW TO PLAY

Before you can play, you will need to hunt down a collection of objects. Nominate yourself as the curator of your collection. It's worth considering what kind of investment you want to make. Although a trip to a secondhand store to find interesting (and cheap) items is a good start, if you are expecting to make a habit out of the exercise, it may be worth the time and expense to look for items more broadly.

Although you will find your own criteria for your collection, one rule of thumb is to collect "things that do things." Functional objects can offer more inspiration. Other things may make it into the collection based on their characteristics or personality, or simply because they are "fun." Here are some types of objects to consider collecting:

- Kitchen gadgets
- Hand tools
- Instruction manuals
- Functional packaging and dispensers
- Containers and compartments
- Sports equipment
- Toys and games

A good collection will evolve over time, and a good curator will get others involved in contributing to the cache of items.

Object brainstorming starts with a question, such as "How will the next generation of [fill-in-the-blank] work?" This question may ask participants to reimagine an existing product or invent something new.

1. Direct the group to explore the objects and to take some time to play with them. The objects may inspire participants to think about how a new thing could function or how it could look or feel. The long, hinged mouth of a stapler may suggest a new way to bend and fasten steel. A telescoping curtain rod might inspire thinking about a collapsible bicycle. Likewise, an object's personality, such as a rugged toolbox, might suggest how a laptop might be designed. Most objects explain themselves, and the results can be very intuitive; participants are likely to stumble on fully formed ideas.

2. After a set amount of time, the participants share their ideas, document them, and decide on next steps. This may be as simple as voting on an idea to pursue in more detail, or it may mean moving into another brainstorming exercise.

STRATEGY

One choice to make before an object brainstorm is whether to use a set of items or a single item. This changes the depth of focus: a group presented with a set will branch into a wider path of ideas, whereas a group presented with one item is "forced" into a deeper study of the object and associations from it, along the lines of random inputs or forced analogy. Try to use a set of items for larger groups and more divergent brainstorming, and a single item for smaller groups and more focused inquiry.

TIPS FOR PLAYING ONLINE

Populate an online whiteboard with pictures of objects in advance. Consider including some objects that are relevant to the topic of the meeting or objectives for the business for priming purposes.

The source for the Object Brainstorm game is unknown.

Pecha Kucha

OBJECT OF PLAY

These fast, structured talks enable people to share ideas quickly and with a mini-mum of distraction. In addition, it puts the pressure on the person conveying the information to do so in a concise and compelling fashion.

NUMBER OF PLAYERS

Any size, from a small working group to an auditorium full of people

DURATION OF PLAY

Can go anywhere from one to four hours. Total time varies widely based on the number of presenters.

HOW TO PLAY

Pecha Kucha is based on a simple idea: that by limiting the number of slides in a presentation and limiting the amount of time a presenter can spend on each slide, presentations will convey information concisely and at a rapid pace. The rule of Pecha Kucha is 20×20: Presenters are allowed 20 slides, and they can spend 20 seconds per slide.

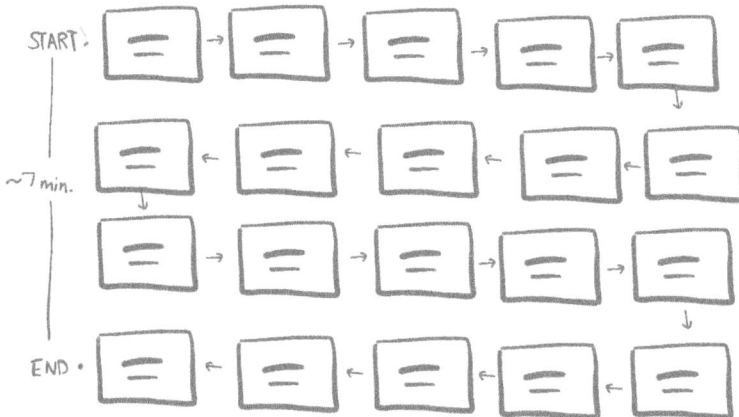

Images are forwarded automatically—they are not under the control of the speaker.

By tradition, Pecha Kucha nights are fun, informal evening events, but the concept will work just as well within any work group or team.

STRATEGY

The goal of these talks is to constrain presenters while keeping things fun. Often drinks and snacks are involved, and the right emcee can make a big difference in the quality of the experience. If you have a lot of people, spend some time on details, like picking a venue with good acoustic qualities and arranging for good sound and video equipment. Make sure not to give presenters control of their laptops!

TIPS FOR PLAYING ONLINE

Instruct participants to add their presentations to an online whiteboard or send them to the facilitator. The order of presenters can be determined using a game, arranged in a 2×2 format based on topic, self-selected, or random. The facilitator has control of advancing slides for the presenters. As the emcee, it's the facilitator's job to keep everything flowing according to a fast, structured pace.

Pecha Kucha (pronounced peh-CHA kuh-CHA—*Japanese for "chit chat") began as an event in Tokyo where designers could share their ideas. The Pecha Kucha presentation format was devised by Astrid Klein and Mark Dytham of Klein Dytham architecture. The first Pecha Kucha Night was held in Tokyo in their gallery, lounge, bar, club, and creative kitchen Super Deluxe in February 2003. Since then, Pecha Kucha has inspired similar events with some minor variations, including Talk20 (short presentations of 20 slides each) and Ignite (short presentations of 20 slides each, 15 seconds per slide).*

Pie Chart Agenda

OBJECT OF PLAY

Many meetings happen in an ad hoc or moment-to-moment fashion. They happen without a formal plan, agenda, or prep work—but despite this, they can be some of the most productive meetings we have. One characteristic that sets these meetings apart is a focused awareness of time constraints—for example, "We have 30 minutes; how should we spend the time?"

Sketching a pie chart agenda answers this question with speed and clarity. In some cases it takes less than a minute, and in the process, it brings into focus both the order and the significance of topics, where a simple list would fall short. What a pie chart agenda lacks in formality it makes up for in speed and flexibility.

NUMBER OF PLAYERS

Small group

DURATION OF PLAY

60–90 seconds

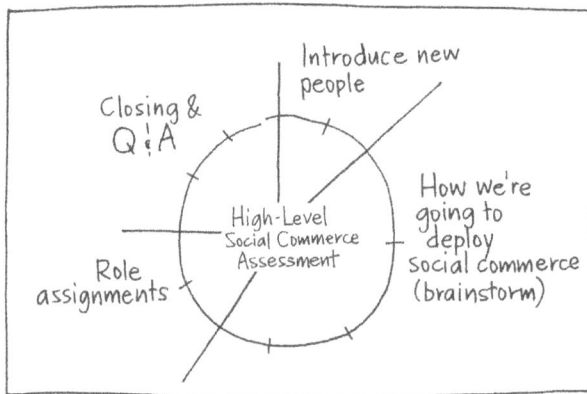

HOW TO PLAY

1. Draw a circle representing your "pie" of time. This may be on a white-board, a flip chart, or even a pad of paper. This circle represents the total amount of time the group has to spend on the objective.

2. Write the objective in the middle of the circle. For instance, it could be "Brainstorm approaches for dealing with Problem X."

3. The group then thinks about how they want to spend the time and adds these items to the clock in a sequence that makes sense for the task at hand, just as they would for a circle-formatted agenda. These are added around the outside.

4. To finish the chart, the group decides how much time they want to reserve for each item. This is captured on the pie chart, as though it were rough sections of a clock face. For instance: "We're going to spend a third of our time on this item, but we need to save the bulk of it for this, and the last five minutes talking about this."

5. Once the group has roughed in the plan and is in agreement, the clock starts ticking, and the meeting begins.

STRATEGY

How is this different from a list agenda? The focal point of a clock does two things. As a metaphor, it emphasizes the notion of time and expediency, which is vital in making ad hoc meetings productive. It also represents the agenda items as parts of the whole, weighted by importance and time to be spent on them. Items at the end of a list have a bad habit of falling off the list or being skipped entirely. When produced quickly and managed through the course of a meeting, a clock agenda helps ensure that the time is spent wisely.

TIPS FOR PLAYING ONLINE

The Pie Chart Agenda works as well online as it does in person and adds a dynamic and flexible element to the meeting space. Draw the agenda in advance and add to the online whiteboard, or draw it in real time for participants to view.

The Pie Chart Agenda is credited to Sunni Brown.

Plane Metaphor

OBJECT OF PLAY

The object of this game (also known as Airplane) is to get a project started while aligning team perspectives on different areas.

NUMBER OF PLAYERS

3–8 people

DURATION OF PLAY

30–90 minutes

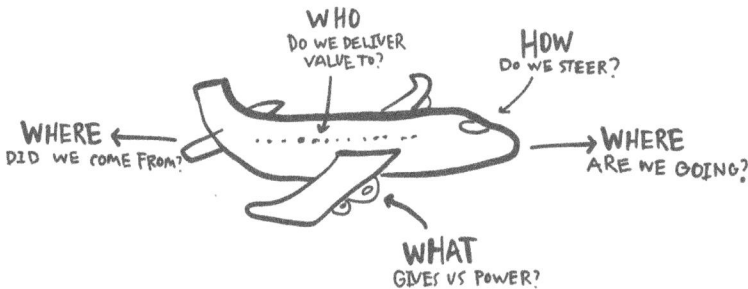

HOW TO PLAY

1. On a white space visible to the players (whiteboard/flip chart) draw a plane or print the template shown and stick it to the wall. The sticky notes, which will be written on, will be placed on the picture in the respective areas.

2. Start with these questions: Where do we come from? What is the reason we are here today? Which challenges do we have right now? Collect answers on sticky notes in silence. Take five minutes for this.

   Take silent time to read the sticky notes. Use red dots for voting for an in-person session. Take five minutes for this.

3. Next, ask the following questions: Who do we deliver value to? Which are the real users that will use what we deliver? Take five minutes to write down the main stakeholders.

4. Finally, ask: Where are we going? What is our project goal? Write one sentence that describes where you are going as a team, and take into

consideration the previous step by thinking about who you're delivering value for. Use the sticky notes and do this exercise in silence. Take five minutes for this.

5. Then, share what you wrote one after another. Take questions if they arrive. Take one minute per person for this.

6. Return to the questions. Now ask: How do we steer? What are the roles that we take in this project, and what we do need from each other? Take five minutes to write in silence on sticky notes, and then share your perspectives in two minutes per person.

7. Next, ask: What gives us the power? What would help us reach this goal together better? Which are the motivators for us? Take five minutes to write on sticky notes in silence. Then share what you wrote in one minute per person.

8. Decide upon the next steps after going through this metaphor. The next steps to help you reach the goal, taking into consideration the challenges you have, for whom you do the work, how are you organized to do it, and what gives you power. Take two minutes per person to share what you think, and the facilitator will write down the proposed steps for each person and then create a common way forward together.

STRATEGY

One way of organizing information is to formulate analogies and conceptual links with other things. The information can be represented by anything that helps you break out of habitual thinking patterns. We all create our reality when getting external information to our brains. We use our values, opinions, previous experiences, etc., to create our reality and react to the outside world based on this. A good metaphor comes with a set of associations that will change your perspective and help you think differently about a topic. This is why it helps your brain to create new associations and get new perspectives, what we call "own realities." This is also what the Plane Metaphor will do for you and your team. The Plane Metaphor can be versatile, but one of the main ideas of its usage is the kick-off of a project. Because it helps to bring all team member's perspectives together, it creates a sense of belongingness and team spirit while everyone is "flying" together toward the same goal.

TIPS FOR PLAYING ONLINE

Include the airplane visual and reveal one aspect at a time. At the end of the game or the end of each aspect, divide participants into breakout groups to discuss and bring the most intriguing ideas to the surface. Use the voting feature to prioritize your challenges and check which ones are the most important for you as a team right now.

The Airplane game template was created by Andra Stefanescu.

Poster Session

OBJECT OF PLAY

If a picture is worth a thousand words, what would 50 pictures be worth? What if 50 people could present their most passionate ideas to each other—without any long-winded explanation? A poster session accelerates the presentation format by breaking it down, forcing experts to boil up their ideas and then present back to each other via simple images.

NUMBER OF PLAYERS

10–100 people

DURATION OF PLAY

20 minutes to develop posters, an unlimited time to browse

HOW TO PLAY

The goal of a poster session is to create a set of compelling images that summarize a challenge or topic for further discussion. Creating this set might be an "opening act" that then sets the stage for choosing an idea to pursue, or it might be a way to get indexed on a large topic. The act of creating a poster forces experts and otherwise passionate people to stop and think about the best way to communicate the core concepts of their material, avoiding the popular and default "show up and throw up."

To set up, everyone will need ample supplies for creating their poster. Flip charts and markers are sufficient, but consider bringing other school supplies: stickers, magazines for cutting up, and physical objects.

Start the game play by first framing the challenge. In any given large group, you could say the following: "There are more good ideas in everyone's heads than there is time to understand and address them. By creating posters that explain the ideas, we'll have a better idea of what's out there and what we might work on."

The participants' task is to create a poster that explains their topic. There are two constraints:

- **It must be self-explanatory.** If you gave it to a person without walking her through it, would she understand?

- **It must be visual.** Words and labels are good, but text alone will not be enough to get people's attention, or help them understand.

When creating their posters, participants may be helped by thinking about three kinds of explanation:

- Before and after: Describe "why" someone should care in terms of drawing the today and tomorrow of the idea.

- System: Describe the "what" of an idea in terms of its parts and their relationships.

- Process: Describe the "how" of an idea in terms of a sequence of events.

Give participants 20 minutes to create their posters. When they have finished, create a "gallery" of the images by posting them on the wall.

Instead of elaborate presentations, ask the group to circulate and walk the gallery. Some posters will attract and capture more attention than others. From here, it may be worthwhile to have participants dot vote (see "Dot Voting" on page 185) or "vote with their feet" to decide what ideas to pursue further.

STRATEGY

As a variation, the posters may be created in small groups. In this case, it's important for the group to have decided ahead of time what their topic will be and to give more time to come to a consensus on what they will draw and how they will draw it.

On a smaller scale, a group may do this around a conference table. A small group of experts may create posters to explain their different points of view to each other at the start of a meeting, to make their models of the world, their vocabulary, and their interests clear and explicit. Twenty minutes spent in this way may save the group from endless discussion later in their process.

TIPS FOR PLAYING ONLINE

Create a virtual game space like the room setup described earlier. Invite participants to create their posters using images, drawings, diagrams, videos, etc. Give everyone time at the end to "walk the gallery" and look at everyone's work in small breakout groups or as a full team. Have them dot vote or add their avatar to the poster and have a group discussion about their observations to decide what ideas to pursue further.

The Poster Session game is based on academic poster sessions, in which authors of papers that are not ready for publication share their ideas in an informal, conversational group.

Pre-Mortem

OBJECT OF PLAY

Often in projects, the learning is all at the wrong end. Usually after things have already gone horribly wrong or off-track, members of the team gather in a "post-mortem" to sagely reflect on what bad assumptions and courses of action added up to disaster. What makes this doubly unfortunate is that those same team members, somewhere in their collective experience, may have seen it coming.

A Pre-Mortem is a way to open a space in a project at its inception to directly address its risks. Unlike a more formal risk analysis, the Pre-Mortem asks team members to directly tap into their experience and intuition, at a time when it is needed most, and it's potentially the most useful.

NUMBER OF PLAYERS

Any, but typically small teams will have the most open dialogue

DURATION OF PLAY

Depends on the scope of an effort; allow up to five minutes for each participant

HOW TO PLAY

A Pre-Mortem is best conducted at the project's kickoff, with all key team members present and after the goals and plan have been laid out and understood. The exercise starts with a simple question: "What will go wrong?" though it may be elevated in phrasing to "How will this end in disaster?"

This is an opportunity for the team to reflect on their collective experience and directly name risks or elephants lurking in the room. It's a chance to voice concerns that might otherwise go unaddressed until it's too late. A simple discussion may be enough to surface these items among a small team; in a larger group, a Post-Up session or list generation may be needed.

To close the exercise, the list of concerns and risks may be ranked or voted on to determine priority. The group then decides what actions need to be taken to address these risks; they may bring these up as a part of ongoing meetings as the project progresses.

STRATEGY

Conducting a Pre-Mortem is deceptively simple. At the beginning of a project, the forward momentum and enthusiasm are often at their highest; these conditions do not naturally lend themselves to sharing notions of failure. By conducting a Pre-Mortem, a group deliberately creates a space to share their past learning, at a time when they can best act on it.

TIPS FOR PLAYING ONLINE

Create a virtual template for the Pre-Mortem. Invite participants to brainstorm their responses. Create an affinity map and review the themes, and then lead a discussion about the primary concerns. At the end of the discussion, make sure the key points are visible to refer to.

The Pre-Mortem game is credited to James Macanufo.

Rose, Thorn, and Bud

OBJECT OF PLAY

This game is used to quickly frame and gain perspective on positives, negatives, and opportunities. Rose, Thorn, and Bud is a quick and simple team exercise that can be performed at the start of a group meeting. The idea is to evaluate a project, a team task, or a status check on your day by having each team member come up with a Rose (positive highlight), Thorn (struggle or challenge), and Bud (opportunity for improvement). The goal of this activity is to open up discussion among team members.

NUMBER OF PLAYERS

2–200 people

DURATION OF PLAY

10–15 minutes

HOW TO PLAY

1. In a space visible to the players, draw or post an image of a rose.

2. Write "Rose" next to the rose. Beginning with the Roses, give participants three minutes to brainstorm responses. What are the positive highlights? Post responses.

3. Next, write "Thorn" next to the thorn. Give participants three minutes to brainstorm responses. Thorns are usually easily identified. One idea per sticky note. What are the pain points or challenges to navigate?

4. Finally, shifting tone, write "Bud" next to the bud. Thank everyone for sharing the positives and negatives and invite them to now consider the possibilities that await. Give everyone three minutes to brainstorm the buds. What opportunities do they see?

5. Take time to discuss observations as a group at the end. Did any themes emerge? Was anything surprising? What does it inspire you to do next?

STRATEGY

This is a simple and versatile framework for coding ideas and opinions as positive, negative, and opportunities. Color code by category to facilitate meaning making and consider emergent patterns in the observations.

TIPS FOR PLAYING ONLINE

Add a visual template to an online whiteboard. Ask participants to brainstorm their responses to each section. Take a few moments to review responses and highlight notable observations as a group. If anything in particular stands out, designate it visually to record the discussion and bring more meaning to the visual.

The source for Rose, Thorn, and Bud is unknown.

Show and Tell

OBJECT OF PLAY

You may remember Show and Tell from kindergarten—kids bring their favorite thing to school and tell the class what it means to them. Well, there's more intelligence in that activity than you may have realized. Meeting leaders can conduct Show and Tell to get a better understanding of stakeholders' perspectives on any topic—a project, a restructuring, a shift in the company's vision, a product, and so forth. Show and Tell lets employees use objects for storytelling around things that are important to the organization.

NUMBER OF PLAYERS

5–15 people

DURATION OF PLAY

20–45 minutes

HOW TO PLAY

1. A few days in advance of a meeting, ask the players to bring an artifact for Show and Tell. The instructions are to bring something that from their perspective represents the topic that'll be discussed at the meeting. If possible, tell them to keep the item hidden until it's their turn to show it.

2. In a white space visible to all the players, write the topic for this play and draw a picture of it. You can do this beforehand if you prefer. When everyone is assembled with their show piece, ask for volunteers to go first.

3. Pay attention to each player's explanation of why they thought an item represented or reminded them of the topic. Listen for how the item is similar to or different from the topic, and listen for emotive descriptions of the item. Write each contribution in the available white space, and if you can, draw a simple visual of the show piece the person brought next to their comments.

4. Summarize what you've captured and let the group absorb any shared themes of excitement, doubt, or concern. Ask follow-up questions about the content to generate further conversation.

Optional activity: Assign a player to be the show photographer. Take snapshots of each person telling their story and create a collage of the images afterward. Hang it in a communal space in the office for continued storytelling, especially if this is a topic that you want the players to continue talking about.

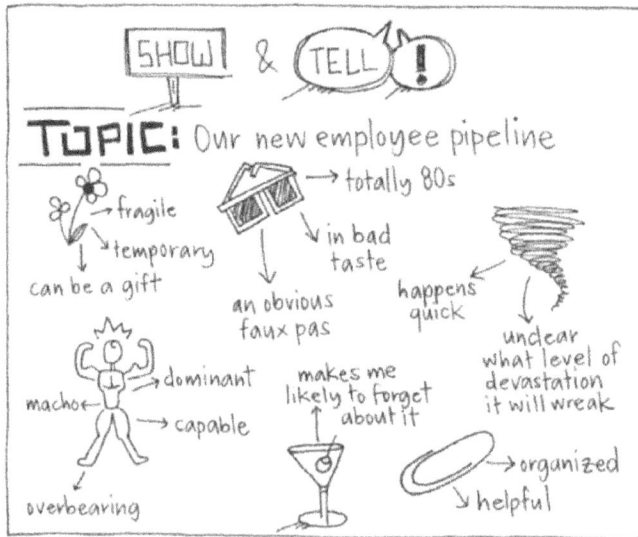

STRATEGY

Show and Tell taps into the power of metaphors to let players share their assumptions and associations around a topic. If you see multiple show pieces that don't exactly represent delight around a topic, that's a signal that the players may have some concerns that need to be addressed. Don't overanalyze the objects; pay more attention to the way the players describe the parallels to the topic. As the team leader, encourage and applaud honesty during the stories, and write down every point that players make that seems important to them. Keep the rest of the players quiet while someone is showing and telling.

For your part, if you feel intimidated by drawing a representation of a player's item in the white space, get through it: attempt to draw it anyway and let the group tease you about your efforts. Show and Tell can be a vulnerable activity for the players—particularly the introverted players—so show some team spirit by being vulnerable yourself.

TIPS FOR PLAYING ONLINE

The artifacts presented can be used throughout the session and future sessions to represent the person and build an association.

The Show and Tell game is inspired by the well-known grade school exercise.

Show Me Your Values

OBJECT OF PLAY

Employees' perceptions of a company's values, whether they're conscious or not, contribute to their morale and their willingness to go the extra mile to support the mission. To get a sense of how employees perceive the values that drive an organization, an initiative, a system-wide change, or any other topic, play Show Me Your Values.

NUMBER OF PLAYERS

5–15 people

DURATION OF PLAY

30–45 minutes

HOW TO PLAY

1. Before the meeting, decide on the topic around which you want players to share stories. Set up a flat surface area on which you can write and they can post their images. Write the name of the topic in this area. This could be a project, division, goal, team assessment exercise, the overall company vision, etc.

2. Tell the players that the goal of the exercise is twofold. First, they'll describe in images and icons what they perceive to be the values underlying the topic. Next, they'll share a work-related story that's indicative of those values. (For example, an image of a turtle may represent patience and longevity, so the player may share an anecdote in which an attractive but high-risk project was not pursued.) Most importantly, when you introduce this game, encourage people to share the values they perceive as honestly as they can. Tell them that it's OK to believe that an underlying organizational value is territoriality and to represent that with an image of a lion. Not only is this behavior appropriate, but it's also desirable—since beliefs that drive behavior often go unstated in public but are repeated and spread through huddles within the organization.

3. Give the players 10 minutes to find images that represent their perception of the underlying values. Realize that some players will think immediately of a value representing a topic and will hunt through the icons and images until they find a suitable representation for what they described. Others will surf the images, looking for something that resonates with a vague

notion they have in their minds and name it afterwards. Either approach is suitable.

Optional activity: Ask the players to find images that represent what the values are not. So, if a player believes expediency is not one of the values around a project, they may choose the aforementioned turtle as a representative image.

4. Ask the players to post-up their image(s) in the designated area and then quietly reflect on a story associated with the value(s) they represented.

5. Next, ask for volunteers to take turns sharing both their images and their associated story. As people share, if someone expresses difficulty in thinking of a story to match their image, give them more time (or let them bow out completely) and move on to someone else to offer a story related to their image.

6. Pay attention as the players describe the values they perceive and write them in the space next to the appropriate image.

7. Go over the values you captured and ask the players to look for overlaps and gaps in their perception. Ask follow-up questions about the content and stories to generate further conversation. Let the group absorb and discuss the perceptions they share as well as those they don't.

STRATEGY

A notable benefit of using pictures to elicit value statements and stories is that imagery is simultaneously one step removed from a straight, verbal declaration, and one step deeper than what you may get when you ask players to share their "intellectual" thoughts. And using pictures gives the players a sort of comfort zone in which to express themselves, since they can choose pictures that represent the entire spectrum of comedy and tragedy around a topic.

So, if someone prefers truth through humor, they can find images that allow them to use it. And if someone else prefers truth through hyperbole, well, they have that option too. Let people be creative during the storytelling section of the game. If two or more participants want to share a story together, encourage them to do so. They can even go so far as to role play an event that unfolded. Your job is to create a space in which people can say something that may be taboo but that *everyone* is thinking.

TIPS FOR PLAYING ONLINE

Show Me Your Values works well in an online whiteboard. Depending on the group size, divide into breakout rooms of 3–5 people. In advance of step 5, bring everyone back together and invite all participants to review everyone's answers on the board.

The source for the Show Me Your Values game is unknown.

Spectrum Mapping

OBJECT OF PLAY

Spectrum Mapping is designed to reveal the diversity of perspectives and options around any given topic and to organize them into a meaningful spectrum. This game gives players an opportunity to express their views without having to assert them vocally or even take ownership of them in front of the group. It's valuable because it unearths information that plays a role in attitudes and behaviors that otherwise may not be visible.

NUMBER OF PLAYERS

5–15 people

DURATION OF PLAY

30 minutes to 1 hour

HOW TO PLAY

1. Before the game begins, brainstorm topics around which you want insight from the group. Write each topic on a sticky note.

2. Introduce Spectrum Mapping by stating that the purpose of the game is to illuminate the team's range of perspectives and to organize those perspectives into a continuum so that everyone gets a view of it.

3. Post the topic sticky notes in a column in the approximate middle of a space on the wall visible to the players. Ask everyone to silently generate a point-of-view preference option around that topic and write it on a sticky note. They are welcome to offer more than one.

4. Ask the players to come to the wall and post their sticky notes in a horizontal line on either side of the topic. Reassure them that the relationships between the sticky notes aren't yet of interest.

5. Once the sticky notes are posted, work with the group to sort them into a horizontal range of ideas. Sticky notes that express similar perspectives or options should go next to each other. Sticky notes that seem to be outliers should stand alone; they may sometimes end up defining the limits of the range. The bookends of the spectrum may be described in advance or emerge based on the response of the group and go to unexpected places.

6. Continue sorting until the group agrees that the sticky notes are in their appropriate places on the horizontal line.

7. Repeat this process if you have more topics to evaluate.

Once the spectrum for each topic has been laid along the horizon, ask for observations and insights on the lay of the land. Discuss the findings with the group and ask if any perspective or option has been excluded. If so, add it and re-sort as necessary.

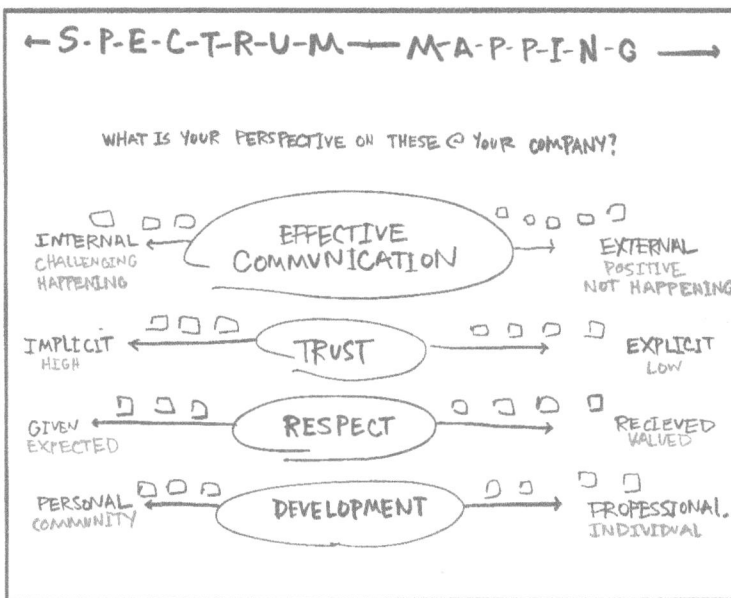

STRATEGY

Not only does Spectrum Mapping reveal individual ideas around important topics, but it tells you *how many* members of your group have certain types of views and where their endpoints lie. After Spectrum Mapping, the players are likely to discern a more holistic view of where they stand. In other words, Spectrum Mapping indicates whether the group tends to lean a certain way—perhaps it's fiscally conservative, oriented toward growth, or reticent about change. Either way, as a team leader, it's good to be aware of the group's natural inclination and openly acknowledge it to enhance future team building, problem solving, and planning.

Assure the players that they're free to write up honest perspectives and preferences around a topic even if those preferences may be considered outlandish by the other players. Tell them that outlier ideas still make it onto the continuum. This play is about mapping and displaying the spectrum, not evaluating ideas for validity, innovation, or popularity. This game has the effect of letting groups see if their behavior skews too far to one side or whether they're taking a reasonable approach when a radical one may be better.

TIPS FOR PLAYING ONLINE

This game translates well online using online collaboration tools. Establish the board in advance and invite participants to add to the spectrum as it is described.

The source for the Spectrum Mapping game is unknown.

Squiggle Birds

OBJECT OF PLAY

Squiggle Birds is a quick exercise that you can use to get people stretching their visual thinking muscles. It takes about five minutes and quickly, clearly demonstrates how little effort is really required to make meaningful, easy-to-read images. The main point of the demonstration is that our minds are already pattern-making machines, and very little drawing is actually required to convey an idea. The mind will fill in the rest.

NUMBER OF PLAYERS

5–50 people

DURATION OF PLAY

3–5 minutes

HOW TO PLAY

1. Ask all participants to make squiggly marks on their page. Draw random squiggles around the page of various sizes and shapes.

2. Participants should then transform them into birds with a beak, an eye, bird feet, and a triangle for a tail and observe how each squiggle bird comes to life.

3. Ask the participants to hold up their drawings for others to see, and reflect on how our brains use marks to interpret and create meaning.

STRATEGY

At the start of creative group sessions, it is often important to help people ease their inhibitions and build a bit of creative self-confidence. People's creativity is often held back because they think they can't draw. Squiggle Birds (*https://oreil.ly/ UJEbA*) demonstrates how easily anyone can draw to represent an idea. In the process, it switches on their curiosity and dissipates self-doubts.

TIPS FOR PLAYING ONLINE

Invite players to draw on paper. Once the game is complete, invite participants to take a photo of their squiggle birds and add it to a collaboration space. Or, if players are more comfortable with this format, have them draw digitally and add an image to the board.

The Squiggle Birds game is credited to Chris Glynn.

Stakeholder Analysis

OBJECT OF PLAY

The concept of a "stakeholder" has deep roots in business and managerial science, appearing as early as the 18th century in reference to any holder of a bet or wager in an endeavor. The term now has come to mean anyone who can significantly impact a decision, or who may be impacted by it. At the beginning of projects big and small, it may benefit a team to conduct a stakeholder analysis to map out who their stakeholders are—so that they can develop a strategy for engaging them.

NUMBER OF PLAYERS

Any; key members of a team who have a collective awareness of all aspects of a project

DURATION OF PLAY

30 minutes to 1 hour, depending on the depth of the analysis

HOW TO PLAY

There are a number of variations in mapping out stakeholders, and a team may change or add variables to the equation, depending on the circumstances.

The most common way to map is by power and interest; one variant is referred to as a "responsibility assignment matrix," or "RACI" matrix.

- **Power** describes a stakeholder's level of influence in the system—how much they can direct or coerce a project and other stakeholders.

- **Interest** describes the degree to which a stakeholder will be affected by the project.

By setting up a matrix with these two axes, you are ready to begin.

Step 1: Create a list of stakeholder groups

If you do not already have a list of the stakeholders, now is the time to generate it. By using Post-Up or a similar method, create your set of stakeholders by answering these questions:

- Who will be impacted by the project?
- Who will be responsible or accountable for the project?
- Who will have decision authority on the project?

- Who can support the project?
- Who can obstruct the project?
- Who has been involved in this type of project in the past?

A typical list of stakeholders may include these groups:

- The customer, user, or beneficiary of a project
- The team or organizations doing the work
- The project's managers
- The project's sponsors, who finance the project
- Influential parties or organizations
- Suppliers or vendors
- Investors or owners
- The local community impacted

Step 2: Map the list on the grid

After generating the list of stakeholders, the group maps them into the matrix based on their relative power and interest. If the stakeholders have been captured on sticky notes, the group should be able to place them into the matrix directly.

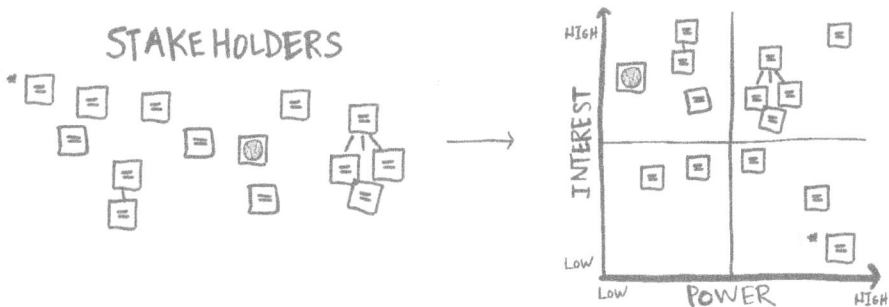

Step 3: Develop a strategy and share it broadly

After each stakeholder has been placed into the matrix, the group will want to discuss specific strategies for engaging their stakeholders. They may ask:

- Who needs to be informed of what, and when?
- Who needs to be consulted about what, and when?
- Who is responsible for engaging each stakeholder, and when and how will they do it?

Creating this draft is a good first step. If the project scope or number of stakeholders is large, it is advisable to share the analysis broadly and transparently with everyone involved. This validates the analysis by filling any gaps, and in the process, it clarifies where people fit in.

STRATEGY

Along with a RACI matrix and other "people + project" activities, Stakeholder Analysis is a basic framing tool for any project. For leaders and managers, it clearly scopes out who has what level of input and interest in a project and can help to align decisions appropriately.

TIPS FOR PLAYING ONLINE

Create a 2×2 game board for Stakeholder Analysis and play as a group, as you would offline. Then, discuss the stakeholders and their positions in breakout groups of 3–7, depending on the group size.

Although it has a long history, the source for the Stakeholder Analysis game is unknown.

Stinky Fish

OBJECT OF PLAY

The Stinky Fish game is used to share concerns and create an environment to "clear the air" for open sharing. The stinky fish is a metaphor for "that thing you carry around but you don't like to talk about; but the longer you hide it, the stinkier it gets." By putting stinky fish (fears and anxieties) on the table, participants begin to relate to each other, become more comfortable sharing, and identify a clear area for development and learning.

NUMBER OF PLAYERS

2–40 people

DURATION OF PLAY

15–30 minutes

HOW TO PLAY

1. Introduce the purpose of the game in your own words and explain that the purpose is to explore and share individual worries and anxieties about the future as a way to start a conversation and begin to confront or overcome them.

2. Give participants five minutes to write down their personal stinky fish for the context of the meeting. Post-up the responses and invite the group to reflect on their responses.

3. Ask participants to share thoughts individually as they feel compelled. Close the exercise by thanking participants and reminding them that in a world of constant change, uncertainty and fear are normal. Explain that by naming the fears, "putting fish on the table" is an important step to confronting and dealing with it. The goal isn't to give advice or fix the problems in the moment, but to have them expressed and acknowledged with a plan to follow up on anything separately where necessary.

STRATEGY

Stinky Fish will invite participants to connect with their fears and concerns. Extra care should be taken by the facilitator to care for participants and close the loop, bringing the group back to an emotionally positive place. This is about clearing the air so everyone can move forward.

TIPS FOR PLAYING ONLINE

Create a visual template of the fish to populate on a shared board. Give participants time to add to the board in step 2. Close the game with a group discussion and by expressing appreciation to everyone for sharing their thoughts.

Stinky Fish is credited to Åsa Silfverberg and based on the overview by Hyper Island.

Trading Cards

OBJECT OF PLAY

People sometimes grumble about the dreaded "icebreaker," but humans are like cars: we perform better when we're warmed up. This meeting starter is great because (1) it lets people self-define, (2) it gives people a "personality" outside the typical work environment, (3) it gives participants quick snapshots of multiple players (since they see many cards as they're being passed around), and (4) it creates memorable visuals that give people conversation pieces as the meeting progresses.

NUMBER OF PLAYERS

Unlimited

DURATION OF PLAY

10–15 minutes

HOW TO PLAY

1. Give the meeting participants access to large-scale index cards and markers.

2. Ask them to take 5–10 minutes to create a personal "trading card"—one that includes a self-portrait, a nickname for their "player," and one thing about themselves that people in the meeting aren't likely to know.

3. Have the players pass the trading cards around the room in no particular manner or order. Tell them to read each trading card that falls into their hands and hold onto one they might ask a question about. They can keep passing until they find one.

4. Ask for volunteers to read their player's name and nickname, then, they'll ask that person a question related to the little-known fact on their card.

5. Let the player who was chosen elaborate on the question they were asked. The player can then opt to ask the person whose card they're holding a question, or they can pass and you can request another volunteer.

6. Keep going around until the players appear to be sufficiently warmed up. But try to keep the play at 15 minutes long or less.

STRATEGY

During this game, there really is no harm and, ahem, no foul. Help meeting participants integrate before the meeting starts.

TIPS FOR PLAYING ONLINE

Invite participants to draw their cards on a piece of paper and hold them up to the group. Then, add a photo to the digital whiteboard. Create a template and add to an online whiteboard. This could segue well into the Low-Tech Social Network.

The source of the Trading Cards game is unknown.

Visual Agenda

OBJECT OF PLAY

In a typical meeting, people walk in and are handed a typed sheet of paper that shows them the meeting agenda. It usually includes the date, the meeting topics, and the time allotted for each topic. Sometimes it acknowledges who is presenting or leading the topic. Most participants give this piece of paper about two seconds of their time. The standard approach for making agendas is perfectly fine for quick meetings among people who work together regularly. But for meetings that matter, for meetings that take a good amount of people's time and attention, and for meetings that bring together people from across disciplines or departments, visual agendas work much better.

When you create a visual agenda, people look it over and linger on it longer. They actually read the desired outcomes and review the steps they'll take to get there. The energy level rises when participants walk into a room and see a large, colorful, hand-drawn display. People start to talk about it with each other. A visual agenda implies that the day might be interesting; it sends a signal to the group that the meeting matters. Visuals also help participants recall later what the meeting was about.

HOW TO PLAY

1. Establish a desired outcome(s) for the meeting and craft an agenda that will get the group there. Choose a visual framework that represents the tone or theme of the meeting.

2. Draw the agenda in a nontraditional and creative way on a large sheet of paper or display it using presentation software.

STRATEGY

A visual agenda is a gesture to the group that you spent time before you took up theirs. So, take the time to build a good roadmap to your outcomes. And when drawing or creating the visual agenda, think of metaphors that represent a theme of the meeting. Draw pictures that symbolize the company's mission or work. If you're working at a vacation rental company, draw a beach scene with each footstep as a stage of the agenda. Draw a forest scene if you're working at an environmental organization; a circuit board if you're with a tech firm.

Brand the agenda in creative ways. If you've got copywriting chops, think of interesting phrases to describe each stage of the meeting. And if you have neither copywriter nor artistic instincts, ask someone who plans to attend the meeting to help you. Creating a visual agenda is a small investment in a meeting, but it offers a good ROI.

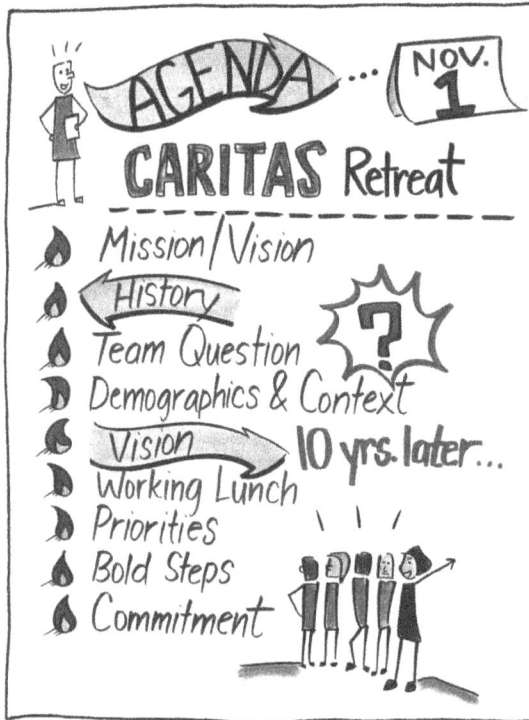

TIPS FOR PLAYING ONLINE

Post the agenda in a collaboration space that's visible to everyone, create an agenda in real time with sticky notes (as shown in the following image), live draw on a shared board, post an image to the chat, etc., to set the tone and intention.

The Visual Agenda game was inspired by The Grove's practice of creating visual agendas before meeting.

9

Games for Exploring

Rarely do we find exactly what we were looking for. The end result often emerges in surprising ways. Games that explore are for navigating, combining, interpreting, and otherwise working with ideas to discover something new.

Exploring games make and break patterns. In some cases they ask participants to create forms, and in others they ask them to split them apart. In most cases, exploring games are best used "in the middle" of an activity—before deciding and committing to action, but after the space has been framed and opened.

If we only opened raw ideas and then closed in on our favorites, we wouldn't create anything new. Games that explore chart the space in between.

The 4Cs

OBJECT OF PLAY

Simple information-splicing games come in handy because, in an intentional way, they disrupt the standard ways we break down topics. The 4Cs game is a quick way to gather and organize information about any subject using four common key concepts.

NUMBER OF PLAYERS

5–20 people

DURATION OF PLAY

30 minutes to 1 hour

HOW TO PLAY

1. Before the meeting, decide on a topic you want the players to explore and draw a 2×2 matrix in a large white space in the meeting room.

2. Write the following categories in each box of the matrix: "Components," "Characteristics," "Characters," and "Challenges." Then, draw something that represents each category.

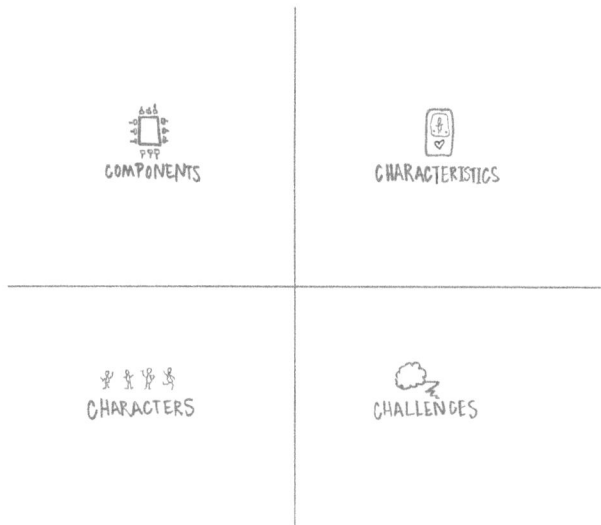

3. Tell the players that this game is about exploring and sharing what they know about the topic based on the 4Cs. Define the terms of each "C":

— **Components** are parts of the topic. For example, a component of a social commerce strategy might be responsive content. Components of a distribution channel might be shipping logistics.

— **Characteristics** are features of the topic. For example, speed of response is a characteristic of a social commerce strategy. A characteristic of shipping logistics might be an inefficient use of fuel.

— **Challenges** are obstacles associated with the topic.

— **Characters** are people associated with the topic.

You don't have to use four "Cs" to conduct this game. You can be creative with other letters that are company or team-specific. Use four "Ds" to create your matrix and name them "Discover," "Design," "Damage," and "Deliver." Just make sure the categories you create will give you a meaningful way to look at a topic of interest.

4. Divide the group into four teams of roughly equal size. (A group of 5–7 people can work as one team.) Give them access to sticky notes and markers.

5. Assign a different "C" to each team and tell them their goal is to collect information about that "C," specific to the topic. Tell them they'll have three minutes to plan an information-gathering strategy, five minutes to collect the information, and three minutes to analyze and organize it. Also explain that they should collect information from as many people in the room as possible.

6. Announce the start of the planning period, and let the teams converse with one another. At the end of three minutes, call time.

7. Tell the players they can use their sticky notes and markers; then kick off the five-minute information-gathering stage and stay out of the way. This stage of the game involves a lot of interviewing and moving around the room. Tell the players when the five minutes are up.

8. Start the three-minute information-analysis stage. In this stage, the players should analyze their data, organize it in a meaningful way, and post the contents in the matrix on the wall.

9. Close the game by asking for volunteers to present their group's findings. After each group presents, ask clarifying questions (Is there anything missing? Do these items mean the same thing?), and encourage the others to reflect and add more information. You can also ask players if they want to share thoughts on their team's information-gathering process—to discuss what worked and what could have worked better.

STRATEGY

The 4Cs is deliberately quick (and slightly chaotic) to avoid a situation in which people simply list information about what they know related to the topic. In this game, the players gathering information may already have a lot of detail about the topic, but they'll inevitably learn something new through the process of interviewing others. Interviewing allows people who may not interact much the opportunity to do so. Because the time is short, they won't dive into a substantive conversation; nevertheless, the chances are higher that someone will take away new content or a new perspective based on an interview.

Avoid shortchanging the closing activity, even though it may be tempting to give the group more time to gather and analyze their content (and some of them will request it). The last stage of the game is important to spend time on because it allows the group to reflect on the content together, as a sort of group mind. If the meeting is based on a familiar topic, there will likely be many players who think they have a corner on information around it, so it's important to discuss the 4Cs as a whole group. It exposes more ground to more people and invites a discussion that can bring new life to old content.

TIPS FOR PLAYING ONLINE

Add a 2×2 template to your game board and include the 4Cs. This game transfers online using breakout groups in step 4 and 6. Divide the group into four teams for breakouts. In step 7, switch the breakout groups 2–3 times depending on the group size, to allow more people to connect with each other. Rather than 1:1 sharing and walking around the room, sharing happens with everyone in the breakout room. Return to the core breakout group in step 8 and the group in step 9.

The 4Cs is based on the same-named activity written by Matthew Richter in the March 2004 publication of the Thiagi GameLetter.

The 5 Whys

OBJECT OF PLAY

Many of the games in this book are about seeing the bigger picture or relating a problem to its context. The 5 Whys game mirrors that motive to move beyond the surface of a problem and discover the root cause, because problems are tackled more sustainably when they're addressed at the source.

NUMBER OF PLAYERS

5–10 people

DURATION OF PLAY

30 minutes

HOW TO PLAY

1. Prior to the meeting, establish a problem your team needs to evaluate. Write the problem in an area visible to all the group members, and if you'd like, draw something that represents it.

2. Distribute sticky notes to each player and ask them to number five of them 1 through 5.

3. Ask the players to review the problem statement and ask themselves why it's a problem. Then ask them to write their first response on sticky note 1.

4. Tell the players to ask themselves why the answer on sticky note 1 is true and write their next response on sticky note 2.

5. Again, tell the players to ask themselves why the answer on sticky note 2 is true and write the response on sticky note 3.

6. Repeat this process in numerical order until every numbered sticky note has a response written on it.

7. Below the problem statement, write the question "Why?" five times in a column and draw lines to create columns for each player's set of notes. Ask the players to approach the wall and post their responses, starting with 1 at the top and ending with 5 on the bottom.

8. Review the "Why" columns with the group and note commonalities and differences. Allow for discussion.

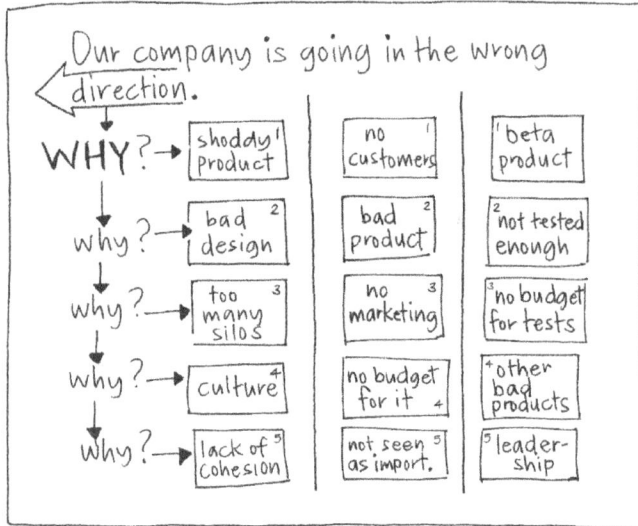

Rewrite the problem statement on a sheet of flip-chart paper. Then give a volunteer five clean sticky notes to write on, and work with the group to build consensus on which of the five "Whys" in the columns offer the most meaningful insight into the problem. Ask the volunteer to rewrite the "Whys"—one per sticky note—as the group agrees on them. Once they're all written, tape the five index cards into a final column under the problem statement. If you have time, move into a discussion around "What's next."

STRATEGY

This game is about reading more between the lines—about understanding the root cause of a problem so that people can get the greatest leverage out of solving it. When leading this game, encourage the players to be honest. This is the single most important strategy. If the players avoid the issues, the game doesn't yield good information. And in a worst-case scenario, you could have people actually addressing the wrong problems. So, as the meeting leader, be aware of the dynamics between the players and foster open conversation around the difficult question of "why."

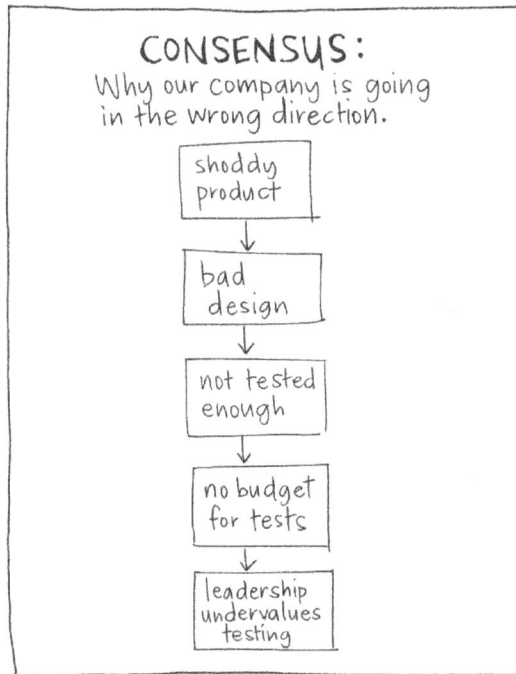

Another important practice is to ask the players to write the first thing that comes to mind each time they ask "Why? If they jump immediately to the perceived root of the problem, they may miss the opportunity to see the stages, which are valuable to know for problem solving at different levels.

Finally, many problems require more or less interrogation to get to the root. Ask "Why?" until you feel the group is really getting somewhere. Five "Whys" is a healthy place to start, but don't interpret it as a fixed number. Build longer "Why" columns if necessary, and keep going until you get the players to meaningful insights.

TIPS FOR PLAYING ONLINE

This game transfers naturally online. Individual game spaces can help create more private thinking and flow. A large shared game space encourages spontaneous combinations and self-editing.

The 5 Whys game is based on a game by Sakichi Toyoda.

Atomize

OBJECT OF PLAY

There is a time to go deep. Just as in science, breaking large structures into their base components is fundamental to knowledge work. It is how we create understanding and formulate new ideas.

This exercise starts with a single item and ends with a layer-by-layer analysis of its components. It is useful for unpacking large but poorly understood structures. Although the applications are numerous, some structures that are well suited for atomization include:

- A firm's offering
- A technology platform
- An enterprise-wide initiative
- A supply or demand chain
- A group's culture or other "intangible"

By breaking the larger system into its components, the group will have an advantage in problem solving or brainstorming. Because they are more discreet and tangible, the smaller components are more easily handled and better understood. Likewise, the overall map that is created will help serve as an explanation of the overall system.

NUMBER OF PLAYERS

Small groups

DURATION OF PLAY

One hour or more

HOW TO PLAY

1. Open the exercise by putting the name of the system on a sticky note at the top of a large whiteboard. Introduce the exercise as a way to understand what the system is made of in tangible terms, by breaking it down into its "atoms."

2. To start the brainstorming, ask the group to "split" the main system into its components. In this step, you are generating a list of things to capture

on sticky notes directly below the main topic. Generally, a short list of three to five large components is the norm.

3. For each item, repeat the splitting process by asking "What combines to create this?" In this manner, you will build a pyramid of components all the way down.

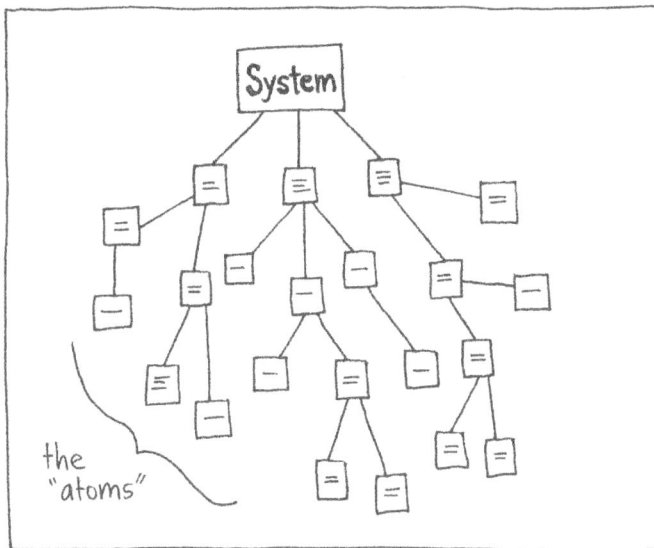

The map and individual components that result may be used as inputs into other activities, or may be documented as an explanation of a system's parts.

STRATEGY

At some point, usually four to five levels deep, there is a natural turning point. Instead of becoming more diverse, the items start to become more fundamental. This is the atomic level, where some of the most interesting results are found. In exploring a group's culture, this is where hidden attitudes and behaviors unique to the group may be discovered. In atomizing a service offering or product, this is where elementary characteristics and differentiation points may live.

TIPS FOR PLAYING ONLINE

Atomize works well online.

With digital scale, the outputs become a repository to remember elements and connections. This game can expand and transform infinitely with tangents and rabbit holes. Breaking apart a concept exposes thinking and can clarify direction.

The Atomize game is credited to James Macanufo.

The Blind Side

OBJECT OF PLAY

Every human being has blind spots, and every company does, too. Knowledge openness can enhance businesses and relationships while knowledge blindness can make things unnecessarily more difficult. In other words, what we don't know can hurt us. The military refers to this as "the fog of war." The premise of this game, therefore, is to disclose and discover unknown information that can impact organizational and group success in any area of the company—management, planning, team performance, and so forth.

NUMBER OF PLAYERS

5–15 people

DURATION OF PLAY

30–45 minutes

HOW TO PLAY

1. Before the meeting, decide on a topic for discussion. Draw a large-scale profile of a person and draw four arrows coming out of the top of the head. Label those arrows "Know/Know," "Know/Don't Know," "Don't Know/Know," and "Don't Know/Don't Know."

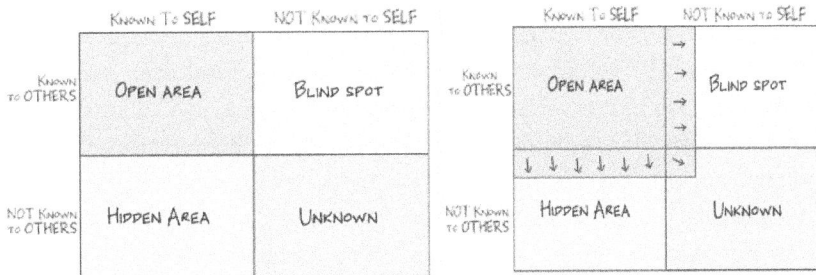

2. Give the players access to sticky notes and markers and tell them that the purpose of this game is to try to make explicit the knowledge they have, and the knowledge they don't have but could use.

3. Start with the Know/Know category. Elicit from the group all information about the topic that they know they know. This category should go quickly and should generate a lot of content. Ask the players to write one bit of

knowledge per sticky note and cluster them near the arrow pertaining to that category. (They'll do this for each category.)

4. Next, tackle Know/Don't Know. This category will go less quickly than the first but should still generate plenty of content. Again, ask them to cluster the sticky notes near the related arrow.

5. Move to Don't Know/Know. This information could be skills people have that are currently not used to solve problems or untapped resources that have been forgotten.

6. Last, move to Don't Know/Don't Know. The group will be stopped here, possibly indefinitely. This category is where discovery and shared exploration take place. Ask the players provocative questions: What does this team know that your team doesn't know it doesn't know? How can you find out what you don't know you don't know?

7. Ask the group what they can do to proactively address the distinct challenges of each category. Discuss insights and "ahas." Even if the players' only revelation is that they have blind spots, this in itself can be a fruitful discovery.

STRATEGY

This game works best with a familiar team when the participants cross disciplines and responsibilities. Having a diverse group enhances the feedback loop for the Don't Know categories, which are where the players are going to get stuck. They'll be confident about what they know—and even about what they know they don't know—but without an outside perspective, it's next to impossible to declare what we don't know we don't know. The nature of this question warrants discussion and the solicitation of others' observations.

Because this game has an obvious trust-building component, start by sharing easy information and move toward more substantive information depending on the players' comfort level. Keep the group on business- or project-related topics and away from personal evaluations. Although The Blind Side can be used as a psychological assessment, the self-help applications of this game should be conducted outside the business setting, unless you're dealing with the rare group that's into that.

TIPS FOR PLAYING ONLINE

The Blind Side works well online. Send smaller groups to breakout rooms and work on a shared board. These groups can be randomly assigned, or curated to prime and support teams with more complex dynamics.

The Blind Side is inspired by and adapted from the Johari Window, a communication model developed by Joseph Luft and Harry Ingham. (Gamestorming, as a practice, helps expand the Johari Window for everyone on the team, individually and collectively in a way that is seen and felt. This is part of the reason gamestorming can be so impactful for individuals and teams.)

Build the Checklist

OBJECT OF PLAY

In all work of reasonable complexity, there is a moment-to-moment risk that equally important tasks will overwhelm the human mind. In knowledge work, this may be doubly true, due to the intangible "fuzziness" of any particular task. For groups that are charting out how they will work, one of the most practical and useful things they can do is build a checklist.

Although creating a checklist may seem like an open-and-shut exercise, often it uncovers a manifest of issues. Because a checklist is a focusing object, it demands that the team discuss the order and importance of certain tasks. Team members are likely to have different perspectives on these things, and the checklist is a means to bring these issues to the surface and work with them.

NUMBER OF PLAYERS

A small team that has deep experience with the task at hand

DURATION OF PLAY

One hour or more, depending on the task to be analyzed

HOW TO PLAY

It's most useful to create the checklist in order of operation, from first to last, but in some cases a ranked or prioritized list is more appropriate. Consider which the group would benefit more from creating.

1. To begin, introduce to the group the topic at hand: "You will be creating a checklist for doing [fill in the blank]." It may be useful to prime the group into thinking about a particular situation or duration of time, as in "Getting from A to B" or "Dealing with an Angry Customer."

2. Have the group brainstorm tasks to put on the checklist using sticky notes. Guide the group to create items that are concrete and measurable, like a switch that is turned on or off. For example, "assess arrival readiness" is not as useful as "deploy landing gear."

3. Once the group has generated a pool of ideas, they may use Post-Up and affinity mapping to remove duplicate tasks. In discussing what has been added to the list, two things may be done:

- Have the group order the tasks into a procedure. Use sticky notes so that the individual tasks can be moved. Given a space with a beginning and an end, the group can discuss and debate the ordering while creating the list in real time.

- Have the group force-rank the tasks. In this case, the group must decide the order of importance of the tasks. By doing this, the group may be able to agree to cut items from the bottom of the list, making their checklist shorter and more direct.

In all cases, the discussion and reflection that come out of the initial brainstorming will be where the most progress is made. It is likely that new ideas will surface and be added to the checklist in the discussion. Coming out of the discussion, the group's next step is to capture the checklist as an artifact and share it with others who can test it and improve it.

STRATEGY

Building a checklist requires atomizing steps into repeatable components.

Players may also realize what cannot be put into checklist form because it is customized or bespoke to the situation or context. In these cases, the checklists that develop are usually most helpful when they are based around values, ensuring best practices, asking the right questions, and documenting learnings.

TIPS FOR PLAYING ONLINE

The Build the Checklist game works well online and can be played on a board. The output can then transfer to any other day-to-day project management system used by the team.

The Build the Checklist game is credited to James Macanufo.

Business Model Canvas

OBJECT OF PLAY

New business models can rapidly disrupt an entire industry—just look what Apple's iTunes strategy did to the music industry. The Business Model Canvas, developed by Alex Osterwalder, is a tool that you can use to examine and rethink a business model.

NUMBER OF PLAYERS

1–6 people. Works well individually to quickly sketch out and think through an idea. To map an organization's existing or future business model, you should work in groups. The more diverse the group of players, the more accurate the picture of the business model will be.

DURATION OF PLAY

Anywhere between 15 minutes for individual play, 2–4 hours to map an organization's existing business model, and up to two days to develop a future or start-up business model.

HOW TO PLAY

Mapping business models works best when players work on a poster on the wall. Print a large-scale version of the canvas or create one by drawing out the categories on the wall. If drawing it out, a version might look like this:

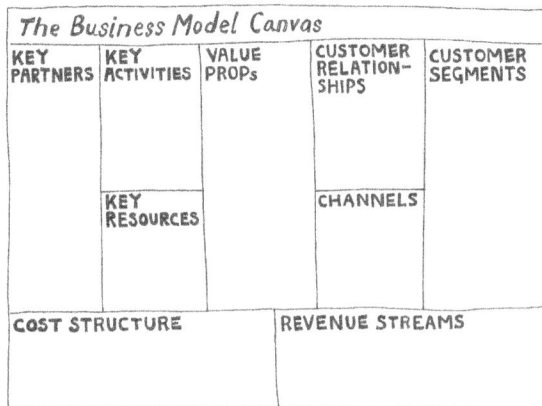

The Business Model Canvas

KEY PARTNERS	KEY ACTIVITIES	VALUE PROPs	CUSTOMER RELATION-SHIPS	CUSTOMER SEGMENTS
	KEY RESOURCES		CHANNELS	
COST STRUCTURE			REVENUE STREAMS	

Make sure all players have access to markers and sticky notes of varying sizes and colors. You will also need a camera to capture the results.

There are several games and variations you can play with the Business Model Canvas Poster. Here we describe the most basic game, which is the mapping of an organization's existing business model, its assessment, and the formulation of improved or potential new business models. This can easily be adapted to the objectives of the players.

1. A good way to start mapping your business model is by letting players begin to describe the different customer segments your organization serves. Players should put up different color sticky notes on the canvas poster for each type of segment. A group of customers represents a distinct segment if they have distinct needs and you offer them distinct value propositions (e.g., a newspaper serves readers and advertisers), or if they require different channels, customer relationships, or revenue streams.

2. Subsequently, players should map out the value propositions your organization offers each customer segment. Players should use the same color sticky notes for value propositions and customer segments that go together. If a value proposition targets two very different customer segments, the sticky note colors of both segments should be used.

3. Then players should map out all the remaining building blocks of your organization's business model with sticky notes. They should always try to use the colors of the related customer segment.

4. When the players have mapped out the whole business model, they can start assessing its strength and weaknesses by putting up green (strength) and red (weakness) sticky notes alongside the strong and weak elements of the mapped business model. Alternatively, sticky notes marked with a "+" and "–" can be used rather than colors.

5. Based on the visualization of your organization's business model, which players mapped out in steps 1–4, they can now either try to improve the existing business model or generate totally new alternative business models. Ideally, players use one or several additional Business Model Canvas Posters to map out improved business models or new alternatives.

STRATEGY

The mapping of an organization's existing business model, including its strengths and weaknesses, is an essential starting point to improve the current business model and/or develop new future business models. At the very least, the game leads to a refined and shared understanding of an organization's business model. At its best, it helps players develop strategic directions for the future by outlining new and/or improved business models for the organization.

TIPS FOR PLAYING ONLINE

In-person work can be summarized and further refined online. The game itself also works well online. Players can play on a hand-drawn board or digital template like the Business Model Canvas shown next. This choice can help set the tone for the activity.

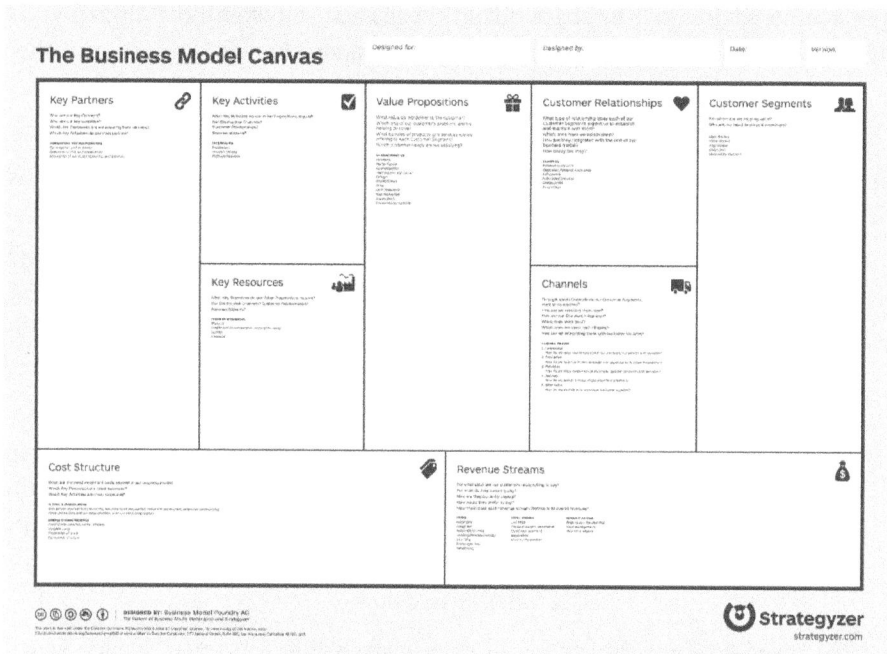

The Business Model Canvas was designed by Alexander Osterwalder and Yves Pigneur. The poster is available under the Creative Commons license as a free download at http://businessmodelhub.com. It is also featured in their book, Business Model Generation.

Button

OBJECT OF PLAY

A common element of brainstorming or group work is the "let's go around and hear from everyone" routine. The rule governing this is a valuable one—that everyone speaks once before anyone speaks twice.

There are two problems with this, however. First, moving from one person to the next in a round-robin fashion can be an energy drain, even with a small number of people. It's predictable, and the participants at the end of the line are often short-changed. Second, and potentially more damaging to the activity, is that often a participant's attention wanes when they are "on deck" and preparing their own thoughts as opposed to listening to others.

The Button is a simple technique that keeps true to the original rule while avoiding the traps of a round robin.

HOW TO PLAY

When the group is asked to report on a question, a small token—it may be a poker chip or something similar—is given to the first volunteer to respond. After their response, they choose a person who has yet to speak to take the button. This continues until everyone has spoken once.

This can be done easily with index cards instead of a button. Participants think about their answers to a question first and write a word on the card along with their name. The cards are passed to the left in a quick manner for a few moments so that in the process of passing, the order becomes scrambled. The participants then call on each other by way of reading the words aloud and asking the writers to explain.

STRATEGY

Randomization keeps the participants' attention. When you don't know if you will be called on next, you will be more present and focused. The Button game also passes control onto the participants, by giving them the power to nominate the next speaker.

TIPS FOR PLAYING ONLINE

Use the "raise hand" feature or designate another symbol visible on video. You could also, or instead, arrange all participants' names on the board and designate a digital token to move from one person to another.

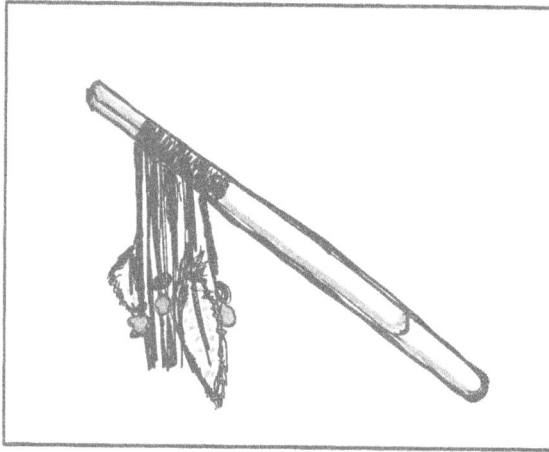

The Button is inspired by the Native American "Talking Stick" tradition, where a ceremonial object such as a stick or feather, representing the right to speak, was passed from one person to another to respect speakers and avoid interruption.

Campfire

OBJECT OF PLAY

Employees spend hours sitting in training sessions, sifting through orientation manuals, and playing corporate e-learning games to learn the know-how for their new positions. But the reality is that the bulk of employee knowledge is gained through storytelling.

Employees train each other by sharing their personal and professional experiences. Campfire leverages our natural storytelling tendencies by giving players a format and a space in which to share work stories—of trial and error, failure and success, competition, diplomacy, and teamwork. Campfire is useful not only because it acts as an informal training game, but also because it reveals commonalities in employee perception and experience.

NUMBER OF PLAYERS

8–20 people

DURATION OF PLAY

30–45 minutes

HOW TO PLAY

1. Before the meeting, brainstorm 10–20 words or phrases you can use as trigger words to start the storytelling session. Write them on sticky notes. Keep the ideas positive or neutral: partnership, venture, first day, work travel, fun project, opportunity, and so forth.

2. Post the sticky notes in the meeting room in a space visible to all the players and give them access to markers and more sticky notes. Tell them that this is a workplace "campfire" and the only thing they're invited to do is share stories back and forth as an informal "company training program." Show them the "wall of words" and ask them to take 1–3 minutes to look them over and recall a story associated with one of them. To help the group warm up, start the storytelling session yourself by removing one of the words on the wall and posting it in a space nearby. Then tell your introductory story.

3. Ask for a volunteer to continue what you started by peeling another word from the wall and posting it next to yours. This begins the sticky-note "story thread."

4. Before the first player begins their story, ask them to read aloud the word they chose and then instruct the other players to listen carefully to their story and to jot down a word or phrase on a sticky note that reminds them of another work-related story. If no words in the player's story jumped out at them, they are welcome to pull a sticky note from your original "wall of words."

5. After the player concludes the first story, ask for another volunteer to approach the wall and to either post their own sticky note or take one from the "wall of words." Ask them to read their word aloud and to then share their story.

6. Repeat this process until the players have created a snake-like "story thread," which acts as an archive of the campfire conversation. Use your best judgment to determine when to end the storytelling session. Before you "put out" the fire, ask the players if there are any lessons learned or final thoughts they want to add.

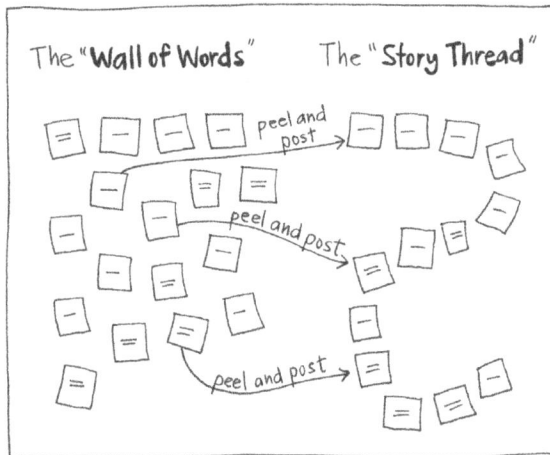

STRATEGY

Your role as the meeting leader is simply to encourage the sharing of work-related stories. If you find a lull in the storytelling thread, refer the employees back to the "wall of words" or ask someone to throw out a "wildcard" story. You can also share work-related stories of your own that are triggered by stories from the players. You can let the stories drift toward less positive or neutral topics if you think the players need some catharsis, but be prepared to manage what may come up, and don't let the meeting conclude on a sour note.

The point of Campfire is simple but powerful. It encourages sharing, shows the many things employees have in common, and leverages the natural tendency of employee training to take place through informal dialogue. Humans want to tell stories; you'll likely find that the players linger to share experiences even after the meeting ends.

TIPS FOR PLAYING ONLINE

Campfire can be easily adapted online using a digital whiteboard. Arrange the digital space to prime for creativity and engagement. The following example is from Dave's School of the Possible, where participants pick a chair and arrange their meeting avatar around the fire. Facilitators need to notice cues and actively intervene where helpful to keep the stories flowing smoothly.

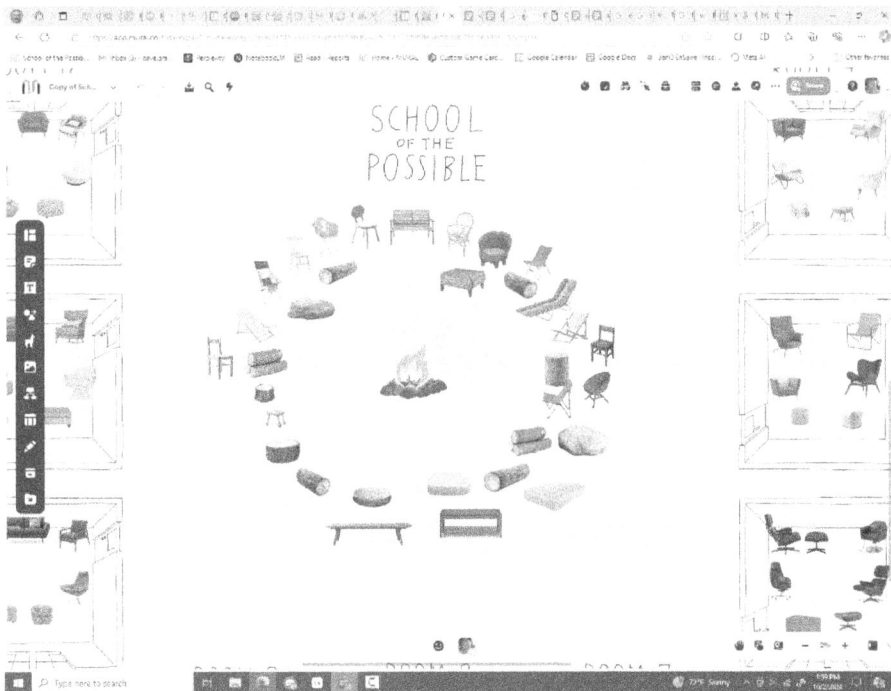

This game was invented by Sunni (Sun) Brown, inspired by Tell Me a Story: Narrative and Intelligence (Rethinking Theory), *by Roger Schank and Gary Saul Morson (Northwestern University Press).*

Challenge Cards

OBJECT OF PLAY

To identify and think through challenges, problems, and potential pitfalls in a product, service, or strategy.

NUMBER OF PLAYERS

Works best with small groups of 5–10

DURATION OF PLAY

30–45 minutes

HOW TO PLAY

Divide each group into two teams. One team, the "solution team," silently brainstorms features and strengths of the product or solution. The other team, the "challenge team," silently brainstorms potential problems or challenges and writes them on index cards, one problem or challenge per card.

When play commences, the two teams work together to tell a collaborative story. The challenge team picks a card from the deck and plays it on the table, describing a scene or event where the issue might realistically arise. The solution team must then pick a card from their deck that addresses the challenge. If they have a solution, they get a point, and if they don't have a solution, the challenge team gets a point. The teams then work together to design a card that addresses that challenge. Play continues in this fashion, challenge followed by solution followed by challenge, and so on, until the story or scenario reaches a conclusion.

STRATEGY

The goal of this game is to improve a product or strategy by thinking through various scenarios and alternatives. By turning the exercise into a competition as well as a storytelling game, players are more likely to get engaged and immerse themselves in the scenarios. Keeping it lighthearted and fun will increase the energy. It shouldn't feel like work.

TIPS FOR PLAYING ONLINE

Challenge Cards can be played online, with scores and story results captured on the board.

This game emerged spontaneously during a gamestorming workshop in London in 2010.

Countdown

OBJECT OF PLAY

Countdown is a practice for self-regulation and self-compassion using sensing and observation of an environment. This can be an unexpected break and energizer. It's a mindfulness practice that can be used anytime, anywhere to bring yourself back to center.

NUMBER OF PLAYERS

1–10 people

DURATION OF PLAY

10 minutes

HOW TO PLAY

1. Ideally outside, while engaging in something physical (examples include walking in a garden, the uphill section of a hike, riding chair lifts), you, as the facilitator, begin by saying you want to play a little grounding game. Start by asking, "What are *five* things you *see*?" Notice and count silently on your fingers then share it with whoever is close to you and compare.

2. Now, "What are *four* things you *hear*?" Share it with those close to you and discuss.

3. Now, "What are *three* things you *feel*?"—like physical sensations on the body. Share it with the person next to you, and contemplate how you are both doing the same thing, yet may be having different experiences based on what you're noticing. Both are true, and valid.

4. Now, "What are *two* things you *smell*?" Notice and share it with the person next to you and appreciate how much we can begin to distinguish when we pay attention.

5. Now, while everyone is thinking about what they taste..., "What's *one* thing you *really like about yourself*?" Answer aloud and share with the group. When listening to answers, notice if it's also something you also like about this person and reaffirm that back to them if you feel so compelled.

STRATEGY

This activity works well in the context of a retreat setting. It helps to ground and regulate in advance of complex topics, visioning, or in an agenda with heavy elements. Use it anytime to ground to the present moment and make decisions, or enter discussions from a place of peace.

TIPS FOR PLAYING ONLINE

This game can be modified for online play. Instead of walking around in nature, invite participants to take a break and walk around their environment while listening to the prompts and making note of their observations in much the same way as they would when playing offline. Write down responses from step 5 and add it to a shared board.

Countdown is based on ancient and modern techniques for nervous system regulation and is now in the creative commons.

Design the Box

OBJECT OF PLAY

Before you begin, focus on the end. In this exercise, teams create the physical "box" that sells their idea—whether that idea will ultimately become a tangible product or not. By imagining the package for their idea, the teams make decisions about important features and other aspects of their vision that are more difficult to articulate.

This game is popular among software developers when setting out to capture the customer's view of a new application, but its use doesn't stop there. The game can help facilitate any vision-oriented discussion and has been used to describe topics ranging from "our future methodology" to "the ideal hire."

In all cases, the box is a focusing device: it wraps up a lot of otherwise intangible information into a nice physical object, prompting decisions along the way. When teams present or "sell" their boxes to each other, a number of things come to life, including the natural translation of features into benefits. Also, it's fun to do. The results of the exercise may be simple drawings or an actual box, which may live on well after as a friendly reminder of the big picture.

NUMBER OF PLAYERS

Although the exercise may be done with a small group, teams working in parallel on different boxes will result in a more robust discussion during the "selling phase."

DURATION OF PLAY

One hour or more, depending on the number of groups and depth of discussion.

SETUP

Although paper and markers will work for drawing a box, don't hesitate to bring heavier craft supplies to bear. Consider acquiring blank white cardboard boxes from an office supply or mailing store. Markers, craft paper, stickers, tape, and scissors are all worth the investment.

It may help get the group's creative gears moving by having sample boxes handy. Cereal boxes, with their free prize offers, bold imagery, and nutritional information, are good thought starters. Likewise, plain "store-label" boxes, gift boxes, and toy boxes offer a range of voices. A group that is heavily entrenched in the business-as-usual paradigm will benefit the most from having this inspiration at hand.

HOW TO PLAY

The exercise moves through three phases: an introduction, box creation, and sharing by "selling."

Phase one: Fill the box

Before a group can jump into creating a box, they need to reflect on what could be in it.

To get people oriented, consider laying out some building blocks:

- Possible names of the idea

- Possible customers, end users, or buyers

- Possible features, functions, or other important defining details

This may be familiar ground, or it may be entirely new to the group. The key in setting up the exercise is to give teams "just enough" information to feel comfortable starting.

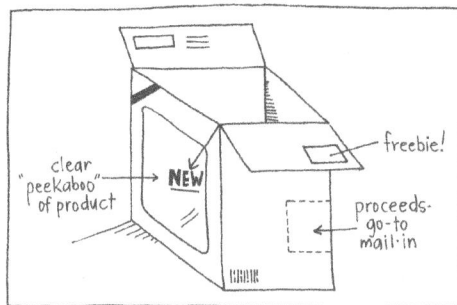

Phase two: Make the box

Give the teams a set amount of time, 30 minutes or more, to create the box for their idea. Ask them to imagine coming across the box on a retail shelf, shrink-wrapped and ready for sale. In designing the box, teams may be helped by a few of these prompts:

- What's it called?

- Who's it for?

- What's its tagline or slogan?

- What are its most compelling features? Benefits?
- What imagery would make it stand out to you?

Teams may self-organize naturally; most participants will want to create their own box, regardless of how they're arranged. Make sure you have ample supplies for them to do so, and make sure they know that there is no wrong way to create their box.

Phase three: Sell the box

Each team or individual should be offered the chance to stand up and "sell" their boxes back to the group. It may be worthwhile to keep a timer for these stand-up presentations, and consider offering a prize to the team that does the best job "selling" their box back to the group.

Look for a naturally occurring breakthrough as they present back their boxes. People put features on the box, but when they sell them, they translate those features into benefits. Listen for the phrases "so that" or "because," which bridge otherwise mechanical features into living benefits.

The exercise works well as an open-ended, divergent process, but may be run so that the teams converge on an agreed-upon, shared box. If agreement and alignment is a desired outcome of the exercise, note the differences and similarities in how each team interpreted their box. Build on the common ground captured in the similarities, and isolate differences for discussion. Consider running a second round, this time incorporating these agreements into a final shared box.

In any case, if there is a prize to be awarded for the best "box seller," make sure it's the teams that cast the votes. And have enough prizes so that if the box was created by a team, everyone on the team will have a prize.

STRATEGY

Keep the boxes and display them in a prominent place. These may be more valuable (and visible) artifacts than any other documentation that comes out of the exercise. It may also be beneficial to record the presentations the teams give around their boxes, if it is not disruptive to the flow of the group.

The core act of "designing the box" may be altered to work for different contexts and participants.

TIPS FOR PLAYING ONLINE

Design the Box can be adapted online among open-minded and engaged participants. Create a game space on the board for each group. Create breakout sessions for the groups to design the box then bring everyone back together to review and discuss. The role of the facilitator is even more important online to keep things moving quickly and flowing well.

This exercise goes by many names, and there are a number of good sources to look to for its variations. This version is based on and adapted from the game Product Box in Luke Hohmann's book, Innovation Games: Creating Breakthrough Products Through Collaborative Play. *Other sources point to Jim Highsmith of the Cutter Consortium, and to Bill Shackelford of Shackelford & Associates for the origination of the concept.*

Desire Mapping

OBJECT OF PLAY

Our thoughts and desires are always changing. Desire Mapping helps identify and uncover the underlying motivation behind what you want.

NUMBER OF PLAYERS

One or more people

DURATION OF PLAY

30 minutes

HOW TO PLAY

1. Before the session, create a template for each participant. Set up the game with the group by explaining that we will explore goals and desires to get a deeper sense of what each participant really wants.

2. First, ask them to consider, what do you really want most right now? One idea per sticky, whatever is on your mind. Let the ideas flow. (3.5 minutes)

3. Now, look at what you came up with and identify the top 3–5 ideas to work with and post them in the first column. (3.5 minutes)

4. Now, we will work with them one by one. Why do you want that thing you wrote in column one? When you have an answer, write it down on a sticky note. Put that in the next column. (7 minutes)

5. Now, ask the same question for column two. "Why do I want that?" (7 minutes)

6. Do it one more time in the last column. "Why do I want that?" The ideas and themes revealed in the last column illuminate your true desires. (7 minutes)

7. Come back together as a group to share insights. (7 minutes)

WHAT I WANT MOST RIGHT NOW IS...	WHY DO I WANT THAT? Because I want...	WHY DO I WANT THAT? Because I want...	WHY DO I WANT THAT? My TRUE DESIRE is...

SO, NEXT ...

STRATEGY

This is an individual activity where each person will work on their own game board. It can be helpful to do in a group setting and brings sharing and closeness to the group. In each step, players look more deeply into *why* they desire what they desire. By the final column, this game almost always goes deep. Allow and acknowledge what occurs. Facilitators hold space for insights and feelings to be shared. This activity can create a powerful experience for participants. At the end of the session, invite participants to take a photo of their work so they can remember what they wrote to refer back to later. If using flip chart paper, encourage participants to roll up the paper and take it home. Holding onto these tangible artifacts creates an opportunity to coincidentally find them later.

TIPS FOR PLAYING ONLINE

Desire Mapping works well online in a group setting. Particular attention should be given to the level of trust among the participants, as there is less opportunity for privacy. Create a shared board with space and a template for each participant to respond.

Desire mapping is credited to Danielle Laporte.

Elevator Pitch

OBJECT OF PLAY

What has been a time-proven exercise in product development applies equally well in developing any new idea: writing the elevator pitch. When developing and communicating a vision for something, whether it's a new service, a company-wide initiative, or just a good idea that merits spreading, a group will benefit from going through the exercise of writing their elevator pitch.

Often this is the hardest thing to do in developing a new idea. An elevator pitch must be short enough to deliver in a fictional elevator ride but also contain a compelling description of the problem you're solving, who you'll solve it for, and one key benefit that distinguishes it from other ideas.

NUMBER OF PLAYERS

Can be done individually, or with a small working group.

DURATION OF PLAY

Save at least 90 minutes for the entire exercise, and consider a short break after the initial idea generation is complete before prioritizing and shaping the pitch itself. Small working groups will have an easier time coming to a final pitch; in some cases, it may be necessary to assign one person with follow-up accountability for the final wording after the large decisions have been made in the exercise.

HOW TO PLAY

Going through the exercise involves both a generating and a formative phase. To set up the generating phase, write these headers in sequence on flip charts:

- Who is the target customer?
- What is the customer need?
- What is the product name?
- What is its market category?
- What is its key benefit?
- Who or what is the competition?

- What is the product's unique differentiator?
- These will become the elements of the elevator pitch. They are in a sequence that adheres to the following formula.

Elevator Pitch sentence structure:
FOR (target customer), WHO HAS (customer need), (product name) IS A (market category) THAT (one key benefit).
UNLIKE (competition), THE PRODUCT (unique differentiator).

To finish the setup, explain the elements and their connection to each other.

The *target customer* and *customer need* are deceptively simple: any relatively good idea or product will likely have many potential customers and address a greater number of needs. In the generative phase, all of these are welcome ideas.

It is helpful to fix the *product name* in advance—this will help contain the scope of the conversation and focus the participants on what the pitch is about. It is not outside the realm of possibility, however, that useful ideas will be generated in the course of the exercise that relate to the product name, so it may be left open to interpretation.

The *market category* should be an easily understood description of the type of idea or product. It may sound like "employee portal" or "training program" or "peer-to-peer community." The category gives an important frame of reference for the target customer, from which they will base comparisons and perceive value.

The *key benefit* will be one of the hardest areas for the group to shape in the final pitch. This is the single most compelling reason a target customer would buy into the idea. In an elevator pitch, there is no time to confuse the matter with multiple benefits—there can be only one memorable reason "why to buy." However, in the generative phase, all ideas are welcome.

The *competition* and *unique differentiator* put the final punctuation on the pitch. Who or what will the target customer compare this idea to, and what's unique about this idea.

In some cases, the *competition* may literally be another firm or product. In other cases, it may be "the existing training program" or "the last time we tried a big change initiative." The *unique differentiator* should be just that: *unique* to this idea or approach, in a way that distinguishes it in comparison to the competition.

The generating phase

Once the elements are understood, participants brainstorm ideas on sticky notes that fit under each header. At first, they should generate freely, without discussion or analysis, any ideas that fit into any of the categories. Using the Post-Up technique, participants put their notes onto the flip charts and share their ideas.

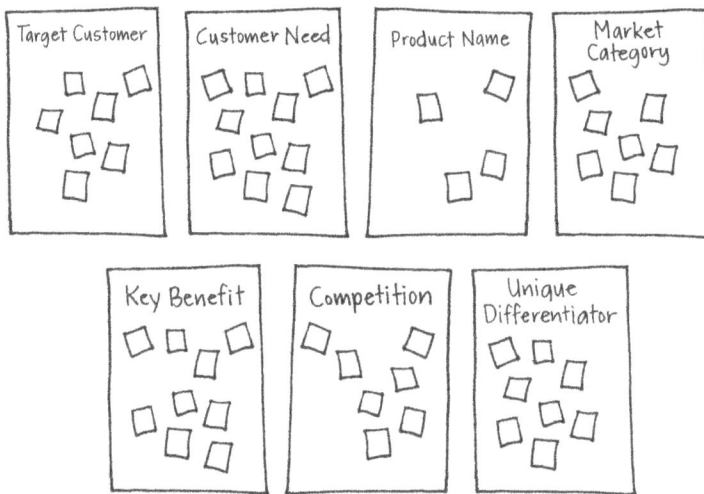

(series of 7 flip charts)

Next, the group may discuss areas where they have the most trouble on their current pitch. Do we know enough about the competition to claim a unique differentiator? Do we agree on a target customer? Is our market category defined, or are we trying to define something new? Where do we need to focus?

Before stepping into the formative phase, the group may use dot voting, affinity mapping, or another method to prioritize and cull their ideas in each category.

The formative phase

Following a discussion and reflection on the possible elements of a pitch, the group then has the task of "trying out" some possibilities.

This may be done by breaking into small groups, as pairs, or as individuals, depending on the size of the larger group. Each group is given the task of writing an elevator pitch, based on the ideas on the flip charts.

After a set amount of time (15 minutes may be sufficient), the groups reconvene and present their draft versions of the pitch. The group may choose to role play as a target customer while listening to the pitch, and comment or ask questions of the presenters.

The exercise is complete when there is a strong direction among the group on what the pitch should *and should not* contain. One potential outcome is the crafting of distinct pitches for different target customers; you may direct the group to focus on this during the formative stage.

STRATEGY

Don't aim for final wording with a large group. It's an achievement if you can get to that level of completion, but it's not critical and can be shaped after the exercise. What is important is that the group decides what is and is not a part of the pitch.

Role-play is the fastest way to test a pitch. Assuming the role of a customer (or getting some real customers to participate in the exercise) will help filter out the jargon and empty terms that may interfere with a clear pitch. If the pitch is truly believable and compelling, participants should have no problem making it real with customers.

TIPS FOR PLAYING ONLINE

This game translates well online. It can be played as a group using a collaboration space. Alternatively, a template of the pitch could be considered individually or in smaller groups and contributed to the board for review by the group.

The elevator pitch, or elevator speech, is a traditional staple of the venture capital community, based on the idea that if you are pitching a business idea it should be simple enough to convey on a short elevator ride.

Event Horizon

OBJECT OF PLAY

Our brain is an incredible, complex adaptive system designed to keep us alive. Because it evolved to survive, not thrive, it more heavily prioritizes negative information and avoids uncertainty, threat, and unpleasant conditions. And hooray for that! If it weren't for the brain's negativity bias, none of us would be here today. But the cost of this bias is that it leaves us less receptive to joy, beauty, wonder, awe—the things that make life worth living. The object of play, therefore, is to unstick from rigid views and projected outcomes of the future in order to imagine other viable possibilities. It serves as a practice anytime we're having a downward spiral in our mind, or our mood, based on rumination or negative fantasizing. Playing in earnest can recalibrate a nervous fixation around any approaching experience by helping the mind consider more options or get a more expansive view. It may also help unlock ideas or beliefs we have around an approaching event that aren't helpful.

NUMBER OF PLAYERS

1–50 people

DURATION OF PLAY

20 minutes

HOW TO PLAY

1. Re-create a good-enough version of the following visual—on a piece of paper, a digital tablet, or in a sandbox!

2. Think of an upcoming event that's causing you stress—a job interview, a difficult conversation, a family event that sounds like a hellscape. (Pardon. Different families?) The event should be something that parts of you are not looking forward to or that creates stress in your system when you think about it. It can be anything, big or small. Write, draw, or doodle that event at the top of the triangle and attempt a brief statement that expresses why the event provokes anxiety. Don't overthink the statement. Just move your pen.

3. On the left, again without overthinking, write the worst thing that could happen. The first thing that comes to your gut. (If you're good at rumination, this part will come easy.) On the right, write the best thing that could

happen. Use an unbridled imagination. Really, what's ideal? Describe it in detail.

4. Now your possibility space gets a workout. The task is to generate as many scenarios as possible in between these endpoints. Some people like to keep these realistic; others like to go far out. Choose your own adventure. Try to find the nuance and gray areas between the extremes. Push past the obvious, because there really are infinite possibilities along this spectrum, depending on how granularly you look.

5. To close, spend a couple of minutes reflecting on what you created and capture any insights it brought to you.

STRATEGY

We are constantly mapping and evaluating the world. This is a game about breaking through some of the thinking distortions we have that make our lives more difficult. The idea is to *play with options*, to pixelate reality and keep pixelating it until not only do you have 20+ scenarios, but you have exploded your endpoints. Because of associative thinking and neurologically constrained spaces of possibility, you may find it initially difficult to generate plentiful outcomes. Don't fret; this is normal, and it's not cheating to add simple details for a new scenario, take as much time as you need, or ask someone close by for alternatives. *Pushing past the obvious is the point*, and that will take mental effort. We invite you to make that effort until you realize unequivocally that reality is so nonbinary that almost anything is possible, and you do not know nor can you precisely predict what challenge, beauty, or instruction will occur. That gut-clenching, stomach-churning, worst-case scenario is just one way to stress yourself out. Even in the most awful worry-based vision, something useful, with a silver lining, can be born.

TIPS FOR PLAYING ONLINE

Show a slide that presents the game template to the participants and ask them to re-create the visual architecture on a piece of paper; then ask them to follow the same steps as previously. Alternately, add multiple versions of the template to a digital mural and let each player have their own game space to work. See the following populated template example.

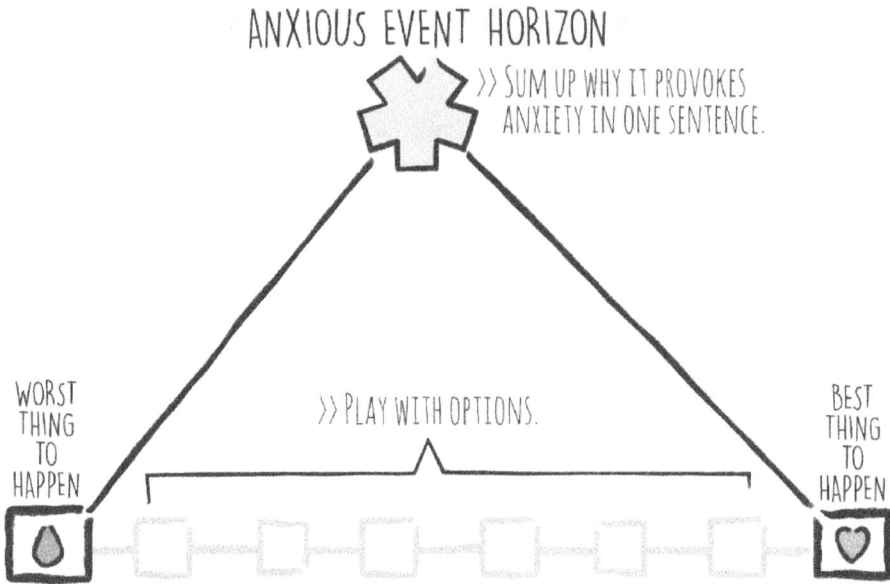

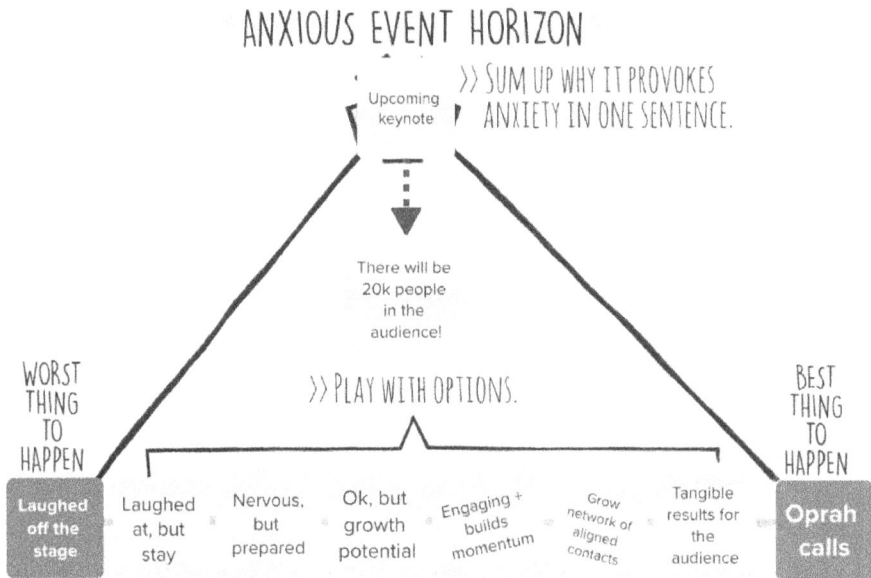

Once the individual drawings are complete or the game board is filled in, invite the group to breakout rooms. Ask them to hold their drawing up to the screen when it's their turn to speak so that people can get a sense of it, or invite participants to look around the digital board and scan each other's work for five minutes. For the next 10 minutes, respond to these questions: 1) What was the experience like for you?, 2) How did that change your sense of the event or relationship to the event, if it did?, and 3) When you imagine the scenarios toward the right, how do you feel in your body?

Event Horizon was created by Sunni (Sun) Brown and can be found at https:// nothingintheway.substack.com/p/it-really-wont-be-that-bad.

Five-Fingered Consensus

OBJECT OF PLAY

This is a technique for managing the feedback loop between a facilitator and a large group. When working in breakouts or as a large group, it may be necessary to periodically gauge the level of perceived consensus, without spending an unnecessary amount of time talking about it. A facilitator may ask for this quickly by using the "five-fingers check."

HOW TO PLAY

The facilitator asks the group to rate their level of consensus on a topic from 0 to 5, with five fingers meaning "absolute, total agreement" and a fist meaning "completely different points of view." This is particularly useful in managing breakout groups, where different topics may be discussed simultaneously. A group that holds up a variety of ones, twos, and threes may have more work to do.

STRATEGY

The "trick" in this technique is in gauging how far apart the individuals feel they are from consensus. A group that is wide apart in the view of its members—with some holding up five fingers and others holding up two—may need outside support and mediation of their discussion.

TIPS FOR PLAYING ONLINE

This game translates well online. It can be played as a group, in breakout sessions, 1:1s, etc., as long as cameras are on.

Hand signals are a commonly found element of consensus-based decision-making and dispute resolution. Related is the thumbs-up, thumbs-down, and thumbs-sideways technique.

Flip It

OBJECT OF PLAY

Often, a change in a problem or situation comes simply from a change in our perspectives. Flip It is a quick game designed to show players that perspectives are made, not born. We can choose to see the glass as either half-full or half-empty, but often when we perceive it as half-full, we get better results. This game is at its best when players begin to see challenges as opportunities and to make doable suggestions around solving problems rather than just rehashing them.

NUMBER OF PLAYERS

5–20

DURATION OF PLAY

30 minutes to 1 hour

HOW TO PLAY

1. Before the meeting, hang four to eight sheets of flip-chart paper on a wall (as shown in the following figure), and on any sheet in the top row, write the name of the game.

2. On the bottom-left sheet write the word "FEAR." If you'd like, spend time drawing a representation of fear on the sheets beforehand or add an image that embodies it. Tell the group that Flip It is about the future—of their department, their organization, their product/service, whatever topic you've agreed on beforehand.

3. Ask the players to quietly spend 5–10 minutes writing concerns, issues, and fears about the topic on sticky notes. Remind them to be honest about their fears because this game gives them an opportunity to reframe their fears. Post-upp the sticky notes on the FEAR sheets, which are all the sheets along the bottom row. Discuss the content with the group and ask for volunteers to elaborate on their contributions.

4. On the top-left sheet write the word "HOPE." Ask the players to survey the content in the FEAR row and try to "flip" the perspectives by reframing in terms of hope. Give them 10–15 minutes to generate sticky notes that respond to the fears.

5. With the group, collect and post the second set of sticky notes on the HOPE sheets along the top row.

6. Discuss the content with the group and ask for volunteers to elaborate on their contributions. Ask the players to dot-vote next to the hopes they can take practical action on. With the group, observe the hopes that won the most votes.

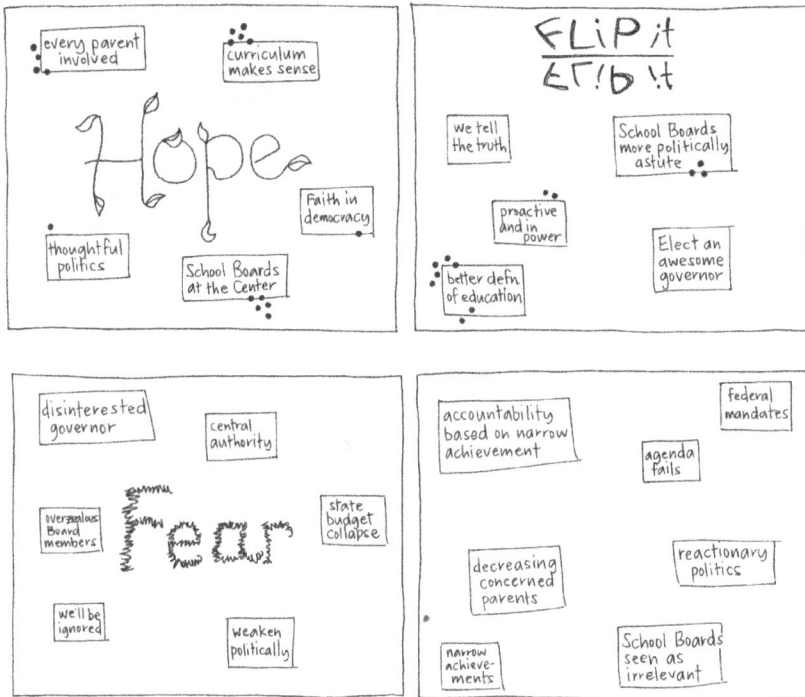

7. Write the word "TRACTION" on another sheet of flip-chart paper. Rewrite (or remove and restick) the hopes that won the most votes on the TRACTION sheet. Ask the players to brainstorm aloud any actionable items related to each hope. Write them down and discuss.

STRATEGY

Because Flip It starts with FEARS, as the meeting leader, you'll need to reassure folks early on that they're not going to wallow in their fears. They just need to spend some time generating fears in order to gather information and get the game moving. You can model the "flip-it" behavior by opening the game with an example of a situation you chose to perceive one way or the other. Once the group writes down their fears and posts them on the wall, let them air any related thoughts, and then spend the majority of the time flipping the fears into positive outcomes. You want the group to see concerns (even if it's a momentary view) as a chance to be hopeful and get motivated around action.

If you're working with a larger group or if the group generates an abundant amount of sticky notes, use the sorting and clustering technique and generate representative categories for each cluster. Then ask the group to vote on those categories and use them during the optional TRACTION activity. Unless directed otherwise, the issues provided by the group will likely focus on both internal and external factors. If you don't want the play to be that all-encompassing, establish a boundary going in.

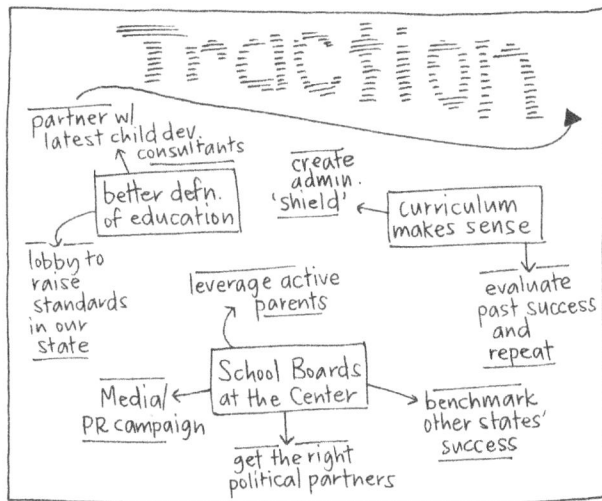

Optional activity: Ask for volunteers to write their initials next to the practical actions they could support. Tell them it's not an intractable commitment, just an indication of where their interest lies.

TIPS FOR PLAYING ONLINE

This game translates well online. Set up the game space in advance for participants to add to, ideally on camera and using a shared collaboration space.

The source of the Flip It game is unknown. The game works well (produces insights and results and offers value to participants) because negativity bias makes identifying our concerns easier—the pain, the challenges, are usually quickly top of mind. With Flip It, we use this bias and quickly name them. Then, we flip it. What is the exact opposite? When we start with this, it gets the concerns out, allowing us to more easily relax and consider the inverse. It can be a good way to help participants uncover what they really want more readily than asking the question directly. This is a practice in shifting perspectives.

Force Field Analysis

OBJECT OF PLAY

The Greek philosopher Heraclitus asserted that change alone is unchanging. This is certainly true in today's competitive global marketplace. As employees, we're often responsible for understanding and even anticipating change in order to stay ahead. The Force Field Analysis game is a time-tested way to evaluate the forces that assist or resist your desired change. Making a deliberate effort to see the system surrounding change can help us steer the change in the direction we want it to move.

NUMBER OF PLAYERS

5–30

DURATION OF PLAY

30 minutes to 1.5 hours

HOW TO PLAY

1. Before the meeting, draw a picture of a potential change in the middle of a large sheet of paper or whiteboard. You can draw a literal representation (e.g., a manufacturing plant) or a more abstract representation (e.g., a metaphor). Label the picture to ensure that everyone participating will be clear on the topic.

2. On the top left of the page, write the phrase "Forces FOR Change." On the top right, write the phrase "Forces AGAINST Change."

3. Draw arrows on both sides pointing toward the image in the middle. These will be the areas that contain categories generated by the group, so make the arrows large enough to write 1–2-inch letters inside. If you like the "wow" factor of drawing live with the group but you're not yet comfortable with freehand, sketch the arrows in pencil or yellow marker and trace them during the meeting.

4. When the group is gathered, introduce the change topic and explain that the goal of the Force Field Analysis game is to evaluate the feasibility of that change.

5. Ask the players to take 5–10 minutes and quietly generate ideas about what elements are driving the change. Tell them to include one idea per sticky note.

6. Ask the players to take 5–10 minutes and quietly generate ideas about what elements are restraining the change.

7. Draw a simple scale with a range of 1 to 5 on your main flip chart. Indicate that 1 means the force is weak and 5 means the force is strong. Ask them to review each idea FOR change and add a number to that sticky note, weighting that idea. Ask them to review each idea AGAINST change and add a number to that sticky note, weighting that idea.

8. Gather all of the sticky notes FOR change and post them to any flat surface viewable by the players.

9. With the group's collaboration, sort the ideas based on their affinity to other ideas. For example, if they produced three sticky notes that say "Can't continue production at current cost," "Materials cost too high," and "Overexpenditure on production," cluster those ideas together. Create multiple clusters until you have clustered the majority of the sticky notes. Place outliers separate from the clusters but still in playing range.

10. After the sorting activity is complete, begin a group conversation to create an overarching category for each cluster. For example, an overarching category for the cluster from step 9 might be "unsustainable costs."

11. As the group makes suggestions and finds agreement on categories, write those categories inside the arrows on the main visual.

12. As you categorize each cluster, direct the group's attention to the numeric scores within that cluster. Get an average for each cluster and write that number next to the related category in the arrow.

13. Repeat steps 8–12 using the sticky notes generated AGAINST change.

14. Add the quantities for and against change and write the totals at the bottom and on the appropriate side of the sheet.

15. Summarize the overall findings with the group, including the numeric totals, and discuss the implications of whether change should occur.

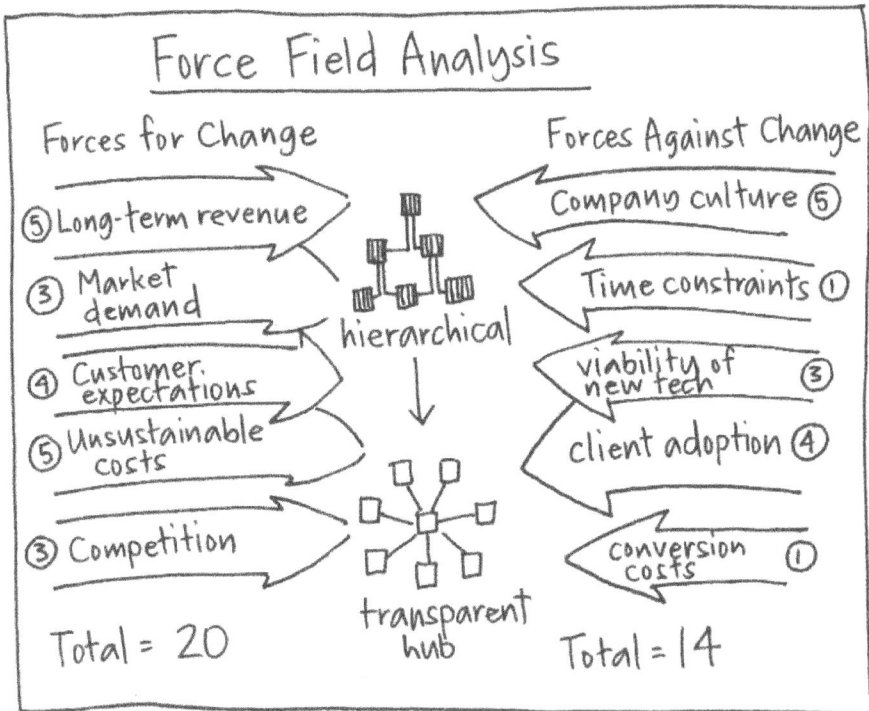

STRATEGY

Often, when you play the Force Field Analysis game, it will not be the first time the players have considered the change under discussion. Many of them will have preconceived beliefs about whether the change should occur. So, be aware of group dynamics—whether they're eager for or resistant to the change. If you sense that they're eager, encourage them to give equal consideration to forces against it. If they seem reluctant, encourage them to imagine their wildest dream with respect to this change and describe what's already in place to support it. Don't let employees with fixed perspectives on either side dominate the conversation.

This game is about exploring the viability of change in an open-minded way. So, be sure to acknowledge and discuss any ideas that end up as outliers in the clusters—they frequently turn out to be valuable by offering unforeseen perspectives. Along that same line, don't assume that the numeric totals resolutely answer the question of whether change should occur. The totals are another gauge by which to measure where the group may stand. Use them as fodder for further conversation and evaluation. And if you want to take the evaluation further, ask the group to look for meta-categories after they've brainstormed the categories within the arrows. Meta-categories should be a level higher than the categories generated from the clusters. They could include "politics," "economics," "company culture," or "mid-level management." Seeing meta-categories can also help the group determine where the bulk of the evaluation may need to be focused.

TIPS FOR PLAYING ONLINE

This game translates well online. Set the game board in advance and add hand-drawn elements live for step 15 for maximum engagement.

This game is based on the Force Field Analysis framework developed by Kurt Lewin.

Give-and-Take Matrix

OBJECT OF PLAY

The goal of this game is to map out the motivations and interactions among actors in a system. The actors in this case may be as small-scale as individuals who need to work together to accomplish a task or as large-scale as organizations brought together for a long-term purpose. A Give-and-Take Matrix is a useful diagnostic tool and helps players explore how value flows through the group.

NUMBER OF PLAYERS

Small group

DURATION OF PLAY

1 hour or more

HOW TO PLAY

To begin, you will need a list of all the actors in the system. This may be prepared in advance or generated at the start of the exercise.

Using the list, create a matrix with the list of actors along both the horizontal and vertical axes.

Each cell in the matrix captures only one direction of the flow. For example, a supplier may give a certain value to a manufacturer, but a manufacturer will give a different value to the supplier. For consistency, the vertical axis can be considered the "from" and the horizontal axis the "to."

Primary motivations

For each actor in the matrix, fill in "what they want" out of the system. This information goes along the diagonal, where the individual actors intersect with themselves. These should be brief phrases that describe a goal or reason the actor participates in the system.

Intersecting interests

The next step is to look at the intersections and capture what value flows between the actors. Start with a single actor and work through each cell, asking "What can I offer you?"

For some intersection points, this will be easier to describe. In other cases, the matrix will expose previously unconnected actors, and possibly those at odds with each other. The goal in completing the matrix is to find the most complete picture of how each actor can benefit all the others.

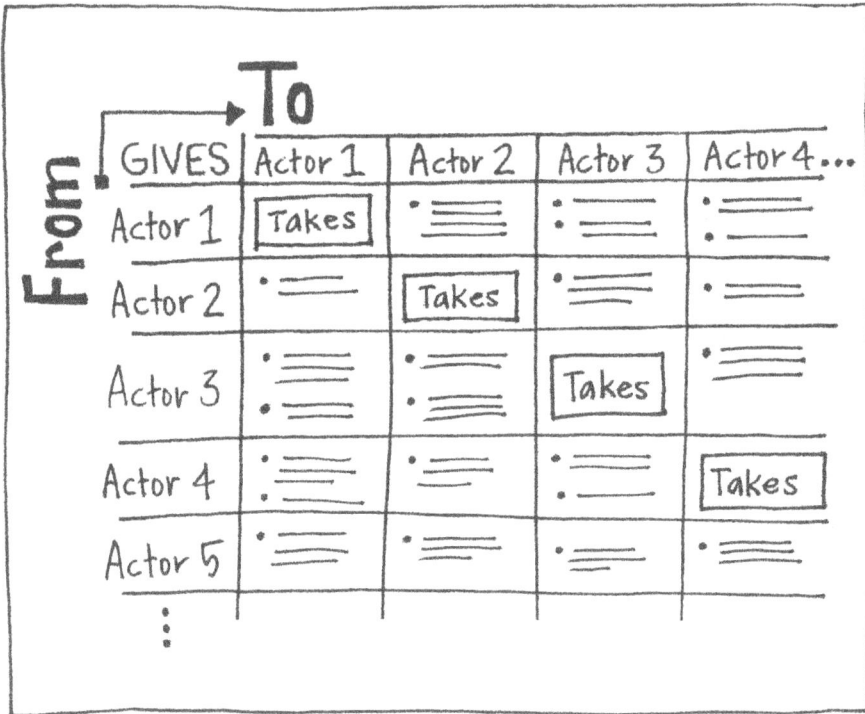

STRATEGY

Completing this matrix may involve research both before and after the initial mapping process. By using surveys or interviews, players may be able to explore and validate both the initial inputs and the intersecting interests.

Along with stakeholder analysis and boundary mapping, the Give-and-Take Matrix helps players explore and define the various actors and interactions within a system.

TIPS FOR PLAYING ONLINE

This game translates well online. Capturing this information digitally encourages further exploration, linking, and connections. Set the game board in advance or collaboratively.

The Give-and-Take Matrix is inspired by a number of techniques used in engineering, chemistry, and design.

Head, Heart, Hands

OBJECT OF PLAY

The object of this game is to examine an issue from another perspective, and find significance in the issue.

NUMBER OF PLAYERS

1–10 people

DURATION OF PLAY

10 minutes to 1 hour

HOW TO PLAY

1. Look at an issue, product, or course of action using these three lenses:

   Head: What makes it logical and sensible?

   Heart: What makes it emotionally engaging?

   Hands: What makes it tangible and practical?

2. List the characteristics or features that appeal to each lens.

3. Score the categories from 1 to 10. Evaluate strengths and weaknesses.

HEAD   HEART   HAND

STRATEGY

Significant products, activities, and experiences appeal to a whole person; they "feed the head, heart, and hands." Use these three lenses as a means of finding, clarifying, or diagnosing the meaning of any endeavor.

TIPS FOR PLAYING ONLINE

This game translates well online. It is a great game for opening, exploring, and closing. It can be used to check in with a group at the beginning of a meeting or workshop; while exploring to consider how a product or solution will appeal to all dimensions; or closing to uncover how the group feels they will take the workshop with them as they move toward a common goal.

The Head, Heart, Hands game was inspired by Swiss educational reformer Heinrich Pestalozzi.

Help Me Understand

OBJECT OF PLAY

Help Me Understand is based on the underlying (and accurate) assumption that a team comes to meetings with widely different questions around a topic or a change. It assumes leadership can anticipate *some* questions and concerns but can't possibly anticipate them all. No one knows the questions employees have better than the employees themselves, so this game gives them a chance to externalize what's on their minds and have leadership be responsive in a setting outside the once-a-year retreat. It also allows the players to discover overlaps with other players' questions and to notice the frequency with which those questions occur—something they may not have known prior to the meeting. It lets some sunshine in around a project, initiative, or change so that employees—who have to implement that change—have fewer lingering questions.

NUMBER OF PLAYERS

5–25

DURATION OF PLAY

30 minutes to 1.5 hours

HOW TO PLAY

1. In a large white space visible to all the players, write the topic of the meeting and the following as headers across the top: "WHO?", "WHAT?", "WHEN?", "WHERE?", and "HOW?". Give all players access to sticky notes and markers.

2. Tell the players that the goal of the game is to let leadership understand and be responsive to any and all questions around the topic.

3. Start with the question "WHO?" and give the players five minutes to silently write down as many questions as they can that begin with the word "WHO."

4. Ask the players to post all of their questions in the white space under "WHO?" and then ask for a couple of volunteers to cluster the questions according to topical similarity.

5. Bring the largest clusters to the group's attention—circle them if you prefer—and ask leadership to offer a response to the most common questions in the clusters and to any outlier questions that look interesting.

6. Repeat this process for the remaining four header questions, each time asking leadership to respond to the questions that seem the most salient to the group.

7. When the meeting closes, gather all of the questions so that leadership has the opportunity to review them later and respond to important questions that weren't covered during the meeting.

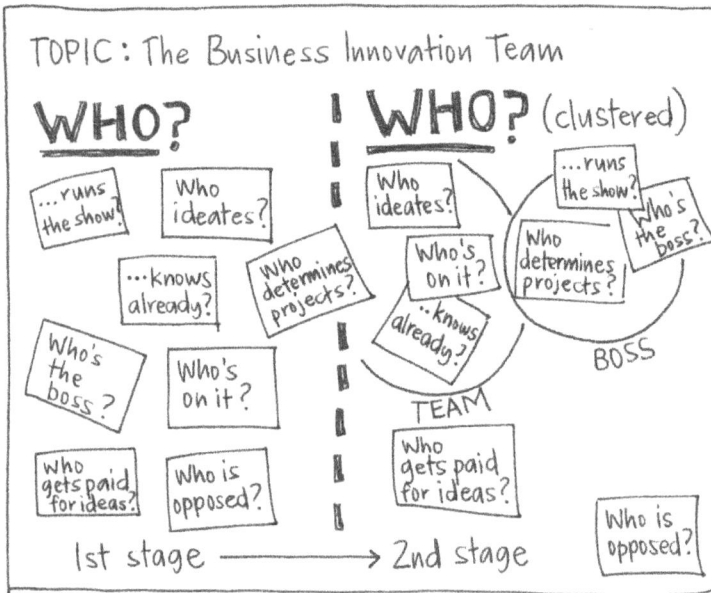

STRATEGY

As the group leader, you can conduct this game in different ways. One way is to ask the five questions back to back, with the players creating sticky notes for all five questions—WHO?, WHAT?, WHEN?, WHERE?, and HOW?—and then posting and clustering them during the first half of the meeting. After they've completed that part of the game, the players ask leadership to address the major clusters during the second half of the meeting. Another approach is to let leadership intersperse responses while the players tackle the header questions one at a time. There are benefits to both approaches.

The first approach allows the players to write questions uninterrupted by content from and reactions to leadership. It also allows leadership to save some time since they only technically need to attend the second half of the session. The second approach breaks up the flow a bit but will inevitably affect the types of questions the players ask since they're getting information from leadership as they go. Choose what's appropriate based on your knowledge of the group.

During the clustering part of the game, you may want to write emergent themes near each cluster to give leadership summaries of where their employees' attention is. This is also helpful for the players to reinforce that they have shared concerns. The themes should be one- to three-word phrases summarizing the general content of the clusters. And as the meeting leader, encourage employees to make the most of this game since it presents an unusual opportunity for them to pose real, substantive questions directly to their company leaders.

TIPS FOR PLAYING ONLINE

This game can be played online, and the private thinking that's done in person can be mimicked using breakout rooms.

This game is an adaptation of WHO WHAT WHEN WHERE and HOW from Facilitator's Guide to Participatory Decision-Making by Sam Kaner. In his book, Kamen notes that his use of this tool was inspired by an exercise called "Five W's and H" in Techniques of Structured Problem Solving, second edition, by A. B. VanGundy, Jr., p. 46 (Van Nostrand Reinhold).

Hidden Variables

OBJECT OF PLAY

The intent of Hidden Variables is to move us away from a binary or, perhaps, a scarcity mindset. It does so by helping us recognize that every single phenomenon in our life is a gift, a challenge, or instruction from processes that circumstances, people, and the universe itself put in place—that a profound creativity made possible. In the quest for staying attuned to your life and the abundance and mystery within, this contemplative, awe-inspiring game is something you can practice anytime.

Used rigorously, Hidden Variables can help you rearrange ideas about how you think things "really are" or are "supposed to be" and instead help you become present to and more embracing of *what is*—even while you may still use energy to change or improve it.

NUMBER OF PLAYERS

One or more people

DURATION OF PLAY

30–45 minutes

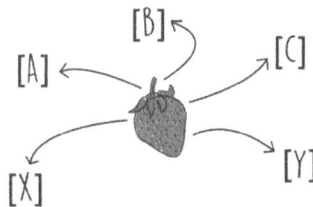

HOW TO PLAY

1. Choosing a strawberry as one example of a phenomenon to place at the center of this game, the question at hand is, *What are all of the processes that made that strawberry possible, and available to you in this moment?*

2. Using a visual structure similar enough to the one shown, draw a strawberry and identify, with sticky notes or simply offshooting branches, as

many hidden variables as possible that have to exist in order for even one strawberry to be available to you. (5 minutes)

3. Think broadly, and consider the following categories if you get stuck:

- Biological
- Circumstantial
- Financial
- Emotional
- Familial
- Socio-policial

- Medical
- Intergenerational
- Psychological
- Spiritual
- Etc.

STRATEGY

Most of the time, we are oblivious to the complex processes—the intelligent flow of information and relationships—that make things available to us. But taking five minutes (or even two minutes!), to do an imaginative visual exercise that invokes the web of life can inspire feelings of appreciation and wonder. There are millions of process flows of energy, matter, and information unfolding around us all the time. We may default to *perceiving* reality as discrete, independent, and disconnected units that don't have interrelationship, but the truth is that reality is a constantly changing, dynamic fabric out of which seemingly infinite things arise, abide, and dissolve. Contemplating the interconnectedness of all things can inspire humility, gratitude, a sense of belonging, and an intimacy with the truth of impermanence, helping us remember that we're part of something—not the center of the universe. We might even conduct ourselves more generously after we play.

TIPS FOR PLAYING ONLINE

Create a space on your mural for this game and pre-populate it with the topic, an icon, any important thematic categories, the following Zentangle template, and sticky notes if your group isn't used to generating many of them at the same time. You can re-create this game template in analog form by doodling it (highly recommended—Zentangles help put you in a contemplative state of mind), download the image and print, or insert the digital image into an online collaboration tool. Here's an example of that last one (*https://oreil.ly/GpRi7*):

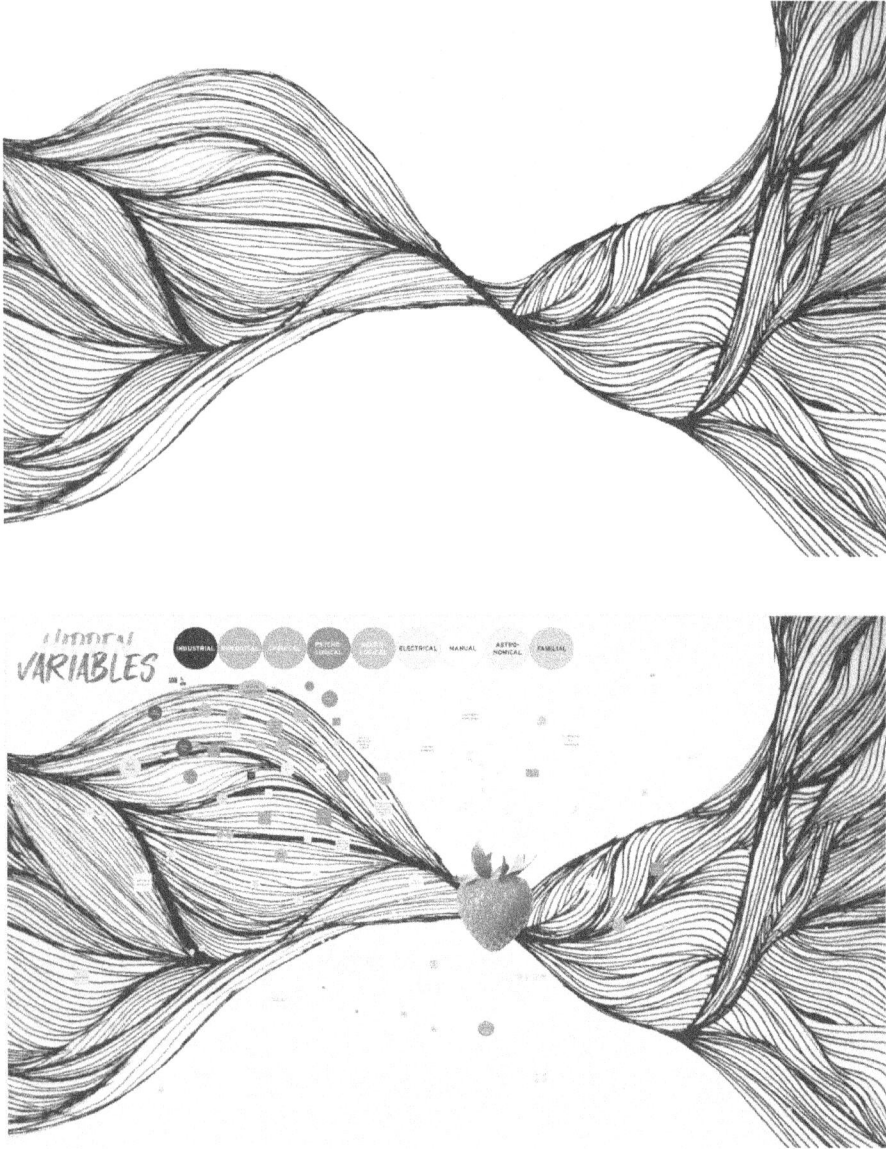

Hidden Variables was created by Sunni (Sun) Brown, inspired by the physicist David Bohm, and is described at nothingintheway.substack.com/p/hidden-variables. Zentangle by Saher Kahn.

Make a World

OBJECT OF PLAY

The Make a World game appeals to visual, auditory, and kinesthetic learners because of its layers of interaction. It's useful (and downright fun) because it lets players imagine the future and take action to create a first version of it. All successful ventures start with a vision and some small, initial effort toward crystallization. Alexander Graham Bell's vision for the telephone started as highly rudimentary sketches. The purpose of Make a World is to create a three-dimensional model of a desired future state.

NUMBER OF PLAYERS

8–20

DURATION OF PLAY

45 minutes to 1.5 hours

HOW TO PLAY

1. Before the meeting, determine a meeting topic. It can be any topic that would benefit from the group advancing it to a desired future state (e.g., "Our new branch location in Austin" or "Our future marketing strategy").

2. Tell the players the meeting topic and give them access to flip-chart paper, markers, sticky notes, pipe cleaners, modeling clay, cards, objects, tape—any art supplies available to help them "make a world."

3. Break the players into groups of three or four and give them 10–15 minutes to agree on a shared vision to make into a three-dimensional world. Explain that the world can include people, scenes, buildings, products, and features, and anything they deem necessary to show an idealized version of the topic.

4. Give the players 20–30 minutes to brainstorm the attributes of the world and physically create it using art supplies.

5. When the time is up, give the players five minutes to create a slogan or tagline to summarize their world.

6. Have each group showcase their "Eden" and give the others insight into what it offers. Make note of any recurring themes or parallel features in these "fantasy lands."

STRATEGY

Any desired state can be visualized. The game isn't confined to creating 3D models of widgets or parks or products or real estate. The "world" that players create could be a new landscape for a video game, a happier and more aligned team, a globally distributed supply chain, and so forth. The challenge for each group will be in the process of ideating and creating without shutting out possibilities. Encourage them to be expansive in their thinking. In this game, players are limited only by their imaginations and their art supplies.

TIPS FOR PLAYING ONLINE

This game looks a little different online, but still works well. Trade cardboard and tangible objects for GIFs and icons, images of landscapes, and digital tokens.

The title of this game was inspired by Ed Emberley's book, Make a World (*part of the Ed Emberly's Drawing Book series, published by LB Kids*).

Mood Board

OBJECT OF PLAY

The object of this game is to create a poster or collage that captures the overall "feel" of an idea. The mood board may be used throughout development as a frame of reference or inspiration. It may be composed of visual or written artifacts—photos clipped from magazines, physical objects, color swatches, or anything that communicates the overall flow and feel of an idea.

NUMBER OF PLAYERS

1–10

DURATION OF PLAY

30 minutes to 2 hours

HOW TO PLAY

Although mood boards are common in design disciplines, creating a mood board does not require professional expertise. Any group that is at the beginning of a project may benefit from creating a mood board; all they need is the raw material and the idea to interpret.

Gather visual material from stacks of magazines, the web, or even corporate presentations. Everything else—scissors, tape, blank paper, and flip charts—can be found in most office supply closets. Bring the group together around the materials and the theme that they will be interpreting. Here are some to consider:

- "Our Culture"
- "Next Year"
- "The New Product"

Small teams may cocreate a single mood board from individual contributions; larger groups may interpret the theme separately and then share them with each other. It's important that every participant gets a chance to contribute elements to the board and to explain their imagery.

STRATEGY

When participants are selecting and contributing elements to a board, they are best advised to do so "from the gut" and not to overly rationalize their choices. A mood board is an artifact that captures the "feel" of an idea—it's not a comprehensive description or a requirements document!

The game is complete when the board is complete, but the board should live on after the process. It is invaluable to keep the board visible and persistent throughout development.

TIPS FOR PLAYING ONLINE

Create an online mood board using a digital whiteboard or other collaboration space. Structure the board in the same way you would offline. Set the activity and create a space for contributions.

Mood boards are a traditional design practice and are often a feature in the architectural practice called charette—*an intense period of collaborative group design activity around a shared goal.*

Open Space

OBJECT OF PLAY

Open Space technology is a method for hosting large events, such as retreats and conferences, without a prepared agenda. Instead, participants are brought together under a guiding purpose and create the agenda for themselves in a bulletin-board fashion. These items become potential breakout sessions, and participants have the freedom to "vote with their feet" by moving between breakouts.

Open Space was founded by Harrison Owen in the 1980s out of a desire to "open the space" for people to self-organize around a purpose. Many meetings and examples have been recorded at Openspaceworld.org. Hosting a small Open Space meeting is fairly straightforward but requires an amount of "letting go" on the part of the organizer, who must trust that the participants will develop a rich approach and solution to the challenge at hand.

NUMBER OF PLAYERS

5–2,000

DURATION OF PLAY

A day or longer

HOW TO PLAY

Setup: An open invitation

Perhaps the most important work of the facilitator is developing a compelling invitation. The ideal invitation will frame a challenge that is urgent, important, and complex enough to require a diverse set of perspectives to solve.

It might sound as simple as "How can we revitalize our city's schools?" or "What's our strategic direction?"

Create the marketplace

At the start of the process, participants sit in a circle, or in concentric circles, to get oriented and start to create their agenda. Given the challenge of the meeting, participants are invited to come to the center and write out an issue they're passionate about and then post it on a "marketplace" wall with a time and place at which they are willing to host the discussion.

All are invited to create an item for the marketplace, but no one is required to. Creating the agenda in this fashion should take between 60 and 90 minutes.

The "Law of Two Feet"

The breakouts then begin, typically lasting 90 minutes per session. Participants may organize their breakouts however they see fit; the host records the discussion so that others may join the conversation at any time. Participants are asked to observe the one law of Open Space, the *Law of Two Feet*, which asks that if you find yourself neither learning nor contributing, use your two feet to go somewhere else. In this sense, participants are given full responsibility over their learning and contributions.

Pulling it all together

Breakouts may last for a few hours to a day or more, depending on the scope of the event. Closing the event may take many forms, the least desirable of which is a formal report from the groups. Instead of a traditional report-back, return to the circle arrangement that started the event, and open the space again for participants who want to reflect on what they've discovered and their next steps.

STRATEGY

Keep in mind the four principles of Open Space that will help set the tone of the event:

1. Whoever comes are the right people. Passion is more important than position on an org chart.

2. Whenever it starts is the right time. Spirit and creativity do not run on the clock.

3. Whatever happens is the only thing that could have. Dwelling or complaining about past events and missed opportunities is a waste of time; move on.

4. When it's over, it's over. When a conversation is finished, move on. Do the work, not the time.

Open Space game rules have been popularized and incorporated into many self-organizing events, which are known under different names, most prominently BarCamps and Unconferences.

TIPS FOR PLAYING ONLINE

Open Space works well organized online with a matrix. Post the invitations and information on which breakout room to join. All rooms, including the main room, stay open, and participants are free to rejoin them at any time.

The concept of Open Space was put forth in Open Space Technology: A User's Guide, *by Harrison Owen (Berrett-Koehler). Dave Gray's School of the Possible uses this regularly to support creative projects.*

The Pitch

OBJECT OF PLAY

It is easy to come up with concepts in a world of imagination, where money, time, and technical capacity are unlimited, or to generate ideas that look good in theory but are impractical in reality. The Pitch is a role-playing game designed to bring attention back to the real world and focus on feasible and viable aspects of concepts (What are the key selling points? How can this make money? Why will people buy it?). The players imagine they are entrepreneurs and need to sell their idea to a group of investors.

NUMBER OF PLAYERS

4–12 people

DURATION OF PLAY

30 minutes to 1.5 hours

HOW TO PLAY

1. Divide people into small groups, ideally pairs or triads. One group should take the role of the investor, while the others are "entrepreneurs."

2. A product or service is defined and agreed on by the group.

3. Individually, each group spends 10 minutes formulating their pitch to be presented to the investors. They can write, draw, and rehearse: the creation is really up to each group. Ideally they should be in separate rooms or breakout spaces while creating the pitches.

4. All groups should be aware that one or two representatives will present the pitch verbally to the investors, but the whole group will answer their questions. It is also important to cap preparation time (around 10 minutes is good), since over-elaborating an idea can take away the true nature of their thoughts.

5. Toward the end of the preparation time, the investors give groups a time warning: "You have two minutes prep remaining."

6. Each group then presents their pitch; a time limit (3 minutes) is given for each presentation, and the investors can ask up to two questions each.

7. It's not essential, but to add a sense of competition, the investors can decide which pitch is the winner at the end.

STRATEGY

The idea behind this game is to capture the different perspectives that different groups have about a product, prototype, service, or concept. Preparing a pitch to a venture capitalist or other investor obliges participants to focus on the really important ideas, and the time limit helps them to concentrate on the core of the proposition. Because different groups will emphasize different aspects, it also provides a range of perspectives on the main idea being discussed. The questions the VCs ask usually expose weak points or help clarify ideas, which can then be shared and discussed by the group.

This game is also good for capturing the type of language people use to define a concept, product, service, or situation, so you should encourage participants not to overthink the words they use in their pitch. If participants don't know each other, it's interesting to make a competition out of it and even offer a prize to the winner: the shared goal of "winning the game" usually brings teams together quickly.

TIPS FOR PLAYING ONLINE

The Pitch game works well online using a shared board. Create groups depending on the group size in step 1. Work through step 3 in breakout groups. Ask participants to create their pitch on sticky notes or slides. If using slides, be sure that everyone adds theirs to the board before presenting in step 6.

The Pitch game is credited to Sarah Rink.

Planning Poker

OBJECT OF PLAY

Planning poker, also known as "scrum poker" and "pointing poker," is a game used in Agile development to prioritize and estimate the relative effort of tasks. Estimates are based on the group's input, so they can be more accurate than other methods of estimation.

NUMBER OF PLAYERS

5–15 people

DURATION OF PLAY

Timeboxed—60 minutes

HOW TO PLAY

1. In advance of the meeting, prepare "decks" of cards for each participant using index cards and the Fibonacci sequence (0, 1, 1, 2, 3, 5, 8, 13, 21, 34…).

2. Present a list of tasks to the group for consideration. These could be results from another game or an ongoing task list for a project.

3. Select one task.

4. To help prioritize, participants select a card from their Fibonacci decks to represent the value of the task.

5. Now, ask everyone to reveal their "hand" simultaneously.

6. Review and pair the participants with the highest and lowest values to debate their views.

7. After 4–6 minutes of discussion, ask the participants to reach a consensus and record the value.

8. Then, move on to the next task and repeat steps 2–6.

9. At the end of a timeboxed Planning Poker session, the group will have a sequence for the list based on the relative prioritization.

STRATEGY

The Fibonacci sequence is used because its exponential nature helps teams more accurately estimate and gauge relative effort between tasks and focus on the bigger picture rather than getting caught up in minute details. It's especially helpful when dealing with more complex items. The numbers on the cards shouldn't be thought of as directly related to an estimate of hours or people needed, etc.; rather, they should be considered in the context of other tasks. For this reason, the first few tasks can be the hardest to estimate, but participants are encouraged to resist the urge to create a formulaic approach to ease this initial discomfort.

TIPS FOR PLAYING ONLINE

Planning Poker can be played online using a digital whiteboard, spreadsheet, or other tool. Online software for planning poker is widely available, but not required. Add a "deck" of Fibonacci cards and make them available to each player. Ask participants to present or unhide their "hands" simultaneously to reveal each participant's estimate.

James Grenning refined an estimation technique called Wideband Delphi, developed by the RAND Corporation, calling it Planning Poker, and tailored it for Agile development teams. Mike Cohn of Mountain Goat Software popularized the game in his book Agile Estimating and Planning *(Pearson).*

Popcorn

OBJECT OF PLAY

A recurring challenge in group work is managing discussions so that every individual has a chance to contribute, and no individuals dominate the meeting. By using simple "popcorn" contributions, a group can self-manage the flow of participation.

NUMBER OF PLAYERS

2–20 people

DURATION OF PLAY

5–20 minutes

HOW TO PLAY

1. Before the meeting starts, each participant draws an object (poker chip, coin, paperclip, etc.) from the center of the table.
2. A participant places their object in the center to speak.
3. Like kernels of popcorn, you only get to pop once.
4. Once all have been placed in the center, participants may remove their items from the center to speak in the same manner, and the process repeats.

STRATEGY

Popcorn-style distributed control makes the value of everyone's contributions tangible and equal and gives everyone a chance to speak. It's just as effective at drawing out otherwise quiet participants as it is at containing dominant ones. This can be dedicated time to offer feedback, or a structure used within a larger agenda.

TIPS FOR PLAYING ONLINE

Play online using digital tokens or icons. Create one for each participant in advance. Ask participants to place their digital object in a designated space on the board to speak, like in step 2.

Popcorn is based on the idea of currency and was developed by Dave Gray, inspired by Byron Reeves's innovative email program, Attent.

Post the Path

OBJECT OF PLAY

The object of this game is to quickly diagnose a group's level of understanding of the steps in a process.

Often, there is a sense of confusion about who does what and when. The team is using different terms to describe their process. The group has no documented process. Things seem to be happening in an ad hoc fashion, invisibly, or by chance.

Through this exercise, the group will define an existing process at a high level and uncover areas of confusion or misunderstanding. In most cases, this can flow naturally into a discussion of what to do about those unclear areas. This exercise will not generally result in a new or better process but, rather, a better understanding of the current one.

NUMBER OF PLAYERS

2–10 people

DURATION OF PLAY

30 minutes to 1 hour

HOW TO PLAY

Introduce the exercise by framing the objective: "This is a group activity, where we will create a picture of how we create [X]." X, in this case, is the output of the process; it may be a document, a product, an agreement, or the like. Write or draw the output of the process on the wall.

Establish a common starting point of the process with the group. This could sound like "the beginning of the day" or "the start of a quarter" or "after we finished the last one." This is the trigger (or triggers) that kicks off the process. If you believe the group will have a hard time with this simple step, decide it for them in advance and present it as a best guess. Write this step on a sticky note, put it on the wall, and then proceed with the exercise.

1. Instruct participants to think about the process from beginning to end. Then give them the task: write down the steps in the process. They can use as many notes as they like, but each step must be a separate note.

2. After the participants have brainstormed their version of the steps, ask them to come up to the wall and post them to compare. The group should

place their steps above and below one another's so that they can compare their versions of steps 1, 2, and so on.

3. Prompt the group to find points of agreement and confusion. Look for terminology problems, where participants may be using different words to describe the same step. Points of confusion may surface where "something magical happens" or no one is really clear on a step.

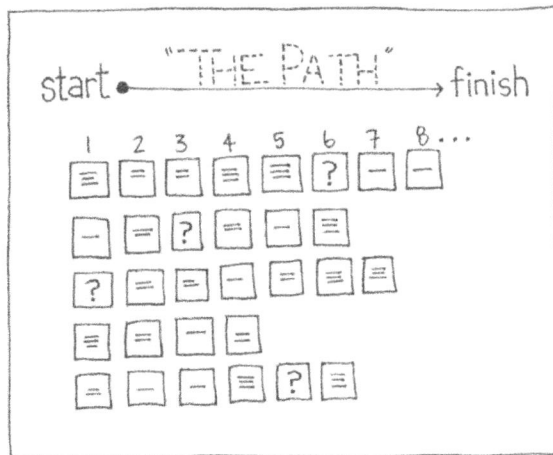

STRATEGY

The group will draw their own conclusions about what the different versions of the process mean and what they can or should do about it.

For a larger group, you may want to avoid individual readouts and instead have people post-up simultaneously.

If you sense in advance that the group will get caught up in the details, ask them to produce a limited number of steps—try 10.

TIPS FOR PLAYING ONLINE

Post the Path works well online using a whiteboard with sticky notes.

The Post the Path game is credited to James Macanufo.

Product Pinocchio

OBJECT OF PLAY

Quite naturally, most of us don't think of products or services as being alive and animate. But there are a lot of benefits to imagining a product as a friend rather than an instrument. By pretending that a product has come to life, we can personalize and evolve its features in a way that is not accessible to us when we think of it as inanimate. Product Pinocchio is a game designed to establish, refine, and evolve the features of a product or service so that it becomes more valuable to the end user. By personifying it, we can better relate to it and better craft it into a "friend" that a consumer might want to take home.

NUMBER OF PLAYERS

5–20

DURATION OF PLAY

One hour

HOW TO PLAY

1. For this game, a "scene" is any simple situation in which the character (the product or service) is required to make a decision or take action. Scene examples might be "you realize you're lost in the desert" or "a driver encounters a hitchhiker on the way to a party" or "a thief steals a woman's purse" or "a child asks for help." Before the meeting, invent four scenes and write them on index cards, one scene per card.

2. Also before the meeting, write each of the following five questions on the tops of flip-chart paper, one question per sheet:

   — What am I like?   — What makes me different?

   — What are my values?   — What is my fight?

   — What is my community?

3. Starting with "What am I like?", draw a picture of the product/service in the middle of the sheet of paper with arms, legs, and a head. (This character should be used throughout the exercise, but in different poses.)

4. Ask the group to imagine that the product or service has come to life and is now a fully developed character that they know well. Ask them to call out adjectives and phrases that describe that character and write their responses around the picture.

5. During this step, you can also ask players who the product/service would be if it were a cartoon character or a celebrity and write down those responses as well.

6. When you have enough information to adequately describe the character, ask the players to dot vote next to the three to five adjectives that best describe the character. Circle or highlight the information that got the most votes and make a note of it with the group.

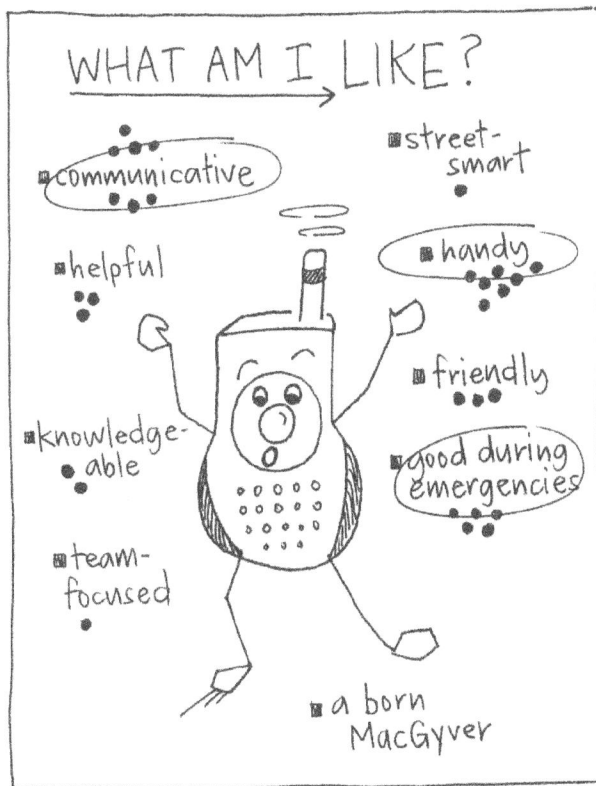

7. Move to the "What are my values?" flip chart and draw a picture of the character. Divide the group into four small groups and give each group an index card describing a scene (or work with all four scenes as one group if you have seven or fewer players). Ask the players to read their scene quietly and discuss in their groups what the character would say or do in that situation.

8. Bring the groups back together and give each one an opportunity to share what they agreed their character would do. Write each response down and then ask the group as a whole what the behaviors suggest about the character's underlying values. Add their responses to the flip chart.

9. Move to the "What is my community?" flip chart and draw another picture of the character in the middle of the sheet. Ask the group who the character spends their time with. What groups do they belong to? Where do they volunteer? Who needs them the most? What do their friends have in common? What are the qualities of their community? Write down the responses.

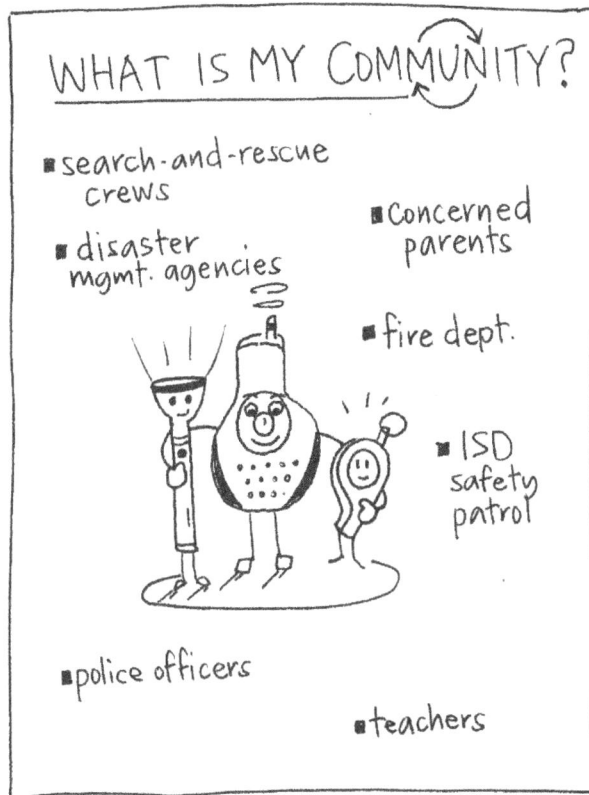

10. Move to the "What makes me different?" flip chart and draw a picture of the character in the middle of the sheet. Ask the group how this character is different from other characters in her community. What makes them stand out? What are their strengths? What could they do better? Why would someone want them on a team? Write down the responses.

11. Move to the "What is my fight?" flip chart and draw a picture of the character in the middle of the sheet. Find out the character's mission in life. What motivates them? What keeps them up at night? What do they do for people? What are they trying to prove? What obstacles are in their way? Write these responses down.

Optional activity: Ask people to toast the character as though they were celebrating their life achievements. Alternatively, ask them to give a eulogy to a competing product or service as though they were at its funeral. Or ask the players to share a true story from the character's life, something that happened to them that makes them who they are.

Summarize the overall findings with the group and reflect on the personality and identity of the character the group created. Discuss the implications of the character traits, values, and behaviors on the features—current or potential—of the related product or service.

STRATEGY

This game works best when the players suspend disbelief and jump into the idea that a product has a personality, a value system, and a life. For some players, it will be a hard leap to make, which is why the picture you draw is important, as are the questions you ask: they both force responses as though the "it" were a "he" or "she." Be receptive even to character names suggested during the group's interactions. Naming it (say, "Cameron") makes it easier to imagine the product or service as a person rather than an object or a process.

Encourage storytelling during this game to flesh out the character's identity based on the scenes you concocted; for example, "What would Cameron do?" Don't discourage the group from creating outlandish characters or personality traits, because the actions taken by a zany character may lead to an innovation in the way people conceive of the use of a product or service. Let the players go as far out as they want; if need be, you can move them toward consensus on a more believable character as the game closes. Just be sure to discuss with the group the parallels between the character traits they created and the benefits those traits may have on the next version of the product or service.

TIPS FOR PLAYING ONLINE

Product Pinococchio works well online using a whiteboard or other collaboration software. In a larger group, facilitators can break up participants into smaller groups and send them to breakout rooms. Each room can start on a different question on the board, and they can cycle through them simultaneously, until each element has been addressed. Then the group comes back together to review, synthesize, and discuss.

The source of the Product Pinocchio is unknown.

RACI Matrix

OBJECT OF PLAY

Sometimes responsibilities aren't clear. Nothing erodes morale and performance faster than a difficult problem that belongs to someone else—or to everyone. When these situations raise their head, it may be necessary to call a group together to sort out who does what. By creating a RACI (responsible, accountable, consulted, informed) matrix collaboratively, a group will tackle the responsibility problem directly.

NUMBER OF PLAYERS

2–6 people

DURATION OF PLAY

1.5 hours

HOW TO PLAY

To set up the matrix, you will need two lists:

A work breakdown
> These are the items or activities that the group shares responsibility for creating or managing. These should be specific enough to answer when a team member asks, "Who does X?"

A list of roles
> Instead of creating a list of individuals, create a list of roles that represent a group of related tasks. For example, "Project Manager," "Business Analyst," and "Architect" are better than "Tim," "Bob," and "Mary" because individuals can play multiple roles on a project, and multiple people can contribute to a single role.

Create the matrix by listing the work breakdown along the vertical axis and the roles along the horizontal axis. Inside the matrix, the group will work through assigning levels of responsibility by coding R, A, C, I:

Responsible
> This is the *doer* of the work. Although this person may delegate or seek support from others, ultimately this one person is responsible for doing the work.

Accountable

> This person is accountable for the work that the *responsible* person does and signs off on the work. The golden rule of RACI is that only one person can be *accountable* for each task

Consulted

> These contributors provide input, opinions, and advice through two-way communication.

Informed

> Although they are not contributors, these people are kept up-to-date on progress or completion through one-way communication.

In working through the matrix with the group, it is best to follow the natural progression of the work breakdown from start to finish. The matrix is complete when every task has a clear set of responsibilities.

R. A. C. I.

Responsible   Accountable   Consulted   Informed

	Expert Witness	Case Manager	Consultant
provides testimony	R	A	A
prepares documents	I	A	R
project manages	I	R	C

STRATEGY

The work breakdown is needed to set up the matrix, but don't be reluctant to change it as the group works through the matrix. In some cases, you may discover that items are unnecessary, redundant, or poorly defined. For example, where it is difficult to assign a single *responsible* role, it may help to split the item into two smaller, better-defined pieces. Other items will have no *responsible* role at all, and the group may decide to eliminate them. This activity can be helpful when structure needs to be created or roles more clearly defined. By defining the tasks and considering the responsibilities of everyone involved, a path forward emerges.

TIPS FOR PLAYING ONLINE

This activity is adapted online with a template and stickies on a shared board. The final outcome created by the group can be recorded in a shared sheet.

RACI Matrix is based on the same-named diagram traditionally employed in the management of cross-functional teams.

Remembering the Future

OBJECT OF PLAY

Remembering the Future is well suited for exploring in groups. It can also be a great opening and closing game for a group that knows each other well.

NUMBER OF PLAYERS

1–1,000 people

DURATION OF PLAY

3–7 minutes

HOW TO PLAY

1. Tell everyone you want to play a game. Get a piece of paper or ask the group to get out their phones and open whatever app they would use to write a note to themselves.

2. Now write the title, "Remembering the Future."

3. Then write one letter per line:

   "X ="

   "Y ="

   "Z ="

4. Starting with X, what's something you do, an activity, that brings you energy and *pure joy* when you do it?

5. Now for Y, who is someone you love?

6. Finally for Z, what's a place you really want to go…that's maybe far away?

7. Confirm everyone has their answers, then set the scene, "It's now one year from today…and you are doing X, with Y, at Z." What's the story for how that came to be? Invite participants to write down the story.

8. Ask for volunteers to share their story.

STRATEGY

This prompt is fun for expanding perception and facilitating connections in a group. It primes for strategy and storytelling. The more outlandish the connections, the better the story. Some people will naturally want to share—allow that to happen and them to express their joy with the group.

TIPS FOR PLAYING ONLINE

Remembering the Future works well online. With cameras on, lead the group through the prompt. Ask participants to keep their mics on and write their responses on paper. The contrast in a digital meeting creates engagement. Invite volunteers to share with the group and add it to the board, to the chat, or in a popcorn-style discussion.

Remembering the Future is a Heuristic Ideation Technique to facilitate visioning, connection, and storytelling. It is credited to Danyelle Faulkner and inspired by Expeditions.

Speed Boat

OBJECT OF PLAY

Speed Boat is a short and sweet way to identify what your employees or clients don't like about your product/service or what's standing in the way of a desired goal. As individuals trying to build forward momentum on products or projects, we sometimes have blind spots regarding what's stopping us. This game lets you get insight from stakeholders about what they think may be an obstacle to progress.

NUMBER OF PLAYERS

5–10 people

DURATION OF PLAY

30 minutes

HOW TO PLAY

1. In a white space visible to the players, draw a boat with anchors attached and name the boat after the product/service or goal under discussion. This picture is the metaphor for the activity—the boat represents the product/service or goal and the anchors represent the obstacles slowing the movement toward a desired state.

2. Write the question under discussion next to the boat. For example, "What are the features you don't like about our product?" or "What's standing in the way of progress toward this goal?"

3. Introduce Speed Boat as a game designed to show what might be holding a product/service or goal back. Ask the players to review the question and then take a few minutes to think about the current features of the product/service or the current environment surrounding the goal.

4. Next, ask them to take 5–10 minutes and write the features of the product/service they don't like or any variables that are in the way on sticky notes. If you'd like, you can also ask the players to estimate how much faster the boat would go (in miles or kilometers per hour) without those "anchors" and add that to their sticky notes.

5. Once they are finished, ask them to post the sticky notes on and around the anchors in the picture. Discuss the content on each sticky note and look for observations, insights, and "ahas." Notice recurring themes,

because they can show you where there's consensus around what's holding you back.

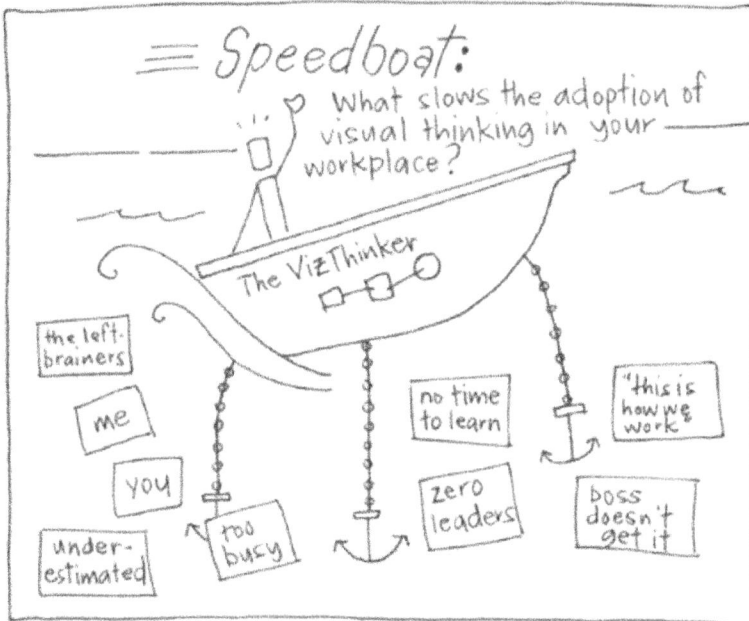

STRATEGY

This game is not about kicking off a complaint parade. It's designed to gather information about improvements or ambitions, so be careful to frame it as such. Tell the players that the intention is to reveal less-than-desirable conditions so that you can be empowered to move the product/service or goal toward an improved state.

That being said, be aware of the fact that many groups have a tendency to move immediately toward analysis of an improved state. They shift into problem-solving mode. However, doing so disrupts the nature of this game play. After the activity, it's probable that you won't have *all* the information or the right stakeholders to respond to the challenges comprehensively. So, if you hear the players critiquing or analyzing the content, gently tell them that problem solving is for another game—try to keep their attention focused solely on description, not solution.

TIPS FOR PLAYING ONLINE

Speed Boat works well online. Draw or add a template to an online collaboration space. Depending on the number of participants, share one game space, or break into smaller groups and collect insights in separate game spaces to share with the group.

Speed Boat is based on the same-named activity in Luke Hohmann's book, Innovation Games: Creating Breakthrough Products Through Collaborative Play.

SQUID

OBJECT OF PLAY

When exploring an information space, it's important for a group to know where they are at any given time. What have we covered, and what did we leave behind? By using SQUID, a group charts out the territory as they go and can navigate accordingly.

SQUID stands for sequential question and insight diagram. It is created progressively over the course of a meeting with sticky notes, capturing questions and answers as the group moves through the space. It is flexible and will move and grow with the discussion, but it also needs to "breathe" by moving between its critical modes of questions and answers.

NUMBER OF PLAYERS

Small groups

DURATION OF PLAY

Timeboxed to 30 minutes provides optimum productivity

HOW TO PLAY

1. Reserve a large area of a whiteboard or several flip charts to create the SQUID. Participants are given two colors of sticky notes to work with, one for questions and one for answers.

2. Start to build the diagram by writing the group's core topic on a sticky note. Put this in the center of the space.

Question mode

To open the exercise, ask individuals to generate a question that is their "best guess" on how to approach the topic. They capture this on a color-coded sticky note, and share it with the group by posting it adjacent to the center of the SQUID. The questions should immediately offer a few different routes of inquiry, and participants will likely start offering thoughts on answers.

Answer mode

Similar to question mode, participants write their "best answers" on color-coded sticky notes. They share them with the group by posting these notes adjacent to the relevant question and connect them with a line. They may answer more than one question, and they may answer one question with multiple answers. As a rule, answers should be succinct enough to fit on one note.

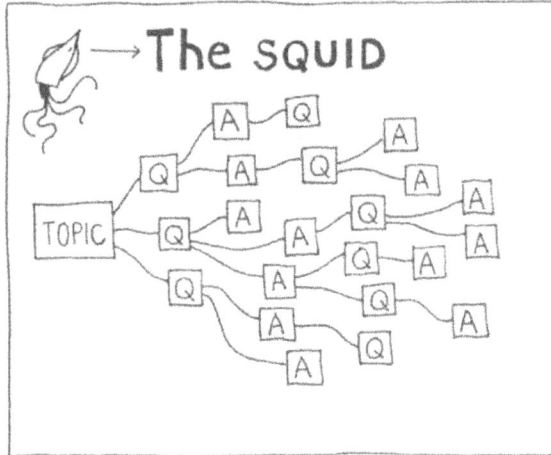

After a discussion, the group then moves back into question mode, generating questions based on the last round of answers. Participants may focus on earlier parts of the SQUID as well. The process repeats over the course of the discussion.

STRATEGY

Keeping with the current mode and not crossing questions with answers requires discipline that can only be acquired by a group through time. By working in this way, a group will train itself on the value of a systematic, rhythmic movement through unknown information, in contrast with a meandering group discussion. The SQUID itself is, of course, utterly flexible and will grow as the group directs it.

TIPS FOR PLAYING ONLINE

The SQUID game works well online. Create space on a shared board and connect sticky notes for questions and answers. Depending on your group size, create breakout groups of 2–5 people to facilitate discussions.

The SQUID game is credited to James Macanufo.

Staple Yourself to Something

OBJECT OF PLAY

The goal of this game is to explore or clarify a process by following an object through its flow. Through this exercise, a group will create a memorable, visual story of their core process. After it is completed, this artifact can be used to identify opportunities to improve or educate others involved in the process.

The notion of "stapling yourself to an order" comes from process improvement but can be useful in a variety of scenarios. A group with no documented process, or an overly complex one, will benefit from the exercise. If the process is taking too long or if no one seems to know how the work gets done, it's time to staple yourself to something and see where it goes.

NUMBER OF PLAYERS

2–10 people

DURATION OF PLAY

30–90 minutes

HOW TO PLAY

1. The group must have an idea of what their object is, the "bouncing ball" that they will follow through the process. It's best to decide on this in advance. Some example objects could be a product, a trouble ticket, or an idea. A familiar example of this type of flow is "How a bill becomes a law."

2. Introduce the exercise by drawing the object. The goal is to focus on telling the story of this one object from point A to point B. Write these commonly understood starting and ending points on the wall.

3. Ask participants to brainstorm a list of the big steps in the process and record them on the wall. If needed, ask them to prioritize them into a desired and workable number of steps. For a high-level story, look to capture seven steps.

4. Before you start to follow the object, work out with the group the vital information you are looking to capture in the story. Ask: in each step of the process, what do we need to know? This may be the people involved, the action they're taking, or the amount of time a step takes.

5. Now it's time to draw. The group will tell the story of the object as it moves step-by-step. As much as possible, capture the information visually,

as though you were taking a picture of what they are describing. Some useful tools here include stick figures, arrows, and quality questions. Questions that produce an active voice in the answer as in "Who does what here?" will be more concrete and visual. Other good questions include "What's next?" and "What's important?"

6. Be aware that the story will want to branch, loop, and link to other processes, like a river trying to break its banks. Your job is to navigate the flow with the group and keep things moving toward the end.

STRATEGY

Use the object as a focusing device. Any activity that is not directly related to the forward motion of the object can be noted and then tied off.

If possible, add a ticking clock to the story to help pace the flow. If the object needs to get to the end by a certain time, use this to your advantage by introducing it up front and referencing it as needed to keep up the momentum and interest of the story.

One trap to be aware of is that participants may move between the way things are and the way they want them to be. Be clear with the group about what state in time—today or the desired future—you are capturing.

Does the process have an owner? If someone is responsible for the process, you can use this person's expertise, but be cautious not to let them tell the entire story. This can be a learning experience for them as well, if they listen to the participants describe "their version" of the story.

TIPS FOR PLAYING ONLINE

The Staple Yourself to Something game works well in an online collaboration tool. Create a game board and set a template to be filled in live by a facilitator. Use an image or drawing of the object to set up the game. Facilitate the group discussion as you would offline and capture ideas visually for refinement. If played in a large group, then create breakouts of 3–7 people to continue this work. Have each group brainstorm the big steps in the process and capture their thoughts on their space on the board.

There are many ways of conducting a "day in the life" type of visualization. This version of the game is credited to James Macanufo.

Synesthesia

OBJECT OF PLAY

By its very nature, knowledge work can be a head-heavy, deeply analytical activity. Even when the results of the work are sensory, the process of getting there is often the opposite: we think our way to solutions and filter out the five senses as irrelevant or frivolous. Through Synesthesia role play, participants examine a topic through a sensory lens and let this inform their decisions and designs.

NUMBER OF PLAYERS

2–5 people

DURATION OF PLAY

15–45 minutes

HOW TO PLAY

1. Participants may choose to examine an existing topic or explore a new idea. It may be something as simple as "the interface for our new site" or as complex as "our global supply chain."

2. Participants choose or are randomly assigned one of the five senses: see, hear, taste, smell, and touch. Also consider including as choices temperature, position, and motion.

3. Participants are given a few moments to interpret a topic from the perspective of their sense and to move on to the other senses as they see fit. They then describe to the group what they perceived. For example:

   "The interface is warm to the touch. And it tastes like oranges."

   "When the app launches, it's as if I can hear an orchestra tuning up to perform. But I can't see anything; I'd like to see what they're doing."

   "The user experience stinks. It smells like a stack of dusty papers, and there is no motion. I wanted to move forward but kept getting slowed down."

STRATEGY

The Synesthesia exercise gives participants a chance to describe in visceral, memorable terms how they feel about an object or how they imagine it to be. It can uncover overlooked aspects of an idea or product or lead to new ones.

TIPS FOR PLAYING ONLINE

Playing Synesthesia online creates a particular contrast. Designate space on the board and identify the topic in step 1. Display the senses to consider and ask participants to spend five minutes brainstorming and recording their responses to the questions in step 3.

The source of the Synesthesia game is unknown.

Understanding Chain

OBJECT OF PLAY

Communicating clearly and effectively is a challenge when there is a lot to say to a lot of people. It can be tempting to try to explain "everything all at once" to an audience and fail in the process. In the Understanding Chain game, a group shifts from a content focus to an audience focus and draws out a meaningful, linear structure for communication.

NUMBER OF PLAYERS

1–10

DURATION OF PLAY

30 minutes to 2 hours

HOW TO PLAY

To set up the game, the group needs to develop two things—an audience breakdown and a set of questions:

The audience(s)

> If there are a large number of audience members, break them down into meaningful groups. The groups could be as broad as "Corporate leaders" or as specific as "The guys in IT who fix the laptops." As a rule of thumb, the more specific the audience, the more tailored and effective the understanding chain will be. Each audience group will need its own understanding chain. This list of audiences could be created as a result of a "WhoDo" exercise.

The questions

> Once the group has a clear picture of their audience, it's time to brainstorm questions. The questions frame what people really want to know and care about. Questions are best captured in the voice or thoughts of the audience, as they would ask them.

The questions may sound like:

- "What's cool about this? Why should I care?"
- "How is this related to a, b, or c?"
- "What makes this a priority?"

Or, they may be more specific:

- "When does your technology roadmap converge with ours?"
- "How will it impact our product portfolio?"

The questions will become the links in the understanding chain. To generate them, the group puts itself in the mindset of the audience and captures the questions on individual sticky notes (see the Post-Up game in Chapter 7 for more information).

Play begins by sorting the questions in a horizontal line on a wall or whiteboard. This is the timeline of a communication, from beginning to end. The group may choose from three options:

Arrange the questions in a simple story format.
In this understanding chain, the group clusters questions under three headings, from left to right:
- *Situation*, which sets the stage, and introduces a topic and a conflict
- *Complication*, in which further conflict is endured and decisions are made
- *Resolution*, in which a course of action that leads to a result is chosen

By constructing the understanding chain as a story, the group may find the "climax"—the most critical question that leads to the resolution.

Arrange the questions in an educate-differentiate-stimulate format.
In this chain, the group arranges the questions from left to right, in three categories:
- *Educate*, in which a topic or idea and its parts are introduced
- *Differentiate*, in which parts of the topic are contrasted to create a basis of understanding
- *Stimulate*, in which actions are asked for or proposed

Arrange the questions as a conversation.
In this chain, the group thinks through or role-plays a conversation with the audience and arranges the questions in an order that flows naturally. Although all conversations are different, one framework to consider is the following:

- *Connecting:* "What's up?" "What do we have in common?"
- *Focusing:* "What's important right now?" "What do you know about it?"
- *Acting:* "What should we do?"

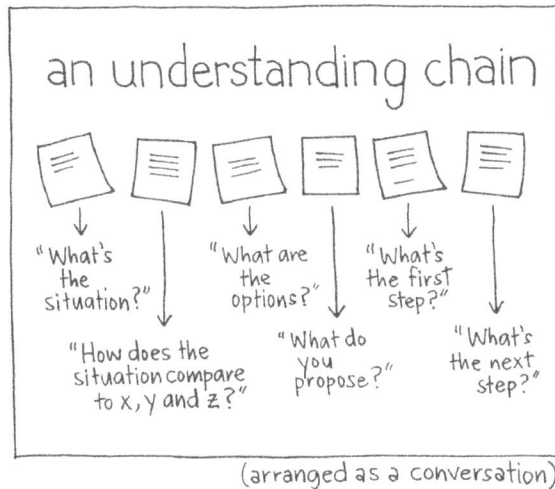

(arranged as a conversation)

STRATEGY

An understanding chain, like any chain, is only as strong as its weakest link. By examining the questions as a whole, the group may uncover an area that needs work or find the "tough questions" that are not easy to answer. A group that tackles the weak questions, and has the courage to answer the tough ones directly and honestly, will win.

TIPS FOR PLAYING ONLINE

Creating an Understanding Chain works well online. In your collaboration space, record the discussion and invite participants to add to it. This can become a helpful artifact that is expanded on after the initial discussion and leveraged to manage the project.

The Understanding Chain game was developed by Dave Gray as part of XPLANE's consulting approach.

Value Mapping

OBJECT OF PLAY

The end goal of Value Mapping is to build a visual matrix that quickly and clearly defines areas of interest for something—it can be a service, a product, a plan, a website. It consists of asking people to choose a limited number of features from a bigger collection and then plotting their choices against a matrix. The result can be presented back in a template that resembles a light box, with items that were chosen more times being lit up by brighter colors and items chosen fewer times by weaker colors.

NUMBER OF PLAYERS

5–30

DURATION OF PLAY

15 minutes to 2 hours

HOW TO PLAY

This game has three main parts:

- Define features and their groups: Draw sketches or write down on cards the features or items you want participants to attribute value to. Group them in a way that makes sense to you and plot them on a table that represents these groups.

- Play: Show the collection of feature cards to participants and have them choose a smaller number than the total, so that they must make choices and leave some features out. A good ratio is 1:3; e.g., if you have 30 cards, ask people to choose 10. Another way of doing this is to provide them with imaginary money—say, $100—and tell them they can use this budget to "shop" for features. Keep a record of each participant's choices.

- Plotting results: Color the cards on the original table according to the number of times they were chosen. Cards that were chosen more times can be colored with stronger or brighter colors, and cards that were chosen fewer times should be colored with light colors. Cards that were never chosen should remain "uncolored." The matrix should now give you a good—and visual—idea of what areas were received with more interest, and which were not.

STRATEGY

Value Mapping lets you quickly visualize things that are valued by others—consumers, members of a team, your department, your stakeholders. Understanding general areas of interest can help focus the work ("Where should we concentrate our efforts?") and settle internal disputes ("Consumers really didn't like any of the social networking features for this application, so we don't need to invest in them now."). Try presenting the matrix in a series of slides that show different color groups—it really makes an impression!

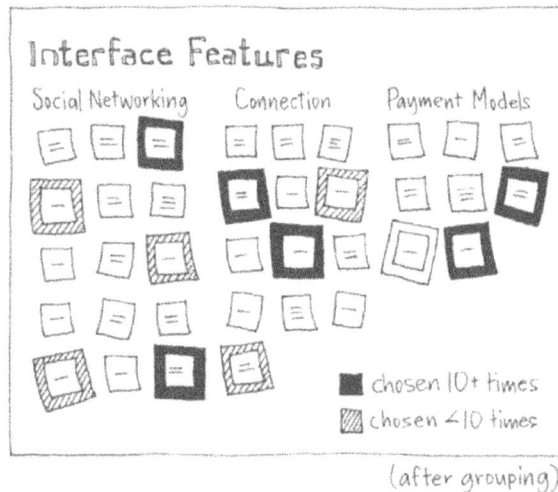

(after grouping)

TIPS FOR PLAYING ONLINE

To play online, create a digital game board and add the features or items to be discussed in step 1. Ask participants to vote or use cards, icons, or other visual markers to designate their choices in step 2. Review and highlight the items with the most votes in step 3. Consider closing by asking the group to discuss any surprises.

The Value Mapping game is credited to Sarah Rink.

The Virtuous Cycle

OBJECT OF PLAY

The goal of this game is to discover opportunities to transform an existing, linear process into a more valuable and growing process by taking a different viewpoint. This is useful in examining processes that are deemed "worth repeating," such as the customer experience.

It might be a good time to play through this exercise if the current process is transactional, compartmentalized, or wasteful. Other indications are a group that is "navel-gazing" and focused primarily on its internal process, or when there is a sense that after the process is complete, no one knows what happens next.

Possible outcomes include that the group may uncover new growth and improvement opportunities in an existing process by "bending it back into itself."

NUMBER OF PLAYERS

3–10 people

DURATION OF PLAY

1–3 hours

HOW TO PLAY

You will need a high-level understanding or documentation of the current state of things. Any existing, linear process will work.

1. Introduce the exercise by "black boxing" the current process. This means that during the course of the exercise, the group's focus will be on what's outside the process, not the fine detail of what's going on inside the box.

2. To make this visual, give each step in the process a box on the wall (medium-sized sticky notes work well) and connect them with arrows in a linear fashion.

3. To start the exercise, ask the group to think about, to the best of their knowledge, what happens before the process: Who or what is involved? What is going on? Repeat this for the end of the process: What comes after the process? What are the possible outcomes?

4. You may ask them to capture their thoughts on sticky notes and post them before and after the process.

5. Next, draw a loop from the end of the linear process back to its starting point. By doing this, you are turning a linear process into a life cycle. Ask: "To get from here, and back again, what needs to happen? What's missing from the picture?"

6. The group is ready to explore possibilities and opportunities. Again, sticky notes work well for capturing ideas. Have the players capture their thoughts along the line and discuss.

Summarize or close the exercise by generating a list of questions and areas to explore.

This may include looking at the internal, defined process for improvement ideas.

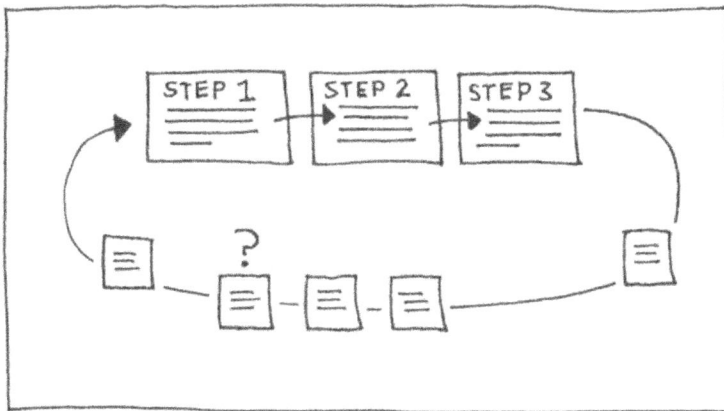

STRATEGY

Pick the right process to do this with. A process that warrants repeating, such as the customer experience, works well. Knowledge creation and capture, as well as strategic planning, are also candidates.

Get the right people in the room. Some awareness of what happens outside the process is needed, but can also hamper the experience. One of the biggest potential outcomes is a visceral change in perspective on the participants' part: from an internal focus to an external focus.

TIPS FOR PLAYING ONLINE

This game works well online. Processes can be drawn on a board or in diagramming software. Depending on the team, you may want to begin in step 3 with an existing process flow diagram.

This game is credited to James Macanufo.

Visual Glossary

OBJECT OF PLAY

The object of this game is to clearly define a set of terms so that a group has a common vocabulary.

It's not in our nature to admit ignorance. When greeted with an unknown or abstract term, many people find it easier to pretend they understand than to ask for clarification. This is dangerous in knowledge work, where a common understanding is necessary to work together.

Groups that make time to define their terms visually will work faster and more effectively by starting on the same page.

NUMBER OF PLAYERS

2–10 people

DURATION OF PLAY

30 minutes to 1 hour

HOW TO PLAY

1. Introduce the exercise as a means to create a common language. The first step is to brainstorm the tough phrases and terms that make up the group's shared language. Have the group brainstorm these individually on sticky notes. Examples might be jargon, slang, technical terms, or acronyms that they use in the course of their everyday work.

2. Have participants post their notes in one large pool and examine them. Discuss which terms were the most common and which are of the highest priority for visual definition.

3. At this point, you are ready to make the glossary. From the pool, assign the most important terms a space on the wall. Pick a term to start with, and ask the group to describe it first with words. The group may uncover points that are foggy, conflicting, or inadequate in their verbiage.

4. Then try to clarify the term with a picture. Ask: what does this look like? If the term is abstract, try a diagrammatic approach. Start with the people or things involved and connect them in a way that visually captures the definition. For example, the word *social* has many definitions and contexts,

but by asking the group to describe a picture of what they mean, you will get a clearer definition.

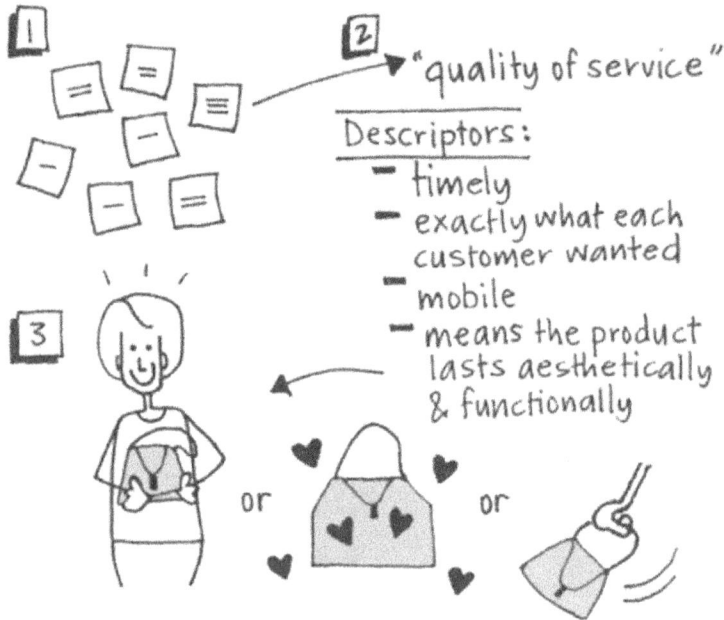

STRATEGY

Don't try to define everything up front. Find the most important terms, where there is the most opportunity to clarify, and do those first.

A good visual glossary will have utility beyond one meeting. Use the visuals in follow-on activities; make them available online, or in training materials, if appropriate. Encourage participants to use the visual elements as shorthand when communicating and working with these terms.

TIPS FOR PLAYING ONLINE

To play online, create a digital game space. Facilitate the group through step 1, and give five minutes of ideation time for step 2. After the facilitator and group review the input, make the glossary in a new space on the board for steps 3 and 4. A good visual glossary can be leverageable and carried forward.

The Visual Glossary game is credited to James Macanufo.

Wizard of Oz

OBJECT OF PLAY

In this role-play exercise, two people prototype a machine–human interaction. The user talks to another who is "behind the curtain," playing the role of the machine. They may use a script to uncover breaking points in an existing design, or improvise to work out a completely new idea.

NUMBER OF PLAYERS

Two, plus observers

DURATION OF PLAY

30 minutes or more

HOW TO PLAY

If a group is testing an existing design, they should prepare a script that outlines the responses and actions that the machine can take. The "wizard" will use this —and only this—to react to the user. For example, a group that is designing a software interface would write a script of information presented to the user and the responses that it understands in return.

If a group is improvising, they can just get started. To open the exercise, the two players should be visually separated from each other. This is the "curtain" that keeps them from inadvertently passing cues or other information to each other. They may be separated by a piece of cardboard, or they may simply turn their backs to each other.

The easiest way to play through the exercise is for the user to initiate some task that they want to accomplish. As the two players play through the experience, they should look for problems, frustration points, or opportunities to do the unexpected. Essentially, the user should challenge the machine, and the machine should stick to what it knows.

STRATEGY

This technique's application goes beyond voice control, as the "curtain" simultaneously eliminates assumptions about the machine and surfaces what the user wants to do and how they want to do it.

TIPS FOR PLAYING ONLINE

To play online, ask the two players to turn off their cameras and use the chat. The person playing the user initiates the conversation about a task they want to accomplish. Other participants can remain on-camera and provide feedback for the user to help guide the conversation. Observers should note findings on a shared board for further refinement.

The technique was pioneered in the 1970s, in the early design and testing of the now-common airport kiosk, and in IBM's development of the "listening typewriter." In these cases, the technique is taken even further: the person playing the machine would interpret voice commands from a user and manipulate a prototype of the system accordingly, like the invisible "wizard" in The Wizard of Oz.

The World Café

OBJECT OF PLAY

What's the difference between a business meeting and a conversation at a café? The World Café is a method for improving large-group discussion by borrowing concepts from the informal "café" conversations that we have all the time: round tables, cross-pollinating ideas, and pursuing questions that matter.

As a conversational process, the World Café may take on many forms. Here is a "quick-start" flow to consider, which focuses on the basics.

NUMBER OF PLAYERS

24–30 people in groups of 4–5 at round tables

DURATION OF PLAY

1.5 hours

SETUP

As the leader, you will need to find the "questions that matter," which will guide the rounds of discussion. A powerful question will be evocative and simple; it should be immediately tangible and relevant to a challenge the group faces. The group may focus on one question or move through a group of subsequent questions. For example, "How might we start having more real conversations with our customers?" may be enough to sustain three rounds of discussion.

Develop your questions that matter, and then focus on creating an inviting and hospitable environment for the event. This may not be an easy task in typical conference spaces. Some things to keep in mind include the fact that round tables are better for conversation than square tables, and each table should be equipped with drawing supplies such as markers, flip charts, and/or paper tablecloths.

HOW TO PLAY

The event consists of three 20-minute rounds of group discussion at tables, followed by a group synthesis. After each round, one person stays behind to serve as a "host" of the next round, while the rest travel to other tables as "ambassadors." In this sense, participants have a chance to go "around the world" and bring their ideas with them from table to table.

During the rounds of discussion, encourage participants to link ideas from one round to the next.

Here are some things to consider:

Spend the first few minutes talking about the last conversation.
The "host" can present ideas left at the table, and the "ambassadors" should talk about what they've brought from their respective places.

Leave evidence.
Draw key ideas out on the table. For the next group to appreciate the previous conversation, they will need some artifacts to respond to and build on.

Connect diverse viewpoints and respect contributions.
If needed, use a "talking stick" or button to manage each other's input.

Look for patterns.
By the second and third rounds, themes and larger patterns will emerge in the discussion. Encourage participants to look for these and make them evident by drawing or writing them toward the middle of the tables.

After the last round, it's time for a town hall discussion to synthesize what the groups have discovered. Referring back to the questions that matter, ask what the answers were at the different tables, and how they are connected.

TIPS FOR PLAYING ONLINE

To play online, create a digital game board or Google Doc in place of the table. Arrange the board and the group in breakout rooms. Facilitators take care that the breakout rooms are organized logically so the participants can do the work of changing "tables" and it's not up to the facilitator to keep track of moving everyone to new groups. Provide clear instructions for breakout rooms to keep the conversations flowing smoothly.

A community of practitioners maintains the evolving methodology, process, history, and design principles at www.theworldcafe.com.

Games for Closing

We don't have the time and resources to do everything, so we make choices. Closing is the act of bringing things to conclusion, in our minds and on paper. Games that close are about finding the endpoint through prioritization, voting, and comparison but are also about finding and creating the commitment and alignment that lead to the next step.

A good closing depends on how well a space is opened and explored. An unsatisfying set of ideas will refuse to be closed. Although closing games often define the end goal—*we need to get aligned on our five priorities*—the closing games can't do it on their own. If you are having trouble with closing, the root of your problem lies elsewhere; consider how well opened and explored the space has been.

$100 Test

OBJECT OF PLAY

In this method of prioritization, participants assign relative value to a list of items by spending an imaginary $100 together. By using the concept of cash, the exercise captures more attention and keeps participants more engaged than an arbitrary point or ranking system.

NUMBER OF PLAYERS

Small groups of 3–5 people

DURATION OF PLAY

Medium; may take up to .5 hour for a group to decide how to spend its money and to reflect on outcomes, depending on the length of the list and size of the group

HOW TO PLAY

To set up the game, you will need a list of items to be prioritized, set up in a matrix with space reserved for the amount spent and reasoning why.

To begin the game, explain the challenge to the group: they have a collective $100 to spend on the list of items. The dollars represent the importance of items, and they must decide as a group how to allocate the dollars across the list.

Give the group sufficient time to assign their values, and ask that they also write a brief explanation for the amount. It is possible that groups may bring up the literal cost or effort of items on the list; this may confuse the primary issue of importance, and it may be best addressed as a separate discussion, or as its own $100 Test.

When the matrix is complete, ask the group to explain their decisions and reasoning. The matrix can then be used as a guidepost for future decision making on a project, specifically, what items are important and of higher priority than the others.

$100 TEST

Item/Topic/Issue	$	WHY?
Internet Access	$21	to tell others & ask for help
alarm clock	$7.50	the only one often available
Telephone	$55	connect with EMS
SMS	$8.50	help during emergencies
camera	$4.25	documentation for insurance
Solitaire	.75¢	stress relief
voice recorder	$3	capture disaster interviews

STRATEGY

This game is commonly used in software development for working with users to create their prioritized feature list. However, it can be applied in any situation where a "false scarcity" would help focus a group's wants and needs. For example, an HR group polling employees about new benefit plans may use the $100 Test to uncover what options would be best received and why.

TIPS FOR PLAYING ONLINE

Create a list for everyone to vote on. Ask participants to claim their spot and add their name to a column. They then have $100 to distribute among the list. Do this with a spreadsheet, sticky notes on a board, or other collaboration tool. Once individual votes have been made, take time to evaluate the result as a group and come up with a group consensus.

The $100 Test is known by many names, including Divide the Dollar and the short-form variation, the $10 Test. The source of the $100 Test game is unknown.

20/20 Vision

OBJECT OF PLAY

The 20/20 Vision game is about getting group clarity around which projects or initiatives should be more of a priority than others. Because employees' attention is so often divided among multiple projects, it can be refreshing to refocus and realign more intently with the projects that have the biggest bang for the buck. And defining the "bang" together helps ensure that the process of prioritization is high-quality.

NUMBER OF PLAYERS

5–10 people

DURATION OF PLAY

30–90 minutes

HOW TO PLAY

1. Before the meeting, write any proposed project or initiative relevant to the players on sticky notes, one item per note. And when you begin, it's important that the initiatives you've written on the sticky notes are posted in random order during both stages of the game. Shuffle them before the meeting starts—you can even blind-post or ask a player to post—so that from the onset there is no implicit prioritization on your part.

2. Introduce the game by explaining to the players that 20/20 Vision is about forced prioritization based on perceived benefits. Verbalize the importance of building consensus on priorities to move the organization forward.

3. In a wall space visible to the players, post an initiative and ask the players to describe its benefits. Write their descriptions on a sticky note posted next to that initiative. If there's disagreement around the benefits of an initiative, write down both or all of the points made. Assume that there's validity to multiple perspectives and let the group indicate the majority perspective through the ranking process. If the group already has a shared sense of the benefits for each initiative, don't spend a lot of time clarifying them. Just move into prioritization and respond to questions around benefits as they organically come up.

4. Repeat step 3 for all relevant projects or initiatives until the benefits have been thoroughly described by the players, captured on sticky notes, and posted.

5. Ask the players if any initiatives are missing from the wall. If so, request that they write them down, post them, and discuss their benefits so that you can capture them.

6. Move onto a neighboring wall space, pull down two random initiatives, and ask the players which they can agree are more or less important to the organization's vision or goals.

7. Post the one that the group generally agrees is more important above the one they generally agree is less important.

8. Move another initiative into the new space. Ask the players if it is more or less important than the two posted and post it accordingly—higher priorities at the top, lower priorities at the bottom.

9. Repeat this process until all initiatives have been thoroughly discussed and prioritized.

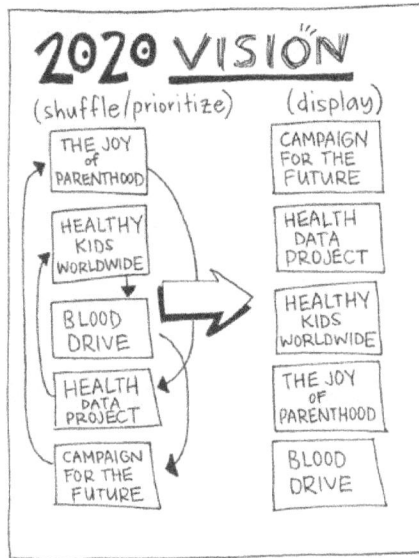

STRATEGY

20/20 Vision is about asking players to thoughtfully evaluate priorities as a group. The first phase of the game—describing and capturing the benefits—is significant because it lays the groundwork for the hard part: determining priorities. It can be challenging to get a group to rank its projects, all of which seem important in some way.

The game works best if you can facilitate general agreement around the benefits and resist the temptation to let the group waffle on prioritizing. They must make the hard decisions. And when the going gets tough, take heart: the players who resist ranking the most may also offer a wealth of insight into the initiatives and ultimately help the players better refine the final ranking.

TIPS FOR PLAYING ONLINE

The simplest way to play this online is to open the game and have players generate a list in a shared space. Then, use dot voting or another voting feature (if the list is succinct enough) to prioritize and rank the items. Create a space on a shared collaboration space or use a template. An example of a template is shown here.

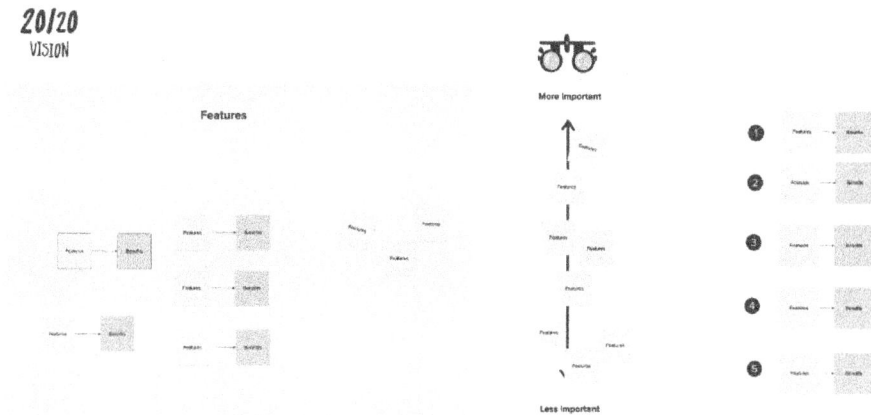

20/20 Vision is based on and adapted from the same-named activity in Luke Hohmann's book, Innovation Games: Creating Breakthrough Products Through Collaborative Play.

Coffee Question

OBJECT OF PLAY

The goal of this game is to clear blocks and imagine an "ideal" future state.

NUMBER OF PLAYERS

One or more people

DURATION OF PLAY

10–15 minutes

HOW TO PLAY

At the closing of a game sequence, or the closing of a meeting, explain you are going to ask a question intended to help clarify goals and objectives. Is everyone okay with that? Perhaps wait for a bit of an uncomfortable silence and a shift in tone, then set the scene...

We are meeting, one year from today, for coffee... You can smell the coffee... The air is cold... We are sitting outside in the café here, awaiting warm cortados...[1]

You are describing how everything is going really, really well! Better than you could have hoped for! What would that look like?

Give participants five minutes to write down their responses. Invite volunteers to share and discuss any surprises or insights.

STRATEGY

The Coffee Question allows players to tap into their subconscious mind to imagine an "ideal" future state, without limitations. The time constraint forces what's known deeply to come forth. Use whatever time frame is most relevant given the goals of the meeting or context of the project.

TIPS FOR PLAYING ONLINE

With cameras on, follow the same prompt and describe a scene familiar to most participants. If you were screen sharing before this activity, stop screen sharing before this to draw attention.

The source of The Coffee Question is unknown. It is practiced in the gamestorming community.

---

1 Help people "ground" into the room by invoking sensory awareness and describe your current environment in detail, or an environment everyone is familiar with.

Ethos, Logos, Pathos

OBJECT OF PLAY

The goal of this game is to channel Aristotle's assessment of your argument.

NUMBER OF PLAYERS

1–10 people

DURATION OF PLAY

10–60 minutes

HOW TO PLAY

Aristotle laid the groundwork for persuasive communication in the fourth century. Although the times have changed, effective communication hasn't. Evaluate a communication, such as a value proposition, by using the three elements of rhetoric.

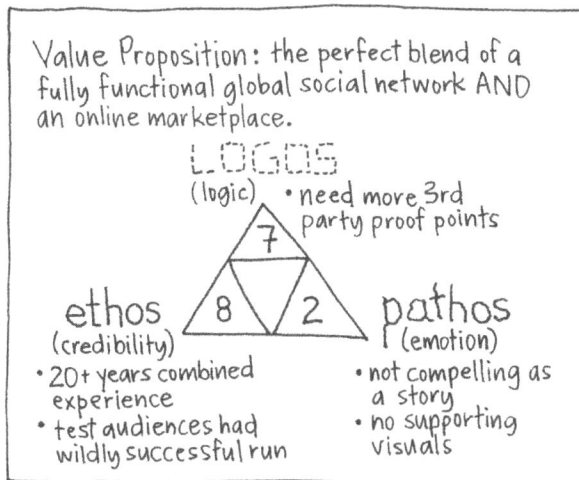

Role-playing as your audience, score your message from 1 to 10 on these categories:

Ethos/Credibility
Who are you, and what authority do you have on the topic?

Logos/Logic

How clear and consistent is your reasoning? How do your facts measure up against my facts?

Pathos/Emotion

How vivid, memorable, and motivating is your message? Look for areas of improvement or imbalance.

STRATEGY

Ethos, Logos, Pathos helps take a holistic view of a value proposition and how it may be received.

TIPS FOR PLAYING ONLINE

With cameras on, invite a group to join a game board with an Ethos, Logos, Pathos template. Using the instructions, invite the group to consider each category. Depending on the group size, you could ask players to respond to each category and, then, based on responses, rank the category.

The Ethos, Logos, Pathos game is credited to James Macanufo.

Fill in the Blank

OBJECT OF PLAY

A way to wrap up a discussion and bring clarity to underlying blocks + next actions. Fill in the blank to illuminate what may be ready to be uncovered.

NUMBER OF PLAYERS

Small groups, but can also be done individually

DURATION OF PLAY

Five minutes

HOW TO PLAY

At the end of a conversation, set up the closing, and ask if it's okay to help close the conversation with a question: *I'm curious, what would you say to this?*

> "If I had more ____, I would ____."

STRATEGY

Fill in the Blank shifts the tone of a conversation to closing, while instigating forward-momentum thought and future discussion. It tends to encourage clarity. This prompt works in many contexts. In meetings, it can help encourage individual accountability and insights. It's simple enough to be used as a discussion tool to close 1:1 conversations and can encourage connection and personal sharing among small groups.

TIPS FOR PLAYING ONLINE

This activity easily transfers online. On camera, pose the question to the group and share it on a board that is visible to everyone. Ask participants to write their responses down on paper (ideal). Depending on the closeness of the group and the themes of the topic at hand, invite them to add their responses to the board.

Fill in the Blank is loosely based on Mad Libs.

Graphic Gameplan

OBJECT OF PLAY

Plenty of us are visionaries, idea generators, or, at the very least, suggestion makers. But ideas never come to fruition without a plan. As Benjamin Franklin said, "Well done is better than well said." Following up on a big idea with an executable action plan is one of the monumental differences between teams and companies that are merely good and those that are outstanding. That's why this activity deserves special attention. The Graphic Gameplan shows you how you'll get where you want to go with a project.

NUMBER OF PLAYERS

Small groups, but can also be done individually

DURATION OF PLAY

30 minutes to 2 hours

HOW TO PLAY

1. Before the meeting, think of one or more projects that need to get traction.

2. In a large, white space, preferably 3–4 feet high by 6–12 feet wide, draw a picture similar to the following.

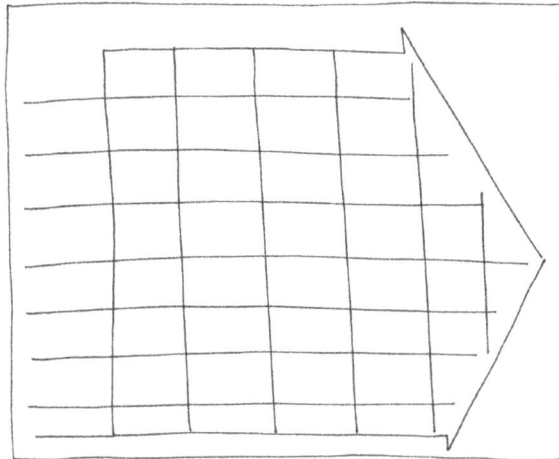

3. Display the graphic on the meeting room wall and tell the players that the goal of the meeting is to get consensus around specific tasks required to complete a project.

4. Write the name of the first project to be discussed at the top left of the first column. As the group leader, you can write all associated projects downward in that same column, or you can ask the players to add projects that they agree need attention. Either way, you should end up with the relevant projects listed in the leftmost column.

5. Based on the projects listed, either tell the group the time frame and write the milestones in days, weeks, or months along the top row, or ask what they think it should be and write that time frame along the top. (Note: you can also establish a timeline after step 8.)

6. Sticky notes in hand, ask the players to choose a project and agree aloud on the first step required to accomplish it. Write their contribution on the sticky note and post it in the first box next to that project.

7. Ask the players for the second, third, and fourth steps, and so on. Keep writing their comments on sticky notes until they're satisfied that they've adequately outlined each step to complete the project.

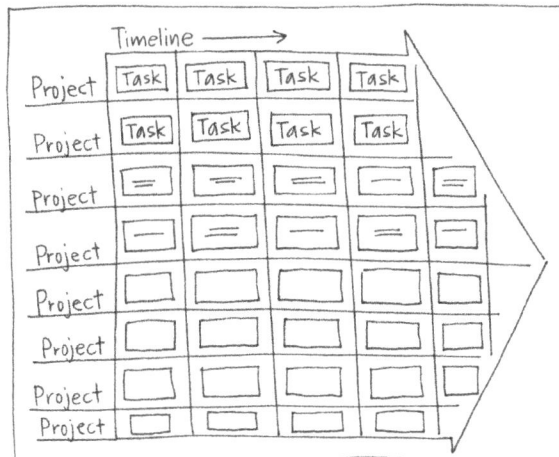

8. Repeat steps 6 and 7 for every project on your display, until the game plan is filled out.

STRATEGY

Completing a game plan as a group has two major benefits. The first is that it breaks big projects into manageable chunks of work, which encourages anyone responsible for a project. The second is that because the "group mind" creates the game plan, it raises the quality of the flow of project management. It becomes less likely that important steps are left out and more likely that the project is approached thoughtfully and strategically. But as you post the sticky notes, don't assume that the first flow the group maps is the best one. Ask the players challenging questions about their comments: Does this have to happen first? Can these two steps be combined? How are steps related across projects? Do steps in one project affect the progress or outcome of another? Ask hard questions to help the group get to the best place, and write any food for thought on a flip chart nearby.

When determining the timeline to write across the top, it's important to note that it can be determined *after* the project steps are established. A time frame written beforehand can impact the steps people are willing and able to take, so think about whether it serves the facilitation process better by assigning time before or after the play is complete.

If you find that the players want to assign tasks to specific people or departments as they go, let them. Simply add the names of the responsible parties to each sticky note (obviously, these assignments should be realistic). And if the players want to discuss available resources, or a lack thereof, ask them to share what they expect to need in order to complete the projects and capture that on a flip chart in the room.

The game plan can be customized with several rows and columns in order to support more complex projects. You can draw however many rows and columns you'd like as long as you have sticky notes that will fit within. Whatever the matrix looks like, the visual that results from this group discussion can serve as the large-scale, step-by-step of a project, or its contents can be funneled into more formal project management software or some other platform used by the organization. Either way, the discussion around creating it will be of significant value.

Optional activity: Draw smaller versions of the game plan on flip-chart paper and have breakout groups tackle specific projects using markers and small sticky notes. Then ask each group to present their approach to the larger group and to get feedback on the steps they proposed.

TIPS FOR PLAYING ONLINE

Play this game online using an online whiteboard and sticky notes. Create a space on a shared board and build the template shown previously. It can be as complex or simple as you like, but the main point is to create the space for a group to identify and write down what needs to be done to achieve a common aim. As the facilitator, you want to encourage the group to get the thoughts out of their head and onto the board so they can be discussed as a group. Help the group if they get stuck by asking questions and capturing their responses on sticky notes.

The Graphic Gameplan is based on the Graphic Gameplan Leader's Guide *(https://oreil.ly/S3lNS) from The Grove Consultants International's strategic visioning process, which involves using a template of the same name.*

I Like, I Wish, I Wonder

OBJECT OF PLAY

The object of this game is to generate constructive feedback.

NUMBER OF PLAYERS

Any

DURATION OF PLAY

10–45 minutes

HOW TO PLAY

Make three columns: one for "I Like," one for "I Wish," and one for "I Wonder."

1. Ask the group to reflect on what they like. Ask what was positive or repeatable about an activity and capture their thoughts under the "I Like" column.

2. Ask the group then to brainstorm about what they wish was different about it, and capture these under the "I Wish" column. These are these changes they would like to see.

3. Ask the group to then brainstorm what they wonder might be possible. Capture opportunities in the "I Wonder" column.

STRATEGY

This feedback method can apply to any activity, idea, work product, or action. By focusing on change and opportunities as opposed to direct negatives, the group will be more likely to share its true assessment while also generating improvement ideas.

TIPS FOR PLAYING ONLINE

Create space on a shared board for the columns "I Like," "I Wish," and "I Wonder." Invite the group to add their thoughts to each category one at a time. Allow 2–3 minutes to generate responses for each category. Depending on time available for the activity, discuss and highlight the main themes at the end, or after each category.

TOPIC: LEADERSHIP RETREAT

I LIKE
+1

_____

+ Quality speakers
+ Interactive exercises
+ Big objectives met
+ Feel motivated and refreshed
+ I know what I need to do

I WISH
△

_____

△ Cross-functional interaction
△ Vegatarian lunch
△ More people heard this message

I WONDER
☁

_____

☁ How can we share learnings?
☁ How can we keep this momentum?
☁ How do we support and hold each other accountable?

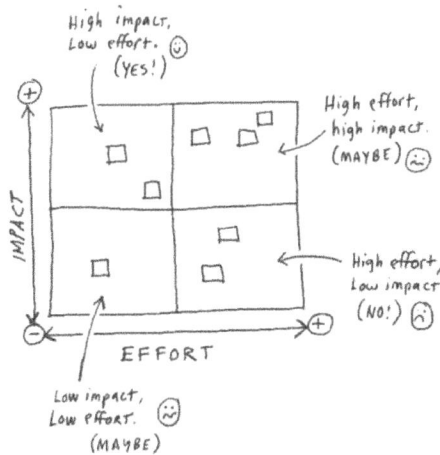

High impact, Low effort. ☺ (YES!)

High effort, high impact. (MAYBE) ☹

IMPACT

High effort, Low impact (NO!) ☹

EFFORT

Low impact, Low effort. ☹ (MAYBE)

The source for the I Like, I Wish, I Wonder game is unknown.

Impact & Effort Matrix

OBJECT OF PLAY

In this decision-making exercise, possible actions are mapped based on two factors: the effort required to implement them and their potential impact. Some ideas are costly but may have a bigger long-term payoff than short-term actions. Categorizing ideas along these lines is a useful technique in decision-making, as it obliges contributors to balance and evaluate suggested actions before committing to them.

NUMBER OF PLAYERS

Based on small groups, but can scale to any size

DURATION OF PLAY

30 minutes to 1 hour, depending on the size of the group

HOW TO PLAY

Given a goal, a group may have a number of ideas for how to achieve it. To open the exercise, frame the goal in terms of a "What to do" or "What we need" question. This may sound as simple as "What do we need to reach our goal?"

Ask the group to generate ideas individually on sticky notes. Then, using Post-Up, ask them to present their ideas back to the group by placing them within a 2×2 matrix that is organized by impact and effort:

- **Impact:** The potential payoff of the action
- **Effort:** The cost of taking the action

STRATEGY

As participants place their ideas into the matrix, the group may openly discuss the positions of elements. It is not uncommon for an idea to be bolstered by the group and to move up in potential impact or down in effort. In this respect, the category of high impact, low effort will often hold the set of ideas that the group is most agreed upon and committed to.

TIPS FOR PLAYING ONLINE

This activity works well online. First ask the group to generate ideas in a shared board. Then, invite the group to move their ideas to a 2×2 template organized by impact and effort. Discuss the results as a group and use the completed template to inform future activities and decisions.

The source of the Impact & Effort Matrix game is unknown.

Memory Wall

OBJECT OF PLAY

Employees are human beings, and every human being likes to be acknowledged. To appreciate employee contributions, celebrate their accomplishments, and build camaraderie among team members, a Memory Wall works wonders.

NUMBER OF PLAYERS

10–50

DURATION OF PLAY

45 minutes to 1.5 hours

HOW TO PLAY

1. During the meeting, give each player markers, paper, tape, and a flat surface to draw on. Make sure you have usable wall space for display purposes.

2. Ask the players to survey the other players in the room and take 10–15 minutes to write down positive, stand-out memories of working together, learning from each other, or participating in some way in organizational life.

3. Once the players have written down a few memories, ask them to draw each memory on a different sheet of letter-sized paper. Tell them they can take 20–30 minutes to draw these "memory scenes." They can partner with any person(s) involved in a memory to conjure up the details of that memory—visually or contextually.

4. When drawing time is up, ask the players to tape their scenes on the wall, forming a visual "memory cloud."

5. As the meeting leader, first ask for volunteers to approach the wall and discuss memories they posted and want to share. When you've run out of volunteers, approach memories on the wall that catch your eye and ask for the owner to share the story.

6. Summarize the experiences and ask the players to take a moment to silently recognize and appreciate those who have contributed to their work life in a positive way. Follow this game up with Happy Hour!

Optional activity: Have volunteer players approach the wall, select a memory, and try to guess who it belongs to. If they get it right, give them a door prize and ask the person whose memory it is to elaborate. If they get it wrong, open it up to the audience to guess whose memory it is. Give door prizes to multiple people if more than one gets it right.

company baseball team won!

threw icewater on Coach Barnes

D'Andra gave me her parking space

welcoming committee changed this — me
everyone else

NETWORK COLLAPSE! — janine to the rescue POW! pop!

Renée stream-lined our processes!

Roadmap perfectly orchestrated thanks to CI team.

Team bonuses for performance hello!

For me? Employee of the Month!!

MAD CLIENT Service Cycle ① ② HANDED TO CHARLOTTE ③ HAPPY CLIENT

I forgot my lunch. Dave gave me his. thank you, Dave!

Bud and our distribution channels are peas in a pod...

Coalition of amazing tech people

STRATEGY

The Memory Wall isn't a game of strategy, but of appreciation. The only rule is that players should recall and draw positive, uplifting memories—nothing offensive or negative. And there is a general guideline about drawing the memory scenes: players should be discouraged from judging their drawings or the drawings of others. Tell them that the activity is designed to share anecdotes and stories—not win a drawing contest. The images are there to illustrate the scenes and, absolutely, to provide good-natured humor.

If you see a player who seems to be having trouble pulling up a memory, ask open-ended questions to bring one to the surface. And when someone has shared a memory at the memory wall, you can ask others to raise their hand if they share that memory and can offer a unique perspective. You also can make the memory wall specific to a project or milestone by drawing a large-scale visual representation of that project or milestone and asking players to recall memories related to that aspect of their work.

TIPS FOR PLAYING ONLINE

This activity works well online. For step 2, invite players to write on sticky notes in a shared board. In step 3, depending on the group and what you are trying to do, invite participants to draw on paper and upload a photo of their work (this will cause the most disruption), draw digitally, or use images, icons, and sticky notes to describe the scene. In step 4, invite participants to add their final scene to the board. In step 5, help facilitate sharing. Close with step 6 and use this at the end of a meeting on Friday with a spirit of appreciation for maximum effect.

The source of the Memory Wall game is unknown.

NUF Test

OBJECT OF PLAY

As a group is developing ideas in a brainstorming session, it may be useful to do a quick "reality check" on proposed ideas. In the NUF Test, participants rate an idea on three criteria: to what degree is it new, useful, and feasible?

NUMBER OF PLAYERS

Small group

DURATION OF PLAY

Short; 15–30 minutes, depending on the size of the group and the level of discussion

HOW TO PLAY

Set up the game by quickly creating a matrix of ideas against the criteria:

New

> Has the idea been tried before? An idea will score higher here if it is significantly different from approaches that have come before it. A new idea captures attention and possibility.

Useful

> Does the idea actually solve the problem? An idea that solves the problem completely, without creating any new problems, will score better here.

Feasible

> Can it be done? A new and useful idea still has to be weighed against its cost to implement. Ideas that require fewer resources and effort to be realized will score better here.

To play, the group rates each idea from 1 to 10 for each criterion and tallies the results. A group may choose to write down scores individually at first and then call out their results on each item and criterion to create the tally. Scoring should be done quickly, as in a "gut" check.

A discussion after the scores have been tallied may uncover uncertainties about an idea or previously underrated ideas. The group may then choose to make an idea stronger, as in "How do we make this idea more feasible with fewer resources?"

	NEW	USEFUL	feasible
promotional bat·mobile	7	2	6 = 15
Facebook Group	Ø	3	10 = 13
Austin bat tours	Ø	6	8 = 14
guano fertilizer	8	9	5 = 22
sponsors for bat colonies	10	4	1 = 15

STRATEGY

The goal of this game is to check big ideas against the realities they will face after the meeting is over. It is not intended to "kill" good ideas, but to identify possible weak points so that they can be shaped and improved before seeing the light of day.

TIPS FOR PLAYING ONLINE

Add the template to a shared space and ask the group to come to consensus for each. Depending on the group size, this could happen in group discussion, in breakout groups, adding sticky notes, or using dot voting to get group consensus, which can then be discussed.

The NUF Test is an adaptation of a testing process used for patents.

Prune the Future

OBJECT OF PLAY

People who work in large organizations know that most change doesn't happen immediately or in broad sweeps. It happens incrementally by taking small, strategic steps. Prune the Future uses a tree as a metaphor to show how the future of anything can be shaped, one leaf at a time.

NUMBER OF PLAYERS

5–15

DURATION OF PLAY

30 minutes

HOW TO PLAY

1. Before the meeting, cut a few dozen sticky notes or index cards into the shapes of leaves. Then, in a white space that will be visible to the players, draw a large tree with enough thick limbs to represent multiple categories of the future. Write the general topic under or above the tree.

2. Tell the group that the inner part of the treetop represents the current states of the topic and moving outward means moving toward the future. For example, if the topic is about growing the customer base, the inner leaves would represent the current customer demographics and the outer leaves would represent future or desired customer demographics.

3. Ask the players to write current aspects of the topic—one idea per leaf— on the leaves and stick them on the inside of the treetop. Remove any redundant comments and cluster similar comments, with the group's guidance, near the appropriate branches.

4. Next, ask the players to write aspects of the future on new leaves. These can be future states or variables already in progress, or simply potentials and possibilities.

5. Tell the players to "prune" the future by posting their leaves around the treetop, related to the categories of the limbs. If you'd like, add thin or thick branches within to show relationships and let the tree grow in a natural way. If it grows asymmetrically, let that be.

6. With the players, discuss the shape of the tree that emerges. Which branches have the most activity? Which areas don't seem to be experiencing growth? Where do the branches appear to be most connected? The most disconnected?

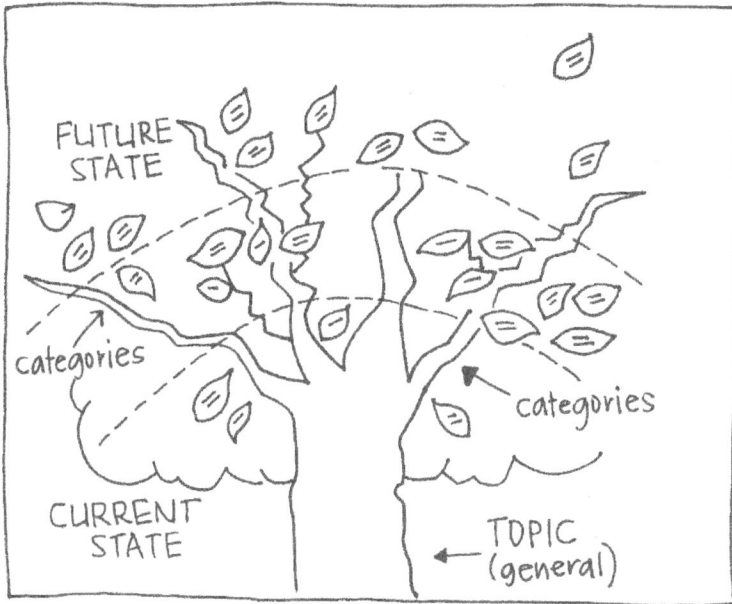

STRATEGY

The picture of the tree is the working metaphor for this game—it represents the roots of the topic, the branches of the topic, and, of course, the topic's growth potential. This game is broadly applicable because you can use a tree as a metaphor for virtually any aspect of your organization that you wish to grow or shape. The topic can be a product whose future features you want to brainstorm. It can be a team whose future roles and responsibilities you want to plan. Or you could use this game to discuss the marketplace and show where the players think it is changing or growing.

When the players start to shape the outer treetop, encourage them to "go out on a limb" with their ideas for the future. This game is about possibilities—realistic and otherwise. And if someone requests fruit on the tree to represent ROI, draw apples where they should be. If the players request another tree (or even a grove!), draw quick rudimentary trees and let the players start adding leaves, following the original procedure. This game works well because it allows for a nonlinear, organic representation of what is likely a complex topic. It results in a visual display of the interconnectedness of future conditions, showing where some parts of the tree may be suffering while others are thriving.

TIPS FOR PLAYING ONLINE

Play this game online using a template and shared collaboration space. Set up the game board in step 1 in a space that is visible to everyone. Play this game as a group in steps 2–5. Consider using breakout groups in step 6 to more deeply explore the topic before discussing it as a group.

The Prune the Future game is based on the Prune the Product Tree activity in Luke Hohmann's book, Innovation Games: Creating Breakthrough Products Through Collaborative Play.

Start, Stop, Continue

OBJECT OF PLAY

The object of Start, Stop, Continue is to examine aspects of a situation or develop next steps.

NUMBER OF PLAYERS

1–10 people

DURATION OF PLAY

10 minutes to 1 hour

HOW TO PLAY

Ask the group to consider the current situation or goal and individually brainstorm actions in these three categories:

- **Start:** What are things that we need to START doing?
- **Stop:** What are we currently doing that we can or should STOP?
- **Continue:** What are we doing now that works and should CONTINUE?

Have individuals share their results.

STRATEGY

This exercise is broad enough to work well as a closing exercise. It's useful in framing discussion at "problem-solving" meetings, or as a way to crystalize aspirational steps toward a vision. The "START" and "STOP" categories require follow-up action; "CONTINUE" requires appreciation.

TIPS FOR PLAYING ONLINE

Create space on a shared board with the columns "START," "STOP," and "CONTINUE." Invite the group to add their thoughts to each category one at a time. Allow 2–3 minutes to generate responses for each category. Take time for the group to share their results and discuss what stands out to them.

The source for the Start, Stop, Continue game is unknown.

Who/What/When Matrix

OBJECT OF PLAY

Identify who will do what, by when.

It's common for people to attend meetings, voice strong opinions, and then waffle and dodge responsibility for follow-up actions. We have all been guilty of this at one point or another; it's a built-in, easy assumption that the person who called the meeting bears the responsibilities coming out of it. We may do this for a number of reasons: we don't have time to commit, we don't believe in the purpose (or people) involved, or there is no clear direction on what needs to be done next.

Many meetings end with a "next steps" or "action items" discussion. These discussions are often abstract, starting with a list of tasks that are then handed out to possibly unwilling participants with no particular deadline attached. By focusing the discussion on a Who/What/When matrix, you can connect people with clear actions they have defined and have committed to.

NUMBER OF PLAYERS

1–10 people

DURATION OF PLAY

15–30 minutes

HOW TO PLAY

On a flip chart or whiteboard, create a matrix that outlines WHO/WHAT/WHEN.

Although instincts may be to start with the "WHAT" (the tasks and items that need to be done), this approach starts with the "WHO" (the people who will be taking the actions). Put every participant's name into the matrix in this column.

Ask each participant what concrete next steps they can commit to. Place this in the WHAT column. Each participant may have a number of next steps that they think are required or feel strongly about. For each item, ask that person "WHEN" they will have the item done.

Actions don't take themselves, and people don't commit as strongly to actions as they do to each other. By approaching next steps "people-first," a few things change. First, it becomes clear that the people in the room are the ones who are accountable for next steps. Second, by making commitments in front of their peers, participants stake their credibility on taking action and are more likely to follow through. And third, it becomes clear WHO is going to do WHAT by WHEN—and who has volunteered little or no commitment.

STRATEGY

In completing the Who/What/When matrix, you are likely to find that there is a lot to do. This is a good time to ask if there is any way for participants who have committed to little or nothing to step up their contribution. They may be able to assist others in completing their tasks—or their attendance may have been unnecessary.

Although participants are more likely to commit to actions they declare in front of the group, ultimately, you, as the meeting facilitator, are accountable for following up with them after the meeting. You may ask participants to email you their commitments, and you may send the group the full list as an update.

TIPS FOR PLAYING ONLINE

Create space on a shared board with the columns "WHO," "WHAT," and "WHEN." Populate the columns based on what you have heard in the conversation thus far, and/or follow the same steps that you would offline. Ask participants to help complete the matrix and get buy-in on the actions. The digital artifacts of this game should be easily leverageable by the team and helpful after the meeting is over.

The source for Who/What/When Matrix game is unknown.

Gamestorming with AI

As we write this in early 2025, AI has already become a significant presence in life and work. It's far too early in its evolution to make sound predictions about its future value for gamestormers and facilitators, but we can acknowledge some of the ways we use it today. Right now, we operate with AI as if it were an assistant, apprentice, and thinking companion.

How We Currently Use AI to Enhance Gamestorming

We're already using AI to do quite a few things:

- Record meetings and provide summaries, tables of contents, videos, and transcripts of online meetings.

- Understand and help refine implicit and explicit meeting goals.

- Design agendas and think through game sequences (ideally based on those sensing interviews we've mentioned).

- Generate draft checklists for materials needed to work a specific game sequence based on group size.

- Rapidly generate variations on a game.

- Evaluate the responsiveness of an agenda to learner diversity, taking into account energy levels, interactions, sensory modalities, and pacing.

- Contemplate an "outside-in" approach—assessing and anticipating participant needs in terms of stuckness or lack of clarity relative to the "ask" of the game.

- Quickly make sense of a wall of sticky notes—with online whiteboards, we can copy and paste content from stickies, and we ask AI to eliminate duplicates and provide a categorized list or spreadsheet of ideas.

- Generate intriguing firestarters and thought provocations or kick the tires on ones we input.
- Ask how it would use itself to enhance gamestorming. :)

It's plausible that AI will get better and better at generating novel ideas, creating robust summaries, and otherwise making sense of large volumes of information. There are many possible future paths, things like AI chatbots and meeting designers or an adaptable, user-centric gamestorming concierge. These would be exciting to see as they could enhance the quality of player experience and minimize agenda design time.

Until these future use cases emerge, however, we hold what's possible as an open question and turn to the past for useful insights. History reveals that almost every new technology is disorienting at the onset. When answering machines were first introduced, for example, many people were offended at the breach of established social norms. When desktop publishing was introduced, many designers feared for their jobs. When phone photography became ubiquitous, documentarians feared they were soon to become obsolete. Today, people are more likely to be offended when they *can't* leave a voicemail; designers have adapted and are now hired to help people with slide decks, websites, apps, and other digital desktop publications; and there are more outstanding documentaries than ever.

We've found that new technologies, when embraced more than resisted, give ordinary people the ability to develop new literacies. Out of this exploration, they develop an emerging awareness of what else is possible, creating new opportunities for work and play. The AI genie is out of the bottle, for better and worse, so perhaps the most productive approach involves a growth over a fixed mindset, or a learner rather than judger way of seeing. The most reliable way to stay fresh and relevant is to be curious and spend time playing with the tools. Experiment with them anywhere it makes sense, be cognizant of the risks, and learn from whatever happens. This kind of experimentation builds confidence and helps you stay prepared for whatever comes next. You might call this becoming a "Learn-it-all" rather than a "Know-it-all."

The Gamestorming
Cheat Sheet

We first met Brynn Evans in 2009, at a small event where a raucous group was prototyping some of the very first gamestorming exercises. Brynn told us that the event changed her life and propelled her into the world of game-based thinking and design. In fact, she credits gamestorming for helping her get her job at Google, using the exercises to tackle a design challenge in her interview.

Brynn brought gamestorming with her to Google, where she began using the activities with her team, even holding monthly sessions to familiarize her colleagues with different games. The *Gamestorming* book became her go-to reference, and she soon realized she wanted to organize the games by the type of problem they could help solve.

That's how Brynn's cheat sheet came into being. It's essentially a table of contents for the book, organized by problem type. She laid out the games into categories like "getting started," "thinking more divergently," and "making a decision." Brynn created it primarily for herself, to use when running sprints and design thinking exercises, but she also distributed it internally at Google and made an external copy available online. This cheat sheet has proven to be incredibly useful. It helps people see how to use the games not just as individual recipes but as a menu that makes it easier to choose the right game for any situation.

Brynn says that the techniques she learned from gamestorming helped her, and her team, to be more effective and to elevate the design craft at Google. We love the cheat sheet and hope you do too. It's been updated and included here in the second edition, with her permission. Enjoy!

Games for Communicating Core Concepts

GAMES FOR FINDING THE ESSENCE OF AN IDEA

"Poster Session": Communicating ideas with images in a poster format

"Draw the Problem": Short drawing exercise to make clear what the "problem" is

"Storyboard": Players use a storyboard format to tell a story about an experience, how to solve a problem, etc.

"Cover Story": To think expansively around an ideal future state; exercise in visioning

"Design the Box": Teams imagine the package for an idea in order to make decisions about important features & other aspects of their vision that are difficult to articulate

"Elevator Pitch": Uses *Mad Libs* structure to come up with a short, compelling description of the problem you're trying to solve

"The Pitch": Players imagine that they're entrepreneurs and need to sell their ideas to investors

"Fill in the Blank": Crystalize a point of view by stating what's missing and what action you would take if it wasn't

GAMES FOR ENVISIONING THE FUTURE

"Make a World": Purpose is to make a 3D model of a desired future state

"Poster Session": Communicate ideas with images in a poster format

"Cover Story": To think expansively around an ideal future state; exercise in visioning

"Mood Board": Create a poster or collage that captures the overall "feel" of an idea

"Remembering the Future": Imagine a future scenario and tell a story about how it came to be

"Coffee Question": Use a prompt to uncover an ideal future state

GAMES FOR BUILDING CONSENSUS (AMONG MEMBERS OF A TEAM)

"Draw the Problem": Short drawing exercise to make clear what the "problem" is

"Elevator Pitch": Uses *Mad Libs* structure to come up with a short, compelling description of the problem you're trying to solve

"Fishbowl": Key listening exercise; inner circle discusses problem, outer circle listens

"Show and Tell": To elicit stakeholders' views, have them bring an object that captures their perspective

"Spectrum Mapping": Designed to reveal the diversity of perspectives and options around any given topic and to organize them into a meaningful spectrum

"Bodystorming": Using improv or "play acting" to feel out what might work a problem

"Visual Glossary": Group starts a meeting by defining their terms visually (everyone starts on the same page = works faster & more effectively later)

"Post the Path": Will help develop a better understanding of a group's current process to uncover areas of confusion or misunderstanding

GAMES FOR EARLY KICKOFF MEETINGS

"The 7Ps Framework": Used before a meeting to plan out an agenda, goals

"Affinity Map": Group creates an "affinity diagram" to find categories within a cluster of ideas (to see which ideas are most common within a group, etc.)

"Stinky Fish": Be up front about unspoken concerns

"Pre-Mortem": Be up front about risks

"Hopes & Dreams": Identify the players, their strengths, and what they hope to achieve

"The 5 Whys": Helps discover the root cause of a problem

"Carousel": Gather the viewpoints of a group from a series of provocative questions

"Elevator Pitch": Uses *Mad Libs* structure to come up with a short, compelling description of the problem you're trying to solve

"Storyboard": Players use a storyboard format to tell a story about an experience, how to solve a problem, etc.

"Context Map": Shows the effect of context

"Cover Story": To think expansively around an ideal future state; exercise in visioning

"Draw the Problem": Short drawing exercise to make clear what the "problem" is

"Poster Session": Communicate ideas with images in a poster format

"Stakeholder Analysis": Identify stakeholders and how to engage them

"Make a World": Purpose is to make a 3D model of a desired future state

"Start, Stop, Continue": Used to spell out what aspects of an issue/product you want to discontinue, introduce, or continue (based on what's going well)

GAMES FOR DESIGN (OR DEVELOPING A HOW-IT-WORKS VIDEO)

"Graphic Jam": Visualize abstract concepts, absorb complexity

"Cover Story": To think expansively around an ideal future state; exercise in visioning

"Elevator Pitch": Uses *Mad Libs* structure to come up with a short, compelling description of the problem you're trying to solve

"The Pitch": Players imagine that they're entrepreneurs and need to sell their ideas to rich venture capitalists (VCs)

"Mood Board": Create a poster or collage that captures the overall "feel" of an idea

"Show Me Your Values": To understand people's deep-seated impressions of something

"Design the Box": Teams imagine the package for an idea in order to make decisions about important features & other aspects of their vision that are difficult to articulate

"Head, Heart, Hands": The goal is to examine an issue from another perspective, and find significance in an issue

"Product Pinocchio": Players personify a product to better identify what features will resonate with and be more valuable for the end user

Games for Ideation

GAMES FOR GENERATING LOTS OF IDEAS

"Brainwriting": Includes everyone in evolving an idea (silent brainstorming, followed by collaborative building on ideas); all done in silence

"6-8-5": Fast way to get initial ideas down, and to iterate through many ideas

"Post-Up": To generate a lot of ideas

"Carousel": Gather the viewpoints of a group from a series of provocative questions

"3-12-3 Brainstorm": Good for generating & developing lots of ideas in only one hour

"Heuristic Ideation Technique": Generate ideas by recombining possibilities

"Object Brainstorm": Uses objects as a starting point for association, exploration, brainstorming

GAMES FOR DEVELOPING A ROADMAP

"WhoDo": Lists out who's involved in the project & what their priorities/next steps are

"Graphic Gameplan": Quickly develop an executable action plan for a project

"Build the Checklist": Team creates a checklist to order, rank, and prioritize tasks

"RACI Matrix": Group creates a matrix/checklist of people who are responsible, accountable, consulted, and informed, to sort out who is doing what (on a team, etc.)

"Plane Metaphor": Used to get a project started while aligning team perspectives on important areas

GAMES FOR AFTER YOU ALREADY HAVE A PROTOTYPE

"Mission Impossible": Take an existing design or idea and change one foundational aspect that makes it "impossible" in function or feasibility

"The Blind Side": Helps to disclose and uncover information that might affect a group's success

"Give-and-Take Matrix": Map out motivations & interactions among actors in a system

"Product Pinocchio": Players personify a product to better identify what features will resonate with and be more valuable for the end user

"Speed Boat": Used to identify obstacles to your goal, things that may slow you down

"SQUID": Used to map out what's been done & what still needs to be done; stands for sequential question and insight diagram.

"Staple Yourself to Something": Used to explore or clarify a process by following an object through its "day in the life"

Games for a Different Perspective

GAMES FOR CONNECTING WITH A USER BASE

"Empathy Map": To develop a customer profile

"Storyboard": To imagine and create possibilities using a storytelling format

"Staple Yourself to Something": Used to explore or clarify a process by following an object through its "day in the life"

GAMES FOR IDENTIFYING STAKEHOLDER VALUES

"Stakeholder Analysis": Identify stakeholders and how to engage them

"History Map": Helps to appreciate an organization's culture

"Campfire": Leverages our natural storytelling capabilities, giving people a format and a space to share work stories

GAMES FOR SEEING THINGS FROM ANOTHER PERSPECTIVE

"Stakeholder Analysis": Imagine many possible futures from different perspectives

"Challenge Cards": Used to identify and think through potential challenges and pitfalls of a product

"The Anti-Problem": For getting unstuck on hard problems: asks people to solve the problem completely opposite to their current problem

"Bodystorming": Using improv or "play acting" to feel out what might work in the real world

"Empathy Map": To develop a customer profile

"Hidden Variables": Consider the nature of reality and the interconnectedness of everything

"Flip It": Quick game to show people that perspectives are made, not born; helps people see challenges as opportunities

"Give-and-Take Matrix": Used to map out motivations & interactions among actors in a system

"Head, Heart, Hands": The goal is to examine an issue from another perspective, and find significance in an issue

"Help Me Understand": Helps to uncover employees' lingering questions or assumptions

"Draw Toast": Notice the diversity of descriptions for a well-known process

"Squiggle Birds": Notice how small changes and visual cues can shift the meaning we assign to something

"The World Café": Improves large-group discussion by borrowing concepts from informal café conversations: round tables, cross-pollinating ideas, and pursuing questions that matter

PRO/CON GAMES

"Challenge Cards": Used to identify and think through potential challenges and pitfalls of a product

"Flip It": Quick game to show people that perspectives are made, not born. Helps people see challenges as opportunities

"I Like, I Wish, I Wonder": To generate constructive feedback by focusing on what was positive or repeatable about an activity, what could change, and what opportunities exist

"Event Horizon": Play with options and cultivate the ability to move beyond thinking distortions and practice joy

GAMES FOR THINKING THROUGH PROBLEMS OR STRATEGIES

"Challenge Cards": Used to identify and think through potential challenges and pitfalls of a product

"The Anti-Problem": For getting unstuck on hard problems: asks people to solve the problem completely opposite to their current problem

"Forced Analogy": Intentionally forces players to think about new concepts to break out of formal categories and help with problem solving & ideation

"Mission Impossible": Take an existing design or idea and change one foundational aspect that makes it "impossible" in function or feasibility

"The 4Cs": Quick way to gather and organize information using four common key concepts (on a 2x2 matrix): components, characteristics, characters, and challenges

"The 5 Whys": Helps discover the root cause of a problem

"Atomize": Good for unpacking large, messy structures

"The Blind Side": Helps to disclose and uncover information that might affect a group's success

"Give-and-Take Matrix": Used to map out motivations & interactions among actors in a system

"Business Model Canvas": Used to examine and rethink a company's business model

"The World Café": Improves large-group discussion by borrowing concepts from informal "café" conversations: round tables, cross-pollinating ideas, and pursuing questions that matter

"I Like, I Wish, I Wonder": To generate constructive feedback by focusing on what was positive or repeatable about an activity, what could change, and what opportunities exist

"Post the Path": Will help develop a better understanding of a group's current process to uncover areas of confusion or misunderstanding

Games for Making a Decision

GAMES FOR VOTING ON CHOICES

"Dot Voting": To converge on ideas that resonate best with the group

"Forced Ranking": To agree on priorities (rank by impact and effort)

"$100 Test": Uses the concept of cash to help prioritize items in a list

"20/20 Vision": To agree on priorities & how to rank initiatives

"Planning Poker": To agree on priorities & how to rank the order of tasks

"Impact & Effort Matrix": Possible actions are mapped out on a 2x2 grid based on the effort required to implement and the potential impact of an idea

"NUF Test": Group rates ideas on three criteria: to what degree are they new, useful, and feasible?

GAMES FOR FINDING PATTERNS IN DATA

"Affinity Map": To discover patterns among similar categories

"Card Sort": General-purpose categorization exercise

"Atomize": Good for unpacking large, messy structures

"Squiggle Birds": Notice how small changes and visual cues can shift the meaning we assign to something

"Rose, Thorn, and Bud": Used to quickly frame positives, negatives, and opportunities

"Start, Stop, Continue": Used to spell out what aspects of an issue/product you want to discontinue, introduce, or continue (based on what's going well)

Other Games

GAMES FOR MANAGING MEETINGS

"Pie Chart Agenda": Quickly agree on an agenda; then use the agenda as a timekeeping artifact during a meeting

"The 7Ps Framework": Used before a meeting to plan out an agenda, goals

"Visual Agenda": A visual agenda creates excitement; people talk about it; it implies the day might be interesting

"Hero's Journey Agenda": A visual agenda created in real time using story structure to frame the day and build emotional engagement

"Hopes & Dreams": Quickly get to know everyone, and their roles, strengths, and objectives

"Code of Conduct": Game to set the tone for a meaningful and pleasant meeting dynamic

"Button": Game where everyone speaks up before anyone speaks a second time; the current speaker passes to the next speaker

"Popcorn": Game where everyone speaks up, "popcorn style," in any order, before anyone speaks a second time

"Five-Fingered Consensus": Quickly gauges extent of the consensus of a group

"Altitude": Used to keep a meeting on track

"Open Space": Method for hosting an event/meeting without a prepared agenda

"SQUID": Used to map out what's been done & what still needs to be done; stands for sequential question and insight diagram

"Who/What/When Matrix": Focuses a "Next Steps" conversation at the end of a meeting on clearly defined actions that people commit to

GAMES FOR TEAM BONDING

"Low-Tech Social Network": Great way to get to know each other; leave nice visual behind, too

"History Map": Helps to appreciate an organization's culture

"Trading Cards": Good opener; also creates memorable visuals for later in the meeting

"Day in the Life": To share our internal system map of reality

"Campfire": Leverages our natural storytelling capabilities, giving people a format and a space for to share work stories

"Mood Board": Create a poster or collage that captures the overall "feel" of an idea

"Memory Wall": Build a visual wall that serves to appreciate & celebrate people on a team

GAMES FOR ASSESSING COMPANY STRUCTURE/LEADERSHIP

"Force Field Analysis": Helps people appreciate the forces both for and against change

"Affinity Map": Group creates an "affinity diagram" to find categories within a cluster of ideas (to see which ideas are most common within a group, etc.)

"The 5 Whys": Helps discover the root cause of a problem

"Stakeholder Analysis": Identify stakeholders and how to engage them

"Hopes & Dreams": Quickly get to know everyone, and their roles, strengths, and objectives

"Help Me Understand": Helps to uncover employees' lingering questions or assumptions

"Let's Count": Count to 10 as a group to illuminate personalities and group dynamics and facilitate awareness of the same

"Prune the Future": Uses a tree as a metaphor to show how the future of anything can be shaped, one leaf at a time (rather than hoping for immediate, broad, sweeping change)

GAMES FOR THINKING THROUGH BUSINESS MODELS

"Business Model Canvas": Used to examine & rethink a company's business model

"Elevator Pitch": Uses *Mad Libs* structure to come up with a short, compelling description of the problem you're trying to solve

"The Pitch": Players imagine that they're entrepreneurs and need to sell their ideas to investors

"Design the Box": Teams imagine the package for an idea in order to make decisions about important features & other aspects of their vision that are difficult to articulate

"I Like, I Wish, I Wonder": To generate constructive feedback by focusing on what was positive or repeatable about an activity, what could change, and what opportunities exist

GAMES FOR UNDERSTANDING THE FEASIBILITY OF CHANGE

"Force Field Analysis": Helps people appreciate the forces both for and against change

"Speed Boat": Used to identify obstacles to your goal, things that may slow you down

"I Like, I Wish, I Wonder": To generate constructive feedback by focusing on what was positive or repeatable about an activity, what could change, and what opportunities exist

GAMES FOR CULTIVATING EMOTIONAL INTELLIGENCE

"Let's Count": Count to 10 as a group to illuminate personalities and group dynamics and facilitate awareness of the same

"I Notice, I Wonder, It Reminds Me of...": A practice of inquiry and a structure for sharing observations.

"Countdown": Grounding practice to prime and anchor to the present moment

"Hidden Variables": Consider the nature of reality and the interconnectedness of everything

"Event Horizon": Play with options and cultivate the ability to move beyond thinking distortions and practice joy

"Desire Mapping": Explore your goals and uncover the underlying motivation behind what you want

"Fill in the Blank": Crystalize a point of view by stating what's missing and what action you would take if it wasn't

The "cheat sheet" was created by Brynn Evans @brynn, brynnevans@google.com and updated by Danyelle Faulkner, danyelle@ideailluminations.com, for the second edition.

Index

About the Authors

Dave Gray's passion has been and continues to be finding ways to help people improve their ability to build shared understanding so they can better coordinate joint action on things that matter to them. In 1993 he founded XPLANE, the visual thinking company, to help people develop shared understanding, so they can make better, faster decisions, and work better together to create more lasting, sustainable impact. He has written three books on design, change, and innovation.

Sunni (Sun) Brown is an author, speaker, facilitator, entrepreneur, and seasoned practitioner of Internal Family Systems and Zen. She founded the creative consultancy Sunni Brown Ink and led a global movement on visual literacy called The Doodle Revolution, garnering 100 Most Creative People in Business recognition from *Fast Company*. She is widely credited with the rise of visual thinking as a tool for deeper inquiry. She more recently founded the Center for Deep Self Design, which uses gamefulness as a method to support inner science and human potential.

Colophon

The cover design is by Susan Thompson. The cover fonts are Gilroy Semibold and Guardian Sans. The text font is Scala Pro and the heading font is Benton Sans.

O'REILLY®

Learn from experts.
Become one yourself.

60,000+ titles | Live events with experts | Role-based courses
Interactive learning | Certification preparation

**Try the O'Reilly learning platform
free for 10 days.**

©2025 O'Reilly Media, Inc. O'Reilly is a registered trademark of O'Reilly Media, Inc. 718900_7x9.1875

www.ingramcontent.com/pod-product-compliance
Lightning Source LLC
Chambersburg PA
CBHW080129220326
41598CB00032B/5001